Learning Microsoft Project 2019

Streamline project, resource, and schedule management with Microsoft's project management software

Srikanth Shirodkar

BIRMINGHAM—MUMBAI

Learning Microsoft Project 2019

Commissioning Editor: Richa Tripathi
Acquisition Editor: Karan Gupta
Senior Editor: Nitee Shetty
Content Development Editor: Tiksha Lad
Technical Editor: Pradeep Sahu
Copy Editor: Safis Editing
Project Coordinator: Deeksha Thakkar
Proofreader: Safis Editing
Indexer: Tejal Daruwale Soni
Production Designer: Shankar Kalbhor

First published: September 2020

Production reference: 1090920

Published by Packt Publishing Ltd.
Livery Place
35 Livery Street
Birmingham
B3 2PB, UK.

ISBN 978-1-83898-872-2

www.packt.com

This book is dedicated to my father, the late R. L. Shirodkar. It is also dedicated to my brilliant wife, (Dr.) Savita, and my lovely daughters, Mahika and Jeevika. Without your love and kindness, this book, and other projects in my life, would not be possible. Special love and gratitude go to my mother, Sadhana (Amma), Pratima, Prashant, and Pavitra for always believing in me through life's ups and downs!

–Srikanth Shirodkar

`Packt.com`

Subscribe to our online digital library for full access to over 7,000 books and videos, as well as industry leading tools to help you plan your personal development and advance your career. For more information, please visit our website.

Why subscribe?

- Spend less time learning and more time coding with practical eBooks and videos from over 4,000 industry professionals

- Improve your learning with Skill Plans built especially for you

- Get a free eBook or video every month

- Fully searchable for easy access to vital information

- Copy and paste, print, and bookmark content

Did you know that Packt offers eBook versions of every book published, with PDF and ePub files available? You can upgrade to the eBook version at `packt.com` and, as a print book customer, you are entitled to a discount on the eBook copy. Get in touch with us at `customercare@packtpub.com` for more details.

At `www.packt.com`, you can also read a collection of free technical articles, sign up for a range of free newsletters, and receive exclusive discounts and offers on Packt books and eBooks.

Contributors

About the author

Srikanth Shirodkar leads online courses relating to Microsoft Project, on which more than 50,000 professionals from 150 countries have enrolled. With a broad range of experience in software delivery management, project and program management, and the design and architecture of software solutions, spanning high-transaction, enterprise-level applications to standalone product development, he has worked with a variety of software development methodologies, including ISV Product Lifecycle, traditional Waterfall, and Agile (Scrum and DSDM).

He has managed global projects and software applications, including one of the world's largest learning management system implementations for online structured higher education, with more than 400,000 students pursuing master's/bachelor's/certificate programs.

This has been my first book, and I wish to thank the entire Packt team for their unflinching support throughout the entire process. Every book is a project and Packt follows a robust process that includes initiation, planning, execution, and reviews every step of the way before the book is closed successfully. This is to ensure that you, the reader, have a highly engaging learning experience. If my book succeeds in achieving this goal, it will all be down to Tiksha Lad (Content Development Editor) and Tanvi Bhatt (PM). If any bugs remain in the book, this will be due to my oversight alone. I also wish to thank Karan Gupta (Acquisition Editor) for reaching out to me first, and Packt's awesome marketing and creative design team. And finally, a very special thank you to the technical reviewer, Vijayendra Shamanna, for providing excellent insights as a result of his extensive industry experience.

About the reviewer

Vijayendra Shamanna is an effective, hands-on leader with a varied technology background and a strong interest in developing innovative technologies for next-generation, cloud-native applications.

He has more than 25 years of extensive and diverse experience as a senior director of engineering/technical manager, architect, senior technical lead, and principal engineer, delivering complex SaaS platforms along with machine learning/AI, storage, virtualization, networking, and data center solutions, from inception to customer deployment.

Packt is searching for authors like you

If you're interested in becoming an author for Packt, please visit `authors.packtpub.com` and apply today. We have worked with thousands of developers and tech professionals, just like you, to help them share their insight with the global tech community. You can make a general application, apply for a specific hot topic that we are recruiting an author for, or submit your own idea.

Table of Contents

Section 2:
Project Initiation with Microsoft Project

2

Fundamentals of Microsoft Project

3

Initiating projects with Microsoft Project

4

Underlying Concepts of Microsoft Project

5

Resource Management with Microsoft Project

Section 3:
Project Planning Like a Pro!

8

Mastering Link Dependency and Constraints

9

Extended Customization – Task and Gantt Formatting

Section 4:
Project Execution – the Real Deal

10
Executing Agile Projects with MS Project

11
Overallocation – the Bane of Project Managers

12
Baselines – Techniques and Best Practices

13
Project Tracking Techniques

Section 5:
Monitoring and Control with Microsoft Project

14
Views, Tables, and Customization

15

Resource and Cost Management

16

Critical Path Monitoring and Advanced Techniques

Section 6:
Project Closure with Microsoft Project

18

Reviewing Projects and Creating Templates for Success

19
Advanced Custom Reports and Templates

20
Book Conclusion and Next Steps

Appendix A:
Using This Book as a Textbook

Appendix B:
Available Fields Reference

Preface

New learners are very often faced with a double challenge: learning Microsoft Project and navigating project management at the same time. Microsoft Project is a beast, and not easy to learn.

So, I promised myself a few things when I started this book:

- To remember and address the key pain-points I faced when I started my own journey into Microsoft Project and into project management

- To introduce topics in the same order as in real-life project management

- To not get lost within the maze of professional jargon, but to show the spirit and practical logic of its intention

- To use storytelling to engage the reader, moving from simple concepts to advanced practical usage

- To leverage all my experience of teaching online courses so that the readers of this book avoid the most common pitfalls

Experienced project managers, too, will benefit from this book. They will be able to plan and estimate, baseline, track progress, monitor and control, and create awesome reports all within a single application. Whether you are a beginner, or an experienced project manager, please start with a complete reading of the book.

Who this book is for

This book is for anyone who grapples with project management in their job role. Your actual designation might vary, but you will certainly be managing projects. Many readers will be brand new users of Microsoft Project – others may have used Project way back and forgotten most of it.

This book will be completely domain-agnostic, as project management (and Microsoft Project) is used in a wide array of domains, including civil construction, industrial production, automobile, architecture, oil and mining, and software and information technology. It is very popular with the armed forces too.

Readers of this book will be at all levels of industry work experience, including people attending college, management trainees, middle managers, senior managers, and start up entrepreneurs.

What this book covers

Chapter 1, *Project Management – the Essential Primer*, explains the project management principles and concepts that are essential for this book with minimum fuss.

Chapter 2, *Fundamentals of Microsoft Project*, introduces Microsoft Project through a simple, hands-on project. We start by making sense of the complex user interface.

Chapter 3, *Initiating projects with Microsoft Project*, reviews the project plan schedule and examines the characteristics and components of a project schedule.

Chapter 4, *Underlying Concepts of Microsoft Project*, explores the logic that makes Project work. This will demystify the automated behavior of Project.

Chapter 5, *Resource Management with Microsoft Project*, explains how to manage the people and machinery required to execute our project. This is an important prerequisite to costing a project.

Chapter 6, *Work Breakdown Structure – the Single Critical Factor*, concerns the most important project management process to succeed with Microsoft Project (WBS the Work Breakdown Structure!).

Chapter 7, *Tasks – under the Microscope*, proceeds from a WBS-based task list to a well-designed project schedule. We will also learn how to import data, organize schedules, and a whole lot of special tasks, all with a new hands-on project.

Chapter 8, *Mastering Link Dependency and Constraints*, creates schedules that are realistic for projecting ground situations through four classic types of task relationships. We also explore the flexibility of time in a schedule represented by date constraints.

Chapter 9, *Extended Customization – Tasks and Gantt Formatting*, explores Project's tools that allow you to fine-tune the textual and graphical aspects of your schedule. Practically every parameter is customizable, as you will see, but you can get by without needing any customization most of the time.

Chapter 10, *Executing Agile Projects with MS Project*, is the beginning of the execution phases of a project. We begin with a discussion of Agile and Kanban supported in Project.

Chapter 11, Overallocation – the Bane of Project Managers, discusses overallocation of resources, which is the most common issue that is faced by users of Microsoft Project. You'll learn how to avoid, diagnose, and resolve overallocation using a plethora of tools and techniques.

Chapter 12, Baselines – Techniques and Best Practices, is a deep dive into the baselining features of Project. You'll learn how to create, maintain, and analyze schedules with the help of baseline best practices.

Chapter 13, Project Tracking Techniques, helps us learn to precisely track the status of your project while adapting to your own ground situations by using a wide spectrum of tools, techniques, and best practices.

Chapter 14, Views, Tables, and Customization, helps us gain an advanced understanding of view architecture in Project. You'll learn which views are used when, as well as sort, filter, and group data. You will also learn how to create your own views.

Chapter 15, Resource and Cost Management, is a deep exploration of Project's resourcing and costing techniques through a new hands-on project.

Chapter 16, Critical Path Monitoring and Advanced Techniques, explains how to work with the foundational methodology used in Project; Critical Path Method (CPM). You'll learn techniques to shorten a project, advanced overallocation techniques, and strategic approaches to resolving scheduling issues.

Chapter 17, Project Reports 101, discusses the many powerful predesigned reports, broad dashboards, and more than a dozen other analytical reports for export that are all shipped with Project out of the box.

Chapter 18, Reviewing Projects and Creating Templates for Success, explains how to identify the most common error patterns within project schedules, use different tools to review projects, and create templates that will help you succeed with future projects.

Chapter 19, Advanced Custom Reports and Templates, explains the logic of Project's reporting architecture to modify existing prebuilt reports and create new custom reports. You'll also learn how to share your customized entities (reports, views and so on) with the world.

Chapter 20, Book Conclusion and Next Steps, is a final big-picture view of Microsoft Project applied to project management. We will tie up the project phases and process groups to everything that you have learned about Microsoft Project. Overall best practices, pitfalls, concepts, and techniques will be mapped to a project life cycle.

Appendix A, Using this Book as a Textbook provides the details of the topics as they are bifurcated in the book in the chapters for quick referencing.

Appendix B, Available Fields Reference explains the types of fields of Project, explained in the various chapters in tabular format. This is beneficial as the tables provide quick reference at a glance.

Appendix C, Keyboard Shortcuts provides a list of shortcuts for the various functions we perform in MS Project 2019. They help provide an ease of access and better user experience.

Appendix D, Glossary has the list of the names, words, phrases which are unique or specific to this book. This helps to provide an easier understanding of the concepts.

To get the most out of this book

A few simple assumptions are made about readers of this book. You are expected to have the following:

- A basic understanding of project management and how teams work in the corporate world.

- A basic familiarity of the Microsoft Office product family, simply because Microsoft Project has the same user interface. Moreover, you should be able to import information from, and export reports to, other products in the Office family.

- You might need some support to install a desktop version of Microsoft Project if you do not already have it. If you do not have it, please make the best use of Microsoft's excellent support system from the Office portal.

Download the color images

We also provide a PDF file that has color images of the screenshots/diagrams used in this book. You can download it here:

```
https://static.packt-cdn.com/downloads/9781838988722_
ColorImages.pdf.
```

Conventions used

There are a number of text conventions used throughout this book.

Bold: Indicates a new term, an important word, or words that you see onscreen. For example, words in menus or dialog boxes appear in the text like this. Here is an example: "This can be done by navigating to the ribbon's **View** tab in the **Data** group, and, in the **Tables** dropdown, choose **Variance**."

> Tips or important notes
> Appear like this.

Get in touch

Feedback from our readers is always welcome.

General feedback: If you have questions about any aspect of this book, mention the book title in the subject of your message and email us at customercare@packtpub.com.

Errata: Although we have taken every care to ensure the accuracy of our content, mistakes do happen. If you have found a mistake in this book, we would be grateful if you would report this to us. Please visit www.packtpub.com/support/errata, selecting your book, clicking on the Errata Submission Form link, and entering the details.

Piracy: If you come across any illegal copies of our works in any form on the Internet, we would be grateful if you would provide us with the location address or website name. Please contact us at copyright@packt.com with a link to the material.

If you are interested in becoming an author: If there is a topic that you have expertise in and you are interested in either writing or contributing to a book, please visit authors.packtpub.com.

Reviews

Please leave a review. Once you have read and used this book, why not leave a review on the site that you purchased it from? Potential readers can then see and use your unbiased opinion to make purchase decisions, we at Packt can understand what you think about our products, and our authors can see your feedback on their book. Thank you!

For more information about Packt, please visit packt.com.

Section 1:
The Iron Triangle – a Quick Primer for Project Management

This section will lay the foundation upon which the whole book is constructed. For new managers, this will be a short and sweet introduction to project management. For experienced managers, this will be a small refresher for the framework used throughout the rest of the book.

This section introduces and explains the phases of the project management life cycle. It provides the terminology scaffolding for the entire book, and with it, defines the book structure by demonstrating the use of Microsoft Project through the life cycle of a project.

This section comprises the following chapter:

- *Chapter 1, Project Management – the Essential Primer*

1
Project Management – the Essential Primer

On a bright hot day 4,500 years ago, in the middle of a desert, a mega civil engineering project was completed. With an estimated 30,000 workers and over 5 million tons of precisely cut rock, the project had taken 20 years to complete.

This project was completed without the help of computers, GPS, or the modern machinery that we have in place today. Yes, we are talking about the Great Pyramid of Giza, in Egypt. This project remained the tallest man-made structure for another 3,800 years!

Humankind has embarked on projects since time immemorial. This knowledge of executing projects has been passed on from generation to generation, being greatly enhanced every time. In more recent times, some notable projects have been putting humans on the moon, building the largest machine in the world—the Large Hadron Collider, and conducting the Olympics and the FIFA World Cup every 4 years.

It can easily be surmised that humanity has studied and practiced project management for a very long time. It is this knowledge of projects and project management, common across time and business domains, that we will now discuss.

Of course, not all projects are mega scale. In your own life, you will have already undertaken several projects. Some examples of personal projects are getting admitted to college, learning a new technical skill, organizing your wedding, or building your own house. The modern world is full of projects running 24 hours a day, 7 days a week, 365 days a year. And most adults in the world have some experience in project management, even if only personal projects.

What has happened since the time of the pyramids? The sharing of project management wisdom between experts from different sectors and domains has led to the identification of activities, tools, techniques, and best practices that are common across domains.

This knowledge is what we commonly call today **Project Management Methodology**. There are a few important, globally accepted standards that we will learn more about shortly.

By the end of this chapter, you will be able to do the following:

- Understand the terminology of Microsoft Project – where the concepts have come from, how they have evolved, and how to learn these standards and techniques further.

- Familiarize yourself with the foundational techniques used by MS Project – especially the **Work Breakdown Structure**, the **Critical Path Method**, and the **Gantt chart**.

- Understand what MS Project is all about, and what to expect.

- Understand when to use MS Project and when not to – Project is a very powerful ally by your side, but it is not a silver bullet for every problem.

If you are reading this book on Microsoft Project, I surmise you are already managing a project, big or small. Or, you are about to start on one soon, and I congratulate you! Actual designations may vary according to seniority, business sector, or domain. Microsoft Project is used in practically *every domain where projects are executed*, in every part of the world. For example, architecture, civil engineering, military, software or information technology, telecommunications, manufacturing and retail, and banking and finance.

If you are in any of the preceding or related domains, you have picked the right book. If you are a new user of MS Project or took a course on Project long back but did not practice it, this book is still perfect for you.

Today, as you have seen, there exists a globally accepted framework of Project Management Knowledge. This chapter will concisely lay out the framework. In the rest of the book, I will show how Microsoft Project's design, features, usage, and pitfalls map to Project Management Knowledge – no matter the specific domain where you will use Microsoft Project.

Projects – what is special about them?

Can any dry textbook definition truly describe the project of climbing Mount Everest for the very first time? Or a project to find new sea routes in uncharted seas?

Yet, when you observe projects in real life a little more closely, you will see a lot that is familiar about them. Big or small, high-risk or no-risk, personal or mega-scale, there are some specific parameters that unify every project.

Project – the definition

In everyday life, projects of every size, budget, risk, and complexity can be found, but here is a definition that defines the soul of a project:

> *"A project is a temporary and unique endeavor with defined objectives."*

While this definition is as generic as it can get, there are some crystal-clear points to break down:

- **Temporary nature**: Projects are temporary in nature – there has to be a clear, time-bound start state and end state. Projects cannot go on forever.

- **Uniqueness**: Pay special attention to this word; it says a whole lot about projects. Manufacturing cars is not a project (because mass-manufactured cars are not unique); it is more of an *operation*. Similarly, providing a car wash is a *service*. However, setting up the factory where cars are mass-manufactured is indeed a *project*.

  Moreover, exactly because projects are unique, they often face more unknown factors. The customer's reaction to a new shoe may really be unknown; a newly engineered door on the Mir space station may not function properly because the conditions cannot be 100% replicated during engineering. Often called *unknown unknowns*, this risk with projects is widely acknowledged and implicitly understood.

  We will discuss risks several times in this book, and how Microsoft Project can help with risks associated with schedules, resources, and budgets.

- **Endeavor**: Projects are purposeful by nature. They don't happen by accident. Or rather, accidental happenings are not called projects. The word *endeavor* also implicitly means that *something has to be accomplished*.

- **With defined objectives**: This means both the result and the limits it must be achieved within. For example, if you are building a house, you will expect to finish it to an acceptable quality, in a reasonable timeframe, and within a limited cost.

> **Note**
>
> Definitions in this book are not the official or standard definitions. It is my humble attempt to make the definitions as easily understandable and memorable for the reader. For the most definitive reference to all the terminology used in this chapter, please *consult Project Management Institute's PMBOK® Guide (A Guide to The Project Management Body of Knowledge)*. In fact, this chapter is based upon this widely accepted standard.

Project management

Project management is the art and science of achieving project objectives by applying knowledge, tools, and techniques.

The science aspect of project management is derived from the body of knowledge. And the *art* aspect of project management becomes evident depending on how you apply the available knowledge to *your* project in your unique situations. This is because there is no single way to execute a project; and the execution is approached based upon the collective wisdom and other resources of the team. Therein lies the art of project management.

Microsoft Project is the preferred software tool. With the scheduling aspects of your project, it can prove to be the most important software project tool that you will use.

Project management done correctly can help you do the following:

1. Achieve your business' end goals
2. Manage constraints in the project – scope, quality, and costs
3. Increase predictability – even for subsequent projects
4. Optimize the usage of precious resources – money, people, machinery, and materials
5. Recover projects in trouble

The application of good project management practices and Microsoft Project will greatly enhance the success of your project.

> **Pitfalls**
>
> A common beginner's pitfall is to use MS Project only to create a schedule. The new user starts enthusiastically, and might even create a schedule at the beginning of the project. But they will not know how to use it to track the project, how to leverage one-click dynamic reports, how to identify risks, or for the long list of other features.
>
> By reading this book, you will identify Microsoft Project's role in all major process groups that you will perform as a project manager.

The project manager

The project manager is the person around whom the project universe revolves. They are directly responsible for the success of the project.

To accomplish such a responsibility, the project manager is expected to bring a great deal of skills and competencies to the table. Project management skills are always expected: awareness of best practices, domain knowledge, business analysis skills, industry standards, and regulatory policy knowledge are just some of the fundamentals. If the project manager also has technical skills, they are highly valued.

Amongst the so-called soft skills, people and organizational leadership skills, good communication, conflict management, administration, and general management are just some of the fundamentals.

Moreover, this is a field where experience can make a big difference to project outcomes and is valued at a premium.

Project management knowledge

As we understood earlier, today, there are multiple global standards for project management. Each of these methodologies provides a holistic set of guidelines, practices, tools, and techniques in self-contained packages.

These methodologies have evolved to cater to different sectors, business domains, geographies, and engineering practices. Organizations that specialize in executing projects, and for whom project success is business critical, will adopt one or more of these methodologies.

Choose your fount of knowledge

Some of the most popular methodologies are the following:

- **Project Management Institute (PMI)**'s – A guide to the **Project Management Body of Knowledge** (shortened to *PMBOK* and pronounced *pimbok*) is a globally recognized standard and is widely used across industry domains. This book will draw upon the PMBOK Sixth Edition.

- The **International Organization for Standardization (ISO)** has several standards published, notably *ISO 9000* for *Quality Management Systems in Projects and ISO 21500:2012 – Guidance on Project Management*

- **PRINCE2 (Projects in Controlled Environments)** is popular in the UK, some European countries, and Australia. This originated in the UK for government usage, and today is also a globally recognized methodology.

- **New kids on the block**: Relatively recently introduced and originating from the software and information technology worlds, there are several other methodologies that are adaptive, iterative, and incremental in nature.

- *Agile* and *Lean* are a couple of the most popular ones in global usage. These methodologies are slowly making inroads into broader acceptance in other fields.

- Hybrid and customized methodologies are also being elaborated and practiced, especially in emerging markets and technologies. These take the best of the predictive and agile methodologies and tailor them according to specific project requirements.

So, what is the bottom line?

- Companies will usually adopt and adapt one or more methodologies, based upon their business domain, customer demands, go-to-market constraints, regulatory guidelines, and other requirements.

- Even with the established traditional methodologies, there is now wide recognition of adaptive frameworks. In fact, PMBOK Sixth Edition is packaged with the Agile Practice Guide included.

- Microsoft Project, starting circa 2017, has started providing some capabilities to support Agile, Kanban, and Hybrid, though widespread adoption by users remains to be seen.

The project life cycle

Since projects have a start date and an end date, the intermediate period (between those two end points) can be described as the life of a project. But in reality, the project manager's role and involvement will usually exceed even the closure of the project, for example, usually in the financial and support aspects.

The duration of all projects, irrespective of size, can be described as a series of phases that together make up the project management life cycle. This describes the stages of development the project passes through to reach completion.

Here is a graphical representation of the project life cycle:

Figure 1.1 – Project life cycle

The phases can be stated as follows:

1. Starting the project

2. Planning, organizing, and preparing the project

3. Executing the project on schedule

4. Completing the project

While the sequencing direction is implied in the diagram, some of the phases can be iterative depending on the nature of the project.

Project management processes

The project manager will execute a large set of activities during the life cycle of a project. These simple activities can be logically grouped together as the **Project Management Process**.

The following diagram depicts a generic Project Management Process:

Figure 1.2 – Representation of a generic project management process

As we can see, a process consists of a set of prescribed tools and techniques applied on some inputs and producing expected results as outputs.

For example, *Develop Project Charter* is one of the very first standard processes, performed by the PM once in the project life cycle. Similarly, *Acquire Resources* is another process, albeit performed on a need basis – as and when required. Another example, *Monitor Communications*, expectedly happens throughout the project life cycle – and many times.

> **Tip**
>
> How many project management processes are there? The current PMBOK Sixth Edition lists 49 processes. The number will vary depending on what methodology and version you reference. The semantics may vary but the philosophy will remain the same.

Every single project management process can be conveniently categorized under two different classifications: as **Process Groups** and as **Knowledge Areas**.

Project management process groups

You, my astute reader, might now have extrapolated that individual project processes themselves can be *logically grouped* – and this is correct.

Before we proceed with understanding process groups, here is a note of caution. A common pitfall is to confuse *process groups* with *project phases* (or the *project life cycle*). You will soon see why such confusion can be prevalent.

Here are the process groups:

- **Initiating Process Group**: Whether it is the start of a new project or a new phase within a running project, initiating processes are performed. These help in defining the project or phase.

- **Planning Process Group**: All planning processes are grouped here – including the scoping of the project (or a phase). **Create WBS** is an important process in this group and we will learn more about it later in this chapter. Every time there is a change in the project requirements, this group will get activated at any point in the project life cycle.

- **Executing Process Group**: Processes in this group deal with the execution of the project. Providing direction for the project, managing quality, building out a project team, and acquiring resources for them – all these are processes within this group.

- **Monitoring and Controlling Process Group**: The processes in this group help the project manager ensure that everything runs according to plan – and within project tolerances. The control of the cost and schedule are some of the important processes within this group.

- **Closing Process Group**: When it is time to officially close a project (or a phase, or even customer agreements), use the processes within this group.

It is easy to see why new learners confuse process groups with project phases, as there is some semantic overlap in the naming convention.

But, as a reader of this book, you should be aware that processes belonging to a group might be executed anywhere in the project life cycle. In particular, the **Monitoring and Controlling Process Group** is something the project manager will perform through most of the project life cycle.

Project management knowledge areas

There are 10 distinct specialization areas utilized by the project manager when managing projects. These are called **Knowledge Areas**. Each of these Knowledge Areas is also a collection of the same project processes that we have discussed so far.

Now, we will learn about the second way in which project management processes can be classified into Project Management Knowledge Areas:

- **Project Integration Management**: This knowledge area will be under the direct control of the project manager and deals with the co-ordination of all other processes utilized in a project. Other knowledge areas, which follow, can potentially be delegated to subject matter experts, such as a technical lead, quality lead, business analyst, or software architect. Another special point to note is that the integration management knowledge area has processes that are performed across the entire project life cycle.

- **Project Scope Management**: Ensuring that the project includes all the work required (and nothing else) to achieve the project objectives.

- **Project Schedule Management**: Concerned with the temporal aspects of the project such as sequencing activities and achieving time-related constraints.

- **Project Cost Management**: Deals with processes to ensure that the project does not exceed budgets. This includes estimating, budgeting, and control of costs.

- **Project Quality Management**: Using appropriate processes to achieve stakeholders' expectations of project quality.

- **Project Resource Management**: Resources include people, machinery, and materials (consumable or otherwise). Often, third-party vendors may be involved, or your own project may be part of a much larger project. In all cases, making sure resources are utilized optimally and on time is covered in this knowledge area.

- **Project Communications Management**: Project information should be periodically disseminated to participants in a project. A good project manager should understand the distinction between raw project data, information, and actionable knowledge.

- **Project Risk Management**: The skill of a project manager is in mitigating risks before they materialize – and if risks do materialize, designing contingency plans for them. All risk-related activities, including identification, analysis, response planning, and implementation, belong to this knowledge area.

- **Project Procurement Management**: Your project will often need products or services from outside your own sphere of control and you will be required to procure them. Procurement processes are within this area.

- **Project Stakeholder Management**: Stakeholders are those people, groups, or organizations that will be impacted by your project. So, a project manager uses appropriate processes to engage appropriate stakeholders, both during decision making and the execution of a project. These stakeholder-related processes belong here.

So far, we have understood project processes and learned about two different categorizations for them: *Process Groups* and *Knowledge Areas*. If you understand these systems, it will enable you to view your project processes from multiple perspectives.

Work breakdown structure (WBS) – a special mention

> *Running a project without a work breakdown structure is like going to a strange land without a road map – J. Phillips*

In this section, we will examine a key project deliverable called **Work Breakdown Structure**. This is encapsulated in the project management processes that we have just familiarized ourselves with as the **Create WBS** process.

So, what is a WBS? The WBS is the breaking down of project work into smaller components to achieve the project scope.

The WBS is created during project initiation to manage the scope of the project. It is an application of the *divide and conquer* technique to break down the project scope into manageable components. After that, we use the WBS to create the project schedule (*using Microsoft Project*). Subsequently, the WBS is referred to, throughout the entire project life cycle, to monitor and control, and to close the project.

Despite its simplicity, WBS creation takes practice and skill to do correctly; and when done, will add significant benefit to the project. Due to the importance of WBS in executing schedules successfully, *Chapter 6, Work Breakdown Structure – the Single Critical Factor*, is dedicated to the practical aspects of creating a WBS.

Pitfall

Projects with a well-defined WBS might also fail, but a project with an incorrect WBS will seldom succeed. If your roadmap is incorrect, how will you reach your desired destination? In such a situation, course correction must happen, starting with the WBS.

How is a WBS different from the task/activity list? If someone asks about your project *What are the project deliverables?* the answer should be listed in your WBS.

> **Pitfall**
>
> The most common pitfall is to include the tasks in the WBS (instead of only deliverables and outcomes). Implementation details (tasks) belong to the task list and not in the WBS. The task list is, in fact, derived in a later stage, using the WBS as a foundation.

Why is a WBS important?

- The most important function of the WBS is *Scope Management*. A WBS helps in ensuring that the project includes all the work required (and nothing else) to achieve the project objectives.

- A WBS helps you to understand the work in the nascent stages of a project. It is also the critical step to proceed from *Scope to Schedule*.

- Changes are inevitable in projects and a WBS helps both in avoiding scope creep (uncontrolled changes to the scope) and as a reference baseline for scope change control.

Who should create the WBS?

The project manager has ownership of the WBS. But the actual bulk of the WBS content should be contributed by the following:

- Domain-specific experts
- Technical experts
- The team that is actually going to work on the project
- Business analysts

Reviews can be done by the following:

- Key identified stakeholders of the project
- Other project managers and teams that have done similar work

Why is a WBS so important in this book?

The WBS of your project should ideally be the input to create your schedule using Microsoft Project. So, it will really help to get familiar with this technique, through repeated practice.

The challenges and benefits of project management

Project management is a truly universal skill, required across all business domains, all geographies, and all the time.

The language of the project manager is the same across all fields: a software project manager can talk about schedule compression and a civil contractor will understand it perfectly, even though the rest of the other's professional terminology might sound like Greek to them.

But there are two misfortunes in this field:

- The first is that people who have been a part of a project at some point in their career will think that they can take on project management with no preparation whatsoever. It is also true that engineers will get promoted to project management roles by their boss, without verification of their aptitude or the downtime required to prepare for the role. Technically competent entrepreneurs start companies based on their passion, and then realize they also must manage organizational projects, which ends up being much more than the amount of work required for their product.

- The second misfortune is that, often, project managers who have had *only* academic training and certifications think they can take on a project beyond their capabilities.

Joel Spolsky, program manager on the Microsoft Excel team between 1991 and 1994, and cofounder of Stack Overflow, jokingly quipped in an essay about the existence of two mutually exclusive sets of genes: one for software development and another for management. The message is that the skills required for a technically oriented person and for a project manager are very different. And it is difficult for both to co-exist (but not impossible). There is more than a grain of truth in Joel's observation, no matter which business domain we look at.

It is all too common that the *rock star performer* of the team gets promoted to be the project manager. And they will find themselves doing something they have never been trained for in their lives, and often do not even have the aptitude for it.

The story is very similar when it gets to Microsoft Project.

The project manager fires up MS Project and because it resembles Excel a little, will innocently expect it to behave similarly. Very soon, they encounter the vast array of options and complexities of automatic scheduling, eventually giving up. *Project management is very complex as it is; how do we use a software tool with a steep learning curve?*

A few PMs might take a course or a book because their organization mandates the use of Microsoft Project. But then, they will not venture beyond creating a draft schedule at the beginning of the project. And there it will remain in the repository—uncared for, unloved, and never updated.

I have already heard a thousand different versions of this same story from my learners. And that is why this book aims to solve these specific challenges. If you complete the book while practicing all the hands-on examples simultaneously, then you will not be intimidated by Microsoft Project and your schedule will be a *living document* because it will reflect the true state of your project. Moreover, your boss (and their boss) will love your reports (which you can pull at the drop of a hat).

The Iron Triangle (Triple Constraint of Project Management)

Every project in real life is bound by constraints. If there was unlimited money or unlimited time, would there be any real challenge in project management?

You will have already heard of the famous **Iron Triangle** (or Triple Constraint) of Project Management:

Figure 1.3 – The famous Iron Triangle of Project Management
(also known as the Triple Constraint)

The story is that, if your customer asks for good, fast, and cheap, you say, choose any two. The third parameter is your room for negotiation.

This concept is grounded on common sense and its origins are probably lost in the sands of time. And you will find multiple interpretations of it, each with a slight variation. But the gist is that any single vertex of this triangle cannot move without also impacting the other two.

Say you were building a house for a project. After all the planning, you start the project. Your significant other and your children now remember that they always wanted a swimming pool and you haven't factored it into your plan. At this stage, you will know that the additional scope means an additional cost and a few extra weeks, right? Moreover, if you don't have the luxury of extra budget or time, the quality of your project will decrease. This is what the Iron Triangle is all about.

And even this **Triple Constraint** model itself has a constraint. There are limits to which you can stretch this model, after which it breaks.

In his legendary book on software engineering and project management, *The Mythical Man-Month*, author Fred Brooks expounded that *adding manpower to a late software project makes it even more late*. This was written way back in 1975, and with the exponential expansion of software complexity and usage everywhere, the book's message rings even truer today.

The reason for this is that given that a project is already under pressure, adding more people to the team leads to added communications, additional requirements in the design interfaces, more training to get team members familiar with the project (requiring key team members to conduct *knowledge transfer* meetings), and so on. This will continue to the point when the project gets even more delayed than it already is.

How MS Project helps with the Triple Constraint

Microsoft Project's powerful automatic scheduling feature makes it a breeze to calculate the impact of additional scope on a project. Moreover, Project also provides some resource costing features that can be layered on top of your scheduling. We will see all these features in action throughout most of the book.

There are, of course, caveats: the additional scope should be well defined enough to be added to the schedule for Project's magic to work.

Microsoft Project and the mythical man-month

The mythical man-month predicts the drop in productivity caused by adding additional resources to a project. This unexpected reduction in productivity will be industry specific and largely depends upon the circumstances of the project. It is also very difficult to objectively quantify this productivity drop due to the unique nature of projects.

While it is possible to simulate such an effect using MS Project (by decreasing the resource units assigned to a task), it is very rarely practiced in real life. In the words attributed to the same author, Fred Books, *everybody quotes it, some people read it, and a few people go by it*, referring to the mythical man-month.

The elephant in the room (failure rates)

Despite the collective wisdom of millennia in project management, all studies show that the failure rates of projects are appalling. What constitutes a failure is generally acknowledged as overrun schedules and budgets, the unacceptable quality of the project result, or ultimately, the desired business objectives not being met.

While the inherently unique nature of projects builds a certain amount of risk into projects, it is also true that certain patterns can be observed from failed projects. We can immediately learn the following points from them:

- A higher complexity, size, and duration leads to failed projects

- Unrealistic schedules lead to real failures

- Not investing in baseline and variance analysis can be detrimental to project health

- Not tracking costs can sink the project ship

Winning – but at what cost (burnout rates)?

Poorly managed projects will cause teams to burn out. We have all heard of project managers leading teams into toxic work schedules, with no downtime to meet the unending *Death March* of projects.

Burnout, a word coined in 1974 by eminent psychologist Herbert Freudenberger, refers to the mental and physical breakdown of individuals caused by work-related stress. Unrealistic project schedules with relentless work hours, Kafkaesque expectations, extreme market conditions, the apathy of management, and any number of other factors, often simultaneous, can cause burnout.

And also, the world has tended to hero-worship the notion of project managers who pull off incredible goals. Steve Jobs, the charismatic cofounder of Apple, created what was half-jokingly referred to as the *reality distortion field* across the software industry. Jobs would use his personal charisma, hype, fear, or any other tools at his disposal to convince teams that anything he said was possible, especially fantastic project timelines.

This discussion would not be complete without mentioning the state of today's multi-billion-dollar video game industry. This industry, perceived by newcomers as fun, modern, and happening, has inordinately high burnout rates. Project schedules are perpetually in crunch mode. There is high *churn* in teams, which means that burned-out developers leave the company and brand-new workers are recruited into the company. Inexperienced developers, mostly fresh from college, are recruited for their ability to work long hours until burnout. Then they are churned out to make way for a fresh set of developers.

Project managers, like you and me, are at the frontline of the battle against burnout. Often the first impact on the team is on the PM themselves. The fight against burnout in all its forms should also begin with us. Today, there is a wealth of information to identify, prevent, and recover from burnout issues.

Where does Microsoft Project figure in the fight against burnout?

When a resource is allocated more work than they can handle in a standard workweek, it is called *overallocation*. Repeated overallocation over a lengthy duration is the first and foremost cause of worker burnout. This is not the same as the occasional crunch time that every real project faces – often during customer demos, or the final launch.

A project is stellar in identifying overallocation, and this is also recognized as the number one bane while creating your schedule. This book will cover overallocation with the highest priority, and we will discuss 10 different resolution techniques throughout the book.

What is Microsoft Project really?

Now, that we have had a tour of the vast landscape of project management, let's understand what Microsoft Project is really about. Of course, it is a software application to manage projects, owned by Microsoft, but it has a rich heritage and it will do you good to understand a bit more about it.

Microsoft Project, despite its modern, slick, and shiny interface, dates to the early 1980s, originally created by PC enthusiast Ron Bredehoeft and written for the DOS operating system. Microsoft purchased the software in 1985 and continued to release a few versions in DOS. The first Windows version of Project was released in 1990.

Three decades later, Microsoft Project is one part of a comprehensive enterprise-level management offering across project, program, and portfolio management. It encompasses desktop, web access, and server-based delivery.

At the core of Microsoft Project is a powerful scheduling engine. This engine is programmed to run according to some simple rules, concepts, and algorithms, all of which have their origins in the same project management theory that you have just learned about.

What does this mean for you? First, in software engineering terms, the application is *robust*. The team responsible for Project has had many decades to iron out all the chinks in the software already.

Second, millions of project managers have already created millions of schedules with the application in every imaginable business domain. Microsoft continues to collect feedback and input from expert PMs across a wide spectrum of business domains. This means that the algorithms have been tweaked and fine-tuned to work predictably for you.

Finally, you must understand that, even with all these big usage numbers, if you understand the simple precepts upon which Project is constructed, then Project becomes a powerful ally in your battle against scope creep, death marches, and burnout.

The Critical Path Method (CPM)

Microsoft Project uses the **C**ritical **P**ath **M**ethod for scheduling projects. Please pay special attention to this section as it is the foundation of the workings of Microsoft Project.

The CPM is a widely popular technique among project managers for sequencing activities (tasks) in a schedule. This special technique is embedded within MS Project as an algorithm. And the reason that I write *tasks* every time activities are mentioned is because "tasks" is the equivalent terminology in MS Project.

The technique involves, as a starting point, the following:

1. **Breaking the project into a list of activities**: This is based upon the WBS method that we discussed earlier in this section.

2. **Estimating the duration (the time taken for the completion) of each activity**: Estimates are usually provided by the people who will do the work, and then they can be verified by subject matter experts.

3. **Identifying the logical dependencies between the activities**: Most activities in a project will have the domain- or project-specific constraints decide the order in which they must be executed, for example:

   - In software development, development has to occur before the product can be tested, and internal testing must occur before customer testing.

   - A professional painter will prepare their canvas before painting it.

   - In civil engineering, the excavation of the foundation will be executed in the early stages of the project rather than later.

4. **Identifying key events (milestones) and deliverable end points**: By making use of these configurations, the CPM technique will calculate the longest path of activities to the end points of your schedule.

The diagram that follows shows a visual representation of the CPM. The whole figure represents a *project schedule*. The boxes represent tasks (or activities), along with the time it takes to execute them (**DURATION**). The arrows represent the sequence of execution of tasks via dependencies. Now notice the special small arrows in red , consecutively between the 5 boxes – they represent the critical path:

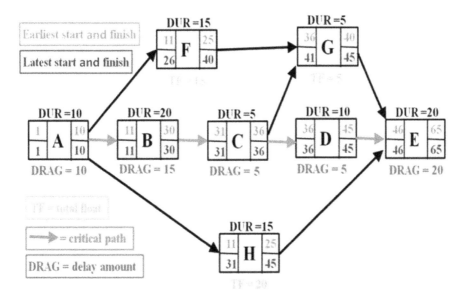

Figure 1.4 – Critical path represented by an activity-on-node diagram

Source: Reproduced without alteration from https://en.wikipedia.org/wiki/File:SimpleAONwDrag3.png under the Creative Commons Attribution-Share Alike 3.0 Unported license.

The advantage of this technique is that it will identify the following for you:

- The **Critical** activities of your schedule: A delay in any of these activities will result in the delay of the entire project. This path is the shortest time to complete the project and must be guarded carefully by the project manager. Any delay with any activity along this path will result in a delay for the entire project. It is often the *longest path* but not necessarily.

- The **Float** of your activities: This is the amount of delay that an activity can accommodate without delaying the entire project. It is often called *Slack* in project terminology. You may also surmise that activities on the critical path will have no slack.

> **Tip**
>
> If you are not already familiar with this technique of scheduling, it will be prudent to invest a few hours in self-learning this topic. This will give you an extra edge when tackling MS Project. You will be fine for the purposes of this book, even if you can't read it right away.

While the CPM technique is used algorithmically by Project, the visual representation of your schedule is predominantly represented by a Gantt chart.

Gantt charts

A Gantt chart is a special type of bar chart that visually represents a project schedule. Today, it is the *de facto* way of picturing schedules in software applications, in standards documents, official publications, and even informally on whiteboards and anywhere else you can imagine.

Gantt charts are named after *Henry Gantt* who first designed them in their current modern form around a century ago, circa 1910. Even though earlier designs were known and in use, Gantt's design revolutionized schedule representation and was promptly put to use in World War I by the United States Army. Here is a sample Gantt chart:

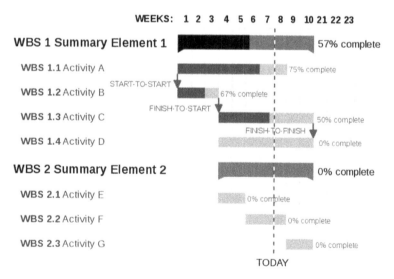

Figure 1.5 – Gantt chart

Image source: `https://commons.wikimedia.org/wiki/File:GanttChartAnatomy.svg`.

This work has been released into the public domain by its author.

Microsoft Project uses Gantt charts as the default representation, so if you are not already familiar with Gantt charts, this is the right time to do so. Project also has other special representations of the schedule (notably the network diagram or PERT diagram) to use for special and occasional analysis.

When to use MS Project (otherwise known as the law of the hammer)

When all you have is a hammer, every problem looks like a nail is a quote often attributed to Abraham Maslow, a renowned American psychologist. This quote refers to a tendency of over reliance on a familiar known tool or technique.

Microsoft Project is suitable for managing single projects of small to medium scale. *Scale* implies scope, project complexity, and the size of the team. The number of projects executed in the business world of this category, that is, of small to medium scale, far exceeds any other type.

How a particular organization categorizes, say, a small - or medium - sized project will vary as regards the obvious parameters. However, a rough rule of thumb would be to use Microsoft Project for projects sized between 10 and 200 person months of work.

When not to use MS Project

If you are looking at tiny projects—say with 1-2 resources and fewer than 10 person months of work—then you might consider simpler tools, because Project might be overkill. Excel is very popular, and Microsoft Planner is another lesser known tool. There are also many open source tools you might consider for tiny projects.

At the other end of the spectrum, if you want to manage a portfolio of multiple projects simultaneously across your enterprise—*including managing resources shared across projects*—then Microsoft Project is just inadequate. You might consider other offerings from Microsoft, such as Project Online/Project Server as a solution.

> **Tip**
> There is a 1980s-style feature called (perhaps loftily) **Master Project**, which allows you to merge multiple projects. But it has several pitfalls when used in today's business requirements and working styles. This feature will not be discussed in this book due to its shaky design. Microsoft probably retains this feature to appease organizations that have not yet made the Enterprise leap.

How this book is structured

The Pareto principle states that for many events, roughly 80% of the effects come from 20% of the causes. In the case of learning Project, it is true that you will use about 20% of the features 80% of the time. These common features will be taught very early in the book.

Mapping to process groups and the project life cycle

Earlier in this chapter, you saw how process groups and the project life cycle are effective ways to organize your project management knowledge.

This book will use the same foundation, making it easy for you to use Microsoft Project as follows:

- Exactly how you need it in your job

- Mapped to the same PM process that you will execute

It is important that you practice all the hands-on assignments and exercises in this book. You can post solutions on my website, `www.learngood.in` (and look at other reader's solutions also).

Truly domain agnostic

Microsoft Project is domain agnostic; that is, literally any business domain can use it. In the same way, this book is also domain agnostic. The examples used in this book are from as varied business scenarios as possible to relate to a large and varied audience of project practitioners.

How to read the book (end to end reading versus pinpoint references)

Here are a few methods to help you to read and understand this book better:

- **First time reading the book**: Read the book end to end and your journey will be from simple to complex topics. After the very next chapter, you will be able to create simple but complete project schedules that can be utilized at work immediately.

- **Pinpoint references**: As a reference guide, you can jump to sections of this book that correspond to the stage your project is at or to the process group that you are executing in your own real-life project.

- **As a textbook:** Several colleges offer project management as a higher education course and strategically match it with Microsoft Project. This book will be a good match as a textbook as it maps to project management concepts.

Summary

In this chapter, we have seen how the global practice of professional project management has evolved and crystallized over the ages into global standards such as the PMBOK. We have gone over the basic framework of definitions and concepts that will enable us to navigate the rest of this book. Microsoft Project is a powerful tool that draws upon the same theory, techniques, and best practices of project management knowledge. At its heart is a powerful scheduling engine that works on the Critical Path method. We have also touched upon other essentials, such as the Iron Triangle, WBS, and Gantt charts. There is a sweet spot to which Project is best suited and it is not ideal for every type of project management.

Armed with this foundational knowledge, we are now ready to take on MS Project. In the next chapter, you will quickly get familiar with Project's user interface, so that the long arrays of buttons and features will not intimidate you in the future. We will also create a simple but functional project schedule! I look forward to meeting you in the next chapter.

Section 2: Project Initiation with Microsoft Project

This section of the book will deal with the use of Microsoft Project in the very first phase of a project – the initiation phase.

This section comprises the following chapters:

- *Chapter 2, Fundamentals of Microsoft Project*
- *Chapter 3, Initiating projects with Microsoft Project*
- *Chapter 4, Underlying Concepts of Microsoft Project*
- *Chapter 5, Resource Management with Microsoft Project*

2
Fundamentals of Microsoft Project

Welcome to your hands-on learning journey with Microsoft Project. Consider first an analogy—*learning to ride a bicycle*. You cannot learn to cycle by just learning about the parts of the bicycle from a book. It is important to actually get on the bike and learn to balance and pedal. In the same way, you will now learn Project by using it to create schedules over the course of this book. This is because being adept at Project requires you to both learn the techniques and then practice them yourself.

The single biggest hurdle to learning and using Project is that it appears complex and intimidating. This is the reason most new learners give up early or don't even start. There are a multitude of switches, buttons, options, and views. To compound the fact, sometimes working on one area of the schedule mysteriously seems to affect other areas. But fear not, my gentle reader, as my goal is to remove that *intimidation factor* and make Project friendly to you, right from this chapter. I will do this by diving directly into Project with you to create our very first simple, fully functional project plan.

In this chapter, we're going to cover the following main topics:

- Understanding the UI basics of MS Project

- Creating your first schedule with MS Project

- Learning the building blocks of Project—Tasks, Schedules, and Views

Technical requirements

You will, of course, need access to Microsoft (MS) Project to follow this chapter from now on. Specifically, I will use **Microsoft Project Professional 2019 Online Desktop Client**, which is a cloud-based offering. The top-tier product offerings will integrate a few Enterprise features that are not required for this book. Also, for the purposes of this book, it does not matter whether you use the *cloud-based* or *on-premise* offering because of the similarities in UI and the algorithmic behavior of Project.

Normally, your company's system administrator should provide you access to MS Project. If you do not have that luxury, then you will have to install it yourself. At the time of writing this chapter, Microsoft's product website is unintuitive to use, even for new users. It is likely that you will find it frustrating to choose, try, install, or even purchase from the six variations of MS Project software currently offered; however, a trial version is available at the same official download site, and it will require a validated registration. If you face difficulty, contact Microsoft's Office 365 support for help. The URL to the site depends on your geographical location, so it is best to search for it online yourself should you wish to install it by yourself.

> **Pitfall**
> Beware of downloading authentic-looking cheap license keys, as there are many horror stories out there on many user forums. Perform your own due diligence before any installation.

This book will be self-contained as much as possible, and won't require you to download anything extra to practice with, except for some complex concepts later on; however, if you want to post your own assignment solutions or get extra practice assignments, visit my site at `www.learngood.in`.

> **Tip**
>
> Are you using an earlier version of MS Project, such as 2016 or 2013? You will be able to follow along perfectly for a large part of this book, except, of course, when we come to look at the newer features; however, if you are coming in from legacy versions, I recommend that you align soon with Microsoft Project 2019's cloud-based future version. A subscription-based pricing model will give you access to all the latest features of Project, as and when they are officially released. It also shifts your license costs from **capital expenditure** to **operational expenditure**.

Understanding the UI basics of MS Project

Let's start our new project by firing up the Project app on your operating system. You should first understand that Project is under the same umbrella of Microsoft's application offerings. Moreover, it is closely knit with the Office suite and is a premium offering. This means that you will already have some familiarity with the ribbon-based interface.

Backstage

The first screen that shows up will be similar to this:

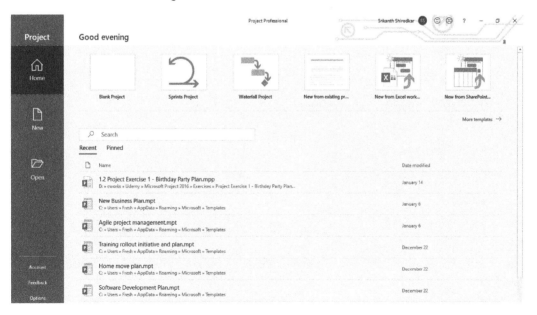

Figure 2.1 – MS Project Backstage screen

This screen is called the **Backstage** and it offers an experience similar to other Office applications. Now, from this screen, you can either create a new blank file, open an existing file, or create a new file from a template.

The green section on the left is the menu and it is contextual, which means that it will change later when you have a file open in the application. The multiple white boxes at the top are templates that you can use to create a new file. There are more templates to choose from than are shown here. Above the templates in the title bar is your account menu. Below the templates are the recently opened existing files. This area will be blank when opening the app for the very first time.

For now, click on the **Blank Project** template (the first one) and you will find that Project will open a completely blank new file. Before we proceed any further, let's pause to understand the project we must undertake next.

Building your first simple project

Legend has it that the original vision for MS Project came to Ron Bredehoeft from an idea of expressing the preparation of a popular breakfast dish called *Eggs Benedict* in project-management terms. And so, just for fun, let's also start with a very simple cooking project: *baking a cake*.

If you break down the work required to bake a cake, you will get a structured list like this:

1.   Decide what kind of cake you want.
2.   Find the recipe.
3.   Procure and assemble ingredients.
4.   Cook from the recipe.
5.   Present the cake.
6.   Clean up.
7.   Finished!

Note that our work breakdown is also arranged chronologically in the sequence of execution. How do we get this list into Project and how do we create a schedule from it? To answer these questions, let's now return to MS Project and continue to understand the new screen.

The following is the screen that should be on your computer now. Much of your work will happen here, so it is important that you get very familiar with this interface:

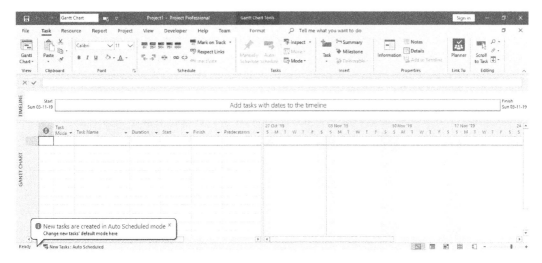

Figure 2.2 – MS Project – a first look

What you see now is called a **view** and is usually made up of a table and chart combination. This view is called the Gantt chart view, and is your first view when you start Project. It is the most widely used view in Project and much of your scheduling work will occur here, so it is imperative that we get familiar with this user interface now.

There are three main areas in this current screen:

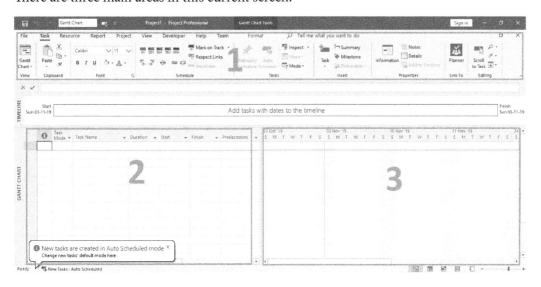

Figure 2.3 – MS Project – main areas of the screen

The various elements of the preceding screenshot are described in detail in the following list:

1. This is the **ribbon** interface. Note the tabs (**Task**, **Resource**, **Project**, **View**, and so on) that smartly group features according to the work you will be performing in your schedule.

2. This is the **Table** area. This is the area where we will enter our project tasks. One row in this table can accommodate one task from your project. Note all of the column headers. Usually, entering data here will start from the **Task Name** column.

3. This is the **Chart** area. Any chart shown here will be tightly linked to the corresponding data in the adjoining table. In other words, the chart shown here is the visual representation of the table data.

Understanding Tasks

Once the scope of the project is known in detail, a top-down approach is used to break down these high-level requirements into smaller and smaller subcomponents. This is the same as creating the **WBS** (short for **work-based schedule**). The WBS is then translated into the tasks actually required to materialize each subcomponent. This breakdown process is repeated until every task is small enough to be meaningfully assigned by you to your team members. Therefore, you can say that tasks are the smallest units of work in a project.

In this way, a top-down design approach is utilized in designing a schedule during the initiation phase of a project. But interestingly, for the execution phase of the project, the perspective reverses completely. When the project starts executing, you will start tracking the work progress from the smallest task upwards, building and integrating bigger and bigger components until the whole project is completed.

Like building blocks, when the tasks are executed in the correct order, with the right resources, and within the allowed tolerances of time, budget, and quality, the project can be said to have been successfully executed. MS Project provides you with a great deal of control over how you can manipulate tasks in your project schedule in both the perspectives we have discussed now. The creation of the WBS and several practical aspects of the process are discussed in detail later in the project-planning part of this book.

To proceed with our exercise project, choose any row at the top of the Table area. In the **Task Name** column, type the first task in our project: *Decide what kind of cake you want*. Hit the *Enter* key, and the task is created. And that's your first task:

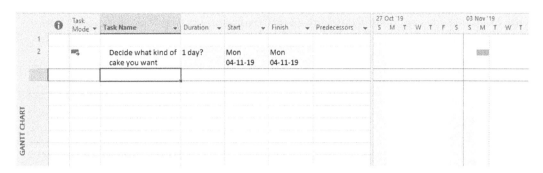

Figure 2.4 – MS Project – first Task created

There are several interesting points to observe from this simple action:

- Note that Project smartly autofilled a lot of data for you. A default duration of *1 day* was set as the duration of your task. The start and finish dates are also set, and they will, in turn, default to the current date. This is also the default start date of the whole project itself. All of these defaults are configurable.

- In the Chart area, note that a small blue dash has appeared. The chart displays a timeline running on the x-axis. The task in the chart exactly corresponds to the dates set for the task.

- The newly created values are highlighted in light blue colors. In fact, when you make *any* changes to the schedule, Project will highlight all the cells impacted by your change.

Now, in the same way, enter all the rest of the tasks, one below the other, as shown in the following figure:

		Task Mode ▾	Task Name ▾	Duration ▾	Start ▾	Finish ▾	Predecessors ▾	27 Oct '19 S M T W T F S	03 Nov '19 S M T W T
1									
2			Decide what kind of cake you want	1 day?	Mon 04-11-19	Mon 04-11-19			
3			Find the recipe	1 day?	Mon 04-11-1	Mon 04-11-1			
4			Procure and Assemble Ingredients	1 day?	Mon 04-11-19	Mon 04-11-19			
5			Cook from the recipe	1 day?	Mon 04-11-19	Mon 04-11-19			
6			Present the cake	1 day?	Mon 04-11-1	Mon 04-11-1			
7			Clean up	1 day?	Mon 04-11-1	Mon 04-11-1			
8			Finished!	1 day?	Mon 04-11-1	Mon 04-11-1			

Figure 2.5 – MS Project – all Tasks created

At this stage, we have completed entering all of the tasks of our schedule. But as you can see, we have not yet tapped into the magic of MS Project. All the tasks take place on the same date, and they have yet to be scheduled.

To create a schedule, first select all of your tasks. Then, under the **Task** ribbon menu tab, locate and click the **Link** button (*it looks like a link in a chain*). As soon as you do this, links will appear, as shown in the following screenshot:

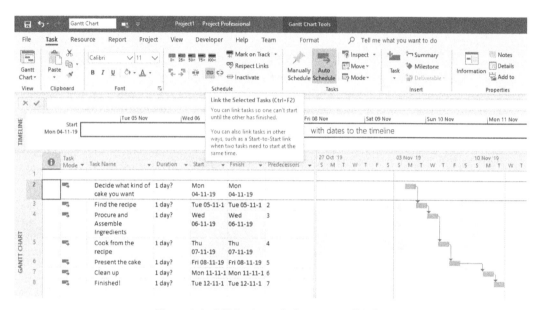

Figure 2.6 – MS Project – linking a set of Tasks

And with a click of that link button, you have just created your first schedule with MS Project. Congratulations!

> **Tip**
> The keyboard shortcut to link tasks is *Ctrl+F2*. Memorizing even a small set of commonly used shortcuts will greatly enhance your speed in creating and maintaining schedules with Project.

Note that a bunch of cells are highlighted in blue in the previous image. This is because your previous action propagated changes to these other tasks' parameters. It is nothing but a visual indication to you. This feature will be incredibly useful when you move on to complex projects that can be multiple screens long and wide, where changes in one part of the screen can affect various other areas in your project. So this is a good thing to note right from the beginning and keep an eye on.

Meanwhile, in the Chart area, a Gantt chart has been created that visually reflects your schedule. Now all the tasks are linked together. More importantly, it means that any further editing of your tasks—such as changing the duration or start date or end date of any task—or the addition of new tasks will mean that Project will automatically keep the overall schedule in shape.

You can see a simple example immediately by just changing the **Duration** of the first task from 1 day to 1 hr. Just type this value directly into the **Duration** field of this task and you will instantly see that Project recalculates everything else in your entire schedule. This is shown in the following screenshot:

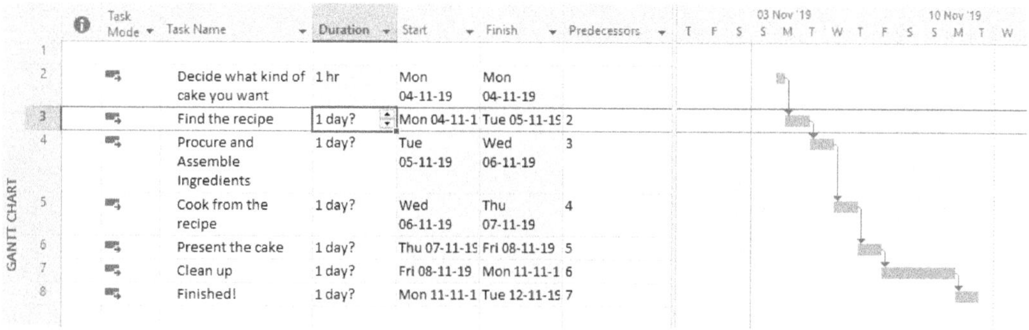

Figure 2.7 – MS Project – impact of changes on linked automatic tasks

Note that in the preceding figure, the first task has a changed duration of **1 hr**. This change was immediately reflected in the Gantt chart by a visually shorter bar representing said task. *One hour* more closely reflects the duration required by all the tasks in this project.

So, you should now change the duration of all the remaining tasks to **1 hr**. Feel free to play with the interface and observe the changes that happen. But I will urge you to only use the features covered thus far. This is to ensure that you do not change any settings that will change the behavior of Project, until we learn the concept at the right time in due course.

> **Tip**
>
> Changes in the schedule as a result of the immediate previous action will be highlighted. If it is not exactly what you wanted, you can immediately undo the change using the *Ctrl + Z* key combination or clicking on the undo arrow in the ribbon.

How does Project know that changes to a single Task parameter have to be propagated to the entire schedule? Project knows this because all the tasks in our schedule are configured to be *automatically scheduled*. We will now learn more about these different task modes in the next section.

Task modes: Automatic or Manual

Any task that you create can be in either one of two modes allowed: **Automatic** or **Manual**. Note that to the left of the **Task Name** column is another column called the **Task Mode**. For a quick reference, see the following figure, which shows a Task in Manual mode:

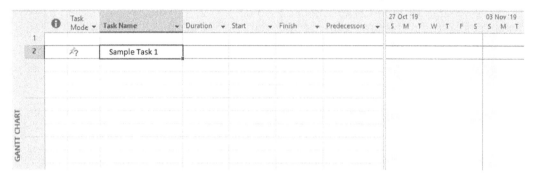

Figure 2.8 – MS Project – first Manual Task created

There are again a couple of important points to observe in the preceding figure:

- Project will not autofill any data for you this time around. It understands that you want to manually configure this task, so it will not make any presumptions this time.

- Look at the corresponding icon in the **Task Mode** column and compare it with the icon for the automatic task in the previous figure. They will be different and signify the specific task's configured mode.

When automatic tasks are created and linked into a schedule, Project takes over the management for those tasks in all respects, and it has several built-in algorithms that are put into use when managing the schedule; however, this doesn't happen with manual tasks.

The vast majority of tasks should be designed to be **Automatic** in order for you tap into the full power and magic of MS Project. The rest of this book will focus largely on automatic tasks.

You should use manual tasks very rarely in situations where you want specific control of a task's properties—for example, if a project's task is hard-bound to a specific date or a certain duration.

> **Tip**
>
> There are some other situations where you might usually need to use manual tasks—for example, when we start a new project and not much is known about a few tasks. Typically, for such tasks, we have to update the parametric information as it gets revealed to us upon designing the project. When sufficient information, such as the duration and dependencies, is known, then we can convert these manually scheduled tasks into automatic tasks. We will touch upon manual tasks once again briefly later in this book.

Manual tasks are highly prone to issues, bugs, and scheduling complexity. You have to avoid them. If they are unavoidable, you should document the reasons why you need to use them.

Until very recently, MS Project used to default to Manual Task mode for new projects that were created. New users would create schedules in Manual mode and not get to experience the scheduling algorithms. On the other hand, even experienced users of Project sometimes trip up with accidental manual tasks in their schedule.

Backstage: contextual changes

Before we proceed further with our project, now is the time to save your project. Click on the **File** ribbon tab. This leads us, once again, into the same Backstage area we saw earlier. The key point to observe on this screen is that, since we have a file open in Project, extra menu options have become available to us, as shown in the following screenshot:

Figure 2.9 – MS Project – Backstage view with a file open

Use the **Save As** link to save the file in a suitable location. To return to your work, click on the return arrow at the very top left of the screen.

Linking and dependencies between tasks

It is important now to look closer into the task links that we created earlier and learn about a new concept called **task dependencies**. For a quick reference, see the following screenshot:

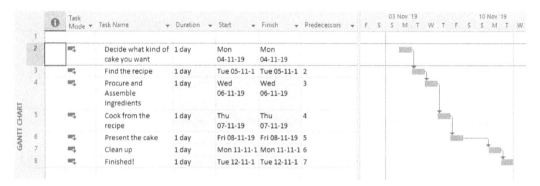

Figure 2.10 – MS Project – linking and dependencies

We saw earlier that tasks originate from a logical breakdown of project requirements. Because of this common origin of a project's tasks, you can naturally expect that most tasks will depend on one another, connected by some meaningful logic. This dependency can be *explicit* or *implicit*. For example, the second task in our project is dependent upon the first task. Obviously, you will find the correct recipe for the cake (*second task*) only after deciding what kind of cake you want (*first task*). This is an example of an explicit dependency.

Often, tasks will also be executed one after another, the order of execution being decided by the fact that the resource can execute only one task at a time. This is an example of an implicit dependency.

For automatically linked tasks, Project calculates new start and end dates for the entire schedule for every change to any of your constituent tasks. Now, you might be wondering what's so great about all this. Consider that what you did now with only a few tasks can be done with hundreds and thousands of tasks, and different resources. Project will automatically calculate and manage a realistic schedule. If you had to do this manually, every change would be a nightmare.

Scheduling a project

The concept of a schedule is primal to the discipline and science of project management, and one simple way of defining it is as follows:

"A schedule is a chronologically ordered listing of tasks or events."

By this definition, our project has achieved a functional project schedule. In fact, MS Project can be understood as a powerful **scheduling engine**. Its built-in scheduling algorithms will help you in organizing, recording, calculating, tracking, reporting, and analyzing schedule data for literally any type of project.

> **Note**
>
> The schedule is not a project plan, even though it is very commonly referred to as such. The schedule is only a part of the overall project plan, which will include other major components, such as the Scope-Management Plan, Risk-Management Plan, Quality-Management Plan, Cost-Management Plan, and so on. For small enough projects, the schedule might constitute the whole project plan.

Resourcing your tasks

Projects are executed by resources. You will assign every individual task in the project schedule to specific resources for the successful execution of your project. In most cases, resources are people from your project plan. They can be your own internal teammates or external vendor team members. It is important to note that resources also include everything else that is needed to execute a project. If your project needs machinery, special budgets, or certain materials, all of these are also considered to be resources.

Adding resources to your schedule is not mandatory in MS Project, and it is perfectly acceptable for tiny projects, such as your currently running exercise project. In any kind of real-life project, however, resources are never infinite and must often be carefully requisitioned for your project execution. This is exactly why using resource capabilities in Project allows you to tap into Project's scheduling magic.

In Project, resources can be one of three predefined types:

- **Material resources**: To understand this type better, think of cement as being a material resource for a house-building project. As your project progresses and walls are being built, naturally, the cement gets consumed. It will often be possible to predict how many units of a certain material resource are required to complete a project. Let's consider another example: your annual subscription license to the MS Project application itself can be considered as a material resource for a project.

- **Work resources**: These are the resources that will not get consumed by the execution of tasks on a project. The most common instances of work resources are the people assigned to your tasks. Work resources are the default and most common type of resource you will find across project domains.

- **Cost resources**: Some of your tasks might require additional costs. Such additional budgets can be assigned to a task as cost resources. For example, consider a fictional task called **Onsite Client Meetings**, which will incur a flight cost, hotel-stay cost, and per-diem expenses as per the company policy. Project allows us to tabulate these costs too.

We will make use of all these different resource types in later examples in this book. But for the meantime, let's revisit our running project and assign some resources.

Allocating tasks to resources

So far, we have discussed tasks and resources separately. The act of assigning one or more resources to a specific task is called *allocation*. This simple concept has many important applications within Project. If you examine this from the perspective of any individual resource, say John Doe, it will be possible to view and manipulate tasks only assigned to them. MS Project has several special views and reports specially designed to analyze your project purely from an assignment perspective.

Let's see how to create allocations in our running project. Locate the column titled **Resource Names** in Project's table. In the cell for the first task, type in your name. You can then drag the edge of the cell to quickly populate all the remaining tasks, just like you can do in Excel. When you are finished, your screen should be similar to the following screenshot:

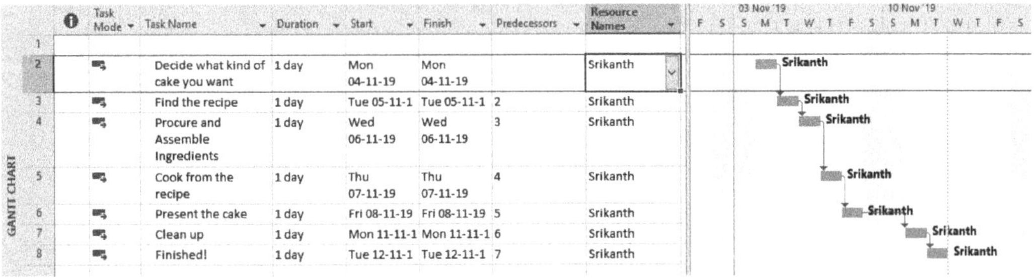

Figure 2.11 – MS Project – resource allocations

Note that the resource names also show up on the Gantt chart, making it very easy to visually identify who is responsible for completing each of the tasks.

This example is the simplest form of task allocation suitable to our current project. In later chapters, we will understand allocations from other perspectives.

Taking a closer look at views

So far into our project, the screen we have been using is called a **View**. It is, in fact, the most popular view in Microsoft Project, and in the whole of the project management discipline, and it is called the Gantt Chart view. There are more than 30 different views available in MS Project.

MS Project can store a lot of information about your project. Views are especially predesigned subsets of this information, presented to you by Project. They offer meaningful ways to analyze and manipulate your project data. Take a moment to notice that there is a complete tab in the ribbon dedicated to Views in MS Project. There, you can access all the other 30+ main views prebuilt into Project. These views cover every imaginable perspective of the project that you can think of.

From the **Task** ribbon tab, the first button on the left is the Gantt chart view. Hover your mouse over this button and note that it is made up of two parts. The bottom part is a dropdown that will list the most popular views available to you. To return from any view, click the top part of the same button and you will return to the Gantt chart view:

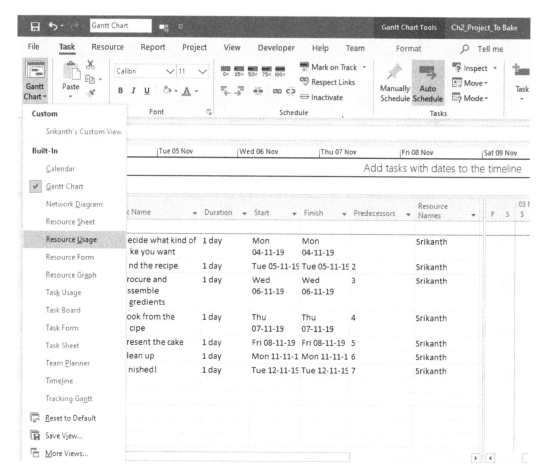

Figure 2.12 – MS Project – changing views

The Gantt chart view is the default view used by MS Project, and for small and tiny projects, it will be almost completely self-sufficient. The Gantt chart view is made up of a chart and a table together, and they are dynamically connected to each other in Project.

For a quick experiment, let's now see a different view. Locate and open the **Resource Usage** view from the dropdown. You should now see a view similar to this:

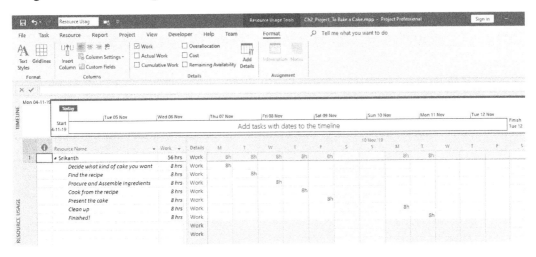

Figure 2.13 – MS Project – Resource Usage view

The Resource Usage view shows the resource assignments for individual tasks in the currently opened project and also displays the summary of the assignments. When you have many resources working on your project, this view is an invaluable tool for resource balancing and identifying problems with allocations, such as overallocations. To return from this view, go to the **Task** tab and click the **Gantt chart** button again.

Every single view is built with individual components, namely tables, charts, filters, groups, and details. In the next couple of pages, we will get a little more familiar with tables and charts.

> **Tip**
> It is possible for you to customize any of the views and then save them as your own new views. You can then even share them in your organization. We will discuss different views throughout this book. We will undertake a deep exploration of views in *Chapter 14, Views, Tables, and Customization*.

Tables

A table can be defined as a set of fields displayed in the sheet portion of a view as columns and rows. Earlier in this chapter, you used the table portion of the Gantt chart view to enter your project tasks. Different views will have different default tables displayed. In the case of our favorite Gantt chart view, the default table is called the **Entry Table**.

It will be possible for you to apply different tables in a view other than the default. To apply a different table, click the **View tab**, click **Tables**, and then select the table you want to apply, as shown in the following image:

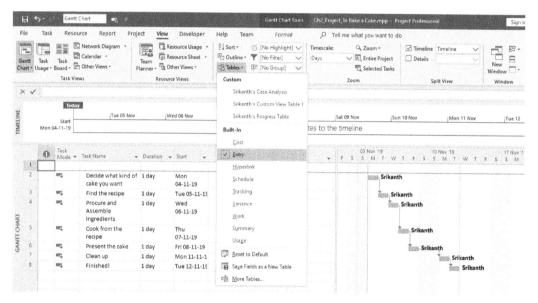

Figure 2.14 – MS Project – applying tables to a view

To return to the default, select the Entry Table for the Gantt chart view.

Tables generally vary from each other depending on the data columns they are configured to display—for example, you have already seen that on the Entry Table, the default columns available are **Indicators, Task Mode, Task Name, Duration, Start, Finish, Predecessors**, and **Resource Names**. This is only a small subset of the hundreds of other data columns available should you ever choose to explore it; however, this small default subset of data columns can even suffice for complex projects.

Pitfall: Resemblance to Excel and limitations

New users to Project are often delighted that the table interface very closely matches that of an Excel worksheet. This is definitely an advantage, and you too would have benefitted from this familiarity while working on the running project in this chapter. *But this is a double-edged sword because the similarity ends there.* Excel is a generic tool; Project is not. I have seen many new learners get disheartened and abandon Project because they do not invest the time and effort required to learn the behavior of Project beyond their comfort zone with Excel.

Charts, diagrams, timelines, and graphs

Different views often provide correspondingly different visual representations of your project data. Once you start the project with the default Gantt chart and build your schedule, you can then use any other visual representation as suitable for the stage of your project, or as mandated by your organizational standards.

For example, consider the **Network Diagram View**. This is a view popular with project managers. It displays your tasks in a flowchart format. This format is especially helpful when fine-tuning and optimizing your schedule. The specialty of this view is that it is built entirely with a chart—that is, there is no table component in this view.

On the other end of the spectrum, there are views that are only built with the table component and no visual representation. The **Resource Usage** view that we explored earlier is an example of such a view.

Which view should we use?

New users to Project are often overwhelmed by the number of views provided. But the fact is that about 80% of your work will be accomplished just within the default Gantt chart view.

You will find the other views useful to optimize your schedule or to discover and resolve issues with scheduling, especially on complex project schedules. Other views are also useful to communicate *different versions of the truth*. For example, you might use the Resource Usage view with your development team leader to show resource loading. You might use the Tracking Gantt view to display weekly progress to your boss.

Over the course of this book, specific concepts and situations will be highlighted with views which are tailor-made for the purpose. This will give you a powerful and quick toolkit to be used in your workplace.

Reports

MS Project ships with a gamut of reports and dashboards. Moreover, every aspect of them is dynamic and customizable. But all of these reports really start to make sense when we proceed to execute and track our progress.

At this early stage of your learning, it's enough to note that there is a full **Report** tab in the ribbon menu provided by Project. Open the **Report** tab, click on the **Dashboards** dropdown button, and select the **Project Overview** dashboard. You should see a screen similar to this:

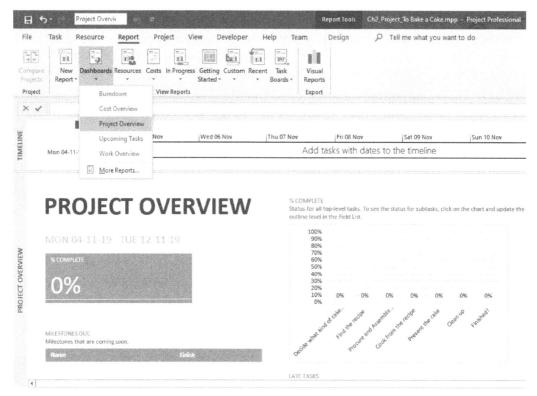

Figure 2.15 – MS Project – Project Overview dashboard

Feel free to explore the reports and dashboards available to you out of the box with MS Project. Be aware that these reports only start to be very useful when you proceed with tracking your project schedule. We will cover all aspects of the tracking, monitoring, and controlling of your schedule as we progress through this book.

Practice assignment

Here is a small assignment that will help you practice everything that you have learned in this chapter.

Objective: Design a small garden for your house. It could be in a small yard, on the terrace, or in any other suitable place of your choice.

Project plan design requirements: Create a plan that covers the garden design, site selection, material procurement, seeking advice from experts on plant selection, testing, and providing some basic amenities in the garden.

What you must do:

Create a Project schedule using only the concepts covered in this chapter.

Explain your plan. What assumptions, constraints, and risk plan will you have in place for your project?

Optional: Submit screenshots of your solution Project schedule to my website at `www.learngood.in`. You will be able to see and discuss solutions from other students.

Summary

In this chapter, you received a warm welcome into the world of MS Project. By creating a simple but fully functional project, you were introduced to the major concepts of tasks, linking and dependencies, Project schedules, resources, and allocations, and finally views and reports. You were also gently introduced to the complex user interface of MS Project, and you should now be able to navigate your way around Project. I urge you to work on the practice assignment, as this will really cement your learning and permanently remove any fear of using Project.

In the next chapter, we will dive deeper in to scheduling concepts and look even more closely at the user interface of Project, specifically aspects related to the Gantt chart. This will give you the skills and knowledge required to start using Project in your professional work.

3
Initiating projects with Microsoft Project

The initiating stage of a project, which is also the first stage, is when you define the whole new project to be executed. Initiation is a crucial stage where the project objectives – that is, the *big picture* – is established with all the people involved. It is also a politically and strategically important stage as you will have to seek the support and resources you require to undertake your project.

Centuries ago, when Christopher Columbus sought to undertake an ambitious project to discover new frontiers by sea, he initiated the project by seeking money and ships from Queen Isabella of Castile. In return, the objectives of the project were aligned to profit the project sponsors.

During the course of this chapter, we will specifically discuss the usage of Microsoft Project in the initiating stages of your project. Using robust techniques for scheduling right from the earliest stages of the project has several advantages and helps you identify risks to the project early on.

In this chapter, we're going to cover the following main topics:

- How to get the best possible start to your projects by harnessing the power of MS Project

- Creating our next hands-on project schedule exercise

- A deeper understanding of all aspects of scheduling – tasks, dependency linking, and resources

- Continued exploration of the Project UI, and uncovering several features that we will use in our exercise project

Initiating projects

In real-life scenarios, the initiation phase of a project often begins when your sales team is pitching a project to a client. The dynamics are very similar even when the project is only in-house with internal customers of the project. The stakes are often high and significant for all the stakeholders and the organizations involved. If the sales pitch is strong enough, the approving authority will want to know the *numbers involved*—budgets, return on investment, the time frame, resources required, and so on. Process-mature and project-oriented organizations will involve the **Project Management Office** (**PMO**), the project manager, and **Subject Matter Experts** (**SMEs**) at this stage.

Using a robust tool such as MS Project in this situation has many advantages, such as being able to do the following:

- Visualize and justify the complexity of the projects.

- Justify the price, resources, and time sought.

- Identify key milestones and mutual deliverables.

- Establish a critical path and schedule risks for the project.

- Make the schedule you have created as the centerpiece of the project-initiating documentation.

- Establish professionalism and confidence with the stakeholders.

It is from this exact perspective that we will view MS Project in this chapter. We will not need to use several features of Project at this stage, such as tracking, reports, and so on.

What the Project Management Book of Knowledge (PMBOK) says

There are two important objectives of the project initiation processes, whether it is for a new project or for a new phase of a running project:

- Managing the expectations of all the stakeholders of the project. This means establishing the initial scope of your project.

- Ensuring appropriate participation of the stakeholders to ensure the success of your project. This translates to you getting all the resources and approvals you need for the project.

Who are the *stakeholders* on a project? Everyone who is impacted by your project and everyone who can impact your project is your stakeholder. For example, this includes your customer, your boss, the PMO, various supporting departments in your organization, and your entire team. If society at large is impacted by certain projects, then it should also be considered as a stakeholder.

So, as the project manager, you must manage the end-to-end expectations of this stakeholder group. By doing so, you must ensure that this stakeholder group will facilitate the execution of your project to successful closure. For example, in the initiation stage, you might establish the following:

- A high-level scope of the project

- Stage-wise customer signoffs required on your project

- The human resources, hardware, software, networking, machines, travel budgets, and so on, required for your project

- The domain knowledge and SMEs required

- The third-party vendor services or tools and libraries to be procured for your project

Key outcomes of the initiating stage

The key outcome of the initiating stage is a document called the **project charter**, according to standard project management terminology. The project manager will develop this document with the help and approval of all the stakeholders.

The gist of this document will often be the project objectives, in and out of scope details, high-level schedule (**Gantt chart developed with MS Project**), and other budgetary details.

Often, for small and medium-sized projects, the Gantt chart will be the most important component of the project charter.

Risk over the project life cycle

Proper initiation of the project will help uncover potential risks (and existing issues) that the project entails. At this early stage, it becomes a crucial part of expectation management to correctly appraise the stakeholders of risk. There are two fundamental ways that risk can be considered:

- Risk mitigation, wherein you plan to reduce the probability of the risk materializing.
- Risk contingency, wherein you plan your action for the circumstances when risk materializes. This is the proverbial *plan B*.

You can see that a high-quality schedule in the initiating stage will include details for these two aspects of risk. There is yet another compelling reason to consider risks right from the initiation stage. The cost of risk mitigation and contingency increases exponentially over the lifetime of the project.

Project for this chapter – digital marketing campaign

Case study: You are the project manager in a fast-growing mobile app company. Your company is ready to launch its first mobile app *in 1 month*. You have been put in charge of the digital marketing campaign project. The objective is to create a marketing leads database from the company's web and social media presence.

The critical success criteria for your project is as follows:

1. Create a web and social media presence for your company.
2. Create a database of prospective customers *(also known as leads)*.
3. Create a functional sales funnel for the new product.
4. Do not exceed 1 month *(20 working days!)*.

The assumptions are as follows:

- You will rely on your company's existing ecosystem of third-party vendors.
- Your company has web and digital marketing content readily available.

A breakdown of the work is as follows:

1. Launch Project.

2. Create the **Business Requirements Specifications** (**BRS**) document. This will form the guidelines for the vendors' work.

3. Contract the vendors to start the work.

4. Vendor 1: Design a blog-based website.

5. Vendor 2: Install the website.

6. Vendor 1: Upload the blog content.

7. Vendor 2: Design a social media presence.

8. Vendor 2: Create social media assets (LinkedIn giveaways, a YouTube channel, contests, a Facebook page, and groups).

9. Vendor 2: Upload social media assets.

10. Close the project.

With this much information, we are now ready to start our new project and replicate the same steps that you would encounter in your real-life work situations.

Scheduling with MS Project – a deeper understanding

Exactly as in *Chapter 2, Fundamentals of Microsoft Project,* fire up your Project application and create a new blank project. But before we proceed further with building the schedule, there are a couple of important configuration aspects that we will now learn about.

Project Information and Project Options

Select the **Project** tab from the main ribbon menu. Locate the button called **Project Information**. In the following reference screenshot, you will see this button highlighted with a red box.

When you click on this button, a dialog box will open called **Project Information**:

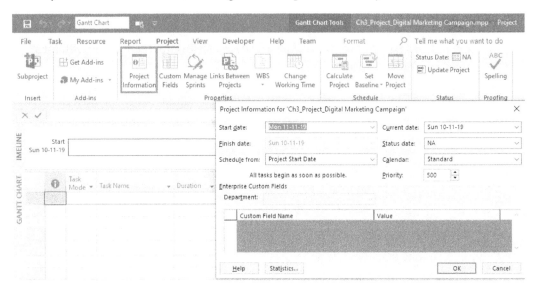

Figure 3.1 – Microsoft Project – the Project Information dialog box

An important aspect of this dialog box is that you can use it to set the start date for the entire project. In the preceding screenshot, I have set the project start date to the next upcoming Monday. For the sake of this exercise, you can also do the same and set the start date to your next upcoming Monday.

The project start date that you set here is used by Project as the default start date of every new task you create. If this date is *not* set, then by default, Project will use *today's date* (that is, the current date) for every new task created. In the same dialog box, you next have the option to tell Project's algorithms to schedule from either the start date or from the finish date. It is also possible to schedule in reverse order, from a fixed finish date. These are for situations when the project has a fixed and "hard" finish date constraint.

Notice that there is an option to set the base calendar for your project. There are pre-built calendars within Project that can be used for most common situations. We will discuss calendars in much greater detail later in *Chapter 4, Underlying Concepts of Microsoft Project*.

At the bottom of the dialog box, there is a **Statistics** button, which is really just a quick and dirty version of the overall project statistics. At this stage of our project, you will not get any useful information, but it is available if you want to use it in the later stages of your project. You can now close this dialog box and return to the main work area.

There is one more important dialog box where most of Project's configurability is presented, and that is the **Project Options** dialog box. Click on the **File** ribbon tab and enter the **Backstage** area. Locate and click on the **Options** tab.

This opens the **Project Options** dialog box, as shown in the following screenshot:

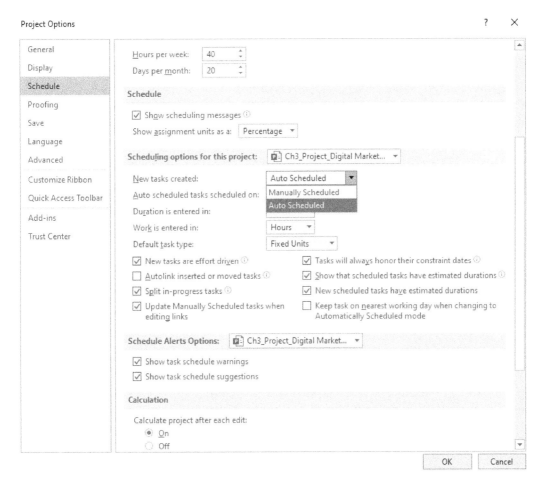

Figure 3.2 – Microsoft Project – the Project Options dialog box

This dialog box has special importance because it is the location where you will find all of Project's default behavior. Specifically, for now, locate the **Schedule** tab and then on the right, locate the section titled **Scheduling options for this project**. Click on the dropdown to select all the new projects and always ensure here that the new tasks created are set to **Auto Scheduled** by default.

By doing this, you have ensured that manual tasks are not accidentally introduced into your newly created schedules.

> **Pitfall – manual tasks**
>
> As we will see continually in this book, it is good practice to avoid manual tasks, except for special situations. Despite this, until recently, MS Project would default to manual tasks. Even now, it is common for new users to inherit project files in their organization that have inadvertent manual tasks. This is a common pitfall that needs to be avoided.

Tasks

We can now fill in the tasks of our project by referring to the task details from before. For every task, start by creating only the task name. For now, do not add other values such as their duration or any of the dates. When you are done, your screen should look similar to this:

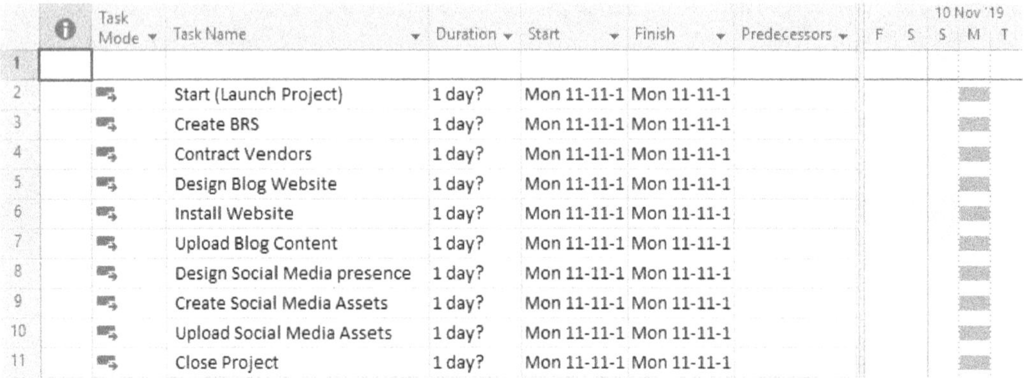

❶	Task Mode ▾	Task Name ▾	Duration ▾	Start ▾	Finish ▾	Predecessors ▾	F	S	S	M	T
1											
2		Start (Launch Project)	1 day?	Mon 11-11-1	Mon 11-11-1						
3		Create BRS	1 day?	Mon 11-11-1	Mon 11-11-1						
4		Contract Vendors	1 day?	Mon 11-11-1	Mon 11-11-1						
5		Design Blog Website	1 day?	Mon 11-11-1	Mon 11-11-1						
6		Install Website	1 day?	Mon 11-11-1	Mon 11-11-1						
7		Upload Blog Content	1 day?	Mon 11-11-1	Mon 11-11-1						
8		Design Social Media presence	1 day?	Mon 11-11-1	Mon 11-11-1						
9		Create Social Media Assets	1 day?	Mon 11-11-1	Mon 11-11-1						
10		Upload Social Media Assets	1 day?	Mon 11-11-1	Mon 11-11-1						
11		Close Project	1 day?	Mon 11-11-1	Mon 11-11-1						

Figure 3.3 – Microsoft Project – tasks have been entered for our project

You will already be familiar with the tasks so far, but before we proceed any further, I will point out some interesting aspects for your careful observation:

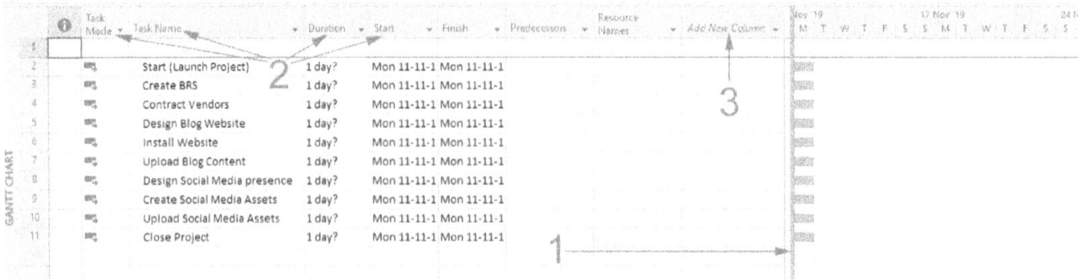

Figure 3.4 – Microsoft Project – observe tasks on the entry table

From the preceding screenshot, we can observe the following:

1. The thin divider that is present between the entry table and the Gantt chart can be dragged to the left and right to uncover areas on either side. If you work on a smaller screen, often, one or more of the default columns might be hidden from your view. Try it out now and get comfortable with this aspect. Observe that we have not yet discussed the standard columns, **Predecessors** and **Resource Names**.

2. Each and every column header on the entry table reveals a different parameter of the task, except for the first column, which is for **Indicators**. The default parameters are **Task Mode**, **Task Name**, **Duration**, **Start**, **Finish**, **Predecessors**, and **Resource Names**.

3. The rightmost column is just a placeholder called **Add new Column**. When you click on the column label, it reveals a dropdown with an enormous list of column data options that you can add to your table. All of these data points are, once again, different parameters of the **Task** entity:

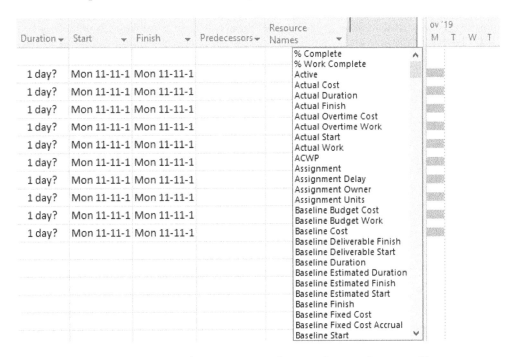

Figure 3.5 – Microsoft Project – new column options on the entry table

You, my astute reader, may now have guessed that this dropdown gives an insight into the data structure used by Project to represent the **Task** entity – and you would be absolutely right! The view that you are currently in, and the table that you have active, will decide what column options are available.

> **Tip**
> Always keep a close watch on the **Indicators** column while working on a schedule. This is where Project whispers directly into your ear. Messages here can be warnings of potential issues, or it can draw your attention to the special nature of the task in question.

Task config dialog box

You can right-click on any task, and in the contextual menu that pops up, choose **Information**. The **Task Information** dialog box will pop up and this is where you can greatly customize any individual task. Notice that there are tabs that group different aspects of the task, including linking and dependency (**Predecessors**), resources, and other advanced options. Feel free to explore the different options but refrain from changing anything for now, or else it will impact our exercise schedule in ways you cannot predict:

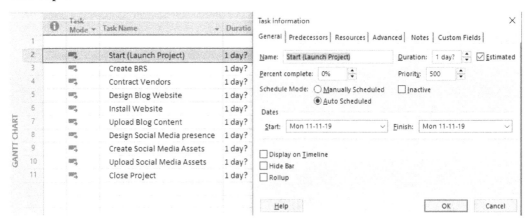

Figure 3.6 – Microsoft Project – the Task Information dialog box

Some of these properties, such as the **Priority** setting, are only used in special advanced situations (for example, resolving over-allocations). However, we will visit this dialog box often in our exercise projects throughout the rest of the book. If you save any inadvertent changes in the dialog box, you can undo your recent action.

Duration

This is one of the most important parameters of a task. MS Project's definition for this column is *the total span of working time for a task*. There are several connotations to this definition, and we will examine them in greater detail in *Chapter 4, Underlying Concepts of Microsoft Project*.

Observe, in *Figure 3.6*, that the default value inserted by Project for a new task is **1 day?**. The question mark denotes that this value is just an assumption made by Project on your behalf. If you enter a value there, the question mark will disappear.

Continuing with our exercise project, now let's fill up estimates for our task durations. Refer to the following screenshot and proceed to enter the values accordingly:

	ⓘ	Task Mode ▾	Task Name ▾	Duration ▾	Start ▾	Finish ▾	Predecessors ▾	10 Nov '19 F S S M T W T F S
1								
2		▤	Start (Launch Project)	1 day	Mon 11-11-1	Mon 11-11-1		
3		▤	Create BRS	2 days	Mon 11-11-1	Tue 12-11-1		
4		▤	Contract Vendors	2 days	Mon 11-11-1	Tue 12-11-1		
5		▤	Design Blog Website	3 days	Mon 11-11-1	Wed 13-11-1		
6		▤	Install Website	3 days	Mon 11-11-1	Wed 13-11-1		
7		▤	Upload Blog Content	3 days	Mon 11-11-1	Wed 13-11-1		
8		▤	Design Social Media presence	5 days	Mon 11-11-1	Fri 15-11-19		
9		▤	Create Social Media Assets	5 days	Mon 11-11-1	Fri 15-11-19		
10		▤	Upload Social Media Assets	5 days	Mon 11-11-1	Fri 15-11-19		
11		▤	Close Project	1 day	Mon 11-11-1	Mon 11-11-1		

Figure 3.7 – Microsoft Project – enter task duration values

It is sufficient for you to just enter the number in the task's **Duration** cell and hit the *Enter* key. You will not need to explicitly type out the *days* every time. There are several small intelligent aspects like this that you will discover when you work hands-on with Project.

At this point in time, we are finished with entering the duration values, but there is still no schedule created, as you can see in the Gantt chart all our tasks lie on the same date. The correct technique for creating the schedule is to now build out the dependency links between tasks and allow Project to work out its algorithmic magic.

Linking and dependency

In the previous simple exercise project, we created task dependencies by using the **Link** button in the ribbon's **Task** tab. In this project, we will hand-craft the links in a different technique, by using the **Predecessors** column. This latter technique easily allows greater customization. Remember that in any given schedule, there are two special tasks. The first task will have no predecessor, and the last task will have no successor. With this guideline, we will create dependency links with all the other tasks, using only the **Predecessors** fields.

Start with the task named **Create BRS**, and in the corresponding **Predecessors** field, enter the row ID of the previous task. In my case, it will be 2. *(I usually leave the first row blank just for better readability of the schedule).* Refer to the following screenshot and you should also get a similar result:

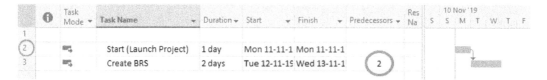

Figure 3.8 – Microsoft Project – creating the first link

When you create this link, there are some interesting points to be observed:

1. In the Gantt chart, an arrow link has been created, indicating the direction of the task execution. Since this is a timeline view, chronological ordering has been established for these two tasks.

2. The second task, **Create BRS**, has been automatically pushed forward in time with a new **Start** date. Notice that this is highlighted to you by the temporary blue coloring of the cells in the table. The new start date occurs *after* the finish date of the **Predecessor** task *(in our case, the first task).*

3. A new **Finish** date is also computed for the second task. This is a function of the said task's duration.

4. Now that the two tasks are linked, any changes to the task's parameters will mean that Project's algorithms will kick in again and recompute the task parameters.

Now, proceed to link all the tasks, as in the following screenshot:

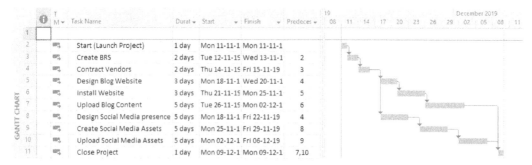

Figure 3.9 – Microsoft Project – schedule fully linked

There are some observations to be made at this stage, referring to the schedule we
have created:

1. The zoom level default in your own Gantt chart will be different, as I have reduced
    the zoom here to fit the whole screen onto this page. This zoom feature will be
    explained later in this chapter, but it does not matter for now as it is just a visual aid
    and just makes your Gantt chart look bigger.

2. The task with ID **4**, **Contract Vendors**, has two branch offshoots, as evident in
    the Gantt chart. Each branch logically represents a different vendor who has been
    contracted.

3. On the other hand, the last task, **Close Project**, has two predecessors. This logically
    represents the fact that both contractors have to finish their respective work for the
    whole project to be considered complete.

4. Pay special attention to the fact that even though the first vendor's branch
    executes a little early, the schedule is driven by the longer branch of the second
    vendor's tasks.

As a project manager, even if you have not been using Gantt charts, you will already be
familiar with this kind of a schedule design, where individual resources (or teams) will
branch out with their tasks and converge at significant stages of your project.

Best practices for task dependency linking

To ensure you derive the maximum benefit of this feature of MS Project, here are some
best practices you must keep in mind:

*   **Minimalism**: Use minimum links to correctly create an executable project schedule.
    This is an implicit golden role and is often abused by new users of Project. Any extra
    complexity adds up quickly, resulting in unmanageable schedules.

*   **Readability**: Use white space intelligently to increase the readability of your
    schedule. Your schedule will have a large and diverse audience, including all of your
    stakeholders. It should be easy to read and follow along even when you are not
    present to explain your design.

*   **Circular references**: Project has some simple constraints in place that will prevent
    you from circuitously making a task dependent upon itself. But these situations
    are possible when you are in the on-paper design stage and also when you are
    working with groups of tasks *(that is, summary tasks, which we will learn about
    later in this book)*. It is best practice to always watch out for circular dependencies
    in your schedule.

- **Orphan tasks**: Avoid tasks with no dependencies (either successors or predecessors). These tasks are harder to track and monitor, especially for complex projects.

- **Manual mode tasks**: When you are in the initiation stages of a project, it is very likely that you will not have complete information about individual tasks and their dependencies. Manual tasks are available in Project exactly for this situation. It is OK if you create some manual tasks in the initiation stage, but it is a good practice to convert all of them into automatic mode tasks by the end of the planning stage of your project. If any remain, they must be watched with special care after every subsequent modification to your schedule.

Resources

The next step in our project is to assign each of the tasks to the people who will execute them. The **Resource Names** column is where this assignment will be made. You can directly start entering names of the resources into this column now; see the following screenshot for a reference:

	M	Task Name	Durat	Start	Finish	Predeces	Resource Names	
1								
2		Start (Launch Project)	1 day	Mon 11-11-1	Mon 11-11-1		PM	
3		Create BRS	2 days	Tue 12-11-1	Wed 13-11-1	2	PM	
4		Contract Vendors	2 days	Thu 14-11-1	Fri 15-11-19	3	PM	
5		Design Blog Website	3 days	Mon 18-11-1	Wed 20-11-1	4	Vendor1	
6		Install Website	3 days	Thu 21-11-1	Mon 25-11-1	5	Vendor1	
7		Upload Blog Content	5 days	Tue 26-11-1	Mon 02-12-1	6	Vendor1	
8		Design Social Media presence	5 days	Mon 18-11-1	Fri 22-11-19	4	Vendor2	
9		Create Social Media Assets	5 days	Mon 25-11-1	Fri 29-11-19	8	Vendor2	
10		Upload Social Media Assets	5 days	Mon 02-12-1	Fri 06-12-19	9	Vendor2	
11		Close Project	1 day	Mon 09-12-1	Mon 09-12-1	7,10	PM	

Figure 3.10 – Microsoft Project – assign resources to all tasks

Each task, when assigned to a resource, becomes an *allocation*. Once again, there are some interesting observations for us:

- It is a common best practice to only use the job roles of the resources that you plan to assign to your task during the *project initiation phase*. This is simply because often, the project plan is not yet approved, and so organizational resourcing is also officially not yet approved. On the other hand, even if named resources are available, your company might choose to reveal *only* the client-facing employee names. In both cases, use only the job roles instead of actual names.

  After resources are officially assigned, should you choose to do so, the job role labels can be replaced by the actual names of the employees, just by simply overwriting the labels.

- Every time you add a resource name, you are actually creating a new resource entry in the internal database maintained by Project. You can see this for yourself, very quickly, by changing the view to **Resource Sheet**. You should be able to see something similar to the following screenshot:

			Resource Name ▼	Type ▼	Material▼	Initials ▼	Gr▼	Max. ▼	Std. Rate ▼	Ovt. ▼	Cost/Use▼	Accrue ▼	Base ▼
1			PM	Work		P		100%	$0.00/hr	$0.00/hr	$0.00	Prorated	Standard
2			Vendor1	Work		V		100%	$0.00/hr	$0.00/hr	$0.00	Prorated	Standard
3			Vendor2	Work		V		100%	$0.00/hr	$0.00/hr	$0.00	Prorated	Standard

Figure 3.11 – Microsoft Project – Resource Sheet view – a first look

From the preceding screenshot, you can observe the following:

1. Be wary of typos when typing in resource names directly. If you type in Jonh instead of John, Project will accept it without complaint, and create a new resource for the misspelled name. This is the cause of many subtle and serious errors when you are balancing the work of your resources.

2. This technique of easily creating resources on the fly is popular with users. However, it is possible to prevent typo errors by setting a simple option. To see this in action, click on the **File** tab and enter the **Backstage | Options**. The **Options** dialog box will open up. Open the **Advanced** tab and locate **General options for this project** section. Uncheck the option labeled **Automatically add new resources and task**. It will be checked on by default:

Figure 3.12 – Microsoft Project – General options – disable the autocreation of resources

3. It's best practice to always review your **Resource Sheet** view after making allocations, precisely to prevent any unwanted typo-created resources.

4. **New UI**: With the exact intention of preventing typo-generated errors while assigning resources, MS Project now has a new UI introduced from the 2019 version: a drop-down UI. If you notice the small arrow button next to the **Resource Name** field, it will open like this:

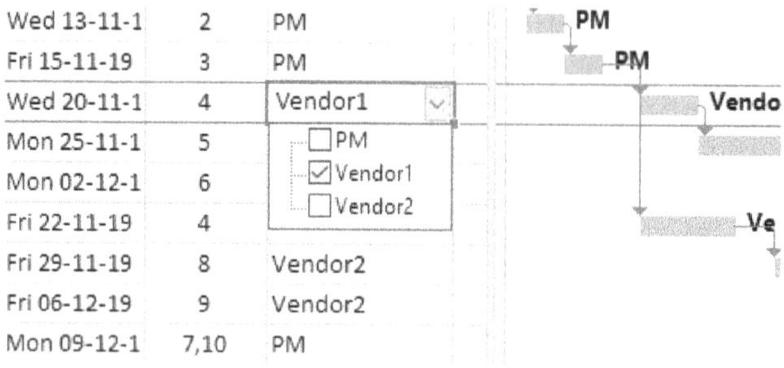

Figure 3.13 – Microsoft Project – the Resource Name drop-down interface

5. It is possible to assign multiple resources to a task just by typing additional names into the same field, separated by commas. However, it is not recommended to do so. The reason will become self-evident when we get to the advanced sections of this book, where we discuss project tracking.

6. There are some exceptions to this recommendation; for example, when certain tasks are designed to be accomplished by multiple resources, or even when the track is small enough to be tracked minutely. Even though this ambiguity exists, assigning multiple resources is a fairly common practice. The best way to avoid assigning multiple resources is by breaking the task down further into assignable chunks.

With that, we have completed our simple schedule of a project in its initiation stage. Now, let's look closer at some of the UI aspects right on your main screen that we have ignored so far.

Revisiting the UI

So far, I have been careful to introduce only those minimum UI features that are needed for us to proceed with our simple exercise projects. Now, let's take a quick look at the other useful features on your Project main screen.

Timeline view

Introduced in the 2010 version of Project, this is a such a loved feature that it occupies prime real estate on the main screen, albeit in a split window, sharing the honor with the Gantt chart view:

Figure 3.14 – Microsoft Project – the Timeline view

Task chronology is the key focus of this view, as the name suggests. The Timeline view starts out blank, and you can choose which tasks get added to it. In the preceding screenshot, you can observe that I have added a couple of tasks to the timeline. You can right-click on any task in the table, and in the contextual menu, select **Add to Timeline**. This action will add your task to the timeline at the right position on the timeline. The same button is also available to you in the ribbon's **Task** tab. We will look at this excellent view in some greater detail later in this book.

Gantt chart UI

You might have already started horizontally scrolling through the Gantt chart area, even with our short projects. The Gantt chart becomes complex very quickly. This is where the Gantt zoom slider buttons come in handy. You can locate these buttons at the very bottom right of the window, just below the Gantt chart:

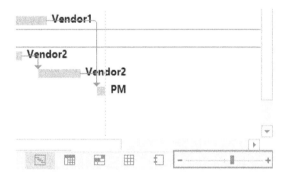

Figure 3.15 – Microsoft Project – zoom slider for the chart

Adjacent to the left of the zoom slider is another set of buttons for the most popular views so that you can access them very quickly. This is just another one of the productivity features and is placed strategically next to the zoom slider.

Quick Access Toolbar

In the same vein, and at the diametrically opposite end of the screen, in the topmost left corner, you will find the **Quick Access Toolbar**. By default, it holds the most commonly used buttons, but you can customize it to add other favorite features of your own choice:

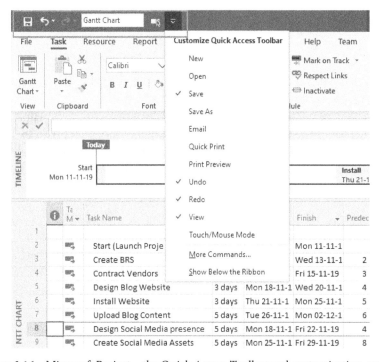

Figure 3.16 – Microsoft Project – the Quick Access Toolbar and customization options

The **More Commands…** option leads you to add practically any of Project's action features. This is a great way to increase your everyday productivity with Project.

The Indicators column

This column on the entry table is your best friend in Project. It can give you several types of information about your task and, sometimes, your whole project in general. It can warn you of some potential risks, such as resource overallocation and date constraints. We will study these indications in most of the later chapters of this book.

Options and configurations

Earlier, we briefly visited the **Project Options** dialog box when working on our exercise project to see how to make sure new tasks are created in automatic mode. Now is a good time for us to visit it once more. You can locate it from **File | Options**:

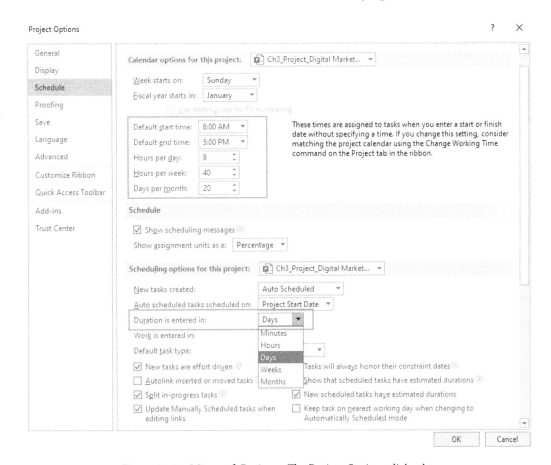

Figure 3.17 – Microsoft Project – The Project Options dialog box

It will be good for you to explore the many different options available from here, but do not change any of the configurations just yet, as they can change Project's behavior in ways that you will not be able to predict just yet.

However, if you want to observe what all the default assumptions that Project makes about your project are, you will find a whole lot here. Once you are more comfortable with Project, this is where you can customize preset parameters to your organizational standards.

Assignment

Here is a practice assignment for you. To solve this assignment, you must create a schedule for a project in its initiation stage. Optionally, your solution screenshots can be posted on my website, www.learngood.in, to share them with other readers and also to see their solutions.

Case study

You are a newly minted project management consultant, starting out on your own. You have rented a new but small office space in a commercial location of your city. Now, you want to prepare the interior of your office so that you can start using it full time.

The critical success criteria for your project is as follows:

1. You need a private working space for yourself and at least one employee.

2. You will also need a separate meeting space for whiteboard presentations to your clients.

3. You need some other basic amenities, such as a coffee machine, water cooler, and so on.

Constraints, assumptions, and instructions

Important: only use the concepts we have discussed so far in this book:

- You have identified that these aspects of work are required: wall painting, simple light fixtures, and creating false wall cabins.

- You have a moderate budget of USD 15,000 for this project, which will limit how fancy you can get with your office.

- You only have 1 month to finish the project. The rent is high, and you have to start making productive use of the office as quickly as possible.

- You have an architect friend who can be consulted *pro bono*.

- You will outsource all aspects to professional workers.

What you must do

1. Create a Project schedule using only the concepts covered so far in this book.

2. Explain your plan – what other assumptions, constraints, dependencies, and risk plans you will have in place for your project.

3. Optional: submit screenshots of your project schedule solution to my website, `www.learngood.in`. You will also be able to see and discuss solutions from other learners there.

Summary

Our focus in this chapter was to understand how MS Project can be best leveraged to initiate projects, such that you will be set up for success. Experienced project managers know that *well begun is half done*, and so it is really effective to start with Project right from the early stages of your project. We then completed another hands-on project exercise in this chapter, during which we holistically explored tasks, linking, and resourcing. While Project offers a great deal of customizability, you must also understand that the default behaviors are often the best suited in the vast majority of situations. However, if you want to finetune any aspect of Project, this ability exists in various configurable dialog interfaces all over the Project interface.

In the next chapter, we are going into very interesting territory. Instead of just learning *how* Project features behave, we will understand *why* they behave the way they do. We will explore the underlying logic of Project's algorithms with simple and relatable examples. This will give you a deeper insight into the automatic behavior of Project, something that often baffles uninitiated users.

4

Underlying Concepts of Microsoft Project

In the vast and complex world of science, a lot of value is placed on the elegant simplicity of scientific equations. Everybody has heard of Einstein's simple but profound equation. In the world of Microsoft Project, there exists a similar, simple formula. This simple formula is the bedrock upon which Project performs a multitude of calculations involving tasks, resources, assignments, calendars, tracking, and so on. But Microsoft did not invent this formula; it has been known to Project Managers from a very long time. You will recognize this formula, and begin to understand how Project really works, in this chapter.

Then, we will explore calendars in Project. If you can compare "managing a project" to "conducting an orchestra", you will find a great deal of similarities. It is the role of the conductor (project manager) to synchronize skilled musicians (team members) to create beautiful music (achieve project objectives). You can take this analogy a long way further. In this context, the calendar is like the metronome of your project. The Project Calendar keeps track of time ticking constantly, and every single aspect of your complex schedule should comply and synchronize with this constant ticking. Every component of Project is connected directly or indirectly to the calendar. Successful project execution requires an understanding of the Project Calendar to build effective and realistic schedules.

In this chapter, we're going to cover the following main topics:

- Demystifying the Basic work Formula

- Identifying, customizing, and using different types of Tasks

- Understanding Project scheduling algorithms

- Learning all about Calendars – creating, setting, and customizing them to your needs

All along the way, you are invited to practice what you learn, right at the place where you're learning it, hands-on. There are also some additional practice assignments at the end of this chapter that will help you understand everything better.

Demystifying the Basic Work Formula

Most Project users expect it to act like a spreadsheet and are often surprised to find that Project appears to have a mind of its own. This is because Project operates within an elegant framework of rules, algorithms, and solid project management techniques. The key to understanding this framework is a simple formula, which we will call the **Basic Work Formula**. Starting from complete basics, let's now proceed to understand this formula and see how it drives complex scheduling behavior.

There are three key parameters associated with every task to be executed in a schedule:

- **work** is the effort required to finish a task, usually measured in person-hours.

- **duration** is the span of working time required to finish a task, usually measured in working days.

- **Unit** is the measure of resources allocated to a specific task, measured by percentage in Project.

These three parameters are related by the **Basic Work Formula** of Microsoft Project:

$$Duration = Work \div Units$$

Using simple algebra, it can also be written as follows:

$$Work = Duration \times Units$$

Alternatively, it can be written as follows:

$$Units = Work \div Duration$$

All three forms are equivalent, mathematically. If you know the total effort (*work*) required to execute a task, and the *units of resources* that will be assigned to the task, then you can compute the *duration* of work time consumed by that task. Furthermore, using simple algebra, you will be able to deduce any unknown parameter if the other two parameters are known.

Let's now break down the meaning of this formula through a few simple examples. Please observe the following screenshot:

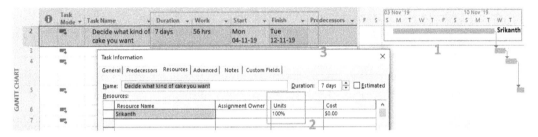

Figure 4.1 – Microsoft Project – Basic work Formula illustration

As highlighted in box 3, we have a task that is **7** days in duration. This is shown on the corresponding taskbar in the Gantt chart. I have also opened the **Task Information** dialog box to show you the **Resources** tab (which houses the **Units** field).

There are some important observations to be made:

- **duration** is neither a consecutive count nor a straightforward elapsed time on the calendar! Observe that the Gantt taskbar extends over 9 elapsed days (as seen in box 1 of the preceding screenshot), even though the duration is 7 days. This is because only the working days of a week are considered, even though the taskbar in the Gantt chart is unbroken over the non-working weekend days. The intervening Saturday and Sunday are excluded from calculations because they are not working days.

  It is possible to customize the working/non-working days and times for your project, as we will see in the latter part of this chapter (in the *Understanding Project Calendars* section).

- *One unit* denotes *one person working full time* on your project. In Project, this is denoted as **100%**. Similarly, a resource working only half their available time is denoted as 50%. So, this can be considered as follows:

  1 Unit = 100% (that is, one resource working full time)

  2 Units = 200% (that is, two resources working full time)

  0.5 Unit = 50% (that is, one resource working half their available time)

- The **work** column is not visible by default on the Gantt table area, though all fields are always available to you. I have included it explicitly in the preceding screenshot. You can see that it shows **56 hrs**. This is derived from the following formula:

$$7\ days\ \times\ 8\ hours\ per\ day\ =\ 56\ hours$$

- Project expects that, by default, for a task, you will start by entering the task's duration. This means that you will have estimated, offline, the work and resources available to begin with. You can, however, choose to start by entering a work estimate in Project instead; for example, if it is mandated by your organization.

> **Tip**
> You can enter the duration using several shortcuts for measures of time, as shown in the following table. This is true for other time measurement fields as well, such as work.

Duration Shortcuts	
1m	1 minute
1h	1 hour
1d	1 day
1w	1 week
1mo	1 month

Table 4.1 – Project's duration shortcuts

Practice mental math and calculating multiples of basic work hours at different magnitudes. Understand the project metrics of your business domain. What is considered a small/medium/large project in your expertise area? Also, there are some basic numbers you can use to make quick approximations. These are invaluable in quick calculations and verbal negotiations, and help you easily size up tasks and projects:

Approximations for ease and speed	
1 workday	8 hours
1 workweek	40 hours
1 person-month	~20 days
1 person-year	~2,000 hours

Table 4.2 – Quick approximations for calculations

Now, let's really cement our understanding of the Basic work Formula by considering some simple examples. Let's say our testing team must execute *80 automated test cases* for the company's software. One engineer can execute one test case in 1 hour. How long does the whole task take?

From the preceding problem statement, we know the following:

work = 80 person-hours (because one test case can be executed in 1 hour)

Units = 1 (because we have one test engineer working 100% on this project)

We can now compute this by applying the Basic work Formula:

duration = 80 person-hours / 1 Unit *(this is the Basic Work Formula)*

duration = 2 work weeks (which is 80 person-hours).

Now, just to make this more interesting, let's say a duration of 2 work weeks is not acceptable to you, and you want to reduce this time further. You decide to speed things up by adding one more test engineer to the task.

Now, we have the following:

work = 80 person-hours (this has not changed)

Units = 2 (because we now have two test engineers working 100% on this project)

We can now compute this again:

duration = 80 person-hours / 2 Units (this is the Basic Work Formula)

Therefore, *duration = 1 work week* (which is 40 person-hours).

By doubling the number of resources, we have halved the duration.

This isn't exactly rocket science but let's continue with yet another example.

A third test engineer has become available to work on your project. But they can only work 50% of their time on your project. Now, your **Units** is 2.5 (which is the same as 250% within Project) and, of course, work is the same at 80 person-hours. What will the new duration of your task be? Take a moment to compute the answer by applying the Basic Work Formula. You should get an answer of 4 workdays (or 32 hours).

An example Project for this chapter – creating online departmental manuals

Now that you have gotten a handle on the Basic work Formula, you are ready to see it in action within Project. Let's start with our next hands-on project, so fire up your Project instance and let's go!

Let's begin with a case study. You are the CEO of a small greenspace management company. You are required to create two online operating manuals, which consist of 100 web pages each. One is a Quality Manual, while the other is a Technical Manual. Remember that the objective of this exercise is for you to observe how Project uses the Basic work Formula to manipulate duration and work automatically, based upon your inputs. So, we will keep this project super simple with only two tasks.

The following are the constraints for these tasks:

- Task 1: Ten web pages can be created by one engineer in one day.

- Task 2: The manuals are independent of each other, and only worked upon by engineers of that department.

With this much information, we are now ready to start our project. The kinds of simple manipulation we will perform now are very common in real-life scenarios, so this is exactly how you will experience Project's algorithms.

Case 1 – Change of duration

Assign two different engineers to both tasks. Since 10 pages can be created in a single day, by each resource, the duration is 10 days to begin with. You already know that when you create a task, the default duration of *1 day?* is auto populated. The question mark appears because Project has assumed this default value for us. As soon as you change the duration, Project's algorithms kick in. A small green informational symbol appears in the duration field of the specific task:

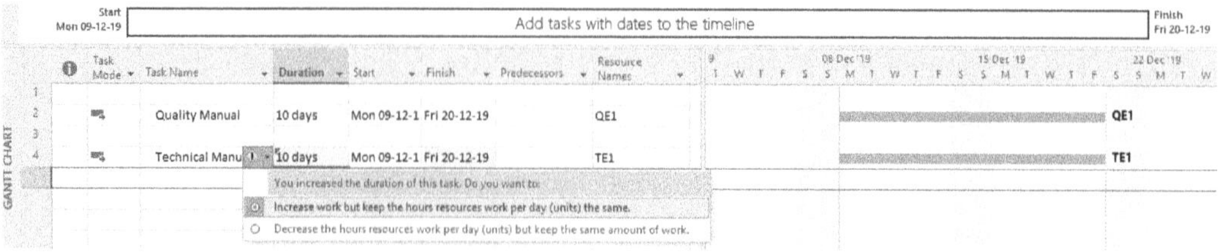

Figure 4.2 – Microsoft Project – Change duration informational message

When you click on the symbol, Project wants to know the reason you increased the duration. There are two reasons you can choose from:

- There's more work to do.

- There are fewer Units (that is, fewer resources).

In both cases, the duration of a task can potentially increase, and Project is not sure what option best reflects your reality. Project is asking you to clarify this in the dialog box. In our case, we modified duration because our task's work requires more time than the defaulted 1 day. Even if you just ignore this query from Project, the defaulted option (increased duration) has already been applied. If you adopt this mode of creating schedules, then it is perfectly fine to ignore this warning when you change the duration of many tasks at once, at the beginning stages of your project.

Note that, if you choose the second option, then duration will increase and work will remain the same, but Unit percentage will decrease. This means that the assigned resource will do less work on the task every day. If this gets confusing, refer to the Basic work Formula from earlier.

Case 2 – Adding additional resources

Now, we will assign an additional resource to the first task. Once again, the first option is the default and it complies with the Basic work Formula. Because we have doubled the number of resources (from one to two), our duration is halved, as shown in the following screenshot:

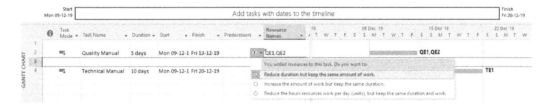

Figure 4.3 – Microsoft Project – work formula, additional resource

This is the expected behavior and it is defaulted by Microsoft. Observe the other two options carefully. They both allow you to retain the same duration without changes, even with an additional resource, but at the cost of either reducing the Units or increasing the work— all under the precepts of the same Basic work Formula. These other options are rarely used, typically in special situations in your real-life projects, but this task customization is available, should you choose to use it.

Case 3 – Increasing Units

There is another technique we can use to increase Units, without adding a new additional resource. We will look at this now. Double-click on Task 2 and bring up the **Task Information** dialog box. Select the **Resources** tab and increase **Units** to **200%**. Refer to the following screenshot:

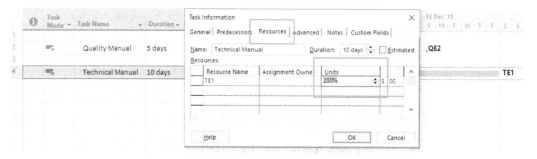

Figure 4.4 – Microsoft Project – Resource Units set to 200%

The effect of performing this change is to halve the duration, similar to what you saw in Case 2. You can observe the decreased duration in the following screenshot:

Figure 4.5 – Microsoft Project – Increased Units results in decreased duration

However, be careful here: this is an interesting and dangerous situation, as I'll explain soon.

What exactly is the meaning of increasing the resource's units to 200%? Can we use this technique everywhere to perform miraculous reductions in duration, without adding extra resources? When you increase the Units of a resource, this means that the resource is working proportionately longer work hours. In our case, we just set the resource's working hours to 200% – and no wonder the duration was halved! And no, we should *not* use this technique of increasing Units as a standardized practice, even by a fraction, because systemic overallocation causes burnout in people, destroys motivation, eliminates all buffers, and also causes hard-to-debug scheduling issues.

This potentially dangerous situation is highlighted to you by Project in the **Indicators** column for the specific task, as shown in the following screenshot:

Figure 4.6– Microsoft Project – Overallocation indicator

It is perfectly normal to expect short periods of *crunch time* in everyday commercial projects. We are all aware of pulling long hours before a demo, or a weekend in the office during a big launch. During the execution of a project, you might have short periods of increased Units for your team. But it is not a good practice to hardcode overwork *(or underwork)* into the planning phases of a project. Project buffers are to be added later if required, in the Planning phase of your project.

This is the first instance where we have encountered significant *overallocation*, though there are other ways overallocations can occur. It is the single biggest bane of project managers while using Project. In this book, first, we will learn to identify and avoid them. Then, we will also examine many techniques and tools we can use to combat overallocations.

---

working smart with Project

There are many methods of working successfully with Project. Every practitioner will eventually evolve their own ways, and so will you. It is my humble attempt in this book to teach you how to flow with and around Project's default values, assumptions, and algorithms with the least possible friction. This method happens to require your hands-on participation.

If needed, adjust your estimation techniques, Units, and standards so that they closely match the defaulted expectations of Microsoft Project. This will save you a lot of conversion and translation efforts. If, for some reason, you can't alter your own techniques, then customize Project to your expectations. This is why it is important to learn how to customize features.

If you choose to pursue neither of these options, then a lot of time will be wasted converting estimations, Units, and so on at runtime. At the same time, you will have a ton of feature customizations available for your tasks. All this increases management complexity.

Deeper scheduling

Now, we will briefly jump into a few more complex topics. You will exercise these task type features and algorithms very rarely in normal projects, but it will be good for your confidence to handle such requirements.

Exploring task types

When you observe your project's real-life tasks in closer detail, you will find that they often have either implicit or explicit restrictions placed upon them. Let's say that you're managing a team of 20 software engineers. Here, you will want maximum utilization for your complete team, which you can do by keeping all of them productively engaged with your project. This is often called *Resource Balancing* or *Resource Leveling*. On the other hand, you cannot sporadically increase your team head count either (for example, to reduce duration). You will want to fix the number of engineers who are working on a specific task. Likewise, you may also have senior experts in your team whose skills might get shared across multiple projects. So, they will be available in fractional resource units to any project. Moreover, you must carefully manage their entry and exit into your different projects. These are only some of the implicit and explicit restrictions you will face, and we haven't even started talking about budget management.

How closely you reflect these team realities/restrictions into your schedule, *with the least complexity*, will largely determine your efficiency with Project. The **Task Information** dialog box that we have been using so far allows you to finely tweak the behavior of your tasks so that they closely reflect your realities. You can open it by double-clicking on any task in the **Entry** table. Refer to the following screenshot:

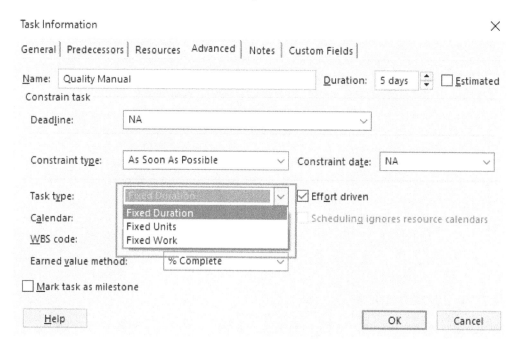

Figure 4.7 – Microsoft Project task types

You can instruct Project to keep one of the three parameters from the Basic Work Formula, as a constant – either duration, Units, or work. Project will comply with your guidelines for that specific task unless you want to overrule it by yourself. But what does this mean? In the following sections, we'll look at when and how you will need to apply this feature to your schedules.

Understanding the concept of Fixed Units

The meaning of making Resource Units *Fixed* is that you have a pre-decided number of people (or machinery) working on a specific task. This is a common situation in real life and, in fact, is the default setting of Project.

You will be familiar with this situation from your working life, where you, as the manager, have been assigned a fixed number of resources, with specific skillsets, whom you can draw upon to execute a project. This is true even in the case of organizations with a *Resource Pool* concept.

Fixed duration

On rarer occasions, you will come across tasks that will take a fixed number of days to complete. The most common example for this condition is the *Curing of Concrete* task, from the world of civil construction. For example, once the roof is laid, a curing period of, say, 7-20 days is often required for the concrete to properly harden as per the requirements. Now, you might assign *n* resources to this task to make sure the concrete is properly maintained during this time, but adding another resource will *not* reduce the duration beyond the curing period.

You will also come across tasks like this in the world of Information Technology. For example, *Automated Backup and Restore* is a task that will take a fixed amount of time. In your own business domains, you will be sure to find tasks like these, which have an irreducible duration.

When you encounter tasks like these, make sure that they are properly configured so that they're of the Fixed duration task type.

Fixed work

The Fixed work task type is when the total amount of effort of the task is known and fixed upfront. This is, once again, very common in actual practice and often forms the bulk of your tasks in a project. Once the task's effort is known and your Resource Units are known, you will be able to compute the duration in Project.

If this type of task is very common, then why is Fixed Units the default type used by Project? One plausible reason for this is that during the estimation process, using a Fixed Units-based calculation enables you to directly proceed to duration computation next – the field that Project expects by default.

Are your tasks effort-driven or not?

At this point, in the **Task Information** dialog box, you might have noticed the **Effort driven** checkbox. An effort-driven task means that if you increase the resources for a task, you can expect a proportional decrease in the duration. Most tasks that you will encounter will be effort-driven in nature and that is the reason, by default, this option will be selected to begin with. Every task that we've discussed so far are all effort-driven tasks. An example of an effort-driven task is as follows: if it takes 10 days to build a wall with one person, then the same task will take 5 days with one resources. That is, if we add more *effort*, we drive the *duration* of the task. In short, this is what we call **effort-driven**.

Now, let's look at a *non-effort driven* task. Consider a 1-day training session, as a task, that you must conduct. Whether two people attend your training or 20 people do, you can expect it will remain a 1-day training session (of course, you might need a bigger venue). Such tasks are not impacted by the number of resources and are statistically rare occurrences in projects. These tasks are **non-effort driven**.

Later in this book, we will look at a more detailed example of a recurring and non-effort driven task.

The impact of using task types

At this point, you might be wondering if you must inspect and modify the task types for every task in your schedule. The answer is no. Instead, you must only identify and modify the exceptions. Even if the size of your project is very large, you will typically set exceptional tasks only once during the initial stages of your project. The reason for this ease is that Microsoft Project has carefully curated, as far as possible, real-life usage into its default values and default behavior. You will understand the significance of this fact in the next section.

Underlying algorithms – How project scheduling works

The big question now is, *how do the three task types affect the Basic work Formula?* We will examine this aspect now. This algorithmic behavior is captured concisely in the following table, for your reference. Note that this table is specifically for making modifications to existing assignments:

Task	Modify Duration	Modify Work	Modify Units
Fixed duration	Work recalculated	Units recalculated	Work recalculated
Fixed work	Units recalculated	Duration recalculated	Duration recalculated
Fixed units	Work recalculated	Duration recalculated	Duration recalculated

Table 4.3 – Project's scheduling behavior

Is it necessary to memorize this table for everyday usage of Project? The answer is no. If you stick with the defaulted Fixed Units and the common form of Basic work Formula, you will be completely conversant with Project scheduling behavior. However, you might occasionally need to cross-check this table when you are modifying assignments for an exceptional task. With that, we have finished our discussion of advanced scheduling features. Now, we will take a look at Project Calendars.

Understanding Project Calendars

By now, you have comprehensively examined the three dimensions of scheduling – work, duration, and Units. But which is the implicit fourth dimension that is hidden within all of these? This fourth dimension is Time. In this section, we will learn how to handle time through the **Calendar** feature of Project.

For the sake of simplicity, so far, we have started all our practice projects by directly entering the tasks into the **Entry** table. This is fine for practice projects, but not for your real-life commercial projects. In the latter case, you should always start by setting a start date for your project.

The proper usage of Project requires that you configure your Calendar. In the sections to follow, we will learn how easy it is to match the calendar to the working time conditions of your organization. Although this will be simple for you, Project, in turn, translates your configurations into internal rules for its algorithms.

When using the calendar that you configure, Project will determine whether work can be scheduled or not for a *day*, *resource*, or *task*. Calendar affects literally every aspect of your schedule. We'll see how this happens and works in the following sections.

Setting the Project Start Date

You can set the start date for your project from the **Project Information** dialog box. The button is aptly located on the **Project** tab. Refer to the following screenshot:

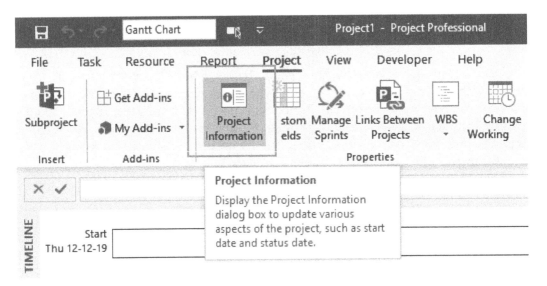

Figure 4.8 – Project Information

The **Project Information** dialog box is chockful of date-related UI controls, as shown in the following screenshot:

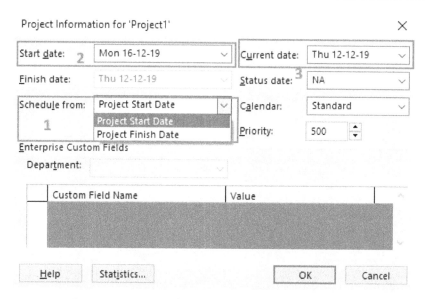

Figure 4.9 – Microsoft Project – setting Project Start Date

It is not very easy to use until you understand the following simple sequence:

1. Select whether you want to schedule from a **Start date** or a **Finish date**. You will almost always schedule in the forward direction of time – from a **Start date**.

2. Select a **Start date** for your project from the Calendar dropdown.

3. **Current date** is picked from your computer's date. You should only change this when you want the **Current date** marker on the Gantt chart to reflect the day of your choice. It is a rarely used feature.

4. Notice that if you choose to schedule from a **Start date**, then **Finish date** is deactivated and vice versa.

5. **Status date** is useful but only significant when we wish to track a project (we will cover this later in this book). You can ignore it for now.

6. Finally, as shown in the following screenshot, there is a **Calendar** dropdown. A **Standard** calendar is selected by default. The whole magic of Microsoft Project's algorithms will dance to the tune of the calendar that you select here:

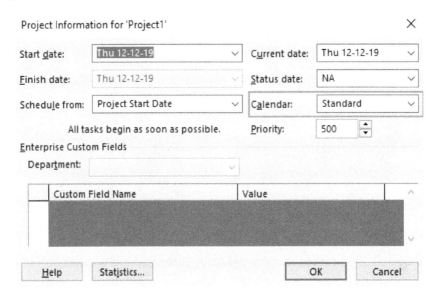

Figure 4.10 – The Calendar option in the Project Information dialog box

We will do a deep dive into calendars in the sections that follow, where we will revisit this option.

However, there is a pitfall to setting this date.

Don't use **Project Finish Date scheduling** in a casual manner if you don't have a grasp of all its implications. This reverse direction of scheduling is useful only on rare occasions, typically when you want to calculate the span of a project. This technique is used only during the initiation and planning stages of the project (just for design and calculation) and never in actual project execution. There are two reasons why it is not used. First, it greatly hampers your ability to interpret the schedule on a day-to-day basis. Second, it affects Project's scheduling and resource algorithms, and you will often be hard pressed to interpret the automatic changes on your schedule. Specifically, it affects the algorithmic constraints designed within Project's scheduling algorithms. For example, when you use normal scheduling from a start date, Project uses a default constraint called **As Soon As Possible** (**ASAP**). But when you reverse this scheduling, the default constraint type changes to **As Late As Possible** (**ALAP**). We will learn more about date constraints in *Chapter 8, Mastering Link Dependency and Constraints.*

Pro Tip

You can also set the project start to a *back date*. It is quite common for project managers to take charge of a project that has already started, and that's when you set a back date to the start date. No matter when you start the project, always ensure that an accurate start date is configured for your schedule.

Creating your new calendar

When you create a new blank project, it will already have made several assumptions about your standard default working times and days. This will be the universal 8 A.M. to 5 P.M., Monday through Friday, with an hour for lunch in-between. Saturday and Sunday are non-working weekends.

These default settings will not include national holidays, company holidays, resource holidays, or any other customized date and time information that might be vital for your project. So, one of the very first activities for you to complete, as a prudent user of Project, will be to configure your calendar customizations, very early in the schedule creation process.

If your organization already provides you with a Project calendar, then use it. Otherwise, you can create a new calendar, as described here:

1. Click on the **Change working Time** button from the ribbon's **Project** tab:

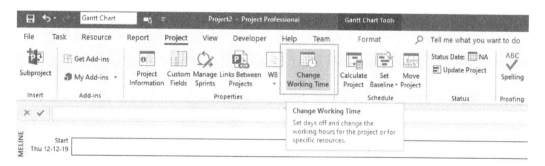

Figure 4.11 – The Change working Time button

This opens the following important **Change working Time** dialog box:

Change Working Time

For calendar: Standard (Project Calendar)

Create New Calendar ...

Calendar 'Standard' is a base calendar.

Legend:

Working

Nonworking

31 Edited working hours

On this calendar:

31 Exception day

31 Nondefault work week

Click on a day to see its working times:

December 2019

S	M	T	W	Th	F	S
1	2	3	4	5	6	7
8	9	10	11	12	13	14
15	16	17	18	19	20	21
22	23	24	25	26	27	28
29	30	31				

Working times for 12 December 2019:

• 8:00 AM to 12:00 PM
• 1:00 PM to 5:00 PM

Based on:
Default work week on calendar 'Standard'.

Exceptions   Work Weeks

Name	Start	Finish

Details...

Delete

Help   Options...   OK   Cancel

Figure 4.12 – The Change working Time dialog box

2. In the top-left dropdown, the Project is pre-packaged with three base calendar instances named **Standard**, **24 Hours**, and **Night Shift**. The Standard calendar is the default selected calendar that you'll see in this dialog box. It is also the default calendar for the project:

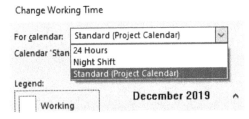

Figure 4.13 – Base calendar instances available (pre-packaged)

Pitfall

Do not modify the pre-packaged base calendars. Instead, create a new calendar that follows your organizational holiday and working policy, based on the existing base calendars.

3. Take a moment to read through the details provided in the **Change working Time** dialog box, but don't change anything yet. It displays, among other details, the working times for the currently selected calendar (**Standard** calendar).

4. Click on the prominent **Create New Calendar** button. This opens a new, smaller dialog box:

Figure 4.14 – Creating a new calendar

5. Give the calendar a distinct name that you will be able to recognize easily as a trial calendar. Name it `Srikanth Lesson Trial` for now.

Pitfall

Every calendar you create ends up in your Project's base data, in a longer storage. So, do not create too many sandbox calendars.

---

6. Make sure you are creating a copy of a base calendar (the second radio button option) instead of creating a new base calendar (the first radio button option).

7. After clicking **OK**, you will have created a new calendar. Verify this in the main dialog box's dropdown:

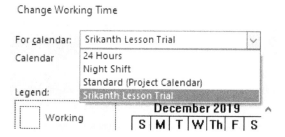

Figure 4.15 – New calendar has been created

Now that you have created a new experimental calendar, you can modify it. We'll create new working timings on this calendar in the next section.

Customizing your new calendar

There are two main types of customizations that you can perform on a new calendar – changing the daily working time and adding holidays. In Project-speak, these holidays are **exceptions** to a normal working week. In the following steps, you will learn how to perform both customizations:

1. Make sure the new calendar is selected in the **For Calendar:** dropdown. You do not want to accidentally modify the base calendar.

2. Open the **work Weeks** tab.

3. Select **Default** in the corresponding listing and click on the **Details** button. Refer to the following screenshot for these steps:

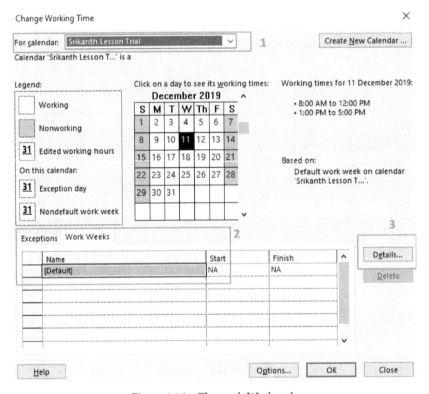

Figure 4.16 – The work Weeks tab

4. Select the day names you want to modify.

5. You can then set these selected days to weekly holidays (nonworking time) or you can set custom working times for them. The latter is shown in the following screenshot:

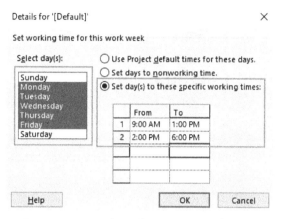

Figure 4.17 – work Week Timings modification

6. Click **OK** and return to the main dialog.

7. You can add holidays (exceptions to the normal work week) by selecting the date in the calendar and typing the holiday's name into the **Name** field. Refer to the following screenshot:

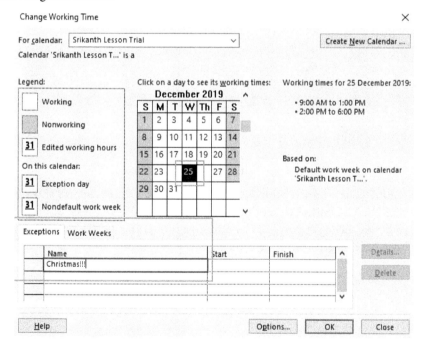

Figure 4.18 – Adding holiday exceptions to the work week

8. After you have marked out all the organizational holidays, click **OK** to save your new calendar.

Now, you are all set to use this calendar for its basic settings. In the next section, we will learn how to use it for the current project.

Setting the Project Calendar

Even though you have created a new calendar, it is not linked to your current running project. Linking a calendar to the open project can be done in the **Project Information** dialog box, which we looked at earlier when we learned how to set the project's start date. Open it once again from the ribbon's **Project** tab, as shown in the following screenshot:

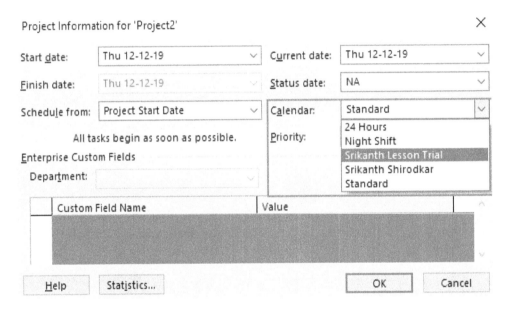

Figure 4.19 – Setting the project calendar

When you open the **Calendar** dropdown, your newly created calendar will show up. Select it and click the **OK** button to set the project calendar. You can now doubly-check that your calendar has been set correctly by once again opening the **Change working Time** dialog box. Refer to the following screenshot:

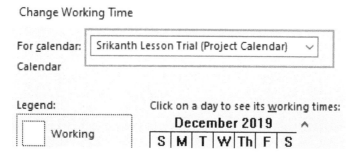

Figure 4.20 – Verifying that the project calendar has been set correctly

Your calendar name should have the designation label **Project Calendar** appended to the end of it. This verifies that you have set up the project calendar correctly.

With that, you have learned enough about Project calendars to cover most of the situations you will encounter in real-life projects. In the next section, we will delve even deeper into the inner workings of calendars.

How calendars really work in Project

Calendars are a major cause of discontent and issues with users of Project. This is because it is a complex feature and users do not take the time to understand it thoroughly.

Calendars are categorized into four essential types:

1. **Base calendar**: Think of these as templates shipped with Project. Every other calendar instance is derived from these base calendars.

2. **Project calendar**: This is the calendar associated with the entire project and is derived from a base calendar. Organizational-level details are then added to the project calendar.

> **Note**
> This calendar is set via the **Project Information** dialog box, as we saw in the previous section.

3. **Resource/Shift-level calendar**: A calendar can be associated with an individual resource, or a group of resources working in a shift, to show their own holiday plans, working times, and so on. This calendar is typically derived from the base calendars, namely **Night Shift** and **24 Hours**.

Resource-specific calendars are set via the **Resource View** interface. The following screenshot shows this:

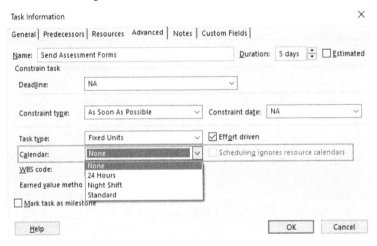

	Resource Name	Type	Material	Initials	Group	Max.	Std. Rate	Ovt. Rate	Cost/Use	Accrue	Base
1	GM-HR	Work		G		100%	$0.00/hr	$0.00/hr	$0.00	Prorated	Standard
2	Personnel Manager	Work		P		100%	$0.00/hr	$0.00/hr	$0.00	Prorated	Standard
3	Admin Manager	Work		A		100%	$0.00/hr	$0.00/hr	$0.00	Prorated	Standard
4	T&D Manager	Work		T		100%	$0.00/hr	$0.00/hr	$0.00	Prorated	Standard
5	QUALITY Manager	Work		Q		100%	$0.00/hr	$0.00/hr	$0.00	Prorated	Standard
6	HR Staff 1	Work		H	Shift Employ	100%	$0.00/hr	$0.00/hr	$0.00	Prorated	Night Shift
7	HR Staff 2	Work		H	Shift Employ	100%	$0.00/hr	$0.00/hr	$0.00	Prorated	Night Shift
8	Microsoft Office Annual License	Material		MSO	Software		$100.00		$0.00	Prorated	
9	Microsoft Project Professional Annual License	Material		MPP	Software		$800.00		$0.00	Prorated	
10	Airfare Tickets (round trip)	Cost		A						Prorated	
11	Lodging	Cost		L						Prorated	
12	Taxi	Cost		T						Prorated	
13	Per Diem cost	Cost		P						Prorated	

Figure 4.21 – Resource/Shift-level calendar

4. **Task calendar**: Sometimes, a task is performed in a different time zone, or perhaps performed using machinery that is only available during certain days. In such situations where you must maintain task-specific dates, it is prudent to use a task calendar.

> **Note**
>
> A task calendar can be set via the **Task Information** dialog box, which you can open by double-clicking on any task.

By default, task-level calendars are not set, and tasks follow the project calendar otherwise. This is shown in the following screenshot:

Figure 4.22 – Task-level calendar

These four calendar types are applied in the same order as we introduced them. First, the base calendar is applied, then the project calendar, followed by the resource and task calendars. Ultimately, on any given day, what, who, and when is decided by Project as it overrides all these calendar settings in the hierarchy.

As a new learner, you must restrict your usage to only the project calendar *(which is mandatory for you to configure)*. As you progress to becoming an intermediate Project practitioner who's handling larger projects, you might also include resource calendars, but only if required. Task-level calendars are rarely used.

> **Tip**
> Calendars are a quick way to debug or triage issues with task behavior.
> Calendar changes not showing up in the Gantt chart.

Sometimes, when you make changes to the calendar framework, such as applying a new project calendar, your exception dates (holidays) might not be reflected on the Gantt chart. This is because the Gantt chart, by default, applies only the default **Standard** calendar. You can just right-click on the Gantt area and configure the Gantt chart in order to apply the calendar that you wish to be visible there.

Summary

The motive of this chapter was to dig deeper into the inner workings of Project's primary pillars – tasks, scheduling algorithms, and calendars. Throughout this chapter, we saw that it is possible to tweak and fine-tune these aspects of Project through the use of methods, interfaces, and techniques. It is important for you to understand the default values and default behavior of Project first, as they have been carefully designed to cater to the vast majority of the use cases that you will encounter.

In the next chapter, we will look at resource assignments in greater detail. First, we will cover all the basic functionalities before opening up the hood and looking closely at the machinations of the scheduling engine.

Assignment

1. Create a new blank project that contains 10 dummy tasks of various durations, 1 day through 20 days.

2. Experiment with the behavior of various tasks that are categorized by the three major task types, as follows:

- Increase resources to halve the duration but retain work

- Increase resources but retain the same duration and work

- Decrease work but retain duration

> **Tip**
> Include the **work** column in your entry table on the Gantt chart view.

3. Create a new calendar that reflects the year 202x holiday schedule for your organization.

4. Many countries do not follow the Monday to Friday, 8 A.M. to 5 P.M. work schedule. Create a calendar for your offshore team in Bahrain, who works on a different schedule Sunday to Thursday, 9 A.M. to 6 P.M.. Apply it as a project calendar.

    If your new custom calendar does not show in the Gantt area, be sure to right-click in the Gantt area and make the new calendar visible manually.

5
Resource Management with Microsoft Project

Imagine for a short while that you are the manager of your national cricket team (or any team sport of your choice). Sporting wisdom requires that you build a team that's highly specific to several playing conditions and requirements. The pitch and weather conditions, the opposition's strengths and weaknesses, and the game format are just some of the parameters that you will need to consider. You will not just choose 11 generic players. Instead, the role of each player will be known, planned, utilized, and passionately debated. Roles are based upon skills, experience, and specializations, such as opening batsman, striker or centre forward, fast bowler, goalkeeper, and so on.

In the same way, as a prudent project manager, you will consider various factors such as specific technical or people skills, prior experience, and domain and subject matter expertise while resourcing your project. Even for small-sized projects, resourcing gets more complicated than this, because *optimization*, *utilization*, and *efficiency* also need to be considered. Microsoft Project recognizes these challenges and provides you with ample features to effectively manage your resources, which we will now discuss.

In this chapter, we're going to cover the following main topics:

- Basic resource management with Project – Creating, allocating, updating, and assigning resources

- Enterprise-level resourcing concepts

- Overallocations, and how to avoid them

- Fine-tuning resource assignments

- Best practices for resource assignment

Basic resource management techniques with Project

For the sake of convenience, Project provides multiple locations from which to create and manipulate resources. If you are working with a particular resource-related view, then there is likely an easy way available to create and inspect resources close at hand, as we will now see.

Creating resources

For our earlier simple project examples, we created resources directly from the main Gantt Chart view. Refer to the following screenshot:

Figure 5.1 – Creating resources directly from the Gantt Chart view

This is the *quick and dirty* method. Quick, because you created the resource *and* also made a task assignment at the same time. Dirty, because this technique is often the source of bugs in your schedule. Any typo in the resource name immediately creates another duplicate resource. These duplicates can cause erroneous algorithmic calculations.

> **Tip**
> You can restrict the creation of new resources to only the Resource Sheet. Traverse to **File | Options | Advanced**. Uncheck the **Automatically Add New Resources and Tasks** checkbox.

The quick technique, however, is perfectly fine for small-sized projects, say between one and five resources. But for most of your real-life projects, you will use the view specially designed for the purpose, the **Resource Sheet** view. You can access this view from the **View** button located on most tabs. Refer to the following screenshot:

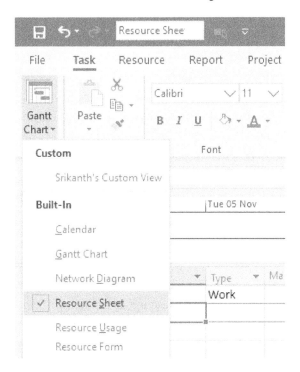

Figure 5.2 – Opening the Resource Sheet view from the View button

Let's now create a new resource from the Resource Sheet. For simplicity, I will use our simple project from earlier, and you can also do the same.

Create a new resource called `Software Engineer` by typing it into the next available free line. Type only in the **Resource Name** column and hit *Enter* when you are done. Refer to the following screenshot:

		Resource Name	Type	Material	Initials	Group	Max.	Std. Rate	Ovt.	Cost/Use	Accrue	Base	Code	Add New Column
1		Srikanth	Work		S		100%	$0.00/hr	$0.00/hr	$0.00	Prorated	Standard		
2		Software Engineer	Work		S		100%	$0.00/hr	$0.00/hr	$0.00	Prorated	Standard		

Figure 5.3 – Creating a new resource from Resource Sheet View

There are a few interesting observations to be made:

1. As soon as you typed in the resource name and hit the *Enter* key on your keyboard, Project auto-populated a lot of columns for you. This behavior is similar to creating a task, which you carried out earlier.

    The **Type** column refers to resource types. The default selection is **Work**. People and machinery are the most common examples of work resources and such resources are not consumed at the end of a task.

2. We will dig deeper into other types of resources, namely, `cost` and `material`, later in the book. The **Material** column that appears next is specifically for the material resource type.

3. It is important to note that the new resource we created, `Software Engineer`, is just a generic job title or a role. This is perfectly fine. During the initiation stages of a project, you can build staffing estimates using this technique.

    If your organization works on a **Resource Pool** concept, then you will not know the actual people who will later be assigned to your project. In this situation, use generic job titles for approximation.

4. The **Initials** column is used purely for aesthetic and readability purposes. The resource names that you create here can appear in the Gantt Chart view and other related views, instead of the **Resource Name** column. If the names are long, they tend to clutter the view and decrease readability on smaller screens, where screen space is valuable. So, it is possible to display only the initials instead of the full resource names. All such options are available from the **Format** tab, and we will visit them later.

5. Optionally, you can use the **Group** column to indicate the team or group that the resource belongs to. This can help you identify resources easily on large projects, but even more importantly, you will be able to sort and filter project data with grouping. For example, `Software Developer` might belong to the **Development Group** and `Software Tester` might belong to the **Testing Group**.

6. It is important to understand that the **Max Units** field needs to be understood carefully. It denotes the specific resource's availability for the whole project. For example, suppose you have a Senior Architect available only 1 day in the week, then you should enter 20% in the **Max Units** field (the decimal value 0.2 is also allowed and is treated as an equivalent).

> **Pitfall**
>
> In *Chapter 4*, *Underlying Concepts of Microsoft Project*, you saw an example in which resource assignment **Units** were increased for *that specific task assignment only*. But here, the **Max Units** field refers to the whole project. You should always be aware of this fact and only make modifications here that impact the specific resource units for the whole project. If unsure, always leave it at the default 100%.

7. The **Std. Rate** and **Ovt.** columns are for standard and overtime rates of pay for the resource. If you want to track the financials of your project, you should fill these up as appropriate for your project. These fields allow for all convenient formats; for example, these are all valid formats: $200/hr., $800/day, or even $6,000/month.

8. If you do not use the rate columns (that is, if you leave them at the default $0.00), you will not be able to track the financials of a project.

> **Pitfall**
>
> Project is not specialized for precise financial analysis, and you should not treat it like precise accounting software. For example, if you work with **full-time employees (FTEs)**, your time tracking might not exactly match the actual outlay. With practice and awareness, however, you will be able to get financial tracking within tolerances. You should also communicate these limitations to stakeholders, just to set expectations accurately.

9. Sometimes, with work resources, there may be an additional cost for every instance of usage. For example, complex machines might have a *setting charge* incurred every time they are used for production. The **Cost/Use** column can be used to hold these costs.

10. Resource cost can be accrued either at the beginning of a task, or as the work progresses (prorated), or at completion. You can fine-tune the cost accrual using the **Accrue** column accordingly. The default value is `Prorated`.

11. The **Base** column refers to the base calendar used for the resource. The default is the standard base calendar, but you can modify it for individual resources from here.

12. **Code** is an optional additional column to hold any other tracking code specific to your organization. This is most commonly used to hold internal resources' specific cost center codes.

> **Tip**
> You are not limited to the dollar ($) currency sign! In the **General Options** dialog box, you can customize currency to any Unicode character. There are a few dozen international currency symbols available, such as ₹. To access this customization, traverse to **File | Options | Display**.

Allocating resources

Users of Project often get confused between *resource allocation* and *resource assignment*, as they are often used interchangeably. Here is a simple way to understand the subtle difference between them. When you use the **Resource Sheet** view, like we just did, you are *allocating* the resources to your project. When you connect a task to a specific resource (like in the Gantt Chart view), then it is an *assignment*.

You can double-click on any resource in the **Resource Sheet** and pull up the **Resource Information** dialog box. Refer to the following screenshot:

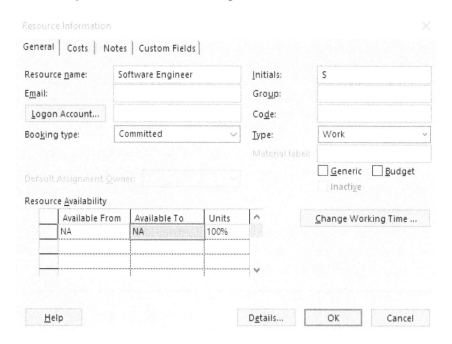

Figure 5.4 – Resource Information dialog box

You might have already guessed that there are a lot of other resource fields available to you apart from the ones presented by default on the Resource Sheet. This dialog box presents a better UI for you to greatly customize your resources. Now that we've covered this, let's move on to assigning resources.

Assigning resources

Project provides the **Assign Resources** dialog box to make all your assignments. This is a powerful alternative to directly entering the resource names against tasks, as we did earlier in the quick and dirty method. Refer the following screenshot:

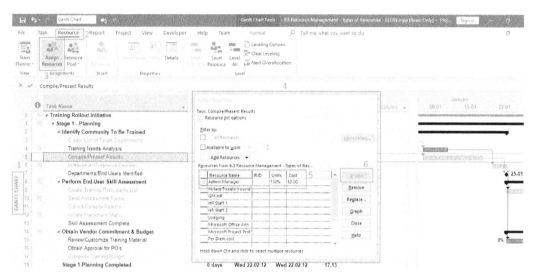

Figure 5.5 – Using the Assign Resources dialog box

A different project file has been used in the preceding screenshot, just to show the availability of multiple resources' data. The steps to use this technique of resource assignment are as follows:

1. Ensure that you are in the **Gantt Chart** view and select the task to which you want to assign resources.

2. Open the **Resource** tab on the ribbon.

3. Find the **Assignments** section and click on the prominent **Assign Resources** button.

4. This opens the powerful **Assign Resources** dialog box.

5. Select the required resources. If your resource list is massive, as in the case of large projects, you can optionally use the **Filter by:** and the **Available to work** options. They provide a multitude of options to pinpoint resources. Refer to the following screenshot:

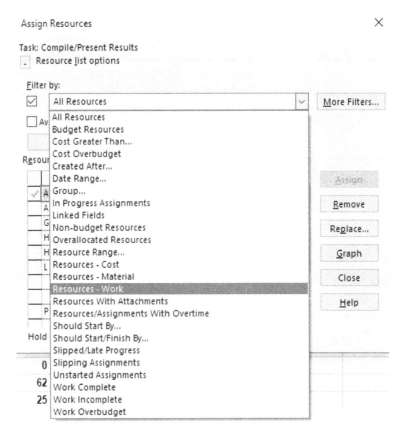

Figure 5.6 – Filter options for the Assign Resources dialog box

As you can see, there are many filtering options that can help you make precise assignment decisions. Using the option selected in the preceding screenshot, **Resources - Work**, will only show you work-type resources. You will get better clarity on these filter option terms later, after we learn how to track and control projects.

6. After you've made your selection, click on the **Assign** button to complete the assignment.

Now that we've covered this, let's see how to update the resources of our project.

Updating resources

It is a good practice to begin your schedule design and estimation process with generic resource names instead of named resources. For example, use **Software Engineer** instead of **John** as a starting point in your design. The typical reasons for this are as follows:

1. Staffing might not be under your control, and in a competitive world, you may not get all the specific resources that you request.

2. An early version of the plan to be shared with eternal stakeholders might be required by policy to show only anonymized resources.

3. Your company might mandate using standardized productivity values. Using named resources often skews estimations.

4. Using job titles instead of actual resource names is often recommended when you share your plan for customer approval for confidentiality reasons.

Taking into account the preceding reasons, you will often start with generic resource names. However, in subsequent project stages, it is possible to update the name of the resource at any time in the **Resource Sheet** view and Project will appropriately change all resource assignments seamlessly.

Pitfall

Do not forget about, or ignore, adding your own project management-related tasks into the project schedule! You might not find this easy to do, due to the amorphous components of project management. But doing so will allow you to quantify and command your own time with higher efficiency. Secondly, this can protect you against becoming overloaded, overworked, and suffering the eventual burnout.

The Resource Pool feature

If you simultaneously manage a few small-sized projects, then Project has a feature that will allow you to create a *Master Project* with a shared **Resource Pool**. The advantages are first that you can manage multiple projects from a centralized view, and secondly, that you can share resources across these projects. Refer to the following screenshot:

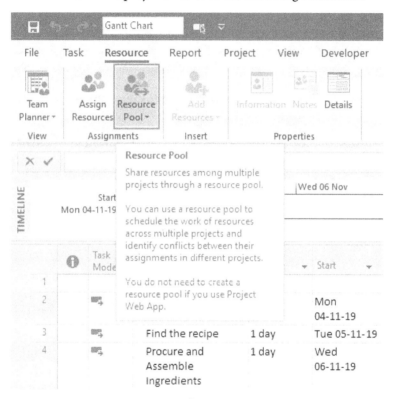

Figure 5.7 – Microsoft Project Resource Pool

While this sounds like a great solution, it is not robust. The challenges stem from the fact that these features are built upon your everyday local filesystem. There are several points of failure, with reported issues including data duplication and loss, the inability to easily archive the resources, and ambiguity in reporting.

The alternative to all this is to consider the enterprise/server-based solutions of Microsoft Project. These enterprise offerings have recently become more financially accessible thanks to Microsoft's subscription-based offerings. Due to the high number of pitfalls, we will not look deeper into the Resource Pool feature in this book.

> **Pitfall**
>
> If you make the mistake of emailing your master Project to someone without all its associated files, it will not function. Similar issues crop for even the simplest tasks such as copying or moving files. Archiving is a challenge. It is not for the faint-hearted, but it is a *viable* solution, nonetheless. If you are in a controlled environment, you can go for it, as do some organizations and experienced Project Managers.

Enterprise-level resourcing concepts

What is the meaning of the term *enterprise level*? To begin with, we know that it implicitly means *complex management at an organizational level* (or even at a departmental level).

From a Project perspective, there are a few immediate implications:

1. **Projects**: The focus shifts from the nitty-gritty of an individual project to a portfolio of related projects.

2. **Resources**: Concerning the usage and optimization of resources across projects, demand is evaluated and fulfilled across a portfolio of projects, or across the whole organization.

3. **Administration**: Instead of the Project Manager creating resources for the project, administrators manage entities across the board.

These Enterprise solutions are based on Microsoft Project Server, integrated with Microsoft SharePoint and the frontend provided by the online/desktop versions of Project. At the time of writing, Project Server offerings are in a state of marketing flux, although it should not affect you as a user. Enterprise-level topics are out of the scope of this book. When you reduce the visibility to an individual project level, all features remain exactly the same, as covered here. Even if you are using Server-based solutions, at the individual project level, almost everything in this book still applies.

Revisiting overallocations

This is an important section, and your special attention is requested. In the previous chapter, you had a quick introduction to the concept of overallocation when we increased the units of a resource to 200%. Project, on its part, immediately escalated this issue to you with a *red person* overallocation warning symbol in the **Indicators** column. Since we are on the topic of resource assignment, let's now examine overallocations in a little more depth.

So, what is an overallocation again? When a resource is allocated more work than it can handle, then there is a potential risk to your entire schedule! And this risk is called an *overallocation*. Refer to the following screenshot, which shows one more way by which an overallocation can be caused. Observe in the Gantt Chart that the resource named **Leonardo** has been allocated two tasks for the same time interval:

Figure 5.8 – Observing a simple overallocation

There is an ambiguity on which task he will perform at that time period. You can observe this represented visually in the overlapping taskbars in the Gantt Chart. Also note, that *both* tasks have the ambiguity and so both tasks are marked as overallocated. This is the most common way in which overallocations occur. You should also now recreate this simple two-task schedule to experiment with overallocation.

> **Note**
>
> When you recreate the preceding example, make sure the task duration exceeds 5 days, as a shorter duration might sometimes not trigger Project's default algorithmic warning.

There are a few dangers of overallocation that we should take into account. In the simplest of words, overallocation is a warning that your resources are set to be overworked over the given time span. This is a direct warning requiring your attention.

You might wonder if real-life overallocations are as simple as the example provided. *Yes and no.* When you create a new schedule with Project and assign resources for the very first time, you will encounter overallocations. This is perfectly fine, and you should strive to resolve all of them before the schedule is considered ready to be shared with the world. There are exceptions to this rule, which we will discuss shortly. But if you retain overallocations, there should be a valid reason. However, the real nastier overallocations creep into your schedule at project execution time. The exploratory and risk-laden nature of projects are a root cause of overallocations.

So, what can we do about these overallocations? From a project management perspective, the strategy will be to identify overallocations, avoid them, plan for contingencies, and finally mitigate the overallocations. From Project's perspective, multiple techniques can be used to resolve overallocations, as we will learn later in this book. Be aware that just like any other project risk, mitigation often involves a cost. This cost can be money, time, or reduced scope or quality, among other things. Our own overallocation example can be resolved simply by linking the tasks together at the cost of the overall project duration. Refer to the following screenshot:

Figure 5.9 – Simple overallocation resolution

Congratulations – that was your very first resolution of an overallocation.

Now comes the million-dollar question, *why does Project allow overallocations in the first place?*

It is a fact of life that most projects do face short crunch times. The upcoming release of a new project, an important presentation to venture-capitalist investors, the release of your new film, or an accidental blowup of a critical component – all of these are examples of when the team will face extra hours at work. In such cases, extra work and effort will be justified in projects with short durations. Overallocation originating from unexpected causes for a short duration—*to recover from issues*—is understandable. But systemic overallocation, hardcoded into the schedule, is what we seek to prevent!

These overallocations can be avoided by the application of both project-scheduling best practices, and also domain-specific expertise. Apart from your own chosen remedies, Project provides a few powerful tools that can also be considered. We will look at the application of each tool and technique throughout the remainder of the book, so the next section provides a quick introduction only to the broader concepts.

Basic concepts of fine-tuning resource assignments

Resource planning involves multiple aspects of design. How many resources are required and for how long? Project managers will also try to assemble the best team possible, that is, they'll plan to get the most bang for their buck (budget). Planning also involves the question of how to load resources during the different phases of the project and for any interim deliverables, such as a customer demo. Project provides some advanced tools to fine-tune resource assignments. We will study such tools later in the book, and will require an understanding of some resource management concepts. While a detailed discussion is beyond the scope of this book, you are urged to explore the following topics further, as relevant to your business domain: **Resource balancing** is a broad and domain-specific collection of ideas, tools, and techniques. The objective is simply to use the optimal resources with the highest efficiency to execute a project.

Resource leveling is a project management technique used to ensure resources are allocated an even amount of work. Within Project, there exists a configurable automated tool for leveling resources.

Task Inspector is another tool with a wizard-type interface to analyze overallocations. This tool is discussed in *Chapter 11, Overallocation – the Bane of Project Managers*, with a hands-on exercise to show you how to use the tool to resolve overallocations.

Best practices of resource management

The following are a few best practices for resource management:

- Smaller projects can be executed without explicitly creating resources. Therefore, resource management is optional in such projects.

- If you do need resource management, then only use the **Resource Sheet** view to create resources until you gain more hands-on experience. Project allows for the creation of resources from multiple views and dialog boxes, such as the **Task Information** dialog box. Using the **Resource Sheet** view as a central location prevents common issues such as duplication.

- Use the **Notes** tab (in the **Resource Information** dialog box) liberally to document your resourcing decisions. This will prove invaluable when you are asked to explain sections of your schedule months or even years after the fact.

- Underallocation of resources is also a significant risk, just like overallocation. But because Project does not flag it with an indicator, it is likely to be overlooked. Use the appropriate resource views to analyze work distribution.

- Watch the indicators column every time you create a new assignment to catch overallocations or anything else that stands out. Issues tend to compound each other, so it is important that you catch any bugs as quickly as possible. On the other hand, a single wrong allocation often creates a whole slew of other issues, and solving one of them can often solve many.

- When multiple resources with different units are assigned to the same task, work distribution will not be intuitive. This is a very frequent cause of confusion and distress for users. If the calculations don't seem intuitive, use different resource views to inspect and analyze Project's work allocation.

Summary

Team selection and management involves choosing the best person to do a specific job. Skills, experience, availability, and costs are only some of the factors to be considered. It also requires you to ensure efficient utilization—that is, one that is well balanced; neither under- nor overallocated. This leads to peak performance. This is true for sports teams just as much as it is for projects. Resource management is one of the pillars within Project. The **Resource Sheet** is the central view from where you have to work your project. In future chapters, we will learn more about other resource-related views, tools, and techniques.

So far in this book, we have already come a far way into our Microsoft Project journey. You already know enough to create simple project schedules in Project. It is important that you keep the same pace as we are unravelling together. While I constantly urge you to be hands-on while learning, ignore the multitude of options and features available until we encounter them in the course of the learning path laid out in this book.

In the next part of this book, we will progress to examining the usage of Project in the planning phases of your project. In the next chapter, we will discuss a critical success factor for your project, the Work Breakdown Structure.

Section 3: Project Planning Like a Pro!

This section of the book will deal with the use of Microsoft Project in the second phase of a project – the planning phase.

This section comprises the following chapters:

6

Work Breakdown Structure – the Single Critical Factor

Welcome to this next section of the book, where we discuss the role of Microsoft Project in the planning phase of a project. This is an exciting phase where the project manager takes complete command of the project, with the initiation stage complete and the execution stage yet to start. From a project perspective, your key objective for this planning stage is to create an *effective* schedule that can be executed by your team.

So, *"What is an effective schedule?"* you might ask. Well, a realistic schedule is a high-level scope that is *translated* into the technical language of your implementation, broken down into small enough activities to be comprehended, and worked upon by your team members. Additionally, it should also map to all your business world logic and constraints. Even more importantly, executing the schedule should deliver all the intended results of the project.

But there are many pitfalls along the way. Have you heard the joke, *"The operation was successful, but the patient died"*? A schedule can be executed accurately, but still the project can be a complete failure. Such a situation occurs if the expected deliverables of the project are not properly translated into a schedule.

So, how do you translate a high-level scope into a detailed schedule (in Microsoft Project or otherwise)? This is the million-dollar question. And the answer is this: by using a **Work Breakdown Structure (WBS)**. The WBS is the critical bridge between scope and schedule. In this chapter, we will have a pragmatic and hands-on discussion of the WBS and why it is crucial to the success of your project.

In this chapter, we're going to cover the following topics:

- A deeper understanding of WBS's origin, rationale, and importance
- Standard techniques to create a WBS
- A collection of 10 simple rules of thumb to create a robust WBS
- The automatic WBS numbering feature in Microsoft Project
- Going from WBS to Tasks

The planning phase in project management

The key objective of the planning phase is to get everything ready for the actual execution of the project. As simple as this sounds, it involves multi-dimensional skills from the project manager to get all stakeholders aligned with the project. The project manager will be expected to integrate scope management, cost management, quality management, and resource management together to develop an effective schedule.

At a bare minimum, the planning process can be visualized as three key project artifacts, as follows:

Figure 6.1 – Key project artifacts in the planning phase of project management

The preceding figure also shows a minimal path to get *from the scope to the schedule*. Depending on the complexity of a project, there may be many other corresponding artifacts, such as the risk management plan, the quality management plan, the cost management plan, and others. The WBS and the schedule are often considered part of the project management plan.

The WBS is the critical factor in creating an effective schedule. However, it is frequently skipped or misunderstood, resulting in project friction. As we will soon see, there are genuine reasons for the confusion that prevails in understanding the WBS.

Delving into WBS

A project can be thought of as a deliverable. This big and final project deliverable can then be broken into a series of smaller deliverables all along the execution route, just like milestones.

As defined in the first part of this chapter, *the WBS is a breakdown of a project into smaller deliverables to achieve the project scope.* This is only a short definition and it has some important implicit connotations that will be clarified now. Here are the characteristics of a well-formed WBS:

- **Hierarchical breakdown**: The high-level scope is decomposed into smaller and smaller components, using a top-down design approach.

- **Deliverables-oriented**: The WBS should have a razor-sharp focus on the deliverables (outcomes) of the project, because it is derived from the scope. Your WBS should answer the question, *"What will be delivered?"* and not *"How will it be delivered?"* These deliverables are not just customer-facing external deliverables. They can be interim, internal, or external deliverables.

The importance of the WBS

The WBS document starts life in the planning phase and is created after the scope document. It is then used in its entirety to create the project schedule. The schedule then takes the central and most important role in the project management plan document.

Not surprisingly, the relevance of a WBS does not decrease after the planning phase, but rather it becomes even more relevant, by constantly aiding the project manager in all major subsequent process groups, such as the following:

- **Planning**: It acts as the primary input to the schedule in the project management plan.

- **Execution**: It is the key reference document for work assignment and serves as the scope baseline.

- **Monitoring and control**: It prevents *scope creep* with effective change control.

- **Closing**: It is the key reference document for the verification of project end deliverables.

What is not included in the WBS

It is important to explicitly list the details that should be excluded from the WBS:

- Tasks/activities (undertaken to achieve deliverables)
- Duration/work estimates
- Resource details

Why are these factors left out of the WBS? This is because most of these parameters should reside within the schedule (which emerges from the WBS), or other associated reference documents. All these other important scheduling entities that are left out of the WBS can be created, stored, managed, and analyzed within a plan created by Microsoft Project.

What does a WBS look like?

Let's now look at a couple of WBS examples, one simple and one complex. The first is an elementary example of the WBS for a *simple one-floor two-bedroom house*:

IDENTIFIER		BREAKDOWN		NOTES (these are just details uncovered during the WBS design phase)
A		Simple House		
	1		Foundation	(Wood and steel forms)
	2		Floor	(Wood frame, 2 weeks)
	3		Room walls	(Windows)
	4		Roof	(Masonry, ceiling fixtures)
	5		Plumbing	(Pipe layouts, control junctions, fixtures)
	6		Electricals	(Wire layouts, control junctions, fixtures, $8,000)
	7		Woodwork storage	(Pantry, household, wash area)
	8		Interior painting and finishing	(Special living finish, waterproof wash, floor)
	9		Exteriors	(Weather-proof exterior finish)
	10		Project management	(Estimates, permits, plans, approvals, meetings, handover, and closure)

Table 6.1 – The WBS for Simple House construction

There are some significant points for you to note from the preceding example:

1. The first WBS level begins from the project name itself—*Simple House*. This is a common best practice to illustrate a tree-structured hierarchical design. In Microsoft Project parlance, this translates to the Project Summary Task, which you will encounter in *Chapter 7, Tasks – under the Microscope*.

2. Every line item should be uniquely identifiable, and you may choose any technique to do this. In the example here, the **IDENTIFIER** column serves this purpose.

3. Observe that this breakdown is entirely focused on the deliverables of the project. The implementation details are not included in the WBS.

    But, if you are from the construction or allied industries, you might say *"This is not how I would break down this project."* And that is perfectly fine, if it is deliverable-oriented.

4. Your own breakdown logic might differ, and it is acceptable as long as it is deliverable-oriented. For example, your breakdown logic might align to the business processes or methodology followed by your organization, or your own technical specialization and expertise, or even by the functional departments in your company.

5. Only the first two WBS levels have been identified in this example. The project manager might often continue this breakdown process as they see fit. This decision to continue the breakdown or not often considers the work estimate implicitly, as we will discuss in the next section. In our current example, the **NOTES** column is included to aid in further decomposition.

6. During the breakdown process, several attributes of the deliverable might be uncovered. This may include implementation details (such as resources required, time or budget constraints, dependencies on other aspects of the project). All these details should be captured in a WBS dictionary document as further attributes of the WBS. In our simple example, the *NOTES* column serves this purpose.

Let's now look at the second example, which is shared under a public domain license by the United States government. Here is the WBS of an aircraft system:

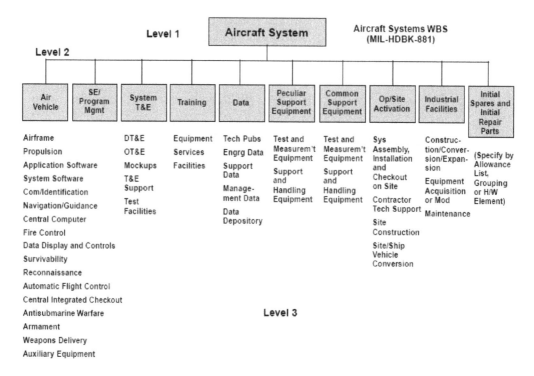

Figure 6.2 – WBS of an aircraft system (License: Public Domain. Source: https://en.wikipedia.org/wiki/File:Work_Breakdown_Structure_of_Aircraft_System.jpg)

You can see for yourself that the observations from the previous example all hold well for this case too. There are a couple of minor variations:

- The WBS is represented here in a hierarchical tree structure, whereas in the previous example it was in a tabular form.

- The decomposition has continued to an additional third level; in actuality, it may continue several levels deeper too.

- A unique identifying code has not been explicitly set. However, the tree traversal path is perfectly unique and can solve the purpose of identifying constituent elements.

Now that we have a fair understanding of how a well-formed WBS should look, let's explore how to create one.

Standard techniques for creating a WBS

The WBS is created with input from multiple documents generated in the project initiation stage, such as the project charter, **Statement of Work** (**SoW**), scope statement, and so on. An iterative decomposition using a top-down approach is utilized. Refer to the following flowchart for the WBS creation process:

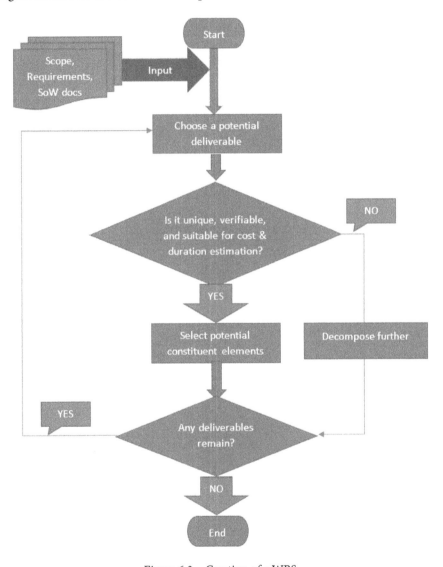

Figure 6.3 – Creation of a WBS

Here are some important observations to be made about this flowchart for WBS creation:

- This top-down iterative decomposition is also known as the **divide and conquer** algorithmic technique in computer science parlance, if you are familiar with it. The directional arrows in the flowchart capture the iterative nature of the technique. In simple language, you break down the deliverables into smaller and smaller components until you decide to stop.

- *How far should a WBS be decomposed?* Effort and cost, among other parameters, can help you make this critical decision.

- When effort is used as a guideline parameter, a rule of thumb known as the *8/80* rule is used. This is explained later in this chapter in the *Creating a robust WBS using 10 simple rules* section.

- The commercial nature of the project can also decide the level of decomposition. For example, if you are on a fixed-fee project, then you might choose to decompose with higher granularity to uncover any cost-related risks. In the case of an exploratory *time and materials* costing based project, you might choose to decompose only enough to progress to the next stage in development. *Build versus buy* decisions are also related to the decomposition factor.

- The WBS should consider all deliverables, implicit or explicit, including internal, external, and interim deliverables.

- *The WBS dictionary* is a by-product of the WBS creation process. In its simplest form, this will be a text-based document that will hold all the notes, context, and other detailed information uncovered for individual WBS elements.

- *Work packages* are the smallest decomposed elements in your WBS. These can be deliverables by themselves or sub-components of a deliverable. Work packages are important to understand, as they are used to create the schedule in the next step of the planning phase.

Some confusing aspects of WBS

WBS practitioners are often confused about whether tasks and other effort-related estimates should be included in the WBS. This confusion exists because until the late 1980s, the standard definitions included a *task-oriented breakdown* instead of a pure *deliverable-oriented breakdown*. You will still encounter training programs and earlier literature that take this approach.

However, in recent decades, the global community of project management practitioners has greatly refined this perspective. It has been observed that a task-based WBS encourages cognitive bias in thinking and design, which adversely affects project design decisions.

But it is a fact that early-stage estimates and hard constraints are discovered during WBS creation, and they can optionally be stored as baseline notes in the WBS dictionary. You should refer to the WBS throughout a project, but only for the project deliverables and not for other estimates.

The drawbacks of a WBS

Project managers might sometimes argue that a WBS is overkill. Indeed, tiny projects do not need a WBS. Such projects do not need a heavyweight tool such as Microsoft Project either. So, I would say that if you are justified in using Microsoft Project, then you are also justified in creating a separate WBS. Roughly, projects that cost 10 months or more in effort need an explicit WBS to be produced and maintained.

Before you proceed, create the WBS for the following two assignments:

1. Create a WBS for a simple bicycle.
2. Create a WBS for a 10-year-old child's birthday party. This could be a half-day event with a venue, games, and cake.

Both assignments should be decomposed to a minimum of 3 levels and 10 work packages. Remember to focus only on the deliverables (not the tasks!). You can upload the solutions to these assignments to `learngood.in` for feedback from peers, and you can also view other submissions there.

Creating a robust WBS using 10 simple rules

There are elements of both science and art to creating a WBS that will eventually lead to project success. WBS concepts and definitions are still evolving rather rapidly, as compared to other aspects of the project management field. At the same time, there is a shortage of books and articles that comprehensively guide WBS development.

Due to this, I have collated 10 handy rules and best practices that can guide your practice. This collection was first introduced in my online courses, with the added benefit of feedback from thousands of my learners, which is also present in this section.

It is important to understand that most of these rules are only *rules of thumb*, with some exceptions that are explained ahead. Most are based on well-known real-world practice and not theory. Following these rules will benefit you, but there will be occasions when you can customize (and break) them too. So, without further ado, let's proceed to examine these rules:

1. **Create the WBS with your team**: All the key players on your project team should be involved in creating the WBS, preferably right from the beginning. There are some key advantages to doing this:

   - As we discussed earlier, there will be more than a single way to break down a project, and your team should help you find the technique that is most suitable to your situation.

   - Project accountability lies with the project manager, *but the responsibility of execution lies with the team*. So, getting the team involved in the WBS ensures a high level of buy-in and ownership within the team.

   - In my personal experience, I have seen software project WBSes that missed out on critical elements of the WBS. For example, there will be high coverage of business logic components, while other important components, such as user interface development, interim demos, testing, deployment, and so on, will tend to be grossly under-represented in the WBS. You will certainly relate to this situation from your own business domains. Proper representation within the team of different disciplines will ensure that such under-representation can be avoided.

   > TIP: RACI Matrix
   >
   > A **Responsible, Accountable, Consulted, Informed (RACI)** matrix is a great tool to use during the planning phase of a project. It will establish the role played by all the stakeholders of a project. With this matrix in place, the person responsible for a deliverable can be identified and their input becomes critical to the WBS. The project manager is both accountable and responsible for the whole WBS document.

2. **A WBS should have at least three levels**: Two levels are the minimum prescribed in **project management** *Practice Standard for Work Breakdown Structures*. But in real-life practice for non-trivial projects, at least three levels will be found. Complex and large projects typically go up to 8-10 levels of decomposition. Not every branch of the decomposition tree needs to have equal levels of depth.

3. **A WBS is not a task list**: It is important to distinguish the WBS (which is part of scope management) from tasks (which is part of schedule management). While creating the WBS, you will often uncover more information related to scheduling. For example, *"Vincent is in charge of the AI algorithms,"* or *"Integrating the open source framework takes 80 hours of automated testing."* These pieces of information can also be documented in the WBS, as attributes of a WBS component. They can be valuable input to the scheduling process.

4. **Follow strong identification and naming conventions**: There are a few simple considerations you should keep in mind, related to the language and naming conventions of a WBS. Firstly, all components should be uniquely identifiable. Organizations will often use a separate unique identifier field (similar to the **IDENTIFIER** column in the *What does a WBS look like?* section's example presented earlier). This will allow the identification of a component not only in the project but also across the organization. In such cases, a mandatory notational rule will be used to generate unique identifiers.

   For example, consider *SRP.prp.2234.XOL Rotor Wheel* as an example. This is an example of a naming convention used universally for WBS identifiers. It can help you deduce that this component is located at the fourth level of decomposition. *SRP* is the root node, and also perhaps the project name code. Any alphanumeric character combination can be used, if something is not already established by your organization. If you are familiar with the hierarchical tree abstract data structure, you can also deduce that the identifier is in fact a traversal path from the root to the specific node.

   Moreover, you should only use nouns to name components of the WBS because they are suitable for naming deliverables. **Do not use verbs** because they are action words that are used for tasks and activities. `Rotor Wheel` is a fine name for a WBS component but not `Design the UI`. The latter is a task, even though it might generate a deliverable. It could have been named better as just `User Interface`.

5. **The 100% rule**: This is an important and mandatory rule. Consider an analogy to understand the 100% rule. On a Sunday afternoon, you decide to completely disassemble and service your car. There are two implicit assumptions within your project:

   - You do not want to introduce any foreign parts accidentally into your car.

   - You do not want any spare nuts and bolts to be found missing after you are finished reassembling the car.

These two connotations form the 100% rule. It states that *every level of decomposition should represent all work (100%) of the higher-level parent component. Conversely, if a component is decomposed, then its lower-level child subcomponents should represent all of the work involved (100%).*

The two excellent results of this rule are as follows:

- Nothing new is added as a result of decomposition (which is **scope creep**).
- Nothing is subtracted due to decomposition (which is **translation loss**).

This is not an optional rule, and neither is it flexible. As the project manager working with your team to create the WBS, it is this rule that you should use to control the iterative decomposition. You should explicitly check in both directions for all major work packages.

6. **The mutual exclusion rule**: This is a significant corollary that follows on from the 100% rule. This rule states that there should be no overlap of deliverable functionality between components of a WBS. Products often have components that have multi-functional or cross-functional uses. You must ensure that such components are accounted for only once in the WBS.

   If this rule is not adhered to, the result is duplication. Such duplication will result in scheduling errors, duplicated work and responsibility, team friction, and costing errors. A common and practical example of where the mutual exclusion rule is to be carefully examined is the **Role-Based Access Control** (**RBAC**) design functionality of software projects. Such a design implementation allows role-based access to features of software and it is cross-functional in nature. An example of RBAC design in web development is a recruitment team having access to the jobs section of a website and a marketing team having access to the press release sections of that website. Unless this access control deliverable is identified and segregated in the WBS, individual teams or developers tend to implement their own design of access control (permissions) in software.

7. **The iterative design rule**: A WBS should be created with multiple iterations, until it is adequately elaborate. This will ensure that the whole project achieves a similar level of decomposition. There is a common tendency to deeply decompose a well-known functionality and ignore unknown sections.

   This rule is also to be applied whenever there are changes to the scope of a project. Any new non-trivial feature request during later stages of a project could potentially cause repercussions to all aspects of the project. In such situations, changes to the WBS will need to be analyzed iteratively across the whole project.

8. **Always include project management**: Every project requires project management. So, every WBS should account for project management deliverables. Such deliverables might often be interim in nature or for internal consumption. Project managers frequently do not add their own deliverables to the WBS because they think that such deliverables are not part of the result itself.

    Nevertheless, significant project manager deliverables should be accounted for in the WBS. It can be safely guessed that project management costs account for approximately 10% of a project's overall costs.

9. **The lowest-level component is called a work package**: In a hierarchical tree, the terminal element is the one that is not decomposed further. In the case of the WBS, such components are called *work packages*. These work packages correspond to a concept called *Summary Tasks* in Microsoft Project. We will explore Summary Tasks in *Chapter 7, Tasks – under the Microscope*. Understanding this rule helps in translating a WBS into a schedule using Microsoft Project that much easier.

10. **The 8/80 rule**: This is another important and practical rule of thumb and is the most misunderstood rule. This rule states that WBS components should be decomposed with neither less than 8 hours of effort, nor greater than 80 hours of effort. This is a rule that clearly has its origins in a time when tasks (and effort) were part of the WBS design. The prevalent confusion about this rule arises from the fact that 80 hours of effort for a work package is often too little for commercial projects.

    This rule can be interpreted from another perspective: *work packages should not take less than a single day (8 hours) nor more than two reporting cycles (80 hours)*. In the first case, if you track tasks that take less than a day in duration, it comes very close to micro-management. In the second case, you do not want to miss tracking things that take longer than two reporting cycles, in order to prevent serious slippage. Notice the subtle change in definition from *effort* to *duration*. If you put the basic work formula into use here, for a single resource, you will see both translate to the same 8/80 rule.

> Tip
>
> The WBS is a critical reference document whose life will often exceed even the closure of a project. So, use the best available version control techniques and tools to maintain the WBS, alongside the other important project deliverables.

Projects can be decomposed in several valid ways. A large global project might have the decomposition start geographically, or your organization might prescribe department-based decomposition to better utilize its resources. The most common approaches are to decompose by key deliverables, or by project phases, or even through a combination of different ways.

The important thing to note is that no matter how the higher levels are decomposed, the terminal nodes (work packages) should constitute the deliverables of the project. Now that we have discussed the generic best practices and several nuances of WBS creation, let's understand how Microsoft Project supports the concept of the WBS in the next section.

Exploring the WBS feature in Microsoft Project

On the positive side, Microsoft Project inherently supports a robust hierarchical tree data structure in all the main views where it is required. You can effortlessly translate your external WBS into a Microsoft Project schedule. We will explore task organization in detail in *Chapter 7, Tasks – under the Microscope*.

On the flip side, Microsoft Project provides only rudimentary *explicit* support to WBS, primarily in the form of special WBS-related columns. This is highlighted in the following screenshot:

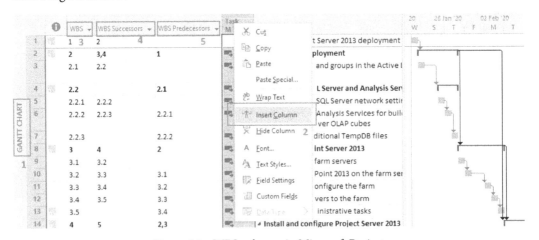

Figure 6.4 – WBS columns in Microsoft Project

From the preceding screenshot, we can observe the following:

1. The Gantt chart view is shown in the preceding screenshot, but this discussion is applicable to all other task-based views.

2. Right-click on any of the column headers and in the pop-up menu, choose **Insert Column**. Type WBS or scroll down the list of predefined fields to locate the WBS-related columns.

3. The **WBS** column is actually a column with automatically generated WBS unique identifiers.

4. **WBS Successors** identifies the task IDs that succeed this particular entry, which are logically based upon the linking applied.

5. **WBS Predecessors** is similar to **WBS Successors** but identifies task IDs that precede a particular entry.

The minor issue with this feature is that Microsoft Project makes no distinction between WBS data and task data. Tasks get automatically numbered too, and not just WBS components. Even with this issue, the WBS numbering column is useful to uniquely identify every component of your schedule.

Going from a WBS to tasks

So far, we have discussed the various techniques, guidelines, and best practices when creating an effective WBS. The question now is, *"How do we turn the WBS into a schedule?"* Specifically, how do we take our WBS into a schedule managed in Microsoft Project? Let's start with a simple definition of the project schedule: *a schedule is the chronological listing from start to finish of a project's tasks, milestones, and deliverables.*

The transition process from a WBS to a schedule is usually accomplished through a series of well-defined steps, which are presented briefly ahead, in line with what's presented in the **Project Management Book of Knowledge** (**PMBOK**):

1. Define tasks (activities).

2. Sequence tasks.

3. Estimate task durations.

    At this point after these first three steps, we will have a functional but minimal schedule. You can stop schedule development at this stage for smaller projects.

4. Estimate costs (and/or determine budget).

5. Resource management plan (estimate and acquire resources – people, machinery, budgets).

6. Activity resourcing (create assignments).

    All the preceding aspects are discussed in terms of Microsoft Project in the next three chapters.

7. Plan communications management, risk management, procurement management, and stakeholder engagement.

All these planning aspects are important from a project management perspective, but they are beyond the scope of this book. However, we will look at these from an execution and tracking perspective in later chapters.

Summary

In this chapter, we have had a comprehensive discussion of the WBS. Starting from the creation of the WBS in the planning phase, we have seen that it plays a vital role in the entire project life cycle. This singular focus on the WBS has been to help us create a Microsoft Project-based schedule that has the highest probability of delivering project success. But there is an aspect of art to WBS management and it involves skillfully getting your whole team involved. As young Goldilocks found in the eponymous story, the decomposition must be *neither too little, nor too much, but just right*.

In the next chapter, we will get hands-on with a well-formed WBS and convert it into a schedule in Microsoft Project. The chapters so far had simplistic exercises, but from here on in, the examples will begin to get closer to the challenges you will face in professional life.

7
Tasks – under the Microscope

Imagine reading a textbook that had no organization to it, with no logical breakup into chapters, or even paragraphs, nor use of punctuation, or a progressive story within it. Such a book would be hard to read, and even more difficult to refer to. It would be an amorphous blob of information and its real-world value would probably be lost.

This same fate often awaits project schedules that are not meaningfully organized. In this chapter, we will learn how to go from a WBS-based task list to a *well-designed* project schedule. There are several aspects of a schedule that will make it well-designed rather than just a functional schedule. These aspects include non-functional requirements such as being able to read the schedule easily, being able to delegate work easily, and being able to track and monitor the schedule easily. In this chapter, we will discuss the techniques you can use to organize your tasks in such a way that these non-functional requirements of a schedule are catered to.

One of the most important schedule-organizing features of Project is the *Summary Task*. Moreover, its functionality extends beyond schedule organization, as we will explore in this chapter.

In this chapter, we're going to cover the following main topics:

- Importing the wizard interface of Project so that it can be used to bring in data from different data sources and formats such as Excel, comma-separated values (CSV) files, and the ubiquitous XML format.

- Different techniques used for schedule organization (including some examples of bad or incomplete design).

- Special types of tasks and their associated features, including milestones and recurring tasks.

- A comprehensive study of summary tasks, including how to create them using multiple techniques, analysis, and applications.

All of this will be replicated within our next project exercise!

The project for this chapter

Now, let's start our hands-on project for this chapter. It is a very common practice to create a task list in Excel or in some other text-based format such as CSV or XML. Such external formats can be easily imported into Project as the foundation upon which to create our schedule.

Case study: ACME Inc. wishes to upgrade their old corporate website to the latest technology. This will involve implementing a software framework, setting up a web server, and migrating data. Since all the components are pre-existing, ground-up development is not involved. You are the PM that's been assigned this prestigious customer-facing project. You have already created a WBS/task list in Excel with the full participation of your team. It looks like this:

⊿	A	B	C	D
1		Task Name	Duration	
2		Project Charter	2 days	
3		Project Estimates Approval	1 day	
4		Project Kickoff		
5				
6		Project Planning		
7		Project Management Plan	1 day	
8		Resource plan	1 day	
9		Launch Execution		
10				
11		DEVELOPMENT		
12		Software Framework		
13		Drupal Installation on Dev	0.5 days	
14		Roles, Permissions	2 days	
15		Content Workflow Setup	2 days	
16		Digital Branding	0.5 days	
17		Server Architecture		
18		Test/Stage setup	1 day	
19		DB automate scripts	1 day	
20		3rd party module integration	2 days	
21		API integration - Newsletter	1 day	
22		Close of Development		
23				
24		DATA MIGRATION		
25		Products Info (all data)	4 days	
26		Corporate Pages	1 day	
27				
28		TESTING		
29		User Acceptance Testing (UAT)	3 days	
30				
31		DEPLOYMENT		
32		Site Admin Training and Handover	2 days	
33		Project Closure		

Figure 7.1 – WBS/task list to upgrade a corporate website

There are some important points to be made about this list, and all these points will be referred to after the import is completed:

1. The very first row of data consisting of Task Name and Duration is the column header. Project will optionally use this header later. It is a best practice to give it a meaningful label, as we have done here.

2. There are two columns with data that should be mapped to two data entities of Project – Task Name and Duration.

3. The first column, labeled **A**, is left intentionally blank, just for legibility.

4. The Duration column has values for some tasks, but not all of them. This is perfectly fine and resembles real-life situations where not all tasks might be estimated early on. Where there is no data present, Project will use a default value of **1 day**.

> **Note**
>
> To follow the project hands-on, please recreate the list in an Excel file and save it on your local filesystem. Alternatively, you can download it from www.learngood.in.

Importing tasks from Excel into Project

The whole import process is encapsulated within a step-by-step wizard interface and is very convenient, as we will see now. This same technique is applicable and valid for other text-based data formats such as XML, CSV, and tab-separated files. Fire up your Project application and then try out the following steps:

1. From the home screen, choose the template entitled **New from Excel workbook**. Click the **Template** button to start the wizard. Refer to the following screenshot:

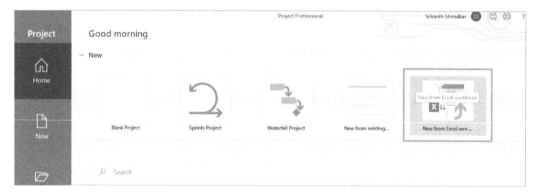

Figure 7.2 – Pre-built template available to import Excel Workbook data

2. A standard **File Open** dialog box will be presented to you. You must now select the file you created earlier (refer to the preceding screenshot), which holds the schedule data. But a small pitfall awaits us now. When this dialog box first opens, the pre-selected file format will be XML format (*.xml). It is very likely that you will not see your file here when you first load it. Due to this, you will have to explicitly open the file format drop-down list and select the correct file format first (for example, *.xlsx). Refer to the following screenshot:

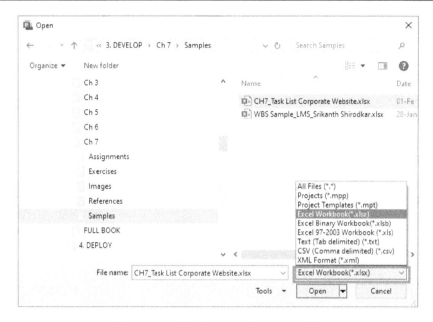

Figure 7.3 – Selecting your data source file

Click on the **Open** button when you have selected your source file.

3.   This is the start of the **Import Wizard** popup, where you will be greeted with the welcome screen. All you have to do here is click the **Next** button:

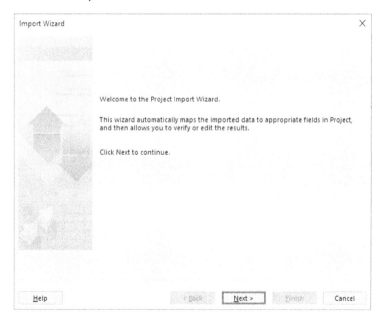

Figure 7.4 – Import Wizard welcome screen

4. Data from the source file has to be mapped to Project entity fields. In the case of organizations that routinely import data, it is prudent to save the mapping instead of creating the map every time. Since we do not have any such map for the time being, we will retain the pre-selected **New map** option on this screen and click **Next**:

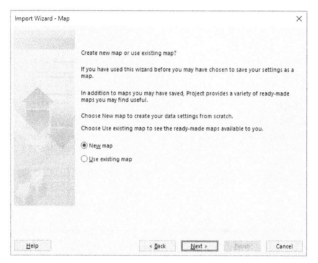

Figure 7.5 – Data map selection on the Import Wizard popup

The mapping technique will become evident during the next steps.

5. There are three file-related options for the data that we are importing. It can be imported into a brand-new file or appended or merged into an open project. For the sake of simplicity, we will go with the first option:

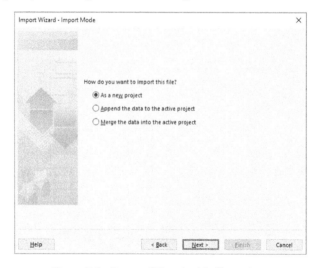

Figure 7.6 – Import Wizard with file options

6. Now, we are presented with data mapping options. The first section will refer to the type of Project entity mapping. In our case, we are importing **Tasks**-related information, so select that checkbox. In the bottom part of the screen, since we have a header in our data (refer to Figure 7.1), choose the first checkbox accordingly:

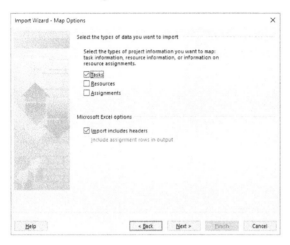

Figure 7.7 – Import Wizard with map options

From this screen, you can see that it is possible to import resource and assignment data using the same current technique. Click **Next** when you're done.

7. Now comes the important data mapping screen. This will begin with a blank slate, as follows:

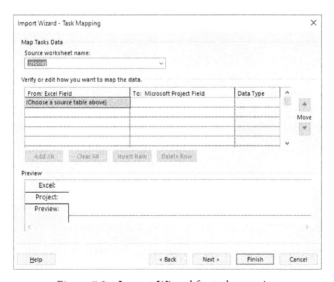

Figure 7.8 – Import Wizard for task mapping

Observe this screen for a moment. This screen is blank because an Excel workbook has multiple worksheets, and Project does not know which worksheet should be plugged in. So, your first action will be to choose the source worksheet from the dropdown at the top.

8. When you select the appropriate worksheet, Project will draw data from the sheet and make its first attempt at mapping the data by itself algorithmically. You can see the result of this algorithmic mapping in the middle UI area, as shown in the following screenshot:

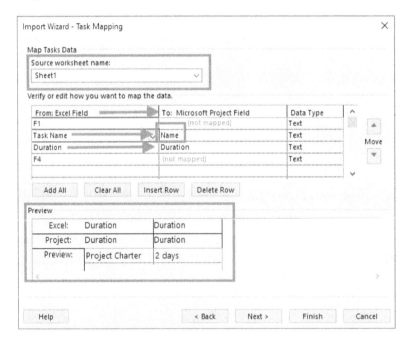

Figure 7.9 – Import Wizard for task mapping, continued

When there is a direct match regarding the data header label to the Project column label (here, this is **Duration**), Project will map directly by intelligence. Otherwise, you will have to explicitly map the correct column name manually (here, the **Task Name** Excel column should be manually mapped to the **Name** column of Project).

After all the source data columns have been correctly mapped, you will be able to see a preview at the bottom of the same screen. Click the **Next** button when you are done.

9. The final screen is now shown. You can optionally save the data mapping so that it can be used for future use:

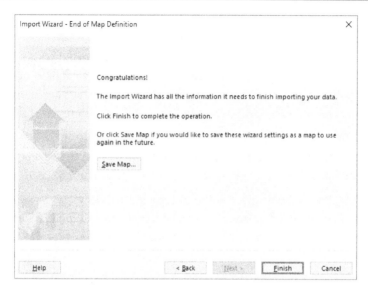

Figure 7.10 – Import Wizard for end of map

Click on **Finish**. Project will create a new file with the imported data. The file on your screen should look similar to this:

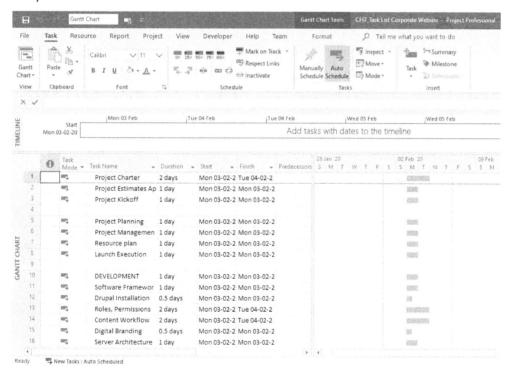

Figure 7.11 – New file populated with imported data

There are some important observations to be made now, as detailed here:

1. Do a quick inspection to ensure that all data has been imported without errors. As we mentioned earlier, empty duration fields in the Excel file have now defaulted to **1 day**. If there are errors, you must carefully debug the steps again until this is rectified. There are no other tools you can use to debug the process, but you can experiment with short pieces of data.

2. It is now the perfect time to set the Project **Start** date (from the **Project Information** dialog box) and configure the project calendar.

3. Notice the title bar (green bar at the top of Project's window), which shows that the current file has been given a default name, which is what happened with the Excel file that we imported from. You still have to use the **Save As** option to save for the first time.

4. All the task bars on the Gantt chart are aligned to the same date because all the start dates are defaulted to the Project Start date and none of the tasks are linked.

> **Best practice**
>
> Use a standardized template for collating task breakdown (and work estimates) from your team members, as shown in this chapter's project. This can then be imported into Project seamlessly, as shown in this chapter, instead of you entering hundreds of records manually. You will find the import technique valuable when collating progress information from your team and vendors if you standardize the information that's sought after into an Excel template. Tracking techniques will be discussed in detail in *Project execution - the real deal* section of this book.

Organizing tasks to create a schedule

In this section, we will discuss three fundamental interconnected techniques that are used to organize tasks into an easy-to-manage schedule. The first aspect is to group tasks within Summary Tasks, the second is based upon chronology, and the third is based upon resourcing.

Technique 1 – Organizing a schedule using Summary Tasks

The Summary Task, despite its name, is not really a task. It is primarily a feature used to organize the schedule. Let's see it in action within our hands-on project. Let's start by observing the first three tasks. These tasks are project managerial in nature and can be grouped together, as shown in the following screenshot:

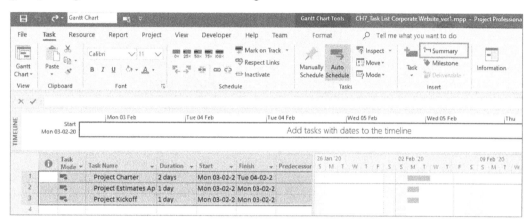

Figure 7.12 – Tasks selected to create a Summary Task

To create a new Summary Task, perform the following steps:

1. Select the tasks that are to be grouped together.

2. Select the **Task** tab on the ribbon menu and, in the **Insert** section of the menu, locate and click the **Summary** button.

3. A new Summary Task will be inserted, as shown in the following screenshot. Correspondingly, in the Gantt chart, a new bracket is also inserted:

	Task Mode	Task Name	Duration	Start	Finish	Predecessors	Resource Names		an '20 M T W T F	S	02 Feb '20 S M T W T
1		◢ <New Summary Task	2 days	Mon 03-02-	Tue 04-02-2						
2		Project Charter	2 days	Mon 03-02-2	Tue 04-02-2						
3		Project Estimates	1 day	Mon 03-02-2	Mon 03-02-2						
4		Project Kickoff	1 day	Mon 03-02-2	Mon 03-02-2						

Figure 7.13 – Microsoft Project showing the new Summary Task that's been created

4. Never directly modify the Summary Task attributes, such as the **Duration** field, **Start** or **Finish** dates, **Predecessors**, or **Resource Names**. Summary Task attributes are computed automatically and the summarized information is displayed for all its child subtasks, as a whole. You will see it in action in the next step.

5.   After adding resources and linking the tasks, the Summary Task will now look as follows. You can replicate this accordingly:

	🛈	Task Mode ▾	Task Name ▾	Duration ▾	Start ▾	Finish ▾	Predecessors ▾	Resource Names ▾	02 Feb '20 T F S S M T W T F S
1		▪️⑤	◢ Project Initiation	4 days	Mon 03-02-	Thu 06-02-2			PM
2		▪️⑤	Project Charter	2 days	Mon 03-02-2	Tue 04-02-2		PM	PM
3		▪️⑤	Project Estimates	1 day	Wed 05-02-	Wed 05-02-	2	PM	PM
4		▪️⑤	Project Kickoff	1 day	Thu 06-02-2	Thu 06-02-2	3	PM	PM
5									
6		▪️⑤	Project Planning	1 day	Mon 03-02-2	Mon 03-02-2			

Figure 7.14 – Changes to subtasks will automatically be reflected in the Summary Task

6.   Here, you can see that the Summary Task attributes are dynamic and have been automatically updated after being linked. Changes to the subtasks will be summarized and reflected instantaneously in the Summary Task attributes.

So far, we've studied a technique through which a brand-new Summary Task can be inserted into the schedule and how it can be used to group and organize tasks.

Technique 2 – Organizing a schedule by chronological sorting

Every schedule is a time-based arrangement of tasks. When transitioning from a plain task list to a schedule, often, multiple iterations are required to get the chronological aesthetics right. While this sounds simple enough, many new users of Project trip up severely here. Proper sequencing can be expressed like this: *"As you step down the task list, the Gantt should execute from the top-left corner toward the bottom-right."* All the hands-on projects we have worked on so far have been examples of proper chronological sequencing.

This is best understood through some illustrative examples, as we will see in the following section. But for now, in the next section, we will look at examples that reflect flawed design and should not be emulated.

Examples of bad chronological sequencing

Properly sequencing tasks might not be evident to the project manager in the first iteration. It is imperative to observe the Gantt chart and reorder tasks until we get the sequencing right. In the screenshot examples that follow, compare the ordering of the task list with the task execution path on the Gantt chart.

Example 1

There is not much wrong in the following example except the sequencing. To understand the issues in linking, notice that the first task to be executed on the Gantt chart is the fourth on the task list. This is the mismatch that can be improved upon. Such problems tend to be compounded in real-life schedules, thus rendering a mishmash of your scheduling:

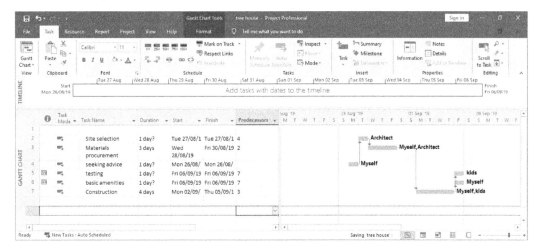

Figure 7.15 – Bad chronological sequencing – example 1

Example 2

The following example shows only one task requiring adjustment:

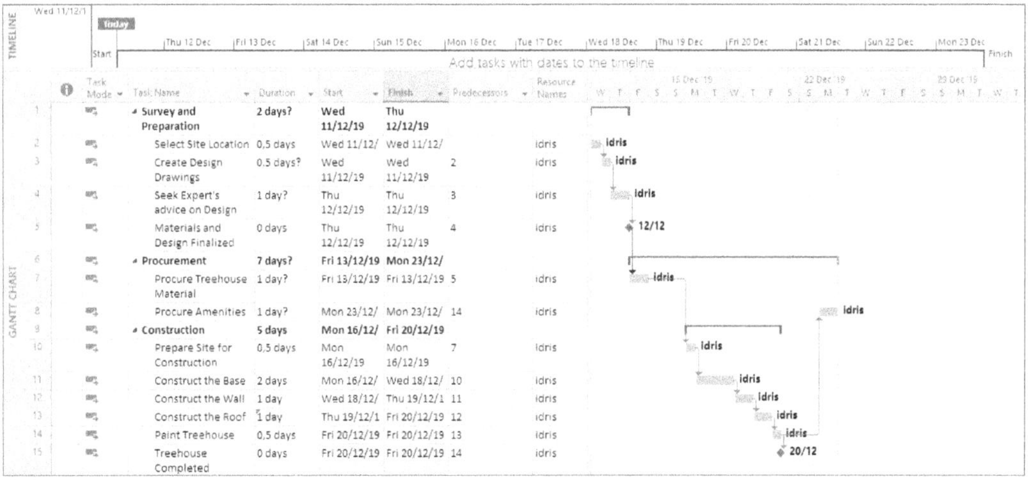

Figure 7.16 – Bad chronological sequencing – example 2

Example 3

There are several issues with the following example, including bad sequencing, disjointed sections of the schedule, and how summary tasks are linked:

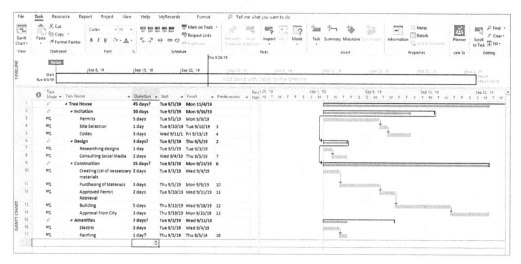

Figure 7.17 – Bad chronological sequencing – example 3

Example 4

The final example shows another schedule that can be simplified with multiple iterations to reorder the tasks:

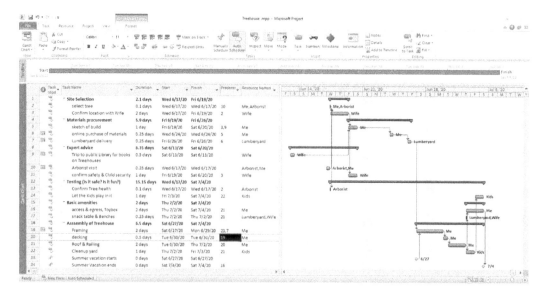

Figure 7.18 – Bad chronological sequencing – example 4

It is a common practice to assemble the small pieces of the schedule iteratively into longer chunks, until the whole schedule is assembled. The best practice is that at every iteration, we have to check the chronological sequencing and fine-tune it if necessary.

Technique 3 – Organizing a schedule by grouping resources

If you group tasks by **Resource Assignment** (that is, assigned to the same resource), the resultant schedule makes delegation easier, readability is improved, and tracking is easier, as we will see in later chapters. We will see this aspect in action in our running project, so let's continue.

Creating Summary Tasks from indentation

The following screenshot shows the state of our project when we'd left it:

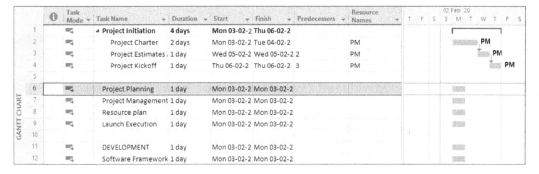

Figure 7.19 – Running Project for this chapter

Some of the tasks shown here had come in from the source WBS and were work packages, not simple tasks. Note the task highlighted in the previous screenshot, called **Project Planning**. This task needs to be converted into a Summary Task.

If you observe the Summary Task that we created earlier, you will see that the subtasks were automatically indented in when we created the new Summary Task. This is a clue that *indentation* can also create a Summary Task:

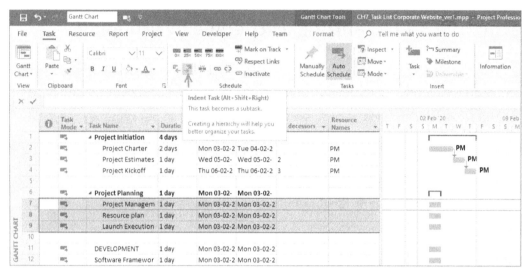

Figure 7.20 – Creating Summary Task by indentation

Refer to the preceding screenshot regarding how to use this technique:

1. Select the tasks that are intended to be subtasks of the Summary Task you will be creating.

2. From the ribbon menu, ensure that the **Task** tab is selected and, in the **Schedule** section, locate and click **Indent Task** (*Alt + Shift + Right*).

3. This creates a Summary Task of the task immediately higher up. The **Project Planning** task is now a summary task.

With that, we have seen two techniques you can use to create Summary Tasks; that is, the **Summary** button on the menu to create a new Summary Task where none existed previously, or use the indentation technique to turn an existing task into a summary task.

Special tasks and task features

Project provides some useful and frequently used special tasks and features, some of which we will explore now. The most commonly used special task is called a *milestone*.

Milestones

In project management, a milestone is used to represent a significant event in the project schedule. It is the project manager's discretion to insert milestones into their schedule as they deem fit. A recommended best practice is to use milestones to mark significant deliverables or achievements in the schedule. For example, showing an interim demo to the client is an important milestone. Similarly, ending the development phase can be another significant event to the project team and can be represented in the schedule.

In any schedule, *a milestone is just a task with 0 (zero) duration*. This makes sense because milestones are just symbolic markers representing certain events, and they should not have any separate work-related duration.

Now, let's create a milestone in our running project. The **Project Kickoff** task can be turned into a milestone by just entering a 0 in its **Duration** field, as shown in the following screenshot:

	Task Mode ▾	Task Name ▾	Duration ▾	Start ▾	Finish ▾	Predece ▾	Resourc Names	02 Feb '20 T F S S M T W T F S S	09 Fe
1	◼	◢ **Project Initiation**	**3 days**	Mon 03-02-2	**Wed 05-02-2**				
2	◼	Project Charter	2 days	Mon 03-02-2	Tue 04-02-2		PM	▬▬▬, PM	
3	◼	Project Estimates	1 day	Wed 05-02-2	Wed 05-02-2	2	PM	▬, PM	
4	◼	Project Kickoff	0 days	Wed 05-02-2	Wed 05-02-2	3		◆ 05-02	
5									
6	◼	◢ **Project Planning**	**1 day**	Mon 03-02-2	Mon 03-02-2				

Figure 7.21 – Milestone creation in Microsoft Project

There are a couple of important points for you to note about the preceding screenshot:

- The milestone is represented as a diamond, shown in the default black color, on the Gantt chart.

- It is possible to assign a resource and add a non-zero duration to a milestone. Both should be avoided as a precaution against inadvertent and hard-to-detect bugs in your schedule.

Using all the techniques we have learned about so far regarding Summary Tasks, milestones, linking, and assignments, we can create a schedule for our running project, as shown in the following screenshot:

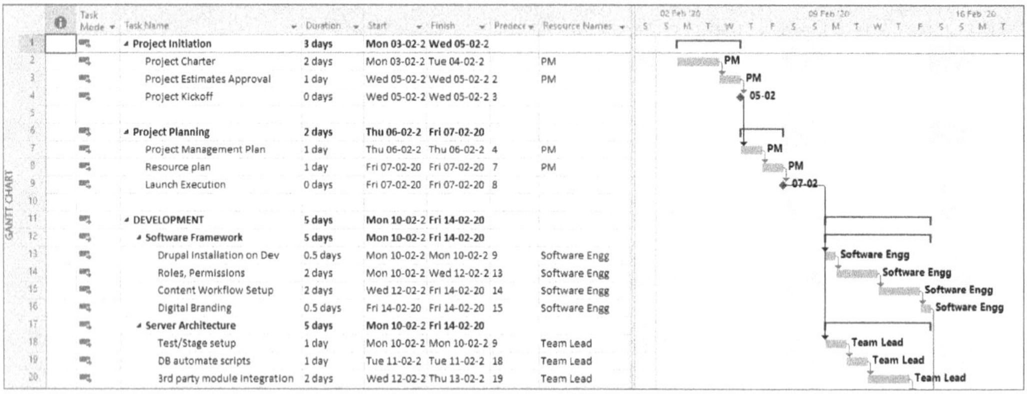

Figure 7.22 – Completed schedule – part one

Just like WBS work packages can be decomposed into a hierarchical tree, the Summary Task feature can be used to recreate a hierarchical structure in your schedule. Such a hierarchical structure is employed in the **Development** section of the schedule (refer to the preceding screenshot). This can be achieved with repeated indentation, as we learned earlier.

The bottom part of the schedule is shown in the following screenshot:

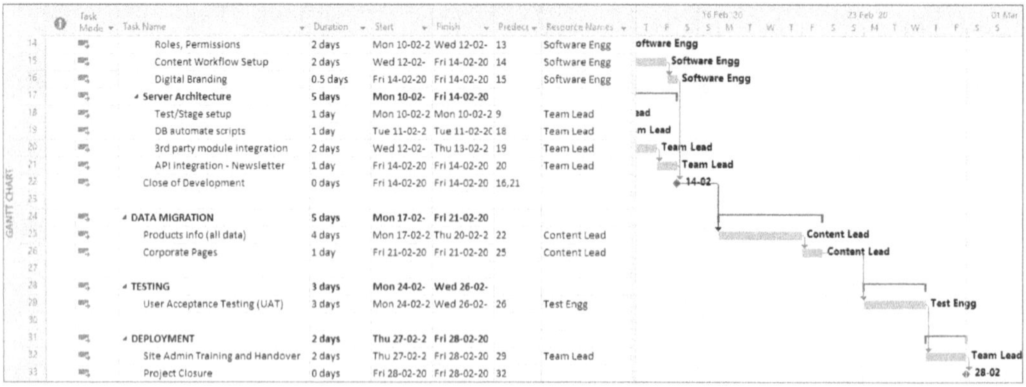

Figure 7.23 – Completed schedule – part two

You are urged to replicate this project exercise as closely as possible by experimenting with all the features we've explored so far. And with that, we have completed the project exercise for this chapter. However, we will continue to explore some more special task-related features in the rest of this chapter, starting from the next section.

Inactivating tasks

By default, every task that is created in the project is active and has a corresponding impact on the schedule and the project as a whole. If the task has been assigned to a resource, then there is an impact on the resource's availability to take on other tasks, too.

But the Professional version of Project has a special button called **Inactivate** in the schedule section, on the **Task** tab of the ribbon menu. If you have this feature available, an interesting experiment can be performed to observe the effect of inactivating tasks. Refer to the following screenshot:

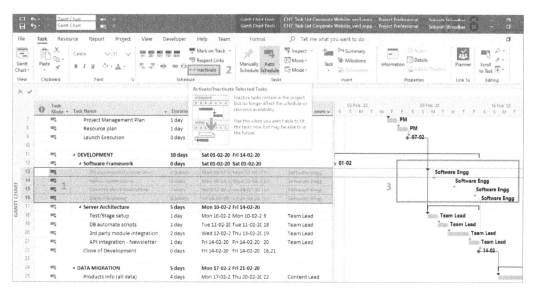

Figure 7.24 – Inactivate tasks feature being used on the current project schedule

Notice that the Summary Task called **Software Framework** is on a parallel branch of the parent Summary Task, which means that inactivating the whole branch should have no impact on the entire project schedule's end dates! Alternatively, the same could be said about the other branch, called **Server Architecture**.

This can be verified using the inactivate task feature, as follows:

1. Select all the subtasks under **Software Framework**.

2. Click on the **Inactivate** button on the **Task** tab of the ribbon.

3. Observe that, in the Gantt chart, the corresponding taskbars have changed their visual representation into hollow rectangles, denoting inactive tasks. You can observe that the Project end dates will not have shifted. You can click the same button again to activate the tasks once more.

Continue to experiment with other tasks and verify that they indeed impact the schedule in subtle ways.

Blank rows

It is possible to greatly enhance the readability of your schedule by judiciously using whitespace. This can be done with empty rows to delineate Summary Tasks. Our current project already has empty rows, but if you wanted more, Project provides a button specifically for this on the dropdown available from the large **Task** button, on the ribbon's **Task** bar, as shown in the following screenshot:

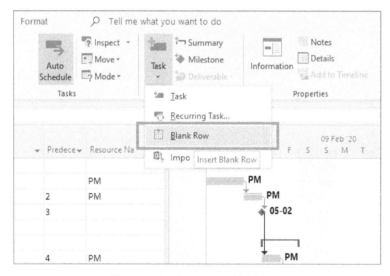

Figure 7.25 – Inserting a blank row

Use blank rows judiciously to improve the readability of your schedule. A much faster keyboard shortcut to achieve the same effect is to select the location where the empty row should be inserted and hit the *Insert* key on the keyboard.

Recurring tasks

Projects often have tasks that repeat with a frequency. Weekly work-status collection meeting is one such example. Fortnightly source code review is another.

Project includes a powerful tool you can use to create such recurring tasks. To see this in action, first, create a couple of blank rows in the same running project. Then, select the row where you wish to insert a recurring task and click on the **Task** button dropdown to select the **Recurring Task** button, as shown in the following screenshot:

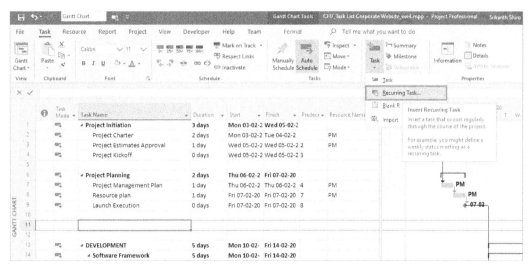

Figure 7.26 – Inserting a recurring task

At this point, the **Recurring Task Information** dialog box will appear, as shown in the following screenshot. Notice that there are four sections in this interface; we will examine them sequentially:

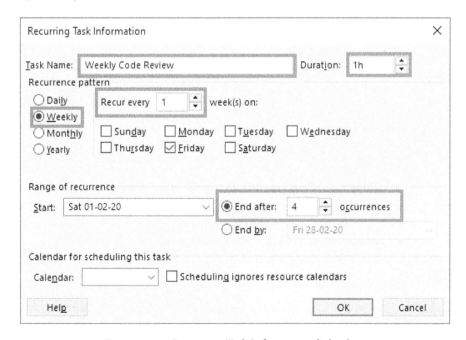

Figure 7.27 – Recurring Task Information dialog box

This interface is highly configurable, and it is possible to design a complicated frequency pattern for your requirements. For the sake of this example, we will keep it simple. Try the following steps:

1. Start by naming the recurring task and setting the duration of the task. Here, it has been named `Weekly Code Review`, with a duration of 1 hour, `1h`.

2. The next section is used to design the recurrence pattern. In our example, a simple weekly recurrence for every Friday has been configured. Note that if you change the value in **Recur every _ week(s) on** to **2**, then it becomes a fortnightly meeting. Similarly, it is possible to design bi-monthly, quarterly, or even annual recurrences.

3. In the next section, we set the meeting's start and end parameters. In our case, we have scheduled for a maximum of **4** occurrences.

4. The final section can be used to choose a specific calendar for which this recurrence is applicable. For example, it may be configured to occur only for the London office timings, if you so choose. In our example, we have left this option in its default state.

Click the **OK** button when you are done. The recurring tasks will be inserted into the project schedule, as shown in the following screenshot:

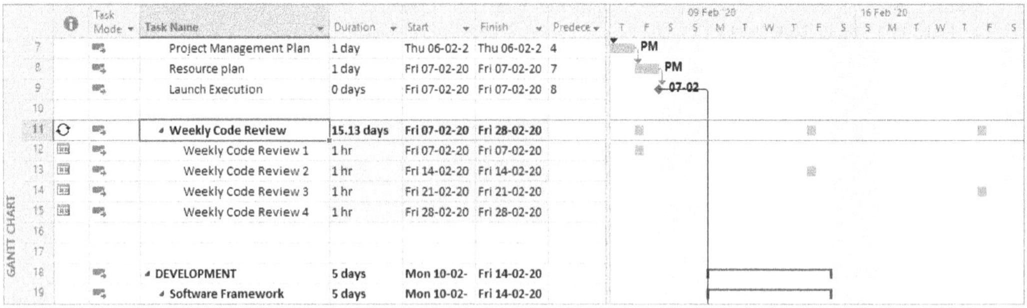

Figure 7.28 – Recurring task inserted into the schedule

There are some salient points to be observed regarding the preceding screenshot:

1. The new tasks have been inserted and encapsulated nicely under a new automatically created Summary Task.

2. Individual subtasks have been uniquely named.

3. Notice the new icon used for recurring meetings in the `Indicators` column. If you hover over it, a summarized message will be displayed.

Pitfalls and extra tips for working with recurring tasks

The following are a few tips while working with recurring tasks:

- Recurring tasks are assigned higher priority than normal tasks by Project and commonly cause overallocation issues when they are assigned resources.

- If you are just scheduling regular meetings with recurring tasks, consider using a calendar tool instead, such as the one available in Microsoft Outlook. This eliminates the complexity of adding a recurring task to your schedule.

- To avoid the possibility of overallocations originating from recurring tasks, you can artificially make the task duration set to 0 (zero).

- It is not possible to convert existing tasks into recurring tasks. This may be desirable if, for example, you are working on older Project schedules that you have inherited.

All in all, use recurring tasks sparingly and only if you cannot justify using other calendar tools.

A deeper understanding of Summary Tasks

So far in this chapter, we have used Summary Tasks from an organizational perspective. Now, we will delve a little deeper into their extended functionality, usage, and hidden connotations.

Making sense of Summary Task information

For this discussion, refer to the following screenshot:

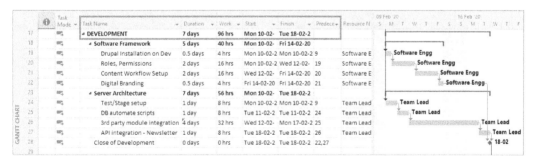

Figure 7.29 – Summary Task information

This screenshot is derived from our running project, but one of the branches has been extended to illustrate the points that we will now discuss. Additionally, the **Work** column has also been included in the table:

- Observe that the Summary Task attributes (**Duration**, **Work**, **Start**, and **End** dates, **Cost**, and so on) represent the collective impact of all the constituent subtasks, as a whole.

- These **Summary Task** attributes are not simple summations for all fields; for example:

- Work is a simple summation, as you can verify from the preceding screenshot, where we can see 96 hours = 40 hours + 56 hours.

- Duration is *not* a summation. It is the span encapsulated within the earliest and the latest date, anywhere within the constituent tasks. It is important for you to understand this sufficiently in order to be able to analyze schedules.

- Similarly, while **Cost** will be a summation, **Baseline** will not be a summation. **Baseline** is an advanced date-based concept, and we will cover it extensively later in this book.

Project Summary Task

Any schedule that you create with Project can be entirely summarized under the Project Summary Task. This is a feature that is always present and camouflaged until you make it visible. Refer to the following screenshot to learn how to enable **Project Summary Task**:

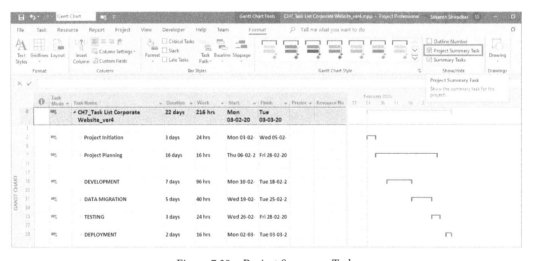

Figure 7.30 – Project Summary Task

Project Summary Task is enabled from a checkbox found in the **Show/Hide** section of the **Format** tab on the ribbon menu. The information it provides pertains to the entire project. In this screenshot, the constituent child summary tasks have been collapsed to show a compact and modular representation. Milestones, active/inactive tasks, recurring tasks, and Summary Tasks are all part of a repertoire of task avatars that you can use to prudently organize your schedule. And with that, we have come to the end of this chapter.

Summary

In this chapter, we continued seamlessly from the WBS into a schedule by learning how to import information into Project. When standardized with repeated practice, this technique can be extrapolated to other data entities, such as resources and assignments.

Once data is brought into Project, it has to be systematically organized. This chapter presented task organization techniques and best practices. Specifically, Summary Tasks, chronological ordering, and grouping by resources were discussed. Special tasks and features were discussed, including milestones and recurring tasks. A special analysis feature that allows us to inactivate tasks was also demonstrated.

Summary Tasks are the best tools available for a well-organized project schedule. There are multiple dimensions to their usage. Firstly, Summary Tasks are used to represent the same work packages that we discussed in detail in *Chapter 6, Work Breakdown Structure – the Single Critical Factor*. Secondly, they can be used to create a hierarchical tree structure within your schedule. Thirdly, they represent the collective impact of their constituent subtasks and hence are excellent analytical tools. Consistent hands-on practice with them will make you well versed in the use of Summary Tasks.

In the same way that we started with very simple tasks and have progressed into complex task features, in the next chapter, we will turn our attention to task linking. So far in this book, we have explored only one kind of linking, but Project provides several ways in which real-life dependencies can be translated into links in the schedule. We will explore all of these in the next chapter.

8
Mastering Link Dependency and Constraints

Every mission into space is a *project*, due to its unique objectives and challenges. Imagine that you are the Project Manager of such a space mission. Your schedule will be highly realistic and reflect the dynamics of the mission's execution. You will be required to cater to special sequencing requirements and hard dates on the timeline. Let's consider some examples of such tasks: only after a new solar battery has been plugged in should the older one be removed. Otherwise, the power could go down and jeopardize the entire mission. This is an example of a special task sequencing requirement. Similarly, within a certain precise date, certain mission experiments should be terminated, and other new ones initiated. This is an example of a special date constraint.

Microsoft Project provides tools and features to reflect such realism in your schedule, as we will explore in depth in this chapter. But the cost of high realism is complexity (of the schedule), and the project will incur some extra cost to retain effectiveness. You should use such schedule customization only on special occasions. We will discuss some best practices to counterbalance realism with effectiveness.

In this chapter, we're going to cover the following main topics:

- Customizing task dependencies and constraints
- Hands-on practice using different task dependencies with a running project
- Incorporating date constraints within your schedule
- Using dependency scheduling best practices with Project
- Let's get started!

Scheduling – a quick refresher

We can define a schedule as *a chronologically ordered listing of tasks or events.* The following screenshot shows an illustration of a schedule:

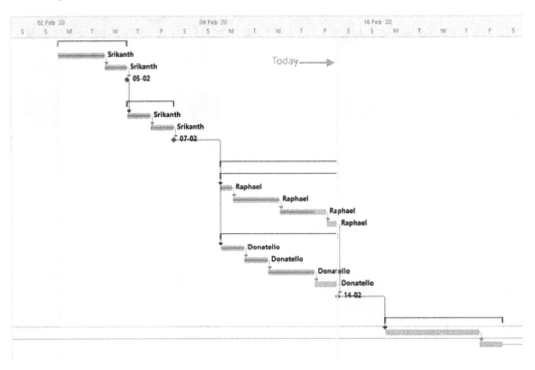

Figure 8.1 – A schedule represented as a Gantt chart

The timeline represents the canvas on which you paint the picture of your project. The single green vertical line represents today's date, and on every new day, this line marches one step ahead on the timeline, from start to finish with regard to the project. Here is a close-up view of the timeline:

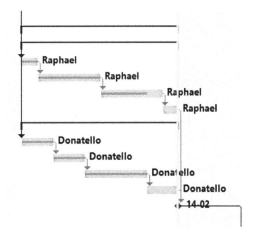

Figure 8.2 – Close-up of a timeline, represented as a Gantt chart

The thick horizontal bars represent tasks. The arrow lines connecting the tasks are their links (or dependencies). They perform another critical functionality – they show the direction of execution.

All the links in the preceding screenshot are of the same type, where the end of one task neatly triggers the start of the next task in line. While such simple links are the most common type, in real-life scenarios, you will come across tasks that have more complicated dependencies between them. We will explore all the different task dependencies in the next section.

Task dependencies and constraints

There are two major aspects that affect sequencing decisions in a schedule. These are as follows:

- The inherent relationship of dependencies between the project tasks
- The inherited set of constraints on the project

We will now investigate how these dependencies and constraints can be realistically reflected in our schedule using Project features.

Task relationships

As the famous saying goes, *no man is an island*, and similarly, within a schedule, no task should exist in isolation. Consider the following diagram, which denotes a relationship between two tasks:

Figure 8.3 – Dependency relationship between two tasks

Tasks in a project derive their meaning only in relation to other tasks. For example, if you are building a house, it is mandatory to build the foundation before your build the walls, and only after you build the walls can the roof be constructed. The universal law of gravity mandates these particular dependencies. Similarly, in software development, an application can only be deployed after you have created it. Dependencies are often rooted in common sense and business logic.

In each of these examples, one task *drives* the other task. Based upon this observation, we can classify the tasks on either side of this relationship as follows:

- **Predecessor**: The controlling task that drives another task. In the preceding diagram, this is Task A.

- **Successor**: The task that is driven. In the preceding diagram, this is Task B.

The process of connecting the predecessor and successor is known as **linking** (or *sequencing* in some texts you may come across).

There are some important points for you to observe from this discussion:

- The definitions of predecessor and successor *only* have relevance in relation to the existence of a relationship between said tasks. These sequences of such predecessors are known as **driving predecessors**. We will encounter this feature in Project later in this chapter.

- A predecessor task in one relationship could be a successor task in a different relationship and vice versa. Terminology is only relevant to the relationship in question.

- If a task is a predecessor, it does not automatically mean that the task occurs earlier than the successor on the schedule's timeline! Rather, it means that the successor is driven (*activated* or *put in motion*) by the predecessor. We will see examples in the next section.

- A predecessor task will drive either the start or finish date of the successor task. Other date parameters of the successor will be driven subsequently by the task's duration.

> **Pitfall**
>
> Do not have disjointed sections in a schedule. Disjointed sections will lose all the power of automatic scheduling when they're disconnected from the rest of the project. Refresh your old network theory class notes on this topic for a refresher. At least connect disjointed sections to the start and end nodes of a schedule. A simple example can be found in *Chapter 7, Tasks – under the Microscope*; please refer to *Figure 7.16*. A detailed discussion of several sequencing error patterns, including the disjointed sequencing of tasks, along with more screenshot examples, are provided in *Chapter 18, Reviewing Projects and Creating Templates for Success*, in the *Sequencing error patterns* section.

Four types of task dependencies

Continuing our discussion from earlier, we can extrapolate that there are four fundamental types of task dependencies. Let's understand each here.

Finish-to-Start (FS)

This is by far the most common type of dependency, and we have been using this dependency in all the examples and projects so far in this book. Refer to the following screenshot:

Figure 8.4 – Finish-to-Start (FS) dependency

In FS dependency, the predecessor is executed earlier than the successor. The predecessor completing triggers the start of the successor. For example, a project has to be approved (predecessor) before it is launched (successor).

Start-to-Start (SS)

The start of the predecessor task drives the start of the successor task. Compared to the previous example, the predecessor doesn't need to be completed before you launch the successor task. Refer to the following screenshot:

Figure 8.5 – Start-to-Start (SS) dependency

The obvious advantage of using this dependency relationship is that you can overlap the tasks to an extent, thereby potentially reducing project duration. For example, if your organization has several departments, often, it is possible to work with several departments at the same time.

Finish-to-Finish (FF)

The FF dependency is the symmetric opposite of the previous SS dependency. The successor task's completion is driven by the completion of the predecessor task:

Figure 8.6 – Finish-to-Finish (FF) dependency

Here, the floor's electrical layout planning is completed as soon as the floor's seating arrangement plan is completed for an office.

Once again, the possibility of overlapping occurring makes the FF relationship attractive, just like SS.

> **Pitfall**
>
> The task-overlapping nature of SS and FF can cause overallocation if both the associated tasks are associated with the same resource. So far in this book, we have learned about two techniques we can use to combat such overallocation: assign to different resources or reduce the Resource Units assigned to the task (that is, say the resource only works for 4 hours/day on each task, thereby increasing the duration of the task).

Start-to-Finish (SF)

Now, we come to the strangest, least used, and least understood of all the relationships – the SF dependency. In the SF dependency, the start of the predecessor triggers the finish of the successor. This is the reverse of the most common FS FS dependency:

Figure 8.7 – Start-to-Finish (SF) dependency

Zero downtime is often achieved by the SF dependency. In the preceding example, consider the case of a running account of payable bills. As soon as we initiate the payables calculation for the existing infrastructure (predecessor), a new account should already be in place for the customer to track newly running payables (successor).

This type of SF dependency is rare, and you must carefully inspect your logic if you encounter this relationship in your project.

> **Tip**
>
> If you encounter and use any dependency other than the default FS in your project, be sure to document the logic. This will be helpful to you for future reviews, to the team members who will execute the task, and to any other project manager who will want to use your plan.

Now, let's look at **constraints**, which are the limitations involved in the project.

Understanding constraints

In *Chapter 1, Project Management - the Essential Primer,* we discussed how every project operates under the triple constraints of scope, cost, and time, just like an iron triangle. In the planning stage of the project, when you are grappling with task sequencing, these constraints translate as follows:

1. **Limited resources**: The **Project Manager** (**PM**) can only overlap a limited set of tasks to reduce overall project duration, and this limit is determined closely by the number of resources in the Project team. Exceeding this limit results in overallocation and should be avoided.

> **Important note**
> The FS dependency may often be used for no other reason than because the resource will work through their set of tasks one after another, even when there are no other explicit dependencies between the tasks. In fact, we have used task linking like this in all our project examples so far in this book.

2. **Hard dates**: When we use automatic scheduling, we do not set either the start or finish date of the sequenced task. However, the PM will encounter tasks that are tied to calendar dates. Such dates are known as *hard dates* for the task. Date constraints will be explained in the *Working with date constraints* section.

Next, we will learn how task dependency selection is an important aspect of project scheduling.

Selecting the correct task dependency

The vast majority of task dependencies you will encounter will be **Finish-to-Start** (**FS**). However, when your project presents special sequencing requirements, the question is, *How do you select the correct dependency?* A handy technique we can use to identify the dependency is a two-step process, as follows:

1. First, identify which task drives the relationship. By doing this, you will have established the predecessor-successor aspect of the relationship.

2. Next, identify whether the *start* or *finish* date is driven. By doing this, you will have identified the *Start-to* or *Finish-to* aspect of the relationship.

With these two initial steps, you will have enough clarity to correctly identify the exact task dependency. It is important for you to get all special dependencies reviewed by your team members, subject matter experts, and all other pertinent stakeholders. To cement all our learning so far, let's work on another hands-on project.

Releasing the latest application version

Case study: You are the project manager for the world's #1 microblogging company – **Chitter**. Your project objective is to upgrade the software application to the latest version.

The following are the critical success criteria for your project:

-   Since millions of users are connected, there has to be zero downtime for the application.

-   Preserve existing customer data and migrate minimal new data.

The following assumptions will be made:

Consider a small subset of tasks from the whole project, pertinent to what you've learned in this chapter.

Breakdown of work

Please enter the following task list into a new blank Project file so that you can follow along. Practice makes perfect!

1. Stage several trials for the new application
2. Launch the project on the production server
3. Migrate consumer data
4. New branding data migration
5. Set up the production server infrastructure
6. Complete production resting
7. Launch the new server, SUNRISE
8. SUNSET server shutdown process

Working with task dependencies

MSP provides many techniques we can use to manipulate dependencies. We used two simple techniques to create the FS dependency earlier. Let's quickly refresh on these before we learn about some new techniques:

- The first technique is to use the link button on the ribbon menu (go to the **Task** tab, then the **Schedule** section). Refer to the following screenshot:

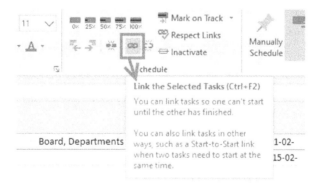

Figure 8.8 – Link button to create a default FS dependency

- The second simple technique we can use to create FS links is to directly enter the table line number of the predecessor task in the column provided for it in the entry table, as shown in the following screenshot:

Duration	Start	Finish	Predecessors	W	T	F	S	S	M	T
2 days	Thu 11-02-16	Fri 12-02-16								
1 day	Mon 15-02-16	Mon 15-02-16	1							

Figure 8.9 – Creating an FS dependency by entering it directly into the Predecessors column

We will now explore another powerful and flexible technique we can use to create SS, FF, and SF dependencies.

Creating special dependencies

Let's start our hands-on project. Start by creating a new blank file, entering the project's start date to the nearest Monday, and entering all the tasks provided earlier. Refer to the following screenshot to prepare the project's task durations:

		Task Mode	Task Name	Duration	Start	Finish		T	F	S	S	M	T	W	T	F	S
1			Staging sever trials for new application	2 days	Mon 17-02-2	Tue 18-02-20											
2			Launch project on Production server	3 days	Mon 17-02-2	Wed 19-02-2											
3																	
4			Consumer data migration	5 days	Mon 17-02-2	Fri 21-02-20											
5			New Branding data migration	5 days	Mon 17-02-2	Fri 21-02-20											
6																	
7			Production server infra setup	5 days	Mon 17-02-2	Fri 21-02-20											
8			Production Testing completion	5 days	Mon 17-02-2	Fri 21-02-20											
9																	
10			Launch new server SUNRISE	3 days	Mon 17-02-2	Wed 19-02-2											
11			SUNSET server shutdown process	3 days	Mon 17-02-2	Wed 19-02-2											

Figure 8.10 – Starting the hands-on project

Software applications are deployed through robust engineering practices that incorporate a multi-stage environment. The new application is fully tested on a staging server (task 1) and only then is the production server project launched (task 2). This denotes an FS relationship. Let's get started:

1. Create a normal FS link for the first two tasks. You can select them together and use the **Task** tab's link button.

2. Now, for the next two tasks we will link, we will open a special split-window view. Traverse to the **View** tab on the ribbon and, in the **Split View** section, enable the **Details** checkbox. In the adjoining dropdown list, select **Task Details Form**. Note that if you do not find the form listed there, click on the **More Views…** button and select **Task Details Form**. Your screen should resemble the following:

Figure 8.11 – Opening the Task Details Form view to create special dependencies

3.   Take a moment to observe this new view and get familiar with it.

4.   The panes at the bottom of the split window can be configured. Your panes should show **Predecessor Name** and **Successor Name**. If they do not, right-click anywhere in the split window and select the **Predecessors & Successors** option. Refer to the following screenshot:

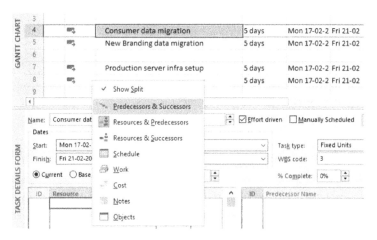

Figure 8.12 – Predecessors & Successors split pane selection

5. In the split window, ensure that the **Name** dropdown shows our predecessor task; that is, **Consumer data migration**; otherwise, select it from the drop-down list. Refer to the following screenshot for the sequence of actions you need in order to create an SS dependency:

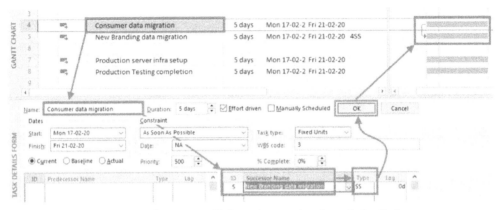

Figure 8.13 – Creating an SS dependency using the task details form

6. In the **Successor Name** column of the split window, click on the first empty row to open a list of all available tasks. Select the **New Branding data migration** task. Click on the **Type** column to show all the task types available and select **SS**. When you are done, click on the **OK** button. With that, you have created your first SS dependency; observe the Gantt chart!

    The reason that the SS dependency was chosen for these two tasks is because these two tasks can be overlapped, and consumer data migration should begin before associated new branding data can be migrated to the database.

> **Tip**
> A very common mistaken belief is that SS dependencies require both tasks to start together. This is not correct, and often, a time interval might be specified between the start of the predecessor and the successor. SS only requires that the predecessor has started before the successor starts.

7. In exactly the same process, create an FF relationship for the next two tasks; that is, **Production server infra setup** and **Production Testing completion**. Here, we mean to say *testing the production environment (the successor task) can't be deemed complete unless the production server infrastructure has been set up completely (the predecessor)*. The only difference in this case will be choosing the FF dependency type instead of SS. Your tasks should look similar to what's shown in the following screenshot:

Figure 8.14 – SS and FF task dependencies in action

Similar to the previous example, the successor can finish any time after the predecessor finishes, and it's not compulsory for the two to finish together.

8. For the last two tasks, create an SF dependency. The technique remains the same and you only have to choose SF this time around. When you create the SF task, the successor task will get pushed back on the timeline, and you can choose to accept that or choose to move both tasks ahead. Refer to the following screenshot:

Figure 8.15 – SF task dependency in action

It is important to understand the meaning of the SF task dependency in the context of our project. Remember that one of our success criteria was to ensure no downtime for the application servers. Here, what we mean is that *starting the new SUNRISE server (predecessor) triggers the completion of the SUNSET server's shutdown process (successor)*. This is a way to ensure low downtime for the servers being swapped.

> **Pitfall**
>
> It is possible to create task links by using yet another technique: dragging and dropping from one task to another. The first task you drag from will be the predecessor and the task you will drop to will be the successor. However, never use the drag-and-drop technique of creating links as they often cause errors, such as linking with incorrect tasks or inadvertently moving the tasks.

When you have finished linking all the tasks, your project should resemble the following screenshot:

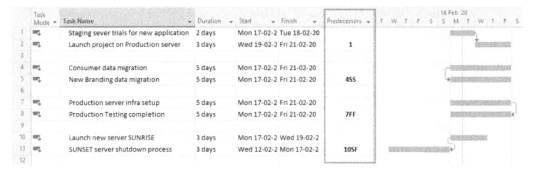

Figure 8.16 – Special task dependencies on the Predecessors column

In a complex Gantt chart, it is not easy to identify the presence of special task dependencies. The best way to do this is to always double-check the **Predecessors** column, which will show the dependency type when you review a peer's schedule, for example.

So far in this chapter, we have learned how to add realism to a schedule from the sequencing perspective. Now, we will explore the same topic from the timeline and date perspective.

Working with date constraints

It is highly recommended that you work in the automatic scheduling mode of Project. All the useful scheduling features and tools that you have been learning about so far are only applicable in the automatic scheduling mode of Project. But sometimes, you may have hard deadlines, such as in the space mission project example from the start of this chapter, where, within a certain precise date, certain mission experiments should be finished, and other new ones should be started.

There are two ways to incorporate specific dates into your project:

- Set manual scheduling mode on for that particular task and set the start date, thereby taking over the responsibility of managing all its parameters. The effect of doing so would effectively be comparable to working with Excel for that task. Moreover, it may also present hard-to-discover bugs in the schedule. Since this is not the recommended technique, we will not dwell on this option.

- Stay within automatic scheduling mode and use the **Date Constraint** feature, which is what we will do for the rest of this chapter.

Let's go back to our running project to understand how to add the realism of time-related constraints to our project. The following screenshot shows how the first two tasks now appear:

Figure 8.17 – Start of the date constraint experiment

Observe that the task relationship between the first two tasks is FS. The second task (which is the successor task) is called **Launch project on Production server**.

Unfortunately, due to some approval review delays, the launch date can only happen the next coming Monday. Let's see how we can handle this date constraint by using automatic scheduling:

1. First, double-click on the second task and bring up the **Task Information** dialog box. You should be familiar with this interface from earlier discussions:

Figure 8.18 – Changing the start date

2. After changing the start date, click on **OK** to return to the Gantt chart view. You will first be challenged by a question from the **Planning Wizard** popup, as shown in the following screenshot:

Figure 8.19 – Planning Wizard challenge upon changing the date

3. Choose the second option to retain the FS relationship. Now, let's look at the impact of our action. Your own screen should be similar to the following screenshot (depending on the dates when your own project starts):

Figure 8.20 – Schedule changes upon date change

There are a couple of interesting observations to be made about the view:

*   A new indicator in the shape of a calendar has appeared in the all-important **Indicators** column on the entry table. Remember that this is the same location where the overallocation warning also appears. You should pay equal importance to date constraints. We'll look at the risk aspects in more detail later in this chapter.

*   The link arrow in the Gantt chart has elongated according to our date modifications.

Now, this task will attach to that date like a magnetic field with a bit of play, even while making any further changes to the schedule. There is more to this than meets the eye, so let's bring up the **Task Information** dialog box once more and open the **Advanced** tab, as shown in the following screenshot:

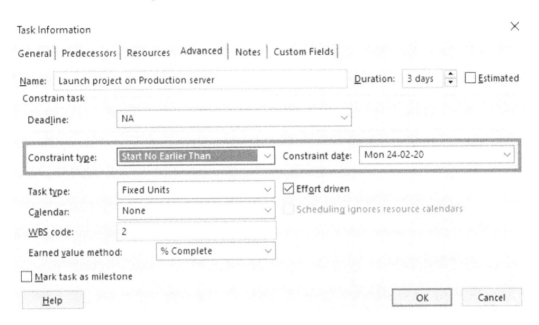

Figure 8.21 – Task information changes upon date change

The most important point to notice is the **Constraint type** field, which has changed to **Start No Earlier Than**. This is tied to the **Constraint date** option that we set in the adjacent field. By *default*, **Constraint type** is very flexible.

As Soon As Possible is an ultra-flexible default constraint. It has been replaced by a relatively more inflexible constraint – **Start No Earlier Than**. Let's explore this concept of date flexibility a bit further.

The real underlying advantage of using this **Date Constraint** technique within automatic scheduling is that it allows us to take advantage of the available *flexibility* within calendar-bound dates. Consider two examples where flexible dates are advantageous within real-life scenarios:

- The final coat of paint on a house is delayed as much as possible before customer handover. This is to make sure any final accidental blemishes can be removed.

- It is better to delay the final training as much as possible before actual practice so that what's been learned stays as fresh as possible in memory.

It is preferable to have this flexibility when future inevitable changes are made to the project schedules. Automated flexibility of Project algorithms is preferable compared to the hard date constraints of manual scheduling. Moreover, Project offers users a broad spectrum of flexibility settings to reflect the reality of your project's situation. If you open the **Constraint type** dropdown list, you will see eight options that have varying degrees of flexibility, as shown in the following screenshot:

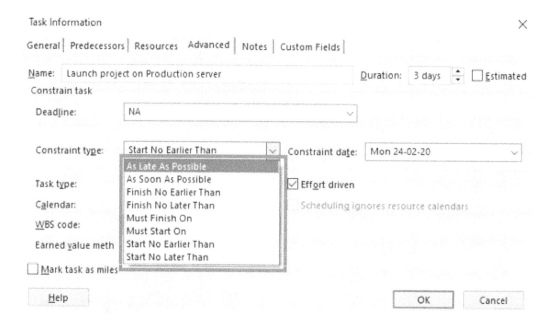

Figure 8.22 – Date constraint types

We'll understand how these different types are arranged in terms of flexibility in the upcoming section.

Types of date constraints

Eight date constraint options are available for us to use, categorized by increasing constraint hardness. Let's see what these are:

1. Most flexible and algorithmically inclined constraints:

- **As Soon As Possible** (often abbreviated to **ASAP**)

- **As Late As Possible** (**ALAP**)

2. Medium flexibility, available on one side of the date:

- **Start No Earlier Than (SNET)**

- **Finish No Earlier Than (FNET)**

- **Start No Later Than (SNLT)**

- **Finish No Later Than (FNLT)**

3. The most inflexible and hard constraints:

- **Must Start On (MSO)**

- **Must Finish On (MFO)**

Depending on the flexibility available to you regarding the task's constraints, the most appropriate constraint should be chosen.

> Pitfall
>
> You should avoid changing the date of any task on your schedule inadvertently. Doing so will immediately introduce a date constraint on the task. I highly recommend that you experiment with changing the date on a task and then inspect the date constraint that was introduced.

A few important best practices

There are a few best practices that we can utilize when considering the use of special dependencies:

- Educate your team members and all the stakeholders about the meaning of special task dependencies and how special dynamics are expected of their deliverables.

- Recognize that the FS dependency (with the ASAP constraint) is the default task mode and easily should make up 90-100% of all dependency types.

- There is an additional maintenance cost to adding realistic complexity to your schedule. It is a project managerial skill to choose the level of abstraction that is suitable.

- It is often possible to avoid special types of task dependencies or convert them into the FS type.

- A thorough study of the schedule network diagram will help uncover the optimal design for your project's plan.

Summary

In this chapter, we unraveled the customization powers of Project. Projects operate under a spectrum of varying risk. Some rare and fortunate projects may be bankrolled by rich corporations with unlimited budgets. Such projects are examples of greater flexibility in the risks they can undertake to ensure greater success. Other projects may be rigid and inflexible due to harsh conditions of Mother Nature or the marketplace. In all situations, your schedule should be as realistic as possible.

There is even further to go on this journey of customizing the interplay of tasks in a schedule. We will encounter manipulating dates in even more advanced situations in further chapters of this book. Once again, we will look at the aspects of exact scheduling science and the art of choosing certain levels of abstraction. In the next chapter, we'll explore a lighter topic; that is, how to make our schedule look visually better. This next chapter also has the objective of increasing the usability of the schedule and making it accessible across all stakeholders.

9
Extended Customization – Task and Gantt Formatting

Imagine that you are a movie director and you have finished planning a dream project. You are in a packed room with the producers, leading actors, technicians, and makeup artists and they are all looking at you. Everyone wants to know what their contribution will be to the project. In your own mind, you already know what the end result looks like. Now, it is your job to convey the important role each person will play and make sure everyone gets crystal clear information about the who, what, when, and why questions. Now that we are at the end of the planning phase, it is time to reveal the final schedule to all the stakeholders. It is the time to put the final polish to the schedule and make it understandable and maintainable.

In this chapter, we will explore Project's tools that allow you to fine-tune the textual and graphical aspects of your schedule. Practically, every parameter is customizable, as you will see, but you will also see that you can get by without the need for any customization most of the time.

In this chapter, we're going to cover the following main topics:

- Customizing the textual format parameters of any view
- Customizing visual format parameters for Gantt charts
- Achieving an aesthetic design for your schedule
- Using diagnostic formatting tools to detect risks and solve issues

Let's get started!

Fundamentals of formatting a view

All the visual customization features of Project are neatly organized under the **Format** tab of Project's ribbon interface. This includes the following:

- Textual element customization (primarily for table-based views, including the entry table of the Gantt chart view)
- Gridlines and layout-related options
- Column-related options
- Task bar styling options (including special diagnostic tools)
- **What You See Is What You Get** (**WYSIWYG**) styled one-click preset options
- Other structural customization (including options for **Summary Tasks** visibility)

Note that all the customizations you add from the **Format** tab can be applied to the current active view open on your screen. Let's explore all these tailoring tools in the same order we will encounter them on the ribbon menu, starting with **Text Styles** in the next section.

Formatting Text Styles

Text Styles are the most commonly changed formatting options and it is apt that it appears first on the ribbon. Observe the following screenshot of the **Format** tab:

Figure 9.1 – Format tab

When changing *any* format option from the ribbon, you should be clear about the context regarding how you want to apply the changes. Four different context levels exist at which changes can be applied, and not all the options are available everywhere. These contexts are as follows:

- **Local level**: For example, formatting a single task, or sometimes even a single cell.

- **Category level**: For example, formatting every *summary task* or every *milestone*.

- **File level**: Changes are applied to every instance of the pertinent elements in the open project file; for example, changing every taskbar in your schedule.

- **Global level**: Changes are applicable even for any other file you may open. Project's formatting options at the file level do not overrule the default global formats preset by Project, and thus are not available at the global level.

> **Pitfall**
>
> Do not experiment with using formatting techniques with your official files, for obvious reasons. Only use dummy files that you can easily create from Project's free file templates. But be aware that prebuilt templates come in all varieties of quality (sometimes dubious) and are not specially endorsed for any specific purpose. Also, get adept at using the **Undo** feature effectively to recover from unwanted edits. Finally, remember that unwanted changes are only retained if you save the file.

Now, let's look at some examples of formatting text styles at different context levels. You can open any new file from an existing template on Project to replicate the following scenarios:

- **File-level context exercise**: You are presenting to a global web-conference online. You have been asked to present with big fonts to ensure readability on all screens, including mobile phones. You must ensure every single piece of text appears larger than it normally would. Fear not – there is a way to do this! Click on the **Text Styles** button on the ribbon and a dialog box will appear:

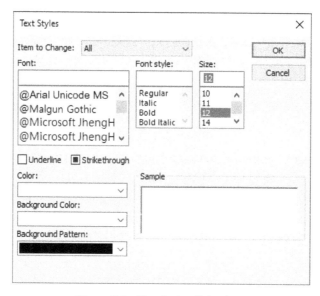

Figure 9.2 – Text Styles dialog box

Don't change anything but the **Size** list box, which pertains to the font size. Set it to **14**. You can play with different sizes to see more dramatic changes. Make sure the **Item to Change** dropdown remains set to **All**. When you return to the Gantt chart, you will observe that every element on the workspace will be impacted by your change, as shown in the following screenshot:

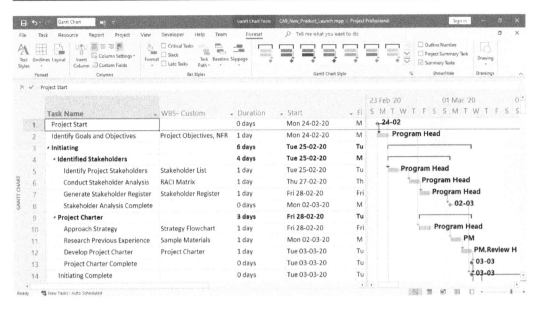

Figure 9.3 – Font size increased at the file level across the workspace

Notice that even the timeline text on the Gantt side and the column text on the table side are impacted by this change. When you are done presenting, you can undo these changes to revert to the original font size.

- **Category-level context exercise**: Now, let's suppose that you want to share the story of your schedule through milestones. Currently, it is hard to discern the presence of several milestones in the schedule and you want to change that. Open the **Text Styles** dialog box once again and make some changes, as shown in the following screenshot:

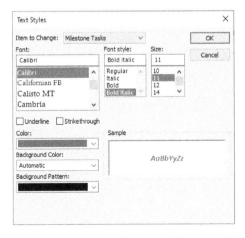

Figure 9.4 – Formatting every milestone task's text in the schedule

The key to this exercise is to set **Item to Change** to `Milestone Tasks`. Then, proceed and modify the look. The **Sample** area is very convenient as it allows you to preview the changes you are making. The Gantt chart will reflect your latest changes, as shown in the following screenshot:

#	Task Name	WBS- Custom	Duration	Start	Finish	Resource Names	Prede
1	*Project Start*		0 days	Mon 24-02-20	Mon 24-02-		
2	Identify Goals and Objectives	Project Objectives, NFR	1 day	Mon 24-02-20	Mon 24-02-2	Program Head	1
3	⊿ **Initiating**		**6 days**	**Tue 25-02-20**	**Tue 03-03-2**		
4	⊿ **Identified Stakeholders**		**4 days**	**Tue 25-02-20**	**Mon 02-03-**		
5	Identify Project Stakeholders	Stakeholder List	1 day	Tue 25-02-20	Tue 25-02-2	Program Head	1
6	Conduct Stakeholder Analysis	RACI Matrix	1 day	Thu 27-02-20	Thu 27-02-2	Program Head	5
7	Generate Stakeholder Register	Stakeholder Register	1 day	Fri 28-02-20	Fri 28-02-20	Program Head	6
8	*Stakeholder Analysis Complete*		*0 days*	*Mon 02-03-20*	*Mon 02-03-*		*7*
9	⊿ **Project Charter**		**3 days**	**Fri 28-02-20**	**Tue 03-03-2**		
10	Approach Strategy	Strategy Flowchart	1 day	Fri 28-02-20	Fri 28-02-20	Program Head	2
11	Research Previous Experience	Sample Materials	1 day	Mon 02-03-20	Mon 02-03-2	PM	10
12	Develop Project Charter	Project Charter	1 day	Tue 03-03-20	Tue 03-03-2	PM,Review Hea	11
13	*Project Charter Complete*	*Project Charter*	*0 days*	*Tue 03-03-20*	*Tue 03-03-2*		*12*
14	*Initiating Complete*		*0 days*	*Tue 03-03-20*	*Tue 03-03-2*		*13,8*
15							

Figure 9.5 – Every milestone task's text specially formatted in the schedule

In the next exercise, we will reduce the scope of change even further and impact the text for just a single task.

- **Local-level context exercise**: Local changes for a single instance of an element are almost always available with the right-click contextual menu. For example, let's highlight a task that is crucial to the success of the project. Right-click the specific task and format it directly from the pop-up menu, as shown in the following screenshot:

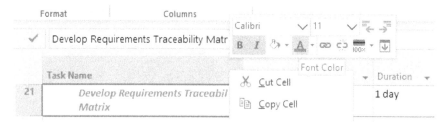

Figure 9.6 – Local level single-task formatting

As we can see, only the specific task is now visually separated from the rest of the schedule. From these exercises, we can conclude that a clear understanding of the formatting context helps in choosing the right tools for the task.

Gridlines

The project schedule is often printed as a handout for all kinds of meetings. At such times, it is not easy to align a particular task's table entry to the Gantt taskbar. An easy solution to this is to use gridlines on the Gantt chart. Let's see how this can be done:

1. Begin by clicking on the **Gridlines** drop-down button on the ribbon, as shown in the following screenshot:

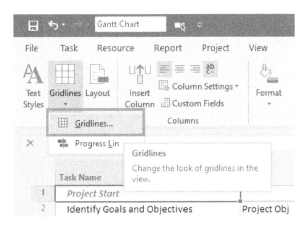

Figure 9.7 – Gridlines drop-down button

We will only focus on the **Gridlines** option here. The second option, **Progress Lines**, is a feature relevant for the next part of this book, where we'll explore project execution.

2. Click on the **Gridlines** link to open a dialog box, as follows:

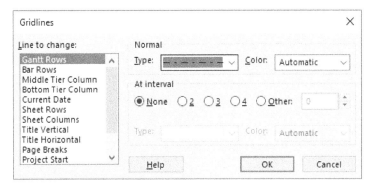

Figure 9.8 – Gridlines dialog box

3. There are only two parameters here that we will modify. Set **Line to change** to **Gantt Rows** and **Type** to any visual style of your choice. The effect of these changes can be observed on the Gantt chart, as follows:

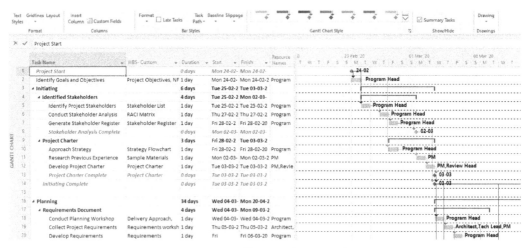

Figure 9.9 – Gridlines on the Gantt chart

As another exercise, using the same **Gridlines** dialog box, locate the **Status date** item and change its color to red. The status date is frequently formatted like this while printing in order to point out where we stand on the timeline.

Layout

The **Layout** dialog box is used to customize the shapes of links and bars on the Gantt chart. As shown in the following screenshot, dependency links can be laid out in three formats:

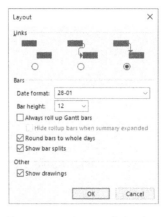

Figure 9.10 – Layout dialog box

The first option will hide all the links on your Gantt chart. Such a configuration is only recommended for tiny screens and should be avoided for normal usage. Your goal in using these features should be purely improving readability. Note that this is also the location where you can modify date formats shown on the Gantt chart. When in doubt, retain all the defaults.

Adding a new customized column

Earlier in this book, we discussed the availability of hundreds of data fields. Each data field will correspond to a single column on the table, with **Task Name** being the most common example. These data columns are available broadly under three categories – task fields, resource fields, and assignment fields. But the question we want to answer now is, *how do I add a completely new column to hold my own data?*

Let's explore a simple technique we can use to add custom data to our table. On the ribbon, in the **Columns** section, click on the **Insert Column** button. A new column will be inserted into your Gantt at the location where your cursor is located. Now, you can choose any of the existing data fields. However, instead of doing this, scroll down until you locate the fields titled **Text1**, **Text2**, and so on. These are purely buffer fields that you can add to your schedule to hold literally any data that you desire. At the time of writing, 30 such fields are available. Refer to the following screenshot:

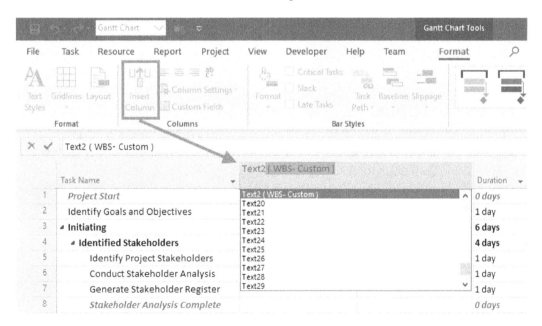

Figure 9.11 – Adding a custom column

It is possible to appropriately rename such a newly added column (data field). In our case, this field is used to hold WBS deliverables corresponding to the task. Using the custom column like this is a useful technique for displaying the traceability of requirements within the schedule.

Before we proceed even further with visual customizations, in the next section, we will study some fundamental design philosophy required to achieve a tasteful and effective schedule.

Achieving an aesthetic design

Do you remember the early days of the internet, when every company scrambled for an online *home page*? Typical designs then included a multitude of fonts, font sizes, and colors. Several elements on the page blinked and flashed, page-wide marquee banners were popular, and every element screamed for your attention. This is precisely the sort of design that you should avoid. Some discrete factors for good design include *using whitespace*, using the **Project Summary Task** feature, and some *naming convention techniques*. We will discuss these options now.

Using whitespace

Whitespace refers to a desirable design incorporating unused space around or within an element in your schedule. Whitespace increases readability and should be used judiciously in your schedule. Less is more! Only use a small subset of fonts, colors, and sizes. The elements of your design that will catch the attention of a user should be decided beforehand.

Using the Project Summary Task feature

This is an important feature and allows you to include your project's name as a part of your schedule, in the form of a base summary task, which is the origin of all other summary tasks in your entire file. As you learned in *Chapter 6, Work Breakdown Structure – the Single Critical Factor*, the **work breakdown structure** (**WBS**) is a hierarchical tree structure. Enabling the **Project Summary Task** checkbox on the ribbon inserts the zeroth row into the entry table, as shown in the following screenshot:

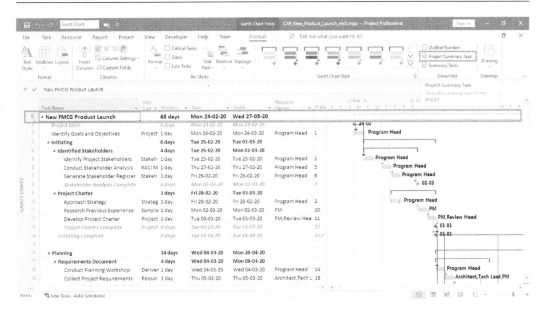

Figure 9.12 – Adding a custom column

The newly visible zeroth row is **Project Summary Task**. Apart from adding an aesthetic value to the schedule, **Project Summary Task** also has practical value. First and foremost, it helps summarize the entire project. As shown in the preceding screenshot, the schedule's duration is immediately available (**68 days**), as well as the start and end dates for the entire project. Such a starting point also allows you to avoid an explicit and additional *start milestone* for the schedule.

Using naming conventions

A few simple conventions that you can use to improve the readability of your schedule are as follows:

- Consider using uppercase capital letters for summary tasks for complex projects. This visually separates the summary and detailed tasks, without the need for additional colors.

- Milestones are used for specific events such as decision points, approval received, specific dates, or special celebratory occasions (such as a new office opening). You should name your milestones according to the event, to better aid your explanation of the schedule.

- Name the detailed tasks (within summary tasks) so that they're neither terse nor wordy. A suitable length between 2 to 5 words is often the most appropriate.

With this short but important discussion on the aesthetics of your schedule, we will, once again, resume our ongoing discussion on the formatting customizations of the schedule. So far, we have discussed the textual aspects. Now, we will focus on the graphical aspects of the view.

Formatting bar styles

We often take how much information is packed tightly into a Gantt chart for granted. Over the next few sections, we will explore the visual design of both single taskbars and the entire Gantt chart in greater detail.

Formatting a single, specific taskbar (local-level formatting)

Any single taskbar can be customized by selecting it and then clicking on the **Bar** link from the **Format** dropdown. Refer to the following screenshot:

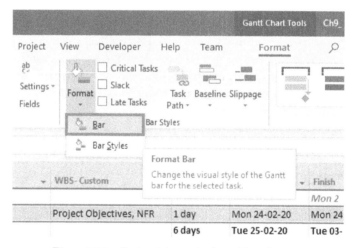

Figure 9.13 – Customizing a single taskbar element

Clicking on this link opens the **Format Bar** dialog box, as shown in the following screenshot:

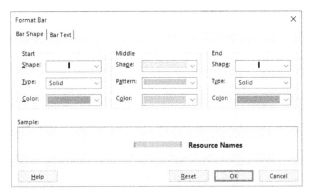

Figure 9.14 – Format Bar dialog box

Take a moment to observe this intuitive dialog box in detail. There are two tabs: one for the visual effects, called **Bar Shape**, and another for textual information, called **Bar Text**. The taskbar is visually composed of three parts – **Start**, **Middle**, and **End**. Furthermore, each of these parts can be customized by **Shape**, **Pattern/Texture**, and **Color**.

Since these customizations are easily comprehendible, we will not delve any further into them. Feel free to experiment with all the choices so that you can apply these techniques to your real-life schedules. Now, let's look at the **Bar Text** tab:

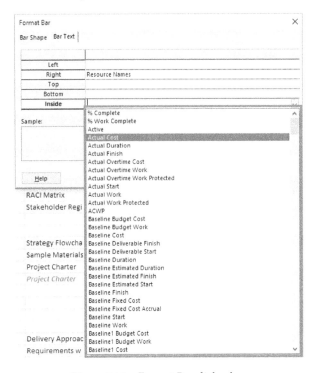

Figure 9.15 – Format Bar dialog box

From this tab, informational text can be placed on five optional locations for a single taskbar (**Left**, **Right**, **Top**, **Bottom**, and **Inside**). More than 400 tasks and assignment-related data fields are available. However, it is not recommended that you use more than 1-2 data values, as doing so will quickly clutter up your screen and greatly reduce readability. The default visual design of Project should be your reference point for an example of good readability.

Formatting an entire category of taskbars

Now, let's expand the scope of impact a little further and consider changing an entire category of taskbars. Under the same **Format** button on the ribbon, click on the **Bar Styles** link to open a dialog box, as shown in the following screenshot:

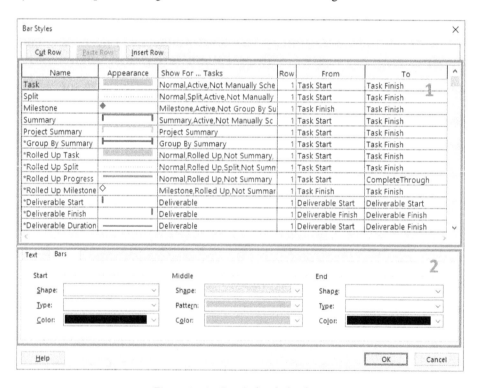

Figure 9.16 – Bar Styles dialog box

While this interface looks intimidating and complex, it is actually easy for us to understand because we learned how to customize a single taskbar in the previous section. Let's take a moment to understand the interface. There are two sections, as numbered in the preceding screenshot. Let's take a look:

1. Each row represents a category of tasks that might appear on the Gantt chart. You will recognize **Task**, **Milestone**, **Summary**, and **Project Summary**. We will encounter other task categories in the appropriate situations in this book.

2. The bottom section of the dialog box is the exact same interface we came across in the previous section, while formatting individual taskbars. So, you will already be familiar with this interface.

Any single task category can be selected in the rows and the *current prebuilt default formatting* will be displayed for it. You can customize any of the characteristics and the change will be reflected for all the task instances in your schedule. Feel free to experiment and observe the widespread impact these style changes can cause. In the next section, we will increase the scope of impact even further.

Formatting an entire Gantt chart

Now, let's consider a feature that can change the visual style of the entire Gantt chart with a single click. This is a WYSIWYG dropdown control, as shown in the following screenshot:

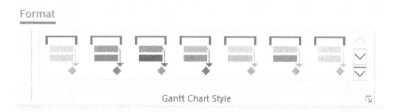

Figure 9.17 – Gantt Chart Style dropdown control

A single click on a particular style will immediately paint the Gantt chart in the colors that you have chosen. Click down to reveal further style types:

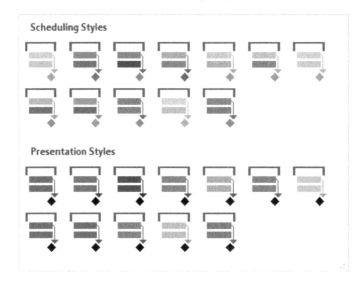

Figure 9.18 – Two types of Gantt chart styles

From the preceding screenshot, we can see that there are two types of styles. The top panel uses two colors, while the bottom panel uses a single color. This design can be explained as follows:

- **Scheduling Styles**: There is a color differentiation between Automatic and Manual task types which makes it possible to distinguish the two task types on your schedule.

- **Presentation Styles**: All task types have the same color, without any task type distinction. Such a style is very useful, as the name suggests, during high-level project presentations, during which you want to elide over intricate scheduling details.

> **Tip**
>
> In the **Gantt Chart Styles** control, the very first choice (a blue-based combination) is the default style applied by Project. If you make changes to your schedule and want to revert, choose this style once again.

With that, we have come to the end of our discussion on the formatting customizations of Project. A few features present on the **Format** tab, such as **Slack**, **Late tasks**, **Slippage**, and so on are related to the execution stages of Project and will be covered in subsequent chapters of this book. For the remainder of this chapter, we will explore two excellent diagnostic tools that will help you with planning-time schedule analysis and execution-time schedule issues.

Diagnostic formatting

Complex schedules will start to look like a bowl of spaghetti when they're suboptimal, with tasks and links in a jumbled amalgamation. In such situations, you will want to study different task paths within your schedule for a network analysis. Project provides a host of diagnostic tools in the same **Format** tab. We will study the two most critical tools in the following sections.

Task Path

Given any task in the schedule, the **Task Path** feature allows you to automatically identify the ecosystem of task relationships that surround the task. There are four options to choose from, but we will only look at **Driving Predecessors** here. Understanding the driving predecessors for a task is important, as any delays on this path can cause delays on the task being analyzed.

Take a look at the following screenshot, where a milestone named **Project Charter Complete** is being analyzed so that the chain of predecessors that drive it can be understood:

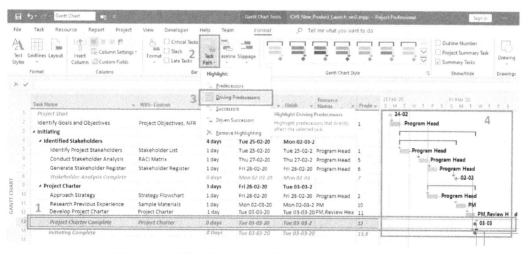

Figure 9.19 – Task Path used to deduct Driving Predecessors

The steps to identify **Driving Predecessors** are listed as follows:

1. First, select the (single) task to be analyzed.

2. Open the **Task Path** dropdown.

3. Notice that four options exist that you need to understand. We will choose **Driving Predecessors** for our exercise.

4. Observe that the **Driving Predecessors** path gets highlighted in a new orange/ochre color, making it very easy to identify the path throughout the project.

Before we move on and look at the next diagnostic tool, please be sure to use the same **Task Path** drop-down button to remove the path's identification by clicking on **Remove Highlighting**. If you don't do this, the highlighting will intervene with our next topic of discussion.

Critical Tasks (critical path)

We first discussed the **Critical Path Method** (**CPM**) and its significance to Microsoft Project in *Chapter 1, Project Management – The Essential Primer*. The critical path is a special sequence of tasks where delays on any one of the constituent tasks will cause a delay for the whole project! Not all tasks on a schedule will be critical, meaning that a slight delay will not affect the whole project. Therefore, it is necessary to identify and carefully guard the critical path tasks against any delays.

The critical path can be easily identified on your schedule by using the **Critical Tasks** checkbox on the ribbon. In the following screenshot, you can see Project algorithmically identifying the Critical Path of a schedule in a highlighted color:

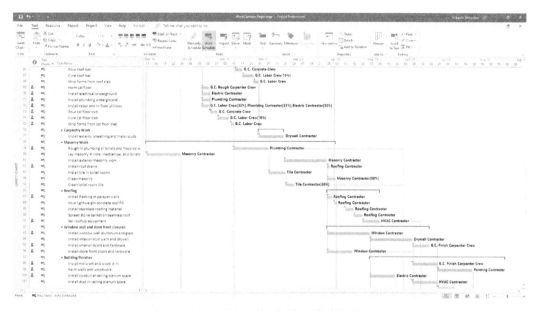

Figure 9.20 – Critical Path identified by Project

As you grow to become adept with Project, you will find these diagnostic tools to be invaluable for your analysis in all the stages of your project. We will close this discussion with a brief but important point about project baselines. As a best practice, a schedule baseline is saved at the end of the planning phase and before we step into the execution phase. However, the real value and applications of baselines (to evaluate project performance) start showing up during the execution phase of the project. So, instead of breaking a discussion of baselines into two discrete steps, we will cover baselines comprehensively in the next part of this book.

Summary

Your schedule is analogous to a highly detailed *manual* on how to execute the project successfully. You have exercised a great deal of skill, planning, theory, and experience to develop it. But the tragedy is that people usually do not read the manual – especially if it looks unfathomable. It is your responsibility to make the schedule readable, understandable, and maintainable. An aesthetically designed schedule goes a long way in satisfying the non-functional requirements of your schedule. In this chapter, we not only discussed how to achieve an aesthetic design but also all the tools and features provided by Project to aid us on this journey. You will mostly work on these aspects during the end of the planning phase.

And with that, we bid farewell to the planning phase and can start steeling ourselves to enter the real game – project execution. The majority of project managers incorrectly associate Project with the planning phase and stop using it thereafter. But we are only midway on our Project journey, yet. We will see how Project proves invaluable when it comes to the *execution* process, *monitoring and control* process, and *closing* process groups. Project's most modern aspect is its Agile capabilities. This is what will be covered in the next chapter.

Section 4: Project Execution – the Real Deal

This section of the book will deal with using Microsoft Project in the execution phase of the project life cycle.

This section comprises the following chapters:

10
Executing Agile Projects with MS Project

In recent years, nothing has ignited the world of Project Management quite like Agile methodologies. *Agile* offers a nimble and adaptive alternative to the traditionally rigid Waterfall methodology, which we have used so far in this book. With the exponential growth of digitization and internet technology in our lives, there was a need to execute software projects where the requirements and the solutions must symbiotically evolve. In such chaotic projects, there is no luxury of deeply analyzing the requirements with highly detailed plans before you hit the market. Applicable mainly to such projects, Agile offers an elegant framework of concepts, philosophy, and practices for successful project management.

Even if your expertise lies outside the software domain, you should still pursue this chapter. The venerable **Project Management Body of Knowledge (PMBOK)**, sixth edition onward, includes the **Agile Practice Guide**. This is because the scope of Agile has extended and evolved beyond the software domain to finding enthusiastic adoption within other traditional domains, such as education and manufacturing. There are many popular frameworks that implement Agile philosophy, such as **Scrum** and **Kanban**. Both these methods are supported by MS Project, as we will see in this chapter.

Meanwhile, in the context of this book, we have now entered the execution stages of Project. So far, we have only looked at the strategic planning stages, but now, we're entering tactile execution. In this chapter, we will look at projects that are going through the process of executing. In this part of this book, you will learn how Project can be used to baseline your schedule, track progress, and fight overallocations. If you were the manager of a football team and every match was a project, then this is where the team would run out from the locker room and onto the stadium to play the game – the plan is being executed!

Please note that we will not cover Agile theory in depth, but a simple roundup is necessary and will be covered early in this chapter. If you are an absolute beginner to Agile, it is better you read up on other sources alongside this chapter. If you are an Agile pro, you will be excited with Project's versatile offerings that do not compromise on the scheduling prowess offered.

In this chapter, we're going to cover the following main topics:

- A brief introduction to Agile methodologies
- Kanban-based Task Board views
- Using Scrum-based Sprint Board views
- Symbiotic usage of different methodologies
- Let's get started!

Technical requirements

Project's Agile features are quickly evolving with every release. Project's versions are also quickly evolving. We can surmise that Microsoft is being *agile* in releasing its Agile features. In this scenario, Agile features are currently *only* available for the Project Online Desktop Client. Even with all these changes, what we'll cover in this chapter will be applicable both at a conceptual level and the practical level to earlier versions of Project, such as Project 2016 and 2013 Professional Desktop version, where similar Agile features were available.

A brief introduction to Agile methodologies

Before we explore Project's Agile feature set, let's go on a whirlwind tour of the Agile universe, starting with the origin story.

The Agile Manifesto

In 2001, 17 thought leaders from the software industry published what was known as *The Manifesto for Agile Software Development,* verbatim as follows:

- **Individuals and interactions** over processes and tools

- **Working software** over comprehensive documentation

- **Customer collaboration** over contract negotiation

- **Responding to change** over following a plan

These are the tenets of the Agile philosophy. In each point, higher value is placed upon the items on the left. To understand Agile better, in the next few sections, we will explore the most common decision-making process that project managers face while adopting Agile practices.

Deciding between Agile and Waterfall

Projects exist on a continuum from *predictive* to *adaptive*. For example, a space mission launch project will obviously need to be planned in advance to a high degree of predictive precision. A traditional Waterfall methodology (a popular and rigid, phase-driven approach) will be best suited for this case. On the other hand, launching an artificial intelligence-based ecommerce website needs to be highly adaptive to the response of buyers. In most real-life projects, a more realistic approach would be *hybrid* – using the best of the Waterfall and Agile techniques combined, as required. Such a hybrid approach can be supported by Microsoft Project, as we will see later in this chapter.

Deciding whether Agile is suited to your project

Is an Agile approach suitable for your project? There are certain project characteristics that make the project suitable for an Agile approach, and these are listed as follows:

- **Requirements are fuzzy at best**: You may have clarity about the end results, but the set of requirements that will get you there are not clearly known.

- **Continuous integration should be possible**: Once a spaceship is in flight, you cannot change its motherboard. However, on a football field, the manager can swap players with some flexibility, as needed by the actual playing conditions. These two examples show that Agile approaches require the ability to integrate continuous changes.

- **Impact of change is low**: Every change in project requirements often has an impact on the entire project, however trivial. This impact can be in terms of money, material, time, customer loyalty, or any other asset. An Agile approach is best suited where it is possible to change product features with a minimal impact to assets. This is often the case with software projects and makes it suitable for an Agile approach.

- **Stakeholder participation is high**: Agile requires swift decision making over the complete life cycle of the project. This means that stakeholders need to be involved in the day-to-day execution of the schedule.

- **Mature and experienced team**: Agile needs an experienced and autonomous team who need minimal or zero project management overhead. You will find high-performing Agile teams that will not build detailed schedules with explicit task resourcing and dependency analysis. On such experienced teams, this is a contributing factor to the team's agility.

The preceding points are only the most prominent characteristics. You may encounter others, depending on your own project situations. If your project does not have the luxury of these characteristics, then Agile may not be suitable for your project.

When you should not use Agile

Agile is not a silver bullet and cannot be applied to every situation. There are several characteristics, both from a project perspective and an industry-based perspective, that will render it unsuitable for an Agile approach. Some such characteristics are as follows:

- Strict compliance-based domains, such as town planning, medicine, aviation, nuclear, and waste management.

- Any project where incremental delivery is not acceptable; for example, civil construction.

- Real-time response systems, such as medical equipment, radar systems, and embedded systems, are not suitable for Agile development.

A careful evaluation of whether Agile is suited for your own project will go a long way toward project success. In the next section, we will discuss some valid criticism regarding Agile.

Criticism of Agile

There are some specific risks when executing projects with Agile. Being aware of these will help us circumvent or mitigate these risks:

- **Technical debt**: Agile facilitates choosing easier and faster solutions instead of more robust, long-term solutions. This can result in an accumulation of additional rework later when the application must scale to larger usage.

- **Rockstar teams**: Agile requires an experienced self-driven team with minimal management overhead. Trying to implement Agile with a new and inexperienced team is fraught with risks.

- **High burnout and risk**: By definition, Agile removes the managerial buffer and puts team members on the frontline of project execution battlefronts.

Now that we have a broad understanding of Agile, let's explore how Project supports Agile through two implementations of Agile, known as Kanban and Scrum.

A project on a simple e-commerce website

Imagine that you are the owner of a widely popular digital marketing blog with millions of readers. You have created a new software tool for your readers. You now want to add a shopping cart to your blog so that you can sell products to your large audience.

You decide that this is a perfect opportunity to try an Agile execution. Your team consists of another two experienced software developers.

Task list for the project

Here is the list of tasks to be performed in order to make the project work:

1. Install the Drupal Opensource framework.
2. Install the UberCart module.
3. Create a Store Configuration page.
4. Build the Drupal taxonomy – 'Catalog'
5. Create an SEO tool Product page
6. Create a Teaser View page
7. Add a suitable theme – "Zircon"

8. Create front page branding.

9. Integrate PayPal with UberCart.

10. Test and launch.

In this particular project, the focus is on integrating existing software components so that your experienced developers can pull off the project with minimal project management overhead. It is perfectly suited for a first-time Agile execution.

Agile frameworks

There are several popular frameworks that implement the Agile manifesto, most notably the Scrum method, Kanban, the **Dynamic Systems Development Method (DSDM)**, and so on. A detailed discussion of these topics is outside the scope of this book. If you are not already familiar with these, I recommend that you read up on them. Scrum and Kanban are supported to an extent within MS Project. We will explore both methods and how they can come together alongside Waterfall in the following sections.

Kanban and MS Project

The word **Kanban** means **signboard** in the Japanese language. Kanban's methodology is a simple but powerful visual scheduling technique. It originated in the Toyota automobile factory, created by engineer Taiichi Ohno.

> Tip
> Kanban is commonly used for an Agile *non-iterative* and incremental execution of the project. Scrum, on the other hand, implements short, iterative, full life cycles that incrementally execute the project.

Let's see the Kanban methodology in action for our hands-on project:

1. Fire up Project and create an empty blank file.

2. Open the **View** tab on the ribbon and locate and click the **Task Board** view button. Refer to the following screenshot:

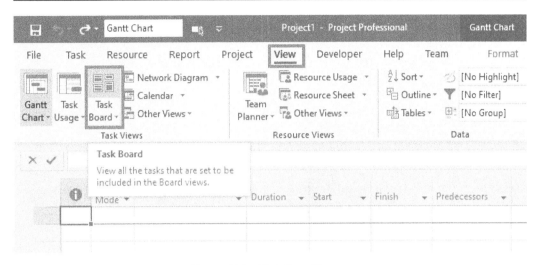

Figure 10.1 – Task Board button

When you click on this button, a new view will open up, as shown in the following screenshot:

Figure 10.2 – Task Board View

There are a few important points to note about this **Task Board** view:

1. This view is visually different from anything we have encountered so far in this book. There are no tables and charts upfront. As you will soon see, this view implements an intuitive drag-and-drop feature.

2. All the Agile features within Project are mapped to existing familiar constructs such as **Views** and **Tables**.

3. Within this Task Board view, there are four primary columns labelled **Not Started**, **Next up**, **In progress**, and **Done**. As you can surmise, these columns represent the stages of task execution.

4. Something that's notably absent is the Gantt chart, which does not have a place in our scheme of things for this chapter – at least for now. Unlike in any other view that you have encountered so far, there is a **New Task** button. This will allow you to add a new task to the schedule.

In Kanban, the primary focus is on visualizing the project schedule's workflow, while the secondary focus is on limiting the **In Progress** tasks as much as possible. With this idea in mind, let's start adding our running project's tasks one by one. Start by clicking on the **New Task** button, as shown in the following screenshot:

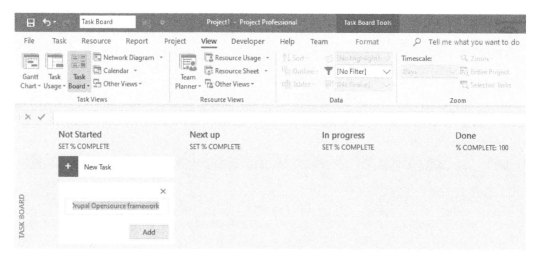

Figure 10.3 – Adding a new task to the Task Board view

A new text area will open, where you can enter the task name and add the task to the **Not Started** column. When you add the second task, you should immediately notice that the newly added second task does not go to the bottom of the list, as you would expect, and stays on top. There is a certain relevance to this, and we will explore this point in the next section.

Every new task that you add will begin its life in the **Not Started** column. You can, however, drag and drop the task cards anywhere on the column list to optionally order them. This behavior emphasizes the experience of a Kanban Task Board. In our case, you should experiment with ordering the tasks so that you get to experience the user interface. When you are done adding all the task cards to the board, your screen should resemble the following screenshot:

Figure 10.4 – All tasks added to the Task Board view

Now, it's time to understand and experience the flexibility promised by Agile Kanban.

Important points to note about Kanban within Project

Remember that Agile is designed for mature and experienced teams who are in constant communication with stakeholders. A fast and autonomous decision-making process is a given. Because of these special conditions, the rigidity of Waterfall scheduling (as we have experienced from the beginning of this book) is not applicable for Kanban. This means that your Kanban board, by default, will have the following properties:

- No strict ordering of tasks required

- No resource allocation required

- No task dependencies required

- No task start date or duration required

Team members can choose tasks to execute by themselves from the **Not Started** column and traverse sequentially through the columns until each task reaches the **Done** column, which is the task's final resting place. With this crucial understanding, let's return to our running project.

For each of the columns, you can set a representative percentage task completion value, which indicates how much of the task has been executed. This is true for all columns except the **Done** column, which, by definition, is preset to 100% completion. A common practice is to set the columns to some meaningful sequence, such as 0% – 25% – 50% – 100%, as shown in the following screenshot:

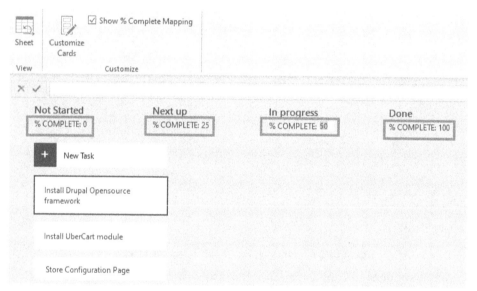

Figure 10.5 – Defining percentage completion for columns on the Task Board view

From the preceding screenshot, we can observe the following:

1. There are several ways you can configure and use such a **Task Board**. It is easily possible to change the labeling and logic to anything of your choice that's suitable. For example, the simplest design of such a board can have three columns: **Requested Features**, **In Progress**, and **Released**. Right-click on the column label to delete it or give it a new name:

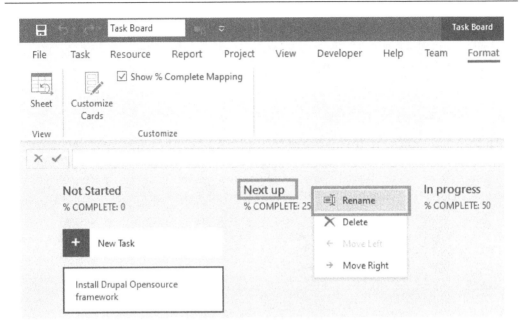

Figure 10.6 – Renaming the column label on the Task Board view

Now continuing, let's consider the flow of events in a normal project:

2. Every new task that is uncovered will be entered into the **Not Started** column. By definition, such new tasks will be at 0% completion.

3. When a task gets logical relevance in the schedule, it is moved to the **Next up** column. A task gets logical relevance when, for example, a dependency is triggered on it.

4. Team members select tasks from the **Next Up** column, and when they are well under execution, they can be moved to the **In progress** column.

5. When the task is 100% complete, it is moved into the **Done** column. This task has completed its life cycle.

6. A task can only be placed in the **Done** column when it is 100% complete. This logic extends all the way back along the sequence of columns.

7. Rinse and repeat until all the tasks reach completion, the **Not Started** column is empty, or the project is otherwise considered complete.

In this way, it is possible to execute entire projects with great flexibility. But sometimes, you might want a little more scheduling power. For example, you might want to set task parameters, dependencies, priorities, or any such parameters. Project allows for that too, as we will see in the next section.

Using the Sheet view for the Task Board view

As we mentioned earlier, the Task Board view is just a facade. The underlying scaffolding is still provided by the familiar tables, views, algorithms, and scheduling engine of Project. This means that we can tap into all the scheduling power on offer. From the **Format** tab, locate and click on the **Sheet** button. Refer to the following screenshot:

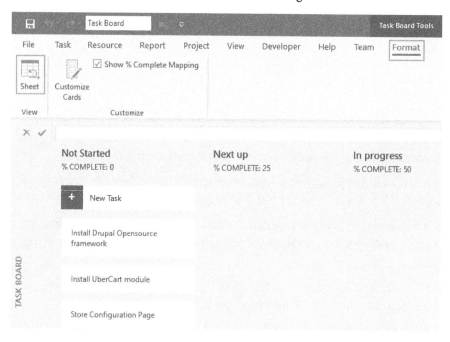

Figure 10.7 – Sheet button to enter the Task Board Sheet view

The **Sheet** button is just a shortcut to the **Task Board Sheet** view. The same view is also accessible from the **More Views** link, which is available in other ribbon tabs. Refer to the following screenshot:

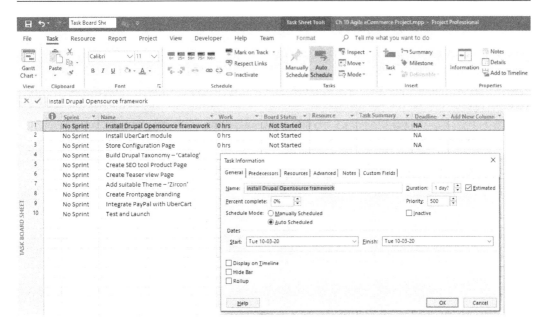

Figure 10.8 – Task Board Sheet view

This view will look very familiar to you as it presents the tasks in a table, very similar to the **Entry** table. From this sheet view, you can add more power to the Kanban board. For example, double-clicking on any task will give you the familiar **Task Information** dialog box. You can then configure any of the task parameters as you so choose.

Despite these similarities, there are some important observations to be made about the **Task Board Sheet** view, as follows:

1. By default, **Work** is used for the tasks, not **Duration**. This is because, as we've already seen, resources are generally not assigned to tasks in Kanban mode. Compare this to all our earlier exercises under the normal Waterfall method, where it is recommended to assign resources to tasks. However, the **Resource** column is readily available, should you need it.

2. The **Board Status** column allows you to assign the task to any of our predefined completion status, similar to what's available in the **Task Board** view.

3. It is also possible to set an external dependency date in the **Deadline** column.

However, the most interesting and new column that we have on this view is the **Sprint** column. As you may have already guessed, this column will connect us to the Scrum aspects of Project. We will explore this in the next section.

Scrum and MS Project

Scrum is the superstar framework for Agile and is widely popular in the software development world. Scrum is iterative, incremental, and lightweight. Development is carried out in small iterations, called **sprints**. In each sprint cycle, a few features are carefully chosen so that the project's value gets delivered continuously. The **Product Backlog** is essentially a list of every deliverable of the project. Sprints, which execute a subset of the Product Backlog, are usually carried out in short durations of 2 to 12 weeks. Within an individual Sprint's execution, the team holds a meeting every day called the *scrum*. Refer to the following diagram, which shows the classic execution model of a Scrum project:

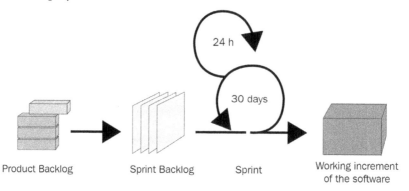

Figure 10.9 – Agile Scrum methodology

Image source and attribution: `https://commons.wikimedia.org/wiki/File:Scrum_process.svg`. This file is licensed under the Creative Commons Attribution-Share Alike 4.0 International, 3.0 Unported, 2.5 Generic, 2.0 Generic, and 1.0 Generic license.

This was just a brief introduction to the Scrum framework, and you are recommended to explore it further if not already familiar with it. Now, let's return to our running project.

There are two equivalent techniques you can use to add sprints to your project. The first technique is from the ribbon's **Project** tab: the **Manage Sprints** button. Refer to the following screenshot:

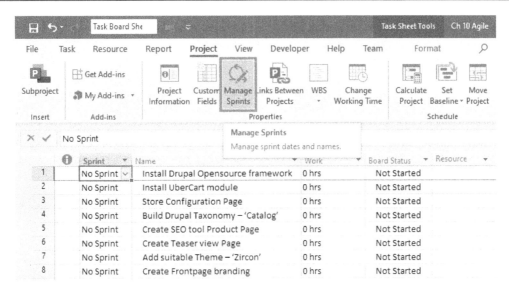

Figure 10.10 – Manage Sprints button on the Project tab

This button is always available so that you can add sprints to your project. But for now, we will move on to the second technique, which we can use to activate sprints from within our current **Task Board Sheet** view.

Click on the dropdown available from any cell on the **Sprint** column. Notice that, at this point, no sprints exist in the project. However, you can use the **Add Sprints** link to create a new sprint. Refer to the following screenshot:

		Sprint	Name	Work	Board Status
	1	No Sprint	Install Drupal Opensource framework	0 hrs	Not Started
	2	No Sprint / Add Sprints	Install UberCart module	0 hrs	Not Started
	3		Store Configuration Page	0 hrs	Not Started
	4	No Sprint	Build Drupal Taxonomy – 'Catalog'	0 hrs	Not Started
	5	No Sprint	Create SEO tool Product Page	0 hrs	Not Started
	6	No Sprint	Create Teaser view Page	0 hrs	Not Started
	7	No Sprint	Add suitable Theme – 'Zircon'	0 hrs	Not Started
	8	No Sprint	Create Frontpage branding	0 hrs	Not Started
	9	No Sprint	Integrate PayPal with UberCart	0 hrs	Not Started
	10	No Sprint	Test and Launch	0 hrs	Not Started

Figure 10.11 – Add Sprints option from the Sprint column

When you click on the **Add Sprints** link, the **Manage Sprints** dialog box opens, as shown in the following screenshot:

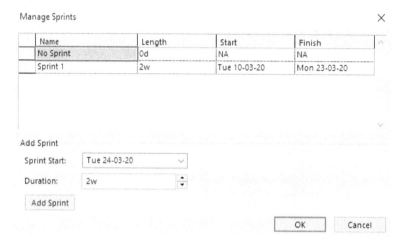

Figure 10.12 – Manage Sprints dialog box

This same dialog box would have opened from the first technique too (the **Manage Sprints** button). In the dialog box, you can see that the top section is for listing the sprints in your project, and the first sprint (**Sprint 1**) is populated by default. You can set the new sprint's start date and duration here, but you cannot change the name label, by design.

If you click the **OK** button now, just a single sprint will be added to your project, but don't do that yet. Notice the bottom section of the dialog box. The details have been populated for yet another sprint, which has been defaulted to 2 weeks. By default, **Sprint Start** will assume contiguous working dates, but you have the freedom to start it when you want. Finally, click on the **Add Sprint** button, at which point your screen should resemble the following screenshot:

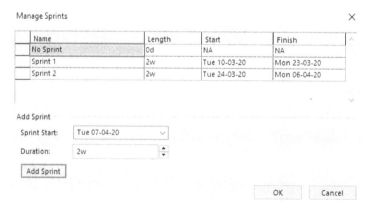

Figure 10.13 – Adding new sprints to the Manage Sprints dialog box

When you finally click the **OK** button, a brand-new tab will automatically appear on the ribbon, called **Sprints**. Refer to the following screenshot:

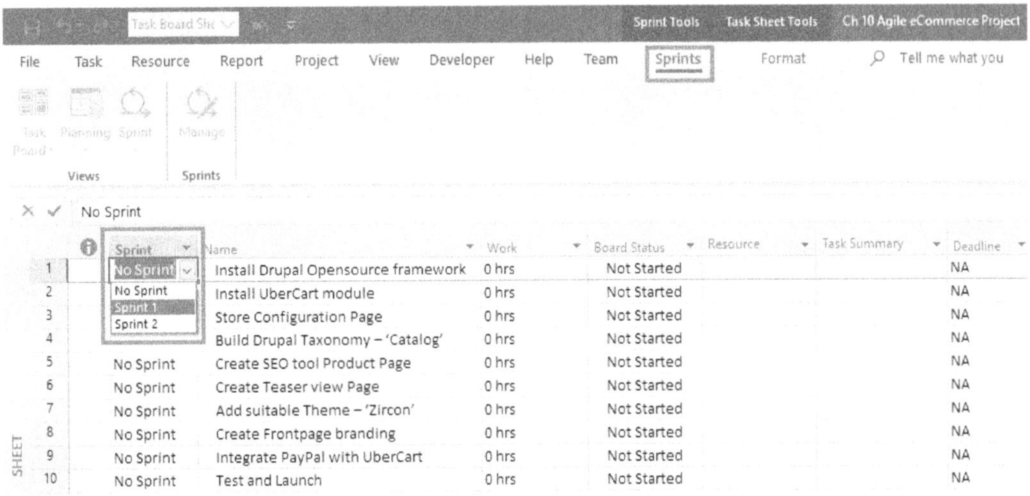

Figure 10.14 – New Sprints tab in the ribbon

Now, it's time to execute the project. We will do so by assigning tasks to the first sprint. Luckily for us, our **Sprint** column dropdown has also updated with the two new sprints that we created. To keep things simple, assign the first five tasks to **Sprint 1**, shown as follows:

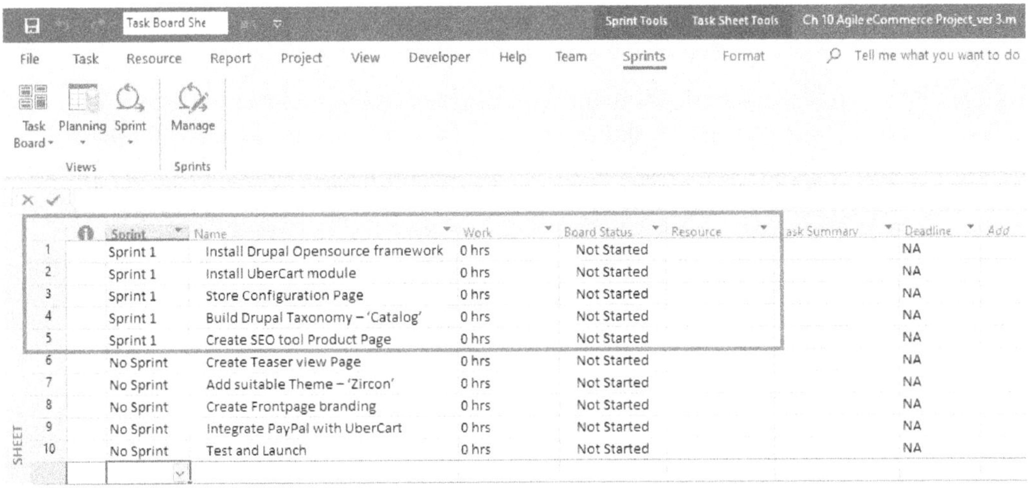

Figure 10.15 – Assigning tasks to Sprint 1

The other tasks will remain unassigned for now. There is one more interesting way to assign tasks to sprints. Observe the **Planning** drop-down button on the new ribbon tab, **Sprints**. Click on **Sprint Planning Board** to see all the sprints currently in your project, as follows:

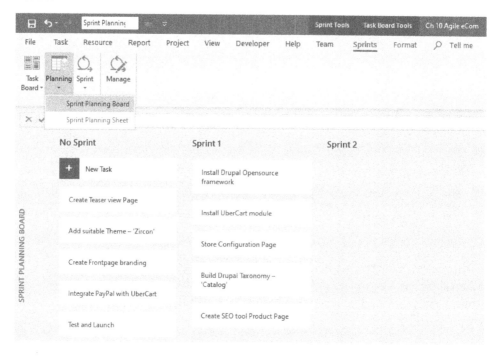

Figure 10.16 – Sprint Planning Board

This is where we come back to the Kanban board style of assigning tasks to sprints. Observe the columns in this new Task Board view. These three columns are as follows:

- **No Sprint**: This has the unassigned five tasks from earlier.

- **Sprint 1**: This has five tasks assigned.

- **Sprint 2**: As expected, this has no tasks assigned.

Using the Kanban Task Board style, drag and drop the remaining five tasks from **No Sprint** to **Sprint 2**. Retain the order of listing. Your result should resemble the following screenshot:

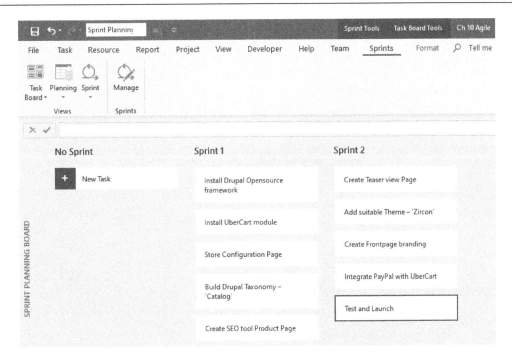

Figure 10.17 – Assigning tasks with Sprint Planning Board

As you might have surmised by now, there's a table view for this drag-and-drop interface too. From the same **Planning** dropdown, open the corresponding **Sprint Planning Sheet**:

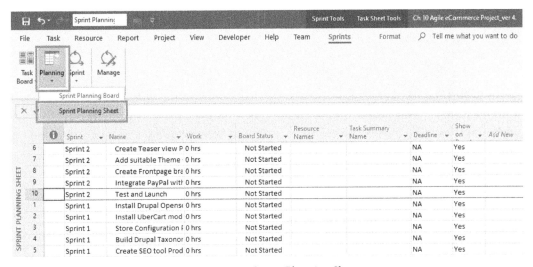

Figure 10.18 – Sprint Planning Sheet

Here, you can see that the tasks that we had dragged from **No Sprint** are now correctly assigned to **Sprint 2** in the **Sprint** column. There's still one more special view to consider. We will explore this now.

Some of you may be thinking by now, *How do I manage the tasks within the current sprint?* The answer is the new **Current Sprint Board**. You can access this view from the **Sprint** drop-down button on the ribbon, as shown in the following screenshot:

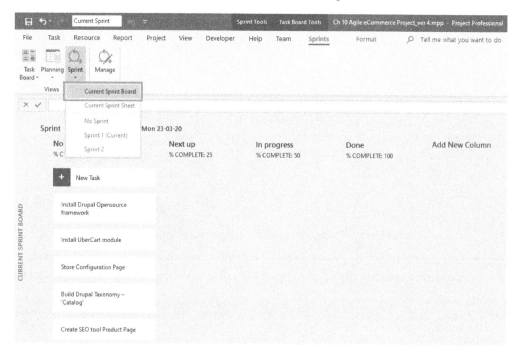

Figure 10.19 – Current Sprint Board

Current Sprint Board has columns that track the execution of the task, exactly like we had for the Kanban Task Board. During project execution, the tasks will traverse a path from **Not Started** (0%) to **Next up** (25%), then to **In progress** (50%), and finally to **Done** (100%). The following screenshot shows such a project in the execution stage:

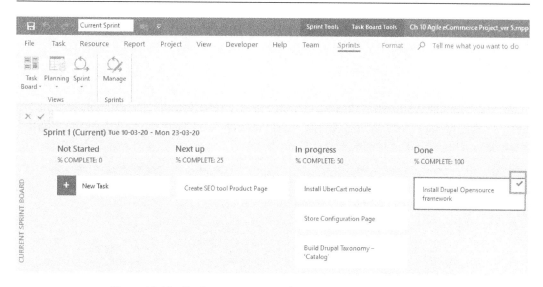

Figure 10.20 – Project execution in the Current Sprint Board view

Notice the small green tick in the tasks that have been moved to the **Done** column, as highlighted in the preceding screenshot. This signifies completion of the task. Once again, this view has a corresponding sheet for your customizations. It is accessible from the same **Sprint** button, as shown in the following screenshot:

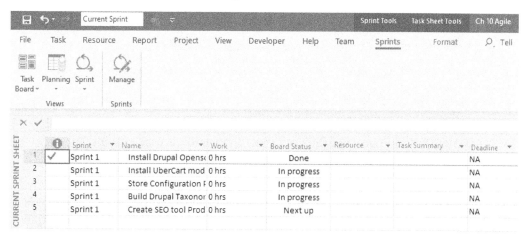

Figure 10.21 – Project execution in the Current Sprint Sheet view

Observe that the **Indicators (i)** column displays a green tick mark, signifying completion. Also, verify that the **Board Status** column has the same task execution status that we updated it to.

To close this discussion, let's return to where we originally started – the original Waterfall model. You can add Waterfall-based linear execution within individual sprints too. To view the same project in our classic Gantt chart view, click on **Task** tab and then the **Gantt Chart** view. Refer to the following screenshot:

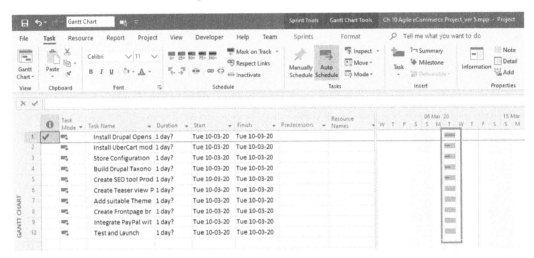

Figure 10.22 – Project execution in the Gantt Chart view

There are a few interesting points to observe from this screenshot, as follows:

- As you can see, the tasks lie in a straight line because we have not used the **Predecessors** column to track linking and dependencies.

- Neither the task duration nor the resources information is used currently in our Agile project. We discussed this earlier in the *Kanban and MS Project* section on Kanban features.

- Significantly, the five tasks in **Sprint 1** have a dark blue internal thinner line. This is highlighted in the preceding screenshot. These lines represent the task's completion information that we had set earlier – 0%, 25%, 50%, and 100%.

- The first task, which is 100% complete, has the same green tick sign that we have been following across recent screenshots.

And with that, we have completed our tour of the latest Agile features in Project. We started from the highly flexible Kanban-style **Task Board** and **Sheet** views. Then, we progressed and looked at the Scrum-style **Sprint Planning Board** and **Sheet** views. These views represented the entire project. But to manage individual sprints, we learned how to use the **Current Sprint Board** and **Sheet** views.

There is an important point to note here. If you choose to use the Agile features of Microsoft Project that were discussed in this chapter, then you will still be able to use all the other features of Project that we will cover in the rest of this book, including the following:

- Resolving *overallocations* using several tools and techniques (*Chapter 11, Overallocation – the Bane of Project Managers*)

- Using all the benefits of *baselines* (*Chapter 12, Baselines – Techniques and Best Practices*)

- Ability to track projects using great flexibility (*Chapter 13, Project Tracking Techniques*)

- Use *monitoring and control* tools for analytics (*Chapter 14, Views, Tables, and Customization*)

- Generate awesome reports using prebuilt graphical reports (*Chapter 17, Project Reports 101*, and *Chapter 19, Advanced Custom Reports and Templates*)

- Using local and global templates (*Chapter 18, Reviewing Projects and Creating Templates for Success*, and *Chapter 19, Advanced Custom Reports and Templates*)

We will not explicitly refer to the Kanban or Scrum methodologies in the remainder of this book. In fact, we will remain mostly methodology-agnostic. However, all these techniques, tools, and features can be applied diligently as per your own requirements. Finally, we closed this chapter by returning to our original starting point – the perennial favorite of the Gantt Chart view.

Summary

Rigidly following any Agile framework to a T defeats the very first statement of the **Agile Manifesto**: *Individuals and interactions over processes and tools*. Understanding the philosophy of Agile is more important than evangelizing any specific process. Importance should be given to customization and choosing the right tool for the job. With this understanding, we can appreciate the ability of Microsoft Project to seamlessly merge Waterfall, Scrum, and Kanban.

We have seen how Scrum and Kanban features in Project can be like Yin and Yang in your Agile project. With all the feature changes in the Agile section in recent years, Project is finally getting the narrative right. Whether you are an avid Agile expert or a newbie, you can customize the Agile features to your own style. Underlying this flexibility is the same scheduling firepower, should you just want to slay the scheduling beast. There is no doubt that Microsoft will continue to improve these offerings.

In the next chapter, we will move on to the important topic of overallocations.

11
Overallocation – the Bane of Project Managers

The famous Parkinson's Law states that *Work expands to fill the time available for its completion*. Soon, every buffer in your project is liable to be overrun with work. In the fiercely competitive world that project managers live in, there is a constant demand to deliver more than expected, for *customer delight*. This aspect is hardcoded into the mission plan of companies. As customers, we too are delighted to receive more than was promised. As a consequence of this universal market condition, the project manager is constantly bombarded with extra work to be accounted for within the schedule.

On the other hand, technology is disrupting every business domain. Along with the obvious benefits, technology also brings extra training needs and unknown risks. As a consequence of this market condition, once again, the project manager has extra work to do that needs to be accounted for.

Whatever the reason, overallocation are inevitable in both well-run projects and otherwise, though for different reasons. Overallocation of resources is the most common issue that's faced by users of Microsoft Project. This is true of both new and seasoned warriors of Project – though the reasons may be different. Fortunately, Project provides you with a plethora of tools and techniques to combat resource overallocation.

In this chapter, we're going to cover the following main topics:

- A brief introduction to overallocation

- How to avoid overallocation

- How to diagnose overallocation

- How to resolve overallocation using several Project tools

Let's get started!

Introducing overallocation

Let's begin with a clear understanding of overallocation. Imagine that you've started working on a report that is to be delivered today. The report will take a whole week to get done. While you are working on it, the CEO assigns you an urgent proposal that is *also* to be delivered this week. Are you familiar with such situations? Congratulations – since you have been allocated more work than the time available to you, you have just been overallocated. In the next section, we will simulate this situation in Project and understand the subtlety that exists within these situations. For all the exercises in this chapter, assume that the calendar defaults are applicable; that is, 8 work hours per day, 5 workdays in a week, adding up to a total of 40 work hours per week.

Simulating an overallocation

Fire up Project so that we can perform a simple experiment to understand how overallocation are triggered:

1. Start with a blank project and enter two task names, as shown in the following screenshot:

Figure 11.1 – Simulating overallocation – starting with two tasks

Notice that both tasks start on the same default date and have the same default duration.

2. The next step is to increase the duration of both tasks to **5 days**, as shown in the following screenshot:

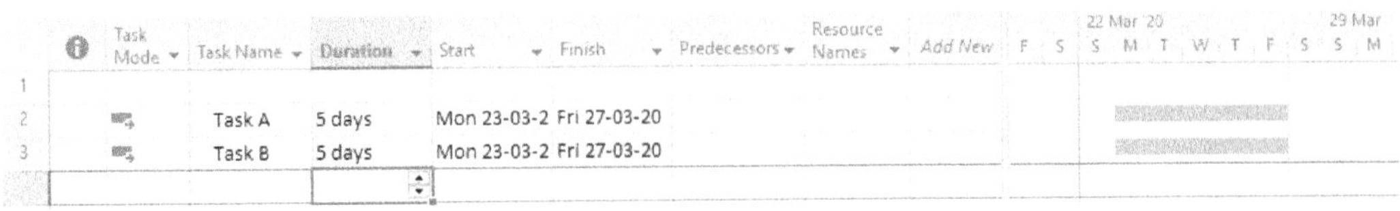

Figure 11.2 – Simulating overallocation – increasing the duration

Both tasks coexist on the same dates. There is no issue yet because these tasks have still not been allocated to any resource.

3. Assign both tasks to the same resource. You will see an overallocation show up. This is an overallocation in its simplest form:

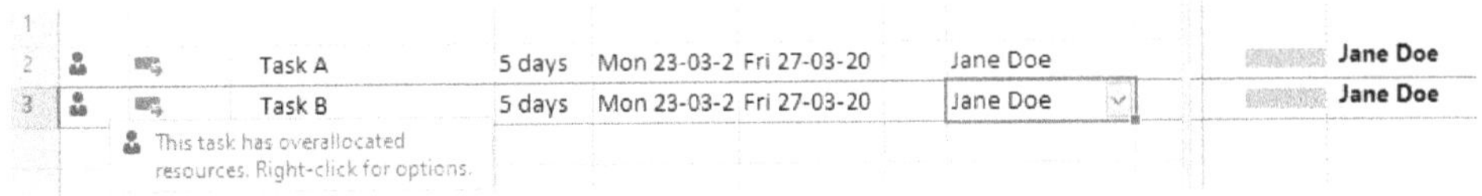

Figure 11.3 – Simulating overallocation – assignment made

You should be familiar with what we've done so far, but this is where things will get interesting. Let's say that this overallocation has caused alarm for you, the project manager.

To resolve this overallocation, you try to reduce the scope of work. Let's try the following steps.

4. Reduce the durations of both the tasks to 3 days and observe the following screenshot:

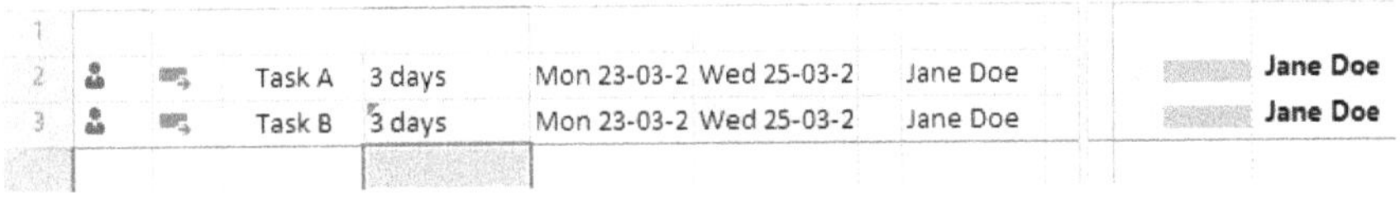

Figure 11.4 – Simulating overallocation – duration reduced to 3 days for each task

As you can see, reduction in duration has had no impact on the overallocation warning.

5. Going further, reduce the duration by one more day for the second task, as shown in the following screenshot:

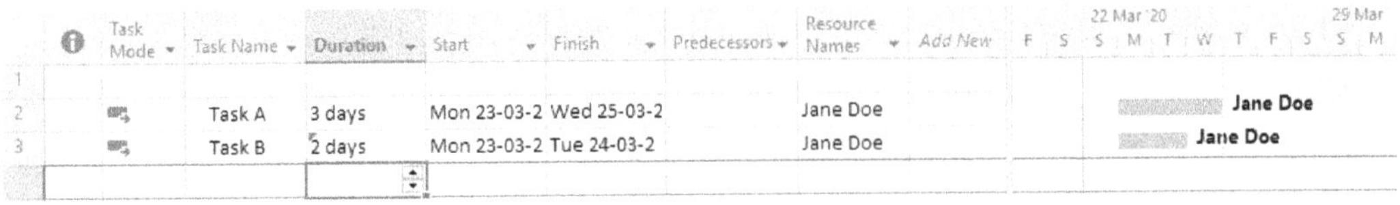

Figure 11.5 – Simulating overallocation – duration reduced to remove overallocation

Here, you can see that the overallocation indicator has gone away. This is a very curious situation since the tasks are still overlapping, but now you do not get the overallocation warning. *Why could this be happening?*

6. For another clue to decipher this behavior, try one more case, as shown in the following screenshot:

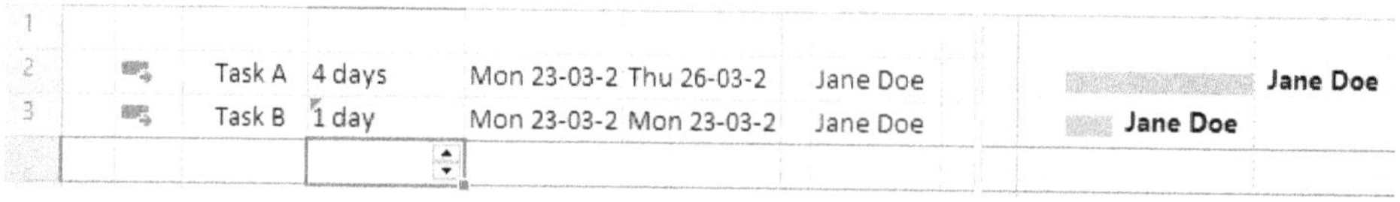

Figure 11.6 – Simulating overallocation – still without overallocation

Increase the first task's duration and reduce the second's task duration, both by one more day. As can be observed in the preceding screenshot, the first task now has a duration of **4 days**, while the second task has a duration of **1 day**. Once again, even though both tasks overlap on the dates and are both assigned to the same resource, Project does not signal overallocation.

The reason for this behavior is that, by default, Project's overallocation-checking algorithm is configured to a default granularity of **1 work week (5 days)**. Only when work breaches *40 hours in a single week* does the algorithm trigger an overallocation. In our previous two examples, the total work that was assigned to Jane Doe was exactly 40 hours in the specific week, so overallocation wasn't triggered.

Let's verify this once again by increasing the duration of the second task, as shown in the following screenshot:

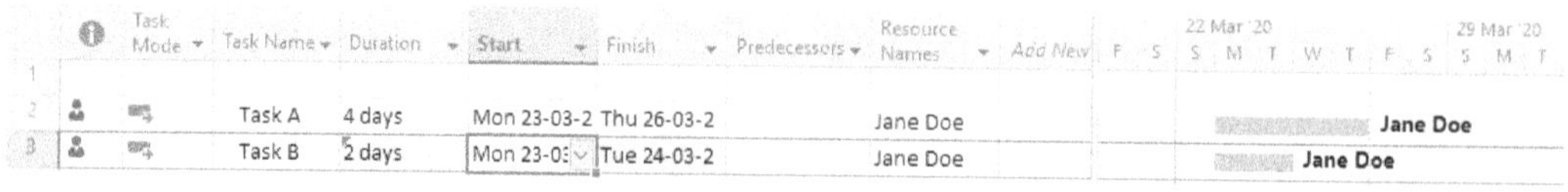

Figure 11.7 – Simulating overallocation – overallocation returns

The overallocation warning reappears now since the resource's allocated work will have exceeded the available weekly 40 work hours. You should be aware of this defaulted behavior and be on the lookout for assignments that suddenly turn into overallocation.

In the next section, we will explore fundamental reasons for the existence of overallocation.

Why does overallocation exist?

As a practitioner, it is common to see overallocation. There are some universal reasons for the widespread existence of overallocation in practice. Let's look at some of them:

- Many project managers don't assign resources to tasks. This is risky as Project cannot detect the presence of overallocation.

- There is a tendency to overestimate efficiency and underestimate risks. Seasoned team members take on more work than possible within the available duration.

- New users of Project neither recognize the warning indicators of Project, nor resolve the issues. In this chapter, we will learn about different techniques we can use to diagnose overallocation.

- In the execution phase of the project, overallocation can occur due to any number of reasons; for example, the scope may increase or change, there might be new pressure from businesses to deliver within shorter timelines, the work estimate might be incorrect, a team member may resign or be replaced, or risks may materialize. We will learn about several different techniques to resolve such overallocation in this chapter.

- Deliberate overallocation is an acceptable practice for certain short durations in the project, especially just before a deliverable. To understand this, we will learn about the best practices to be used for deliberate overallocation.

> **Tip**
> You will often find overallocation warnings in professionally created Project templates. This is not an indication of bad design. These overallocation often only exist because the author of the template would have used generic resources, for you to replace as you deem fit for your project. It will be your responsibility to resolve all overallocation resulting from the usage of any template.

The negative impact of overallocation increases over the project's life cycle. So, it is best to proactively avoid overallocation as early as possible. We'll discuss this in the next section.

Avoiding overallocation with the Assign Resource feature

Project provides a nifty tool we can use to avoid overallocation, right at the time of assignment. Let's see it in action, continuing with the same example from earlier. Refer to the following screenshot:

Figure 11.8 – Avoiding overallocation with the Assign Resource dialog box

To replicate this exercise, corresponding to the preceding screenshot, follow these steps:

1. Select the task to be assigned. In our case, this is the second task.

2. Go to the **Resource | Assign Resources** tab.

3. The **Assign Resources** dialog box will pop up and present you with a list of all the resources available to you. These will appear on the **Resource Sheet** dialog. A new resource called **John Doe** had previously been added to the resource list for this exercise.

If you select **Jane Doe** from the list and use the **Assign** button, you will have the same overallocation that we encountered earlier. So, instead, we will ask Project to find us all the resources who have at least 40 hours of work time available to take on **Task B**. This helps us avoid assigning to resources that will create an overallocation:

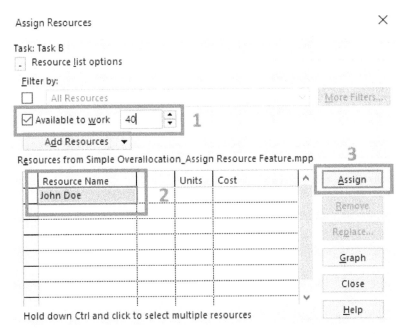

Figure 11.9 – Avoiding overallocation by filtering by the resources available

We can avoid assigning the task to resources who do not have the time available to work. To use this feature, perform the following steps:

1. Enable the **Available to work** checkbox. Enter the minimum work hours availability in the text box provided. In our case, this will be 40 hours (which is 5 days). This will now act as a filter that will remove resources from the listing who are not available for the hours specified.

2. **Jane Doe** is not available anymore in the listing. Select **John Doe**, who is available.

3. Click on the **Assign** button for the resource to be assigned on the Gantt chart.

This is a great tool to use in the planning stages or when you have the luxury of using resources with available working time. In the next section, we will discuss the tools and techniques that are often used in the execution stages of a project.

Diagnosing overallocation

We will follow a systematic path to understand overallocation:

1. Learn how to recognize overallocation warnings from Project.
2. Learn how to diagnose the source of overallocation.
3. Learn techniques to resolve overallocation.

We will study each of these in the following sections.

Recognizing overallocation (the Indicators column)

The overallocation warning in the **Indicators** column is so important that it was introduced earlier in this book, which means you should familiar with it. Refer to the following screenshot:

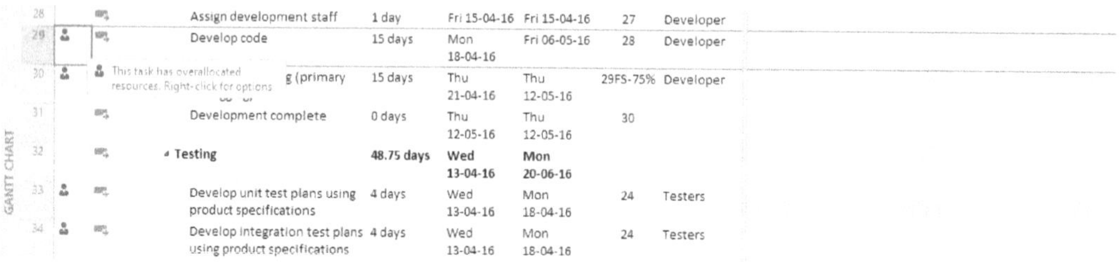

Figure 11.10 – Overallocation with the red man indicator

Sometimes, an overallocation indicator might not be visible when you expect to see one. This might happen when Project has been explicitly instructed to ignore the warning. Project provides a special field called **Ignore Warnings** for every task in your project. You can include this column in your table, as shown in the following screenshot:

Figure 11.11 – Overallocation with the Ignore Warnings column

It is not recommended that you hide (ignore) warnings, but this is a useful tool, should you ever need to hide warnings temporarily.

Before we move on to the next topic, we will look at another useful navigation tool, since this is an opportune time. Notice that, in the previous two screenshots, tasks are not visible on the Gantt chart. This is because of limited screen space, and the tasks are out of view. To instantly readjust the Gantt chart, click on the **Scroll to Task** button on the **Task** tab. Refer to the following screenshot:

Figure 11.12 – Usage of the Scroll to Task button

Next up, we will explore a series of tools that will help us diagnose the root cause of overallocation.

Checking for Max Units and duplication of resources

Overallocation (and underallocation) can occur from incorrectly modeling resource requirements. This is one of the first aspects that you should explore while debugging overallocation. For this discussion, refer to the following screenshot, which shows the **Resource Sheet** view of a project:

		Resource Name	Type	Material	Initials	Group	Max.	Std.	Ovt.	Cost/Use	Accrue	Base	Code
1		Management	Work		M		100%	$0.00/hr	$0.00/hr	$0.00	Prorated	Standard	
2		Project Manager	Work		P		100%	$0.00/hr	$0.00/hr	$0.00	Prorated	Standard	
3		PM	Work		P		100%	$0.00/hr	$0.00/hr	$0.00	Prorated	Standard	
4	👤	Analyst	Work		A		50%	$0.00/hr	$0.00/hr	$0.00	Prorated	Standard	
5	👤	Developer	Work		D		100%	$0.00/hr	$0.00/hr	$0.00	Prorated	Standard	
6	👤	Testers	Work		T		100%	$0.00/hr	$0.00/hr	$0.00	Prorated	Standard	
7	👤	Trainers	Work		T		100%	$0.00/hr	$0.00/hr	$0.00	Prorated	Standard	
8	👤	Technical Comm	Work		T		100%	$0.00/hr	$0.00/hr	$0.00	Prorated	Standard	
9		Deployment Tea	Work		D		100%	$0.00/hr	$0.00/hr	$0.00	Prorated	Standard	

Figure 11.13 – Resource Sheet view used to debug resourcing requirements

Notice that there are several resources that are overallocated. Specifically, observe the **Analyst** resource on line 4. This resource has been set to a **Max. value** of just **50%**. In a normal 8-hour working day, *this resource should not be assigned more than 4 hours!* Otherwise, there will be an overallocation. If this is, in fact, the reason for **Analyst** being overallocated, then increasing **Max. Units** to **100%** should probably resolve this issue. Refer to the following screenshot for the solution:

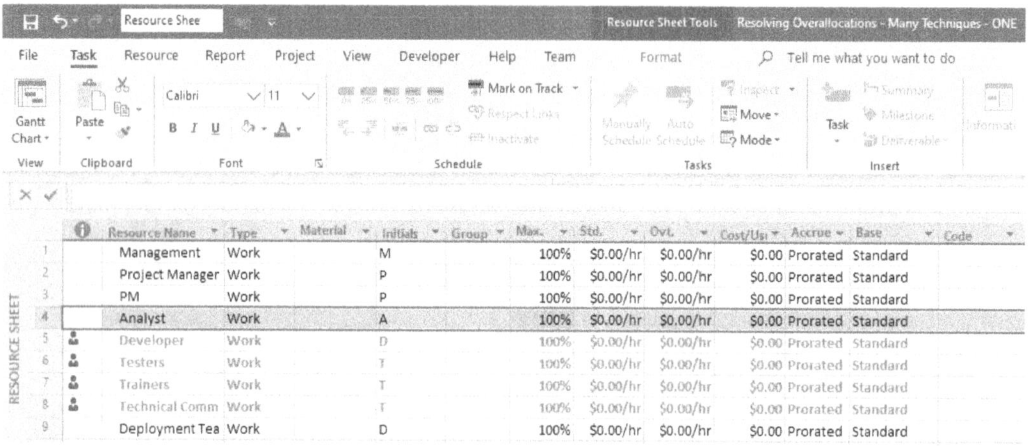

Figure 11.14 – Max. Units resolution regarding overallocation

As can be verified in this specific case, a mismatch between **Max. Units** set for a resource versus the actual work assigned was indeed the cause for the overallocation.

But wait – there's more. You must have noticed one more error in this **Resource Sheet** view. Notice that lines 2 and 3 both refer to the project manager (**Project Manager** and **PM**). This is an example of resource duplication. This resource will almost certainly end up being overallocated when their work is consolidated for solving this issue. You should watch out for such duplication errors that can slip through the door.

Resource Usage view

Now, we are going to start looking at an important topic, so special attention needs to be paid here. Project provides a powerful tool we can use to manage resource workload. This tool is the **Resource Usage** view. It will help you ensure that your resources are optimally utilized. *Both* overallocation and underallocation should be minimized or, even better, eliminated. The following screenshot shows the **Resource Usage** view:

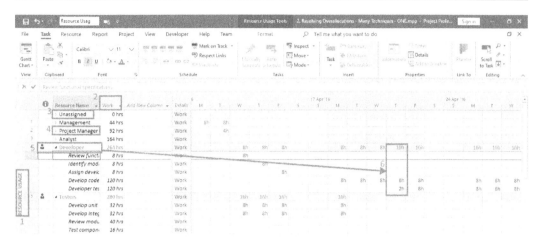

Figure 11.15 – Resource Usage view

There are a few important points to be observed in the screenshot, detailed as follows:

1. The current view's name (**RESOURCE USAGE**) is displayed on the left-most panel, as with every view of Project. If you lose your way around Project, look here to quickly identify which view you are on.

2. The **Work** column shows the total assigned work hours for a resource when collapsed and shows individual detailed tasks when expanded. The data here will help you understand if any individual resource is overallocated or underallocated.

3. A grouping of **tasks by resource name** is applied to the entire table. The first group is the **Unassigned** tasks. Milestones, which are usually not assigned any resources, should end up in this grouping. You should ensure that no orphan normal tasks remain here unassigned.

4. Expand individual resource name groupings to view all the tasks assigned to that resource. Correspondingly, on the right-hand side, you will be able to view the same task data in a time-phased manner. Any overallocation will be marked in the color red.

5. The **Developer** resource is overallocated. This can be identified because the resource name appears in red. In the corresponding time-phased details, the specific tasks that are overallocated will again be in red, with a breakdown of individual dates, which will also appear in red.

6. One such overallocated task is highlighted in the preceding screenshot. The resource is allocated two tasks that add up to 10 hours (instead of the normal 8-hour day).

If overallocation is found, the **Resource Usage** view will help you identify *where* it is, *when* it occurs, and *who* is impacted. This detailed information can be used to resolve overallocation. As you might have surmised, the **Resource Usage** view is the gold standard for resource allocation analysis.

Team Planner view

The next tool that we'll explore is available only on the Professional versions of Project. It's called the **Team Planner** view. Please refer to the following screenshot:

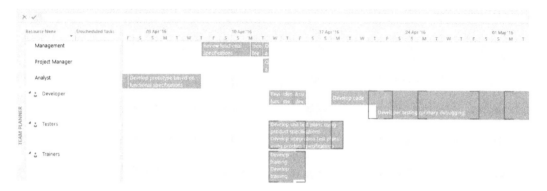

Figure 11.16 – Team Planner view

This view can be compared to the **Resource Usage** view, as follows:

- Similar to **Resource Usage**, both views consist of a left and right panel.
- The left panel lists all the resources available for the project, but the expand feature will not list the individual tasks right below on the table, as you saw in the **Resource Usage** view. When expanded, it lists the tasks on the right panel. This is explained in the next point.
- The right panel is a time-phased **WYSIWYG** interface. This is a significant difference (and advantage) compared to the **Resource Usage** view. This interface allows tasks to be dragged and dropped.
- Similar to the **Resource Usage** view, overallocation are highlighted in red on both panels of the view.
- Note that the task dependencies are neither visible nor obvious.
- The disadvantage of the **WYSIWYG** interface is that it is possible to inadvertently move tasks, thereby creating more overallocation or errors in your scheduling.

In conclusion, the **Team Planner** view is great for analyzing overallocation, but care should be exercised so that you don't accidently drag the schedule out of coherence.

> **Tip**
>
> If you do not have access to the premium **Team Planner** view, there is no reason to fret. While this is a convenient tool for analyzing resource allocations, anything you do here can be done elsewhere using a combination of the other standard workhorse views – Gantt Chart, Resource Usage, Task Usage, and Resource Sheet, among others.

Summary task assignments

In the diagnostic process, the next important aspect to look out for is overallocation originating from summary tasks. It is possible to assign resources to summary tasks, but you should not do so without carefully understanding the consequences. This will be illustrated with an example; please refer to the following screenshot:

Figure 11.17 – Summary task overallocation

In the preceding screenshot, **Scope** is a summary task that has been assigned a resource: **Project Manager**. Some of the detailed tasks within the summary task also have the project manager assigned to them. The end result is overallocation, both to the summary task and to the constituent detailed tasks! If the summary task's allocation is removed, the overallocation will resolve immediately, as shown in the following screenshot:

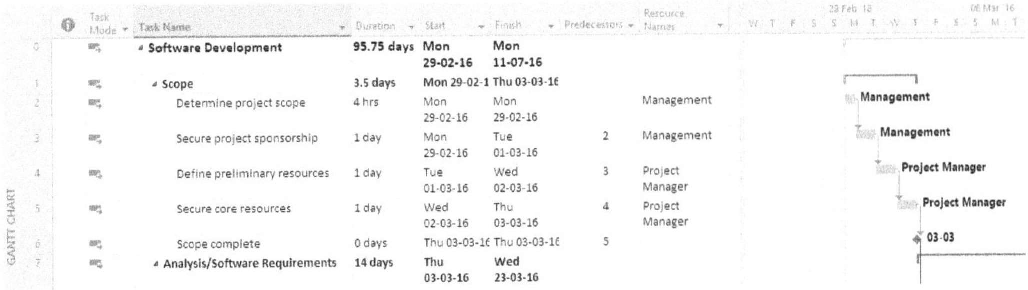

Figure 11.18 – Resolved summary task overallocation

While this example is simple to understand and easy to debug, other overallocation caused by summary tasks will not be because the schedule itself will be complicated. They will often cause bugs at remote sections of the plan that are usually hard to detect and debug. New users of Project should especially guard against this usage of summary tasks.

> **Tip**
> Completely avoid allocating resources to summary tasks, even in the planning stage. The summary task is *not* a task, but just a tool for organizing tasks. Assigning resources to it does not make logical sense and causes hard-to-debug overallocation, mistakes in effort estimation, and resource availability bugs.

The Resource Allocation view

The **Resource Allocation** view is a special combinatorial view, both powerful and useful for the analysis of overallocation. To enable this view, follow these steps:

1. Go to the **Task | Gantt Chart | More Views** tab.

2. From the list of views that shows up, select the **Resource Allocation** view. Please refer to the following screenshot:

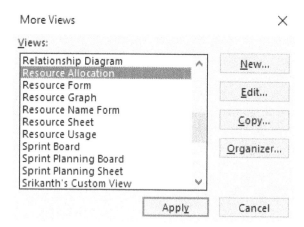

Figure 11.19 – Selecting the Resource Allocation view

The key advantage of this view is that when a specific resource is selected in the **Resource Usage** view, the bottom view will only show the tasks associated with that specific resource in a familiar Gantt-based chart. However, there is more to the Leveling Gantt, and it can be used to resolve overallocation by shifting tasks suitably. Please refer to the following screenshot:

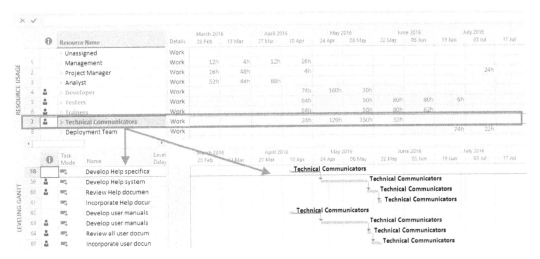

Figure 11.20 – Resource Allocation view

A deeper understanding of this view will become evident later, when we cover other concepts of resource leveling both in this chapter and later chapters in this book. However, it is good to know about this powerful diagnostic tool.

Best practices for deliberate overallocation

We will end this discussion on overallocation diagnosis with some best practices. If short periods of deliberate overallocation are inevitable in the nature of your project, then follow the following best practices:

- Address overallocation across all your projects, as resources who work across projects are also accounted for.

- Set your own limits to the deliberately overallocated hours (at daily/weekly/monthly levels, as suitable to your project). For example, *120% for no more than 5 days* can be a guideline for a single release cycle.

- Verify your overallocation diagnosis with the team. This human factor outweighs other diagnosis techniques.

Now that we have seen plenty of tools and techniques we can use to diagnose overallocation, let's proceed to resolving them.

Resolving overallocation

If you choose to resolve overallocation, there will be an engineering trade-off. This trade-off will be to the constraints of your project. For example, the impact could be on duration, scope, budget, or other important non-functional aspects such as team morale. Your goal is to manage this trade-off. Let's proceed and analyze resolution techniques in the same order that they're normally approached in, starting with the simplest techniques first.

Assigning overallocated work to other resources

Starting with the simplest type of resolution, overallocated work can be assigned to another resource. Refer to the following screenshot for an illustration of such a case:

Figure 11.21 – Overallocated resource

In the preceding screenshot, notice that there are two tasks with an FS relationship so that the successor can start when at least 25% of the predecessor has been completed. This overallocation exists because the parallel tasks are assigned to the same developer. This issue can be easily resolved by assigning one of the tasks to a different resource, as shown in the following screenshot:

Figure 11.22 – Resolving overallocation via different resource allocation

This technique assumes the availability of a free resource with the required skillset being available to take on the task. If there is no free resource available, we will have to consider other options.

Increasing workdays and workhours

The next option we can use to resolve overallocation is to increase the workdays through the calendar. For example, you might add a working Saturday in the standard calendar, thereby increasing the workdays from 5 days to 6 days for a specific week. If this is not an option, you can increase the allowable max working hours for the specific resource.

The advantage of increasing workhours is that the resource can choose when these hours are utilized, if at all. The correct location to set the increased work hours is the familiar **Resource Sheet**. Let's look at an example where this technique is used to resolve overallocation. Refer to the following screenshot:

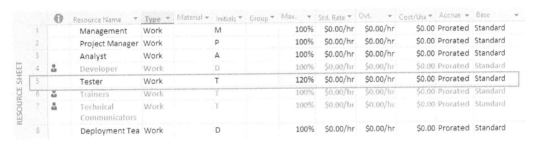

Figure 11.23 – Overallocations on the Resource Sheet

The preceding screenshot shows multiple resources with overallocation. It has been diagnosed that the **Tester** resource will be suitable for increasing **Max. Units** to resolve overallocation, as low hanging fruit. Refer to the following screenshot:

		Resource Name	Type	Material	Initials	Group	Max.	Std. Rate	Ovt.	Cost/Use	Accrue	Base
1		Management	Work		M		100%	$0.00/hr	$0.00/hr	$0.00	Prorated	Standard
2		Project Manager	Work		P		100%	$0.00/hr	$0.00/hr	$0.00	Prorated	Standard
3		Analyst	Work		A		100%	$0.00/hr	$0.00/hr	$0.00	Prorated	Standard
4		Developer	Work		D		100%	$0.00/hr	$0.00/hr	$0.00	Prorated	Standard
5		Tester	Work		T		120%	$0.00/hr	$0.00/hr	$0.00	Prorated	Standard
6		Trainers	Work		T		100%	$0.00/hr	$0.00/hr	$0.00	Prorated	Standard
7		Technical Communicators	Work		T		100%	$0.00/hr	$0.00/hr	$0.00	Prorated	Standard
8		Deployment Tea	Work		D		100%	$0.00/hr	$0.00/hr	$0.00	Prorated	Standard

Figure 11.24 – Max. Units increased to resolve overallocation

By increasing **Max. Units** by just **20%**, the overallocation is resolved. However, the key assumption in this technique is that the resources will work extra hours to stay on track with the schedule.

Task Inspector/Reschedule tasks

In the situation where it is neither possible to assign overallocated tasks to other resources, nor to increase the working hours, then we can consider the third option – moving overallocated tasks to the next available dates so that overallocation is resolved.

Project has a nifty tool called **Task Inspector** to help you move tasks automatically. Let's look at an example of such a resolution. Refer to the following screenshot:

48			⊿ Training	45.75 days	Wed 13-04-16	Wed 15-06-16				Alice
49	▲		Develop training specifications for end users	3 days	Wed 13-04-16	Fri 15-04-16	24	Alice		Alice
50	▲		Develop training specifications for helpdesk support staff	3 days	Wed 13-04-16	Fri 15-04-16	24	Alice		Alice
51	▲		Identify training delivery methodology (computer based training, classroom, etc.)	2 days	Wed 13-04-16	Thu 14-04-16	24	Alice		Alice

Figure 11.25 – Overallocations to be resolved

Notice that the three tasks assigned to the resource **Alice** are causing an overallocation. It makes logical sense to adjust the second (or the third) task, and not the first one, because they are the ones causing the overallocation. Right-click on the second task to bring up a contextual menu, as shown in the following screenshot:

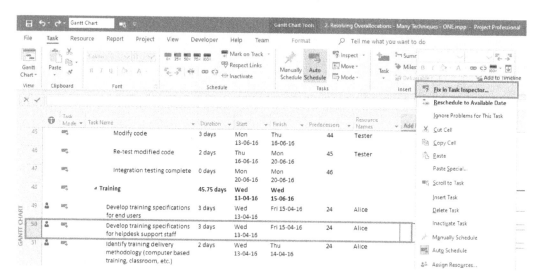

Figure 11.26 – Contextual menu of an overallocated task

A new panel will open up on the left called **Task Inspector**. It presents a couple of diagnosis and resolution options to help you. The diagnostic option is to view the overallocated tasks and resources in the **Team Planner** view. We covered this in the previous section, so ignore this option for now. The other option is **Move task to resource's next available time**, and this is the option that we are interested in. Refer to the following screenshot:

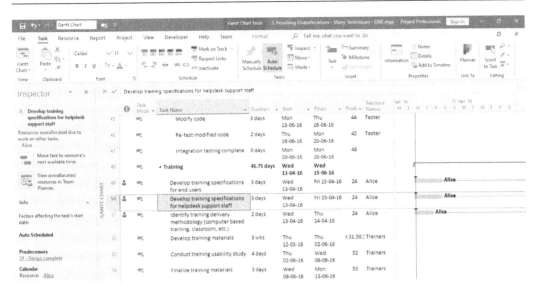

Figure 11.27 – Task Inspector for overallocated tasks

When we accept the offer of **Task Inspector** to move the task to the resource's next available time, the overallocation gets resolved, as shown in the following screenshot:

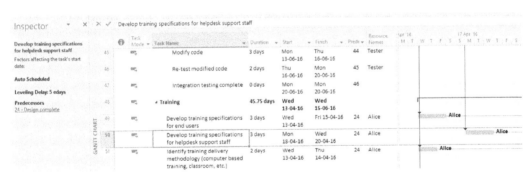

Figure 11.28 – Overallocations resolved by Task Inspector

Obviously, you will want to fine-tune any automatic task movement made by **Task Inspector** and ensure that the logic of the schedule remains valid for your project.

Notice that Alice's third task (line 51) is unchanged, and even though it is concurrent to the first task, it still does not trigger an overallocation. What could be the reason for this? The reason is that both tasks add up to 5 days (40 hours), which does not breach the weekly overallocation granularity.

Manually balancing allocations using the Resource Usage view

Uneven distribution of work within a team can cause overallocation. This is because some resources can be allocated more work than others. Refer to the following screenshot for an illustration of this scenario:

Figure 11.29 – Resource balancing issue

The **Resource Usage** view can best visualize this situation. The whole project has 800 work hours, with 5 equally adept resources. But **Plant** has been allocated more work, resulting in an overallocation. On the other hand, the resource **Sri** has extra bandwidth to take on more work. A careful redistribution of work can be done manually to alleviate this overallocation. The important assumption regarding this technique is that the team members have the skillsets and expertise to take on work from an overallocated resource.

> **Tip**
> Uneven distribution of work is common within teams. A conscious redistribution often goes a long way in both avoiding and alleviating overallocation.

Changing overallocation granularity (leveling options)

With a mature and experienced team, it is possible to handle overallocation by doing nothing. Here, the project manager will not attend to overallocation on a day-to-day or even the default week-by-week basis. With a longer view and nothing else, you can take advantage of the resource's downtime to resolve overallocation. Project recognizes this fact and you can configure the granularity at which overallocation is inspected. Refer to the following screenshot, which shows a **Resource Sheet** with the default **Week by Week** granularity:

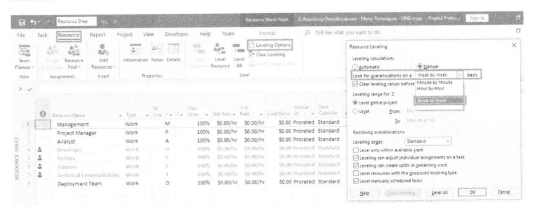

Figure 11.30 – Overallocation checking granularity – Week by Week

In this case, every time a 40-hour boundary is crossed, an overallocation is triggered. Now, let's see the same **Resource Sheet** with the granularity set to **Month by Month**, as shown in the following screenshot:

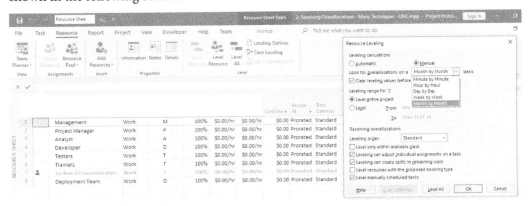

Figure 11.31 – Overallocation checking granularity – Month by Month

Note that this technique may appear like a hack and should not be used lightly. There is an obvious risk attached to this technique as we are consciously ignoring overallocation for a longer duration. But there will be situations where this technique can be suitably employed; for example, when certain conditions are met, such as the following ones:

- Tasks are of lower priority.

- These tasks are **not** on the Critical Path and don't need to be specially guarded.

- There is slack available on these tasks (that is, some *downtime* is available without impacting other tasks).

Depending on only these and your own project factors, this technique of adjusting granularity can be suitably employed.

The Move Task tool – adding delays

Project provides another tool we can use to change the start dates of overallocated tasks, similar to the one we saw with **Task Inspector**, but with more flexibility. To see this tool in action, first, consider the following screenshot:

Figure 11.32 – Overallocations to be resolved

Notice that the resource **Dijkstra** has been overallocated. To solve this, select the second task, which is causing the overallocation. We will use the **Move (Task)** button on the **Task** tab here. Let's understand the options this feature provides, as shown in the following screenshot:

Figure 11.33 – Move Task feature for overallocation resolution

As can be seen from the dropdown, plenty of automated flexibility is available. You can move tasks either forward or backward on the schedule, either by a present amount or by customizing the shift duration. The options for moving parts of the task are not important for now and we will explore this when we cover project tracking, later in this book. It is also possible to automatically reschedule the task to when the assigned resource is available next, just like we did for **Task Inspector**.

In the specific example that we have, there is more than one arrangement for the tasks to resolve this overallocation. But for the sake of this exercise, we will move the second task 1 week forward. Refer to the following screenshot:

Figure 11.34 – Overallocation resolved with the Move Task tool

As a result of moving the task by a specific amount of days, the overallocation has been resolved. But a date constraint (flexible, **Start No Earlier Than**) has been introduced to the task, and we should live with this. In this particular example, there was no impact on the entire project's end dates, but this will not always be the case.

Automated tools

There are even more overallocation resolution tools within Project, including automated ones. We will explore these tools in *Chapter 13*, *Project Tracking Techniques*. The effectiveness of overallocation resolution normally reduces with higher automation tools, as we will see.

With that, we have come to the end of this chapter. Before you move ahead, it is recommended that you simulate and practice the examples demonstrated in this chapter.

Summary

For every issue your project has, the common symptom is often overallocation. In this chapter, you have been provided with a lot of ammunition to combat these issues. You should use the tools provided by Project to recognize the presence of root causes, diagnose them, and finally resolve overallocation.

There are even more advanced techniques we can use to resolve overallocation, and we will explore them in combination with project tracking techniques later in this book. Such problems on Project often cause the schedule to deviate from its original intended course. We need powerful tools to continuously navigate our project's course.

In the next chapter, we will explore the concept of baselines and learn about Project's support when it comes to baselining our project.

12
Baselines – Techniques and Best Practices

In today's world of ubiquitous mobile devices, it is common practice to take a quick snapshot of anything significant that we want to remember or reference later. In the same way, a baseline functions as a snapshot of your project. It acts as storage for project artifacts that you can reference at a later date. A baseline stores the best estimates for the scope, cost, and timeline of a project at any point in time. A reference point in the project life cycle is defined by the baseline.

Microsoft Project provides a comprehensive solution for storing a project *schedule* baseline. Approximately 20 parameters are recorded for every task. These parameters are related to the start and end dates, work, duration, and cost. If there is any change in the project's scope, cost, or timeline, you rework your project plan and store another baseline. Project provides a generous 11 storage spaces for your baselines.

Moreover, Project provides several special views and tools to help you compare your project against a baseline. In this chapter, we will understand the underlying logic of these features. Without this understanding, the experience of baselining the schedule can be quite daunting to a new user of Project.

In this chapter, we're going to cover the following main topics:

- A deeper understanding of baselines in Project Management
- Significance and usage of Project's Variance Table
- Creating baselines within Project
- Best practices when using Project's baseline features
- Maintaining baselines within Project
- Let's get started!

A deeper understanding of baselines

The **baseline** is a critical concept in Project Management – specifically under the discipline of configuration management. A baseline is the reference point on which all project performance measurements are based. At a minimum, the scope, cost, and schedule are to be baselined for any project. In practice, this means the documents holding the approved scope, cost, and schedule are saved with a *version control* tool.

Once a document has been version controlled, such documents can only be changed through a formal process known in the PMBOK as the **Perform Integrated Change Control Process**. Version-controlled documents can be both physical and digital. In the PMBOK, baselining is categorized within the **Project Integration Management** knowledge area.

The need for baselines

Baselines are needed to evaluate the variance of *actual* versus *planned* parameters. Only with the aid of such evaluation is it possible to manage performance. When you enter the execution stages of the project, your schedule, which was static so far, comes alive because resources start the actual project work. Once approved and put into action, the schedule now has multiple roles and responsibilities, as follows:

- It reflects the contractual scope.
- It reflects the execution plan.
- It reflects the best estimates for dates, durations, costs, and work.
- It reflects the resourcing promised for your project (people, machinery, and expenses)

But the inherently risky nature of projects means that, at any time, any of these parameters can change. The scope of the project may change, as may the execution plan or the resources. Unless the original design of your schedule is carefully saved and controlled, you will not have a reference point to track the execution of your project.

The traditional technique of creating baselines is through version-controlled physical blueprints, architectural models, registers, and any other kinds of artifacts. At a minimum, you may save the baseline in different files named "version 1", "version 2", and so on. This can be cumbersome, but we have all been there.

Project provides an ecosystem of tools we can use to manage baselines, neatly recorded within the same file that holds your schedule. This means that you save the extra cost of maintaining the baseline elsewhere. It also means that when you share your project file, you are also sharing the baseline with it for a ready reference. Of course, all these benefits are available only if you baseline your project and keep it up to date. In this chapter, we will learn everything needed to baseline a project and maintain it. In the next chapter, you will learn how to keep your schedule up to date by tracking its progress. All of this learning will be hands-on through a project, which we'll start in the next section.

Project for this chapter

Case study: You are the vice president of marketing for a luxury watch manufacturing company. Your project is to launch the latest watch, named **SeaMaster 5300**, at a company sponsored event. The task list for your project, in order of their execution, will look like this:

1. Event roadmap approval
2. Budget approval
3. Set up an internal team
4. Event website – CVENT
5. Channel promotion
6. Engage venue vendor
7. Engage advertising vendor
8. Worldwide press release
9. Independent media release
10. Loopback production database

Fire up Project and key in the tasks so that you can follow along and get some hands-on experience. We will keep the project's logic simple so that the focus remains on baselining. When you have finished linking the tasks, your schedule should resemble the following screenshot:

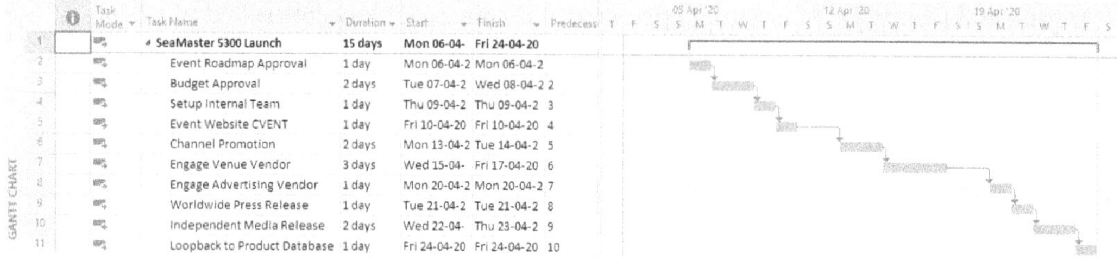

Figure 12.1 – Hands-on project for this chapter

Remember that baselines are purely a project managerial concept and they do not directly impact the schedule in any way. Correspondingly, the baselining toolkit provided by Project includes a special table called the Variance table, which we will inspect in the next section.

Understanding the Variance table

The act of baselining is analogous to taking a snapshot of your project at a point of time. Approximately 20 parameters are saved by Project in five major classifications (start and finish dates, durations, work, and cost). The Variance table is specially designed to work with some of these baselined parameters. For our running project, first, let's see Project's behavior when no baselines have been stored yet.

In the same existing **Gantt Chart** view that we currently are on, switch the table that's displayed from **Entry** to **Variance**. This can be done by navigating to the ribbon's **View** tab, going to the **Data** group, and then, from the **Tables** dropdown, choosing **Variance**. Refer to the following screenshot:

Figure 12.2 – Variance table before setting the baseline

In this new **Variance** table, the **Task Name**, **Start**, and **Finish** columns are exactly the same as in the familiar **Entry** table. However, the **Baseline Start**, **Baseline Finish**, **Start Variance**, and **Finish Variance** columns are fields you have not encountered yet. The significant point to note here is that these columns will not hold any data for a schedule that has not been baselined yet. They display the letters **NA**, which signifies **Not Applicable** here.

In the same vein, this is an opportune time to inspect one more location where baseline data can be viewed. Open the familiar **Project Information** dialog box, from the **Project** tab, and navigate to the **Project Information** button. The **Statistics** button will open a dialog box, as shown in the following screenshot:

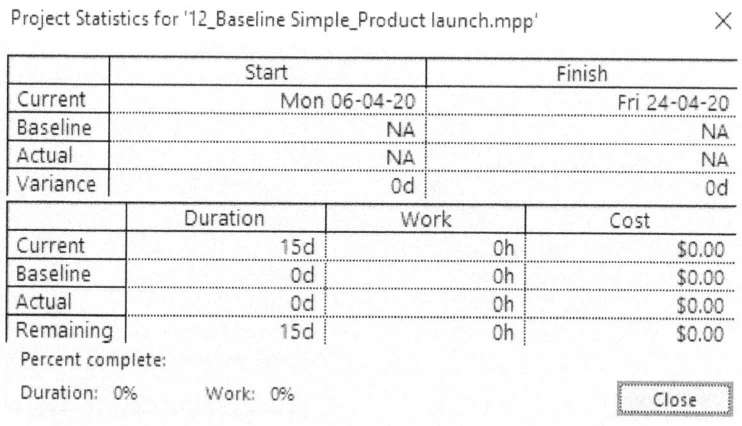

Project Statistics for '12_Baseline Simple_Product launch.mpp'   ✕

	Start	Finish
Current	Mon 06-04-20	Fri 24-04-20
Baseline	NA	NA
Actual	NA	NA
Variance	0d	0d

	Duration	Work	Cost
Current	15d	0h	$0.00
Baseline	0d	0h	$0.00
Actual	0d	0h	$0.00
Remaining	15d	0h	$0.00

Percent complete:

Duration: 0%   Work: 0%   Close

Figure 12.3 – Statistics dialog box before setting the baseline

As can be observed in this dialog box, **Baseline** data forms a prominent aspect of your project statistics and it will be mostly marked as **NA**, if the baseline has not been set for your project. With this understanding, it is now time to create the first baseline for our project.

> **Tip**
> The **Project Statistics** dialog box is the fastest way to check the health of the project. If you have diligently baselined your project and have been tracking it regularly, the **Statistics** dialog box presents a quick way to check the pulse of your project.

Creating a new baseline

The first baseline is sacrosanct for the project as it will signify the first and best estimates for the schedule of your project. To set the baseline, go to the **Project** tab | **Set Baseline** and choose the **Set Baseline** option.

This opens the **Set Baseline** dialog box, as shown in the following screenshot:

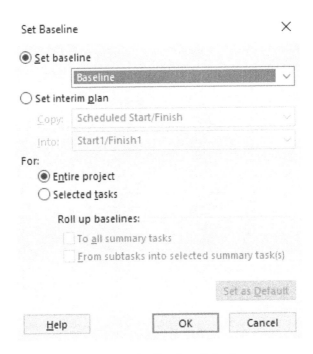

Figure 12.4 – Set Baseline dialog box

Let's begin by understanding this important interface and what it offers to us.

The first two radio buttons indicate that you can now set either a *baseline* or an *interim plan*. You can think of the interim plan as a *junior baseline* for now; we will explore it later in this chapter.

Let's move on to the next set of radio buttons, under the **For:** label. They present the option of saving the entire project within a baseline, or just a set of selected tasks. Two further checkboxes are present, which are only relevant when you are saving a set of selected tasks. However, the first baseline should always be saved for the entire project, and that is what we will do now.

Retain all the default options and save the first baseline of your project. Immediately, the baseline data will be populated in the **Variance** table, as shown in the following screenshot:

	Task Mode	Task Name	Start	Finish	Baseline Start	Baseline Finish	Start Var.	Finish Var.
1		SeaMaster 5300 Launch	Mon 06-04-20	Fri 24-04-20	Mon 06-04-20	Fri 24-04-20	0 days	0 days
2		Event Roadmap Approval	Mon 06-04-20	Mon 06-04-20	Mon 06-04-20	Mon 06-04-20	0 days	0 days
3		Budget Approval	Tue 07-04-20	Wed 08-04-20	Tue 07-04-20	Wed 08-04-20	0 days	0 days
4		Setup Internal Team	Thu 09-04-20	Thu 09-04-20	Thu 09-04-20	Thu 09-04-20	0 days	0 days
5		Event Website CVENT	Fri 10-04-20	Fri 10-04-20	Fri 10-04-20	Fri 10-04-20	0 days	0 days
6		Channel Promotion	Mon 13-04-20	Tue 14-04-20	Mon 13-04-20	Tue 14-04-20	0 days	0 days
7		Engage Venue Vendor	Wed 15-04-20	Fri 17-04-20	Wed 15-04-20	Fri 17-04-20	0 days	0 days
8		Engage Advertising Vendor	Mon 20-04-20	Mon 20-04-20	Mon 20-04-20	Mon 20-04-20	0 days	0 days
9		Worldwide Press Release	Tue 21-04-20	Tue 21-04-20	Tue 21-04-20	Tue 21-04-20	0 days	0 days
10		Independent Media Release	Wed 22-04-20	Thu 23-04-20	Wed 22-04-20	Thu 23-04-20	0 days	0 days
11		Loopback to Product Database	Fri 24-04-20	Fri 24-04-20	Fri 24-04-20	Fri 24-04-20	0 days	0 days

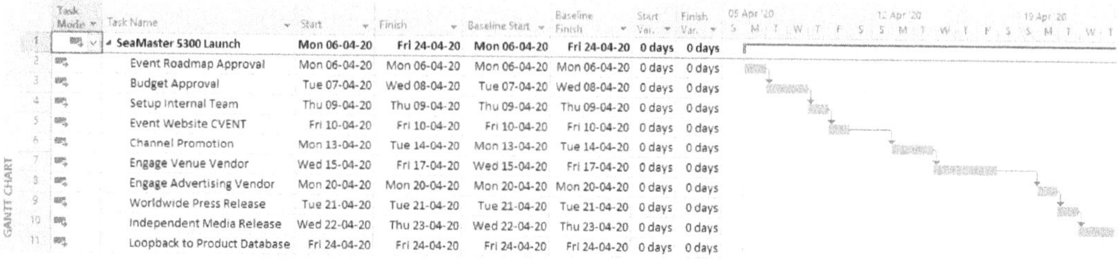

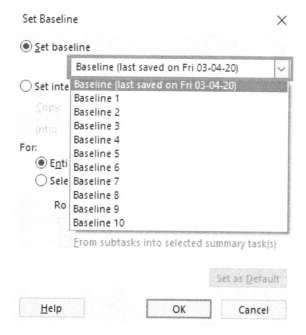

Figure 12.5 – Variance table with baseline data populated

With that, the **Baseline Start** and **Baseline Finish** columns are now populated. These columns will have replicated the same values as the **Start** and **Finish** columns, individually for every task in the schedule. Of course, other parameters such as duration, work, and cost (if available) are also recorded, but they are not currently visible on the table. There is another small consequence of setting the baseline. To see this, open and observe the **Set baseline** dialog box once again. Refer to the following screenshot:

Figure 12.6 – Baseline name saved with date automatically

There are four important points to note from this screenshot, as follows:

- Project allows you to save a maximum of 11 baselines in your project. You can imagine them as 11 storage slots where you can save your data.

- You can save in any slot at any time. The first slot is named **Baseline** and is selected by default. It is a best practice to save your first baseline into this slot.

- The other slots have a number concatenated to the name. You cannot manually change any of these baseline names.

- When you save in any baseline slot, the current date automatically gets affixed to it, as can be observed with the first baseline slot that we have saved in.

With that, we have seen how to create the first baseline. In the next section, we will understand the big picture view of how multiple baselines are created and used within a project life cycle.

A flowchart for controlling changes with baselines

In Project, baselines are intended to record changes to the project *schedule*, whereas interim plans are intended to track deviations to project *execution*. This design can be illustrated with the help of the following flowchart:

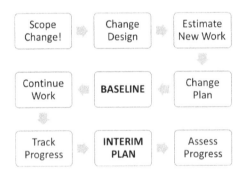

Figure 12.7 – Flowchart to show baselines in action during project execution

There are at least two distinct purposes for a baseline within Project, as follows:

- To record a snapshot of the schedule: With multiple baselines, a series of snapshots can be recorded throughout the life cycle of the project.

- To assess deviations in the project. Deviations in the actual schedule versus the planned schedule can be detected.

Returning to our hands-on project, let's see these two aspects in action. While we were away, some new changes have emerged within our case study project:

- A new task is to be added to the schedule.

- The duration of one existing task has increased due to some resourcing issues.

These are very common situations that you will face within your project. Let's see how Project baselines will help us deal with these situations. Apply these changes to the project and replicate with the help of the following screenshot:

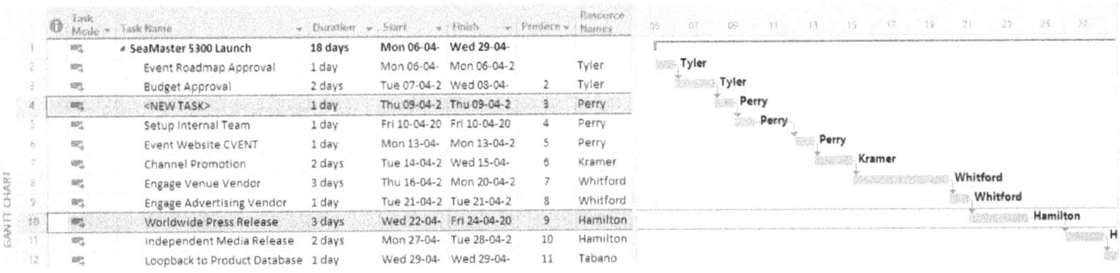

Figure 12.8 – Changes to the hands-on project

In the preceding screenshot, the **Entry** table has been reapplied to the Gantt chart, from the **Tables** dropdown in the ribbon's **View** tab. You should observe the following points in particular:

- A new task was added on line 4. You can use the **Insert** key to add a new task. You will also be required to readjust the linking. Refer to the **Predecessors** column in the preceding screenshot to key in the links. Alternatively, use the **Link** button on the **Task** tab.

- The duration of the **Worldwide Press Release** task on line 10 has increased from 1 day to 3 days.

What is the impact of these changes on our project schedule? Is every task in the schedule impacted? We'll answer these questions in the next section with the help of our friend, the Variance table.

Variance table revisited

Once again, reload the **Variance** table within the **Gantt Chart** view and observe the following screenshot:

Task Mode	Task Name	Start	Finish	Baseline Start	Baseline Finish	Start Var.	Finish Var.	Add	05	07	09	11	13	15	17	19	21
1	⊿ SeaMaster S300 Launch	Mon 06-04-20	Wed 29-04-20	Mon 06-04-20	Fri 24-04-20	0 days	3 days										
2	Event Roadmap Approval	Mon 06-04-20	Mon 06-04-20	Mon 06-04-20	Mon 06-04-20	0 days	0 days		Tyler								
3	Budget Approval	Tue 07-04-20	Wed 08-04-20	Tue 07-04-20	Wed 08-04-20	0 days	0 days			Tyler							
4	<NEW TASK>	Thu 09-04-20	Thu 09-04-20	NA	NA	0 days	0 days			Perry							
5	Setup Internal Team	Fri 10-04-20	Fri 10-04-20	Thu 09-04-20	Thu 09-04-20	1 day	1 day			Perry							
6	Event Website CVENT	Mon 13-04-20	Mon 13-04-20	Fri 10-04-20	Fri 10-04-20	1 day	1 day				Perry						
7	Channel Promotion	Tue 14-04-20	Wed 15-04-20	Mon 13-04-20	Tue 14-04-20	1 day	1 day					Kramer					
8	Engage Venue Vendor	Thu 16-04-20	Mon 20-04-20	Wed 15-04-20	Fri 17-04-20	1 day	1 day							Whitford			
9	Engage Advertising Vendor	Tue 21-04-20	Tue 21-04-20	Mon 20-04-20	Mon 20-04-20	1 day	1 day								Whitf		
10	Worldwide Press Release	Wed 22-04-20	Fri 24-04-20	Tue 21-04-20	Tue 21-04-20	1 day	3 days										
11	Independent Media Release	Mon 27-04-20	Tue 28-04-20	Wed 22-04-20	Thu 23-04-20	3 days	3 days										
12	Loopback to Product Database	Wed 29-04-20	Wed 29-04-20	Fri 24-04-20	Fri 24-04-20	3 days	3 days										

Figure 12.9 – Variance table after making changes to the project

Let's analyze the changes to our schedule from the perspective of the **Variance** table's columns, specifically the **Start Variance** and **Finish Variance** columns. These columns indicate the deviation in the actual (*currently estimated*) **Start** and **Finish** dates to the planned (*baselined*) dates. Notice that different tasks have different variance and they can be explained as follows:

1. **Zero (0) days variance**: These tasks have not been impacted at all. These tasks were scheduled to be executed prior to the newly added/modified tasks.

2. **One (1) day variance**: These tasks are impacted *only* from the newly added task, which had a 1-day duration. Note that *all* tasks scheduled after the newly added task were impacted.

3. **Three (3) day variance**: These tasks are impacted by *both* changes (1 day for the newly added task, *plus* 2 days increase for the task on line 10).

Also, note that the **Start** and **Finish** columns hold the newly calculated task dates, whereas the **Baseline Start** and **Baseline Finish** columns hold the unchanged baselined dates from earlier, as a reference point. There are even more techniques we can use to readily analyze the baseline data, and we will continue to examine them in the following section.

Analyzing baselines

The **Project Statistics** dialog box provides baseline information for the whole project, so it is perfect to continue our analysis from there. Once again, open this dialog box from the **Project** tab by clicking on the **Project Information** button and then the **Statistics** button. Your statistics should be similar to the ones shown in the following screenshot:

Project Statistics for '12_Baseline Simple_Product launch_ver 2.mpp'

	Start	Finish
Current	Mon 06-04-20	Wed 29-04-20
Baseline	Mon 06-04-20	Fri 24-04-20
Actual	NA	NA
Variance	0d	3d

	Duration	Work	Cost
Current	18d	144h	$0.00
Baseline	15d	0h	$0.00
Actual	0d	0h	$0.00
Remaining	18d	144h	$0.00

Percent complete:

Duration: 0% Work: 0%

Close

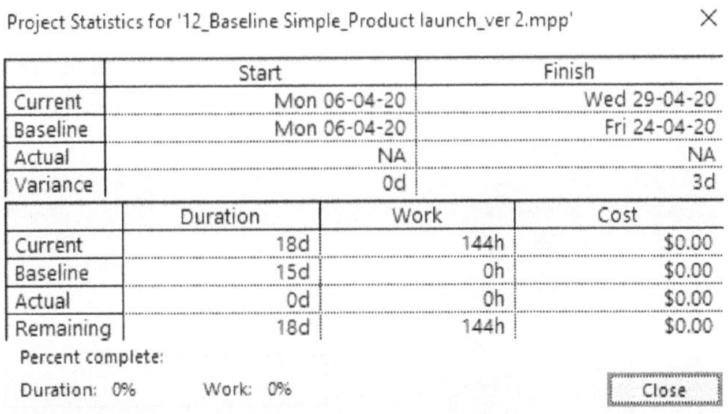

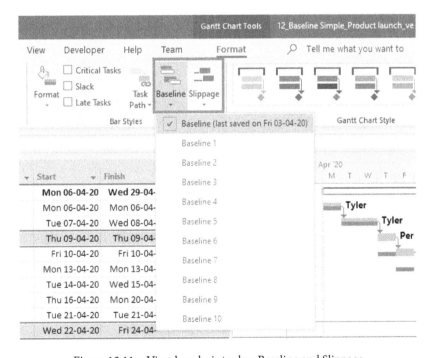

Figure 12.10 – Project Statistics dialog box with baseline information

If you look at the finish date's variance, you will be able to immediately tell that the project has already been extended by 3 days. This concise view is the key value of the statistics dialog box. So far, we have been looking at numeric variance values, but a visual comparison is also possible! There are two excellent visual tools that we will explore now, and they can be found on the **Format** tab. Refer to the following screenshot:

Figure 12.11 – Visual analysis tools – Baseline and Slippage

Notice the two buttons, **Baseline** and **Slippage**, next to each other in the preceding screenshot. They both deliver the same baseline options, but their functionality is different, as we will see now. Start with the **Baseline** button dropdown and select our saved baseline. Refer to the following screenshot:

Figure 12.12 – Baseline Gantt chart

This chart shows an additional slimmer bar in gray, juxtaposed for every task. These are the baselined tasks. If you carefully observe the chart, you will see that the first two tasks have zero (0) deviation and hence they overlap. There is no slippage for these tasks.

The third task has no baseline information since it was newly added, and so it has no baseline bar at all. The next few tasks will have a single working day's slippage. Finally, the last two tasks will have a total of 3 days of deviation. This is, of course, an exact match with the **Variance** table values that we saw earlier, represented graphically.

We can ramp up the visual imagery now by displaying both the baseline tasks and corresponding slippage. From the **Slippage** button dropdown, select our saved baseline. Refer to the following screenshot:

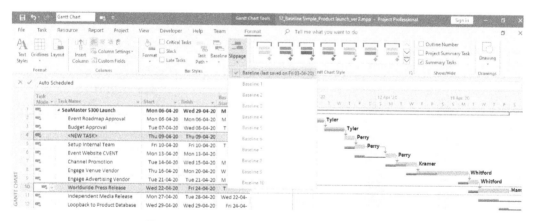

Figure 12.13 – Baseline and Slippage Gantt chart

As you may have guessed, *slippage* is the same as *variance*. This is shown in the form of a line extending from the start of the baseline task to the start of the actual task.

You will now be able to fully appreciate the value of baselines in your project. If your baseline had not been created, you would not be able to see this numerical and visual history of the project and its evolution over time. While we have only used a single baseline, we can potentially trace our project's history through 11 different baselines and get specific reference points dating back in time.

As an additional exercise, add another new task and, immediately after, save it to the **Baseline 1** slot. Then, view the Gantt chart with the latest baseline, **Baseline 1**, activated. You will find that the taskbars coincide perfectly. *Why is there no slippage now?* Refer to the following screenshot:

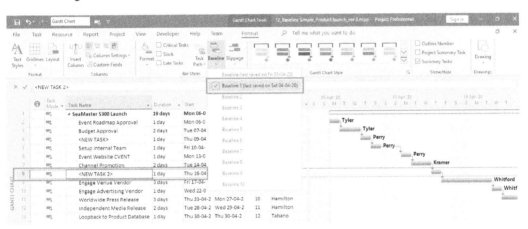

Figure 12.14 – Second baseline Gantt chart

There is no slippage in the preceding screenshot because no changes have been made to the project since the baseline. Due to this, there's been no deviation between the baselined values, but the actual values are shown.

Comparing multiple baselines

Complex projects often need more baselines. It is possible to compare baselines against each other. Project provides a very special view for this purpose and it is appropriately called the **Multiple Baselines Gantt** view. To enable this, first, navigate to the **Task** tab. Then, from the **Gantt Chart** button's dropdown, select the **More Views** option. From the ensuing dropdown, select **Multiple Baselines Gantt**. Refer to the following screenshot:

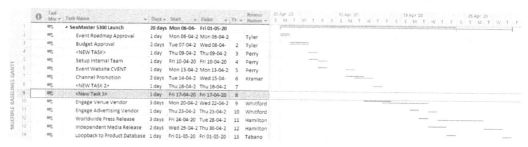

Figure 12.15 – Multiple Baselines Gantt view

In the ensuing **Multiple Baselines Gantt** view, be aware that if you have tasks that haven't been saved within any of the baselines, such tasks will not have any taskbars visible.

From the preceding screenshot, we can observe the following:

- There are two baselines in our project currently. Each baseline in the preceding screenshot is represented by a different color. These colors are decided by the **Bar Style** formatting that's applied.

- Notice the task on line 9, creatively named **<New Task 3>**, which is used to highlight its addition after the last baseline save. This task has no visual representation on the corresponding Gantt chart because it is not in any baseline. Similarly, you can find tasks with a single bar represented on the Gantt side, and others with two bars.

- As the project progresses, there is a divergence in the bars. This represents the presence of variance days. It increases over the schedule due to new tasks being added. Observe the top **Summary Task** bars; they immediately convey the delays that were introduced to the project.

There is a minor inconvenience to this view, though, which will examine in the next section.

Multiple baselines issue and its resolution

Only the first three baselines are visible on this **Gantt Chart** view, as the default behavior. These are **Baseline**, **Baseline 1**, and **Baseline 2**. If you want more to appear here, you will have to create a **Bar Style** specifically for your baseline.

To do this, navigate to the ribbon's **Format** tab, click the **Format** button, and then click the **Bar Styles** button. Refer to the following screenshot:

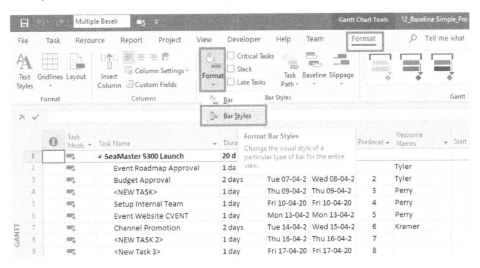

Figure 12.16 – Adding a Bar Style for the new baseline

The **Bar Styles** dialog box will appear. You can scroll through the list to see the default styles for the three baselines that appear in the **Multiple Baselines Gantt** view – **Baseline**, **Baseline 1**, and **Baseline 2**. You have to create a new style for the baseline that you want to see. In the screenshot that follows, this process is demonstrated for **Baseline 3**:

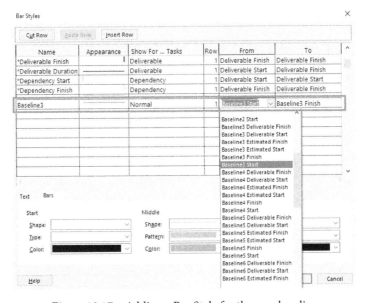

Figure 12.17 – Adding a Bar Style for the new baseline

The **Name** cell can have anything in it, but it is wise to name the style using the same convention followed by Project. When you have created a new bar style for your baseline, it will automatically appear in the **Multiple Baselines** view. This technique gives you a useful debugging and reporting tool. There is a lightweight alternative to using multiple baselines, which is using interim plans. We'll discuss this in the next section.

Pitfall

Is just 11 baselines enough for my own complex project? The answer is, *Yes*. If you find yourself requiring more baselines, there may be other serious problems with your project. Remember, using baselines in Project requires practice and you will soon be able to work within its limitations.

Understanding interim plans

Interim plans are similar to baselines, but they only record the current *start* and *finish* dates for the project tasks. In comparison to the interim plan's limited data storage, the baseline records approximately 20 parameters tracked for every task in a project. The date values stored in an interim plan reflect the execution data for a project and are generated when you record the progress of a task. There are a total of 10 slots available to save interim plans. In spite of the differences between interim plans and baselines, all the techniques and tools available for baselines are equally applicable to interim plans.

We will discuss the tracking techniques of a project, along with execution data, later in this book. In the meantime, there are some important best practices to be understood.

Best practices when using baselines

The following best practices will help you maximize the power of baselines and prevent potential pitfalls:

- If you miss the opportunity to set the baseline at an opportune time, there is no going back. You cannot revert to the original configuration of your schedule if you have subsequently saved design changes. So, don't miss out on creating a baseline.

- You can baseline either at the *end-of-planning* phase or at the *beginning-of-execution* phase. The latter is better. This is because in the planning phase, you might not use the names of the real people who will work on your project, and instead you are likely to use generic resource names. You will not want to baseline with generic resource names because they are likely to hide overallocation issues. During the start of execution, the generic resources will be replaced by the actual names of people who will execute the schedule. Baseline after resolving all the resourcing issues in your schedule, and before your execution starts!

- The first baseline, named **Baseline**, has a special place in Project. It is used by default to calculate variations, by the relevant algorithms of Project.

- The first baseline is to be permanently preserved and should not be overwritten. This is because it will show the original state of your plan.

- Do not set multiple baselines unless it is well justified. They have an associated maintenance overhead.

- You cannot change the default baseline names or store other additional information. Due to this, you cannot easily identify a baseline by its purpose for existing. So, use an external document to store any other information about a baseline, such as why the baseline was created, and the pertinent approvals required.

- In many business domains, it is difficult to estimate work reliably. But you can learn from your mistakes and get better in your game by using baselines. Use **Variance** information to improve your estimations over time. Variance shows the difference between what was originally planned and how the project situation changed subsequently. If you track this over multiple projects, your estimates can improve.

Starting from the execution phase, you should maintain not only the running schedule, but baselines too. Project expects you to understand the underlying logic required to maintain your baselines. Otherwise, there may be disastrous results, such as accidentally overwriting a baseline. We will discuss baseline maintenance techniques for the remainder of this chapter.

Maintaining baselines

Everything we discuss in this section applies to both baselines and interim plans. For the sake of brevity, we will refer to only baselines, though you should suitably extrapolate to interim plans too. Just like other features of Project, there are multiple ways to maintain your baselines.

Updating a baseline

Sometimes, you may prematurely save a baseline while design changes are still underway. At such a time, you will want to update your baseline again after all the changes have been done. The correct way to do this is to just overwrite the baseline in question, exactly as if you were creating a fresh baseline, but now you select the existing baseline that you want updated.

Optionally, you may want to select only a few tasks to be updated into the baseline. For example, in the following screenshot, **Baseline 3** is being updated only for selected tasks:

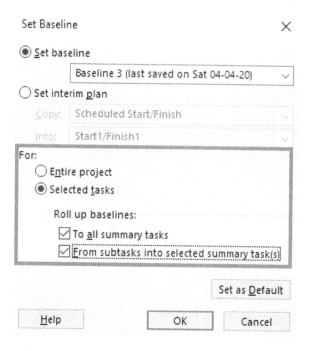

Figure 12.18 – Updating a baseline with selected tasks

There are two checkboxes here, as shown in the preceding screenshot. Enable both checkboxes if your project contains summary tasks. Otherwise, the baseline's summary tasks may not reflect proper data for the updated subtasks. This issue is probably a vestige of old design carried over into Project.

Deleting (clearing) a baseline

Sometimes, project managers are trigger-happy with baselines in the early stages of the project and find themselves running out of baseline slots in the execution phase. In such situations, it is perfectly fine to delete unwanted baselines.

Since baselines are saved into existing slots, the appropriate term to use would be *clearing baselines* instead of *deleting them*. You can clear baselines from the same **Set Baseline** dropdown button, but now you use the **Clear Baseline** option. The **Clear Baseline** dialog looks as follows:

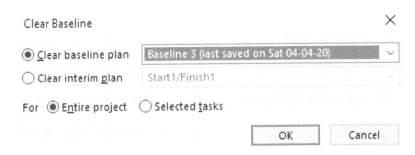

Figure 12.19 – Clear (delete) Baseline dialog box

In this dialog box, you can clear both baselines and interim plans equally well. Exercise caution as it will not be possible to undo this action and you will lose the baselined data permanently.

And with that, we have come to the end of this chapter. With 11 baseline slots, 10 interim plan slots, and a flexible architecture, we can conclude this chapter with the understanding that Project's baselining feature is robust and sufficient for all projects.

Summary

Baselines form the bedrock for tracking the execution of a project. They also form the foundation for monitoring and controlling projects. In this chapter, we have comprehensively learned how to work with baselines within Project by going through a hands-on exercise. Do not miss the opportunity to set baselines even for simple projects.

However, it is possible to overwrite or delete baselines easily. A good understanding of the implementation logic will go a long way in helping you maintain baselines for your project. We also discussed the best practices that are suited for Project.

In the next chapter, we'll learn how to track project execution progress within Project.

13
Project Tracking Techniques

"No plan survives contact with the enemy."

This is a quote of military origins, often used in project management. It eloquently highlights the fact that actual execution often deviates from the plan. This may be due to any number of real-life factors impacting the project. A project manager needs to know precisely where they stand on the schedule on any given day in order to combat this situation. Frequently tracking a schedule is what enables the project manager to know exactly where the project stands. With this critical information, the best remedial action can be deployed.

Remember that the first project baseline is only a prediction based upon the best estimates that are understood in the planning phase. Once the chaos of the execution phase begins, there will be unknown and unpredictable factors that impact your schedule, causing the actual schedule to deviate from the plan.

Project is stellar in terms of the numerous tools it provides to track a project. Moreover, there is great flexibility to customize the features to your schedule tracking techniques. In this chapter, we will navigate all the features systematically and understand their underlying logic. We'll start with the simplest and most commonly used techniques and progress to complex and more accurate techniques. As always, it is advised that you follow along with the hands-on project. You will learn to precisely track the current status of your project while adapting to your own ground situations by using a wide spectrum of tools, techniques, and best practices.

In this chapter, we are going to cover the following main topics:

- The importance of project tracking
- A project tracking flowchart applicable to the entire project and to individual update cycles
- Simple techniques of project tracking
- Advanced techniques of project tracking
- Best practices for project tracking
- Let's get started!

A deeper understanding of project tracking

There are some distinct advantages and functions when it comes to tracking a project, as follows:

- Tracking identifies existing issues within the schedule. These issues can then be resolved by making changes to the schedule, within the constraints of the project. Potential upcoming risks can also be identified so that mitigation can be planned.
- Tracking introduces realism into the schedule so that the future course of the project can be forecasted with greater reliability.
- Customers and other stakeholders require accurate project tracking information to make critical decisions. Scheduled data tracking is important to approve changes for the budget or scope.
- Alternatively, without tracking data, project stakeholders will be potentially blind to the progress of a project.

These are the key reasons why a project should be tracked and updated periodically. *How do we start tracking our own project?* We have to understand that Project distinguishes between three types of data that your schedule can contain, as follows:

- **Planned data**: This is contained in the baselines of your project. Baselines hold pertinent information about start and finish dates, durations, work, and the budget for the entire schedule. This data is considered to be unchanging compared to the other types of schedule data. If you have missed out on creating a **baseline**, then you will not have access to this critical comparative data. A comprehensive discussion of baselines was covered in *Chapter 12, Baselines – Techniques and Best Practices*.

- **Scheduled data**: This is contained in the current state of your schedule and can be ever-changing. As the story of your project execution unfolds, it should be tracked back into your schedule using the techniques discussed in this chapter. As a result, Project's algorithms will forecast the future of your schedule.

- **Actual data**: When did a task actually start? How much work was actually expended? This and all other such data that tracks the reality that has occurred in your project schedule is captured within this kind of actual data. Project will use this data for both completed tasks and in-progress tasks.

In the rest of this chapter, all our discussions will be based upon these types of information. Correspondingly, within Project, data fields will be available within various interfaces so that you can record and present these types of information. Before we progress further with the actual project tracking techniques, we will become familiar with some other important tracking aspects.

Considerations for project tracking

MS Project presents many techniques you can use to track your project. You must choose the tracking technique employed within your schedule, based on the following considerations:

- **The cost of tracking**: Tracking involves extra time and effort. This applies to every working member of the team, including the project manager. Time spent tracking should otherwise be utilized actually completing project tasks.

- **Accuracy of tracking**: Task progress estimations are precise only when they haven't been started yet (0% completion) or when they've been finished (100% completion). At any other point in the task's progress, the tracking accuracy will only be a best estimate. In some business domains, task completion can be better estimated than others.

- **Team data collation format**: The progress of a task can be communicated in a number of ways. One team member might say *The task is 90% complete*, while another might say *I need just 2 more days to complete the task*. If you have a 100-member team and each person communicates progress information in a different format, you will have a serious challenge on your hands. You will need a standard format to collect task information that's applicable to all tasks and resources. However, Project allows great flexibility in the techniques you can use to collect data from the team in a consistent fashion.

- **Task update versus assignment update**: This aspect is included here only for the sake of completeness. You can update *task* progress or update *assignment* progress. But assignment updates require a lot of overhead in terms of time and complexity. It is almost never recommended within standalone Project. We will explore assignment updates briefly toward the end of this chapter. Otherwise, every technique discussed in this chapter only pertains to task updates.

- **Update frequency**: Due to the cost involved with tracking a project, you will only want to track the project just before you send a report to the customer. Most projects follow a reporting cycle ranging anywhere between a minimum of 1 week to a maximum of 1 month.

Going further with this discussion, all the tasks that you track on the project will belong to one of the following categories:

- Completed tasks that were executed as scheduled

- Completed tasks that started early or finished late (or both)

- In-progress tasks that are being executed as scheduled

- In-progress tasks that started earlier than scheduled

- In-progress tasks that are running behind schedule

- Tasks that should have started but haven't been yet

Tasks that are scheduled to start later are not taken into consideration for the current tracking and reporting cycle. With this background understanding, we are now ready to see the entire tracking flowchart for a project.

Project tracking flowchart

A complete flowchart for the project tracking process is depicted in the following flowchart. Setting the baseline is a foundational activity for project tracking. Subsequently, the project manager will establish the tracking frequency and data collection format. Once within the execution phase, every project update thereafter is cyclic:

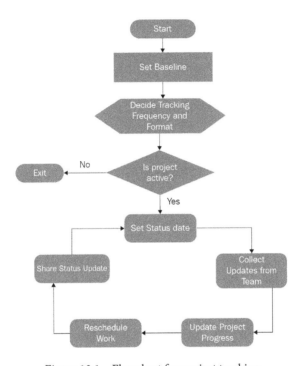

Figure 13.1 – Flowchart for project tracking

There are a few important points to be noted about the steps in this flowchart, as follows:

1. The first step of project tracking is to set the status date. Your project schedule will be updated until this date. This is explained further in the next section.

2. The next step is to gather task information for **completed** tasks and **in-progress** tasks from your team.

3. Update the schedule with tracking information. This is the key topic of this chapter.

4. If your project is off the acceptable track limits, then you have to reschedule the tasks and take other remedial actions. This is the topic of discussion in the next part of this book.

5. The final step is to share the project's tracking status with all relevant stakeholders.

We will now proceed to explore a wide variety of techniques you can use to track and update your project.

Project for this chapter

We will continue with the same hands-on project from *Chapter 12, Baselines – Techniques and Best Practices*. It will have a baseline saved within it and we can continue from that point, without repeating all the steps we went through earlier. If you do not have this project readily available, you can recreate it easily by going back to *Chapter 12, Baselines – Techniques and Best Practices*. The following screenshot is for reference:

Figure 13.2 – Current state of this chapter's hands-on project

If your project does not have the same start date as in the running example, then your schedule will look a little different from what will be shown in the following examples. This will only be because of different week starting dates and intervening weekends. Use your hands-on experience from your project work so far to simulate this logic in the exercises that follow. This will help you in real-life tracking situations.

Relevance of the status date

There will often be a difference between the date you collect project information from your team and the date when you share your project report with the larger world. The former date, until your tracking information is accurate, is known as the *status date*. You can set the status date by going to the **Project** tab, then to the **Status** group, and clicking the **Status Date** button. Refer to the following screenshot:

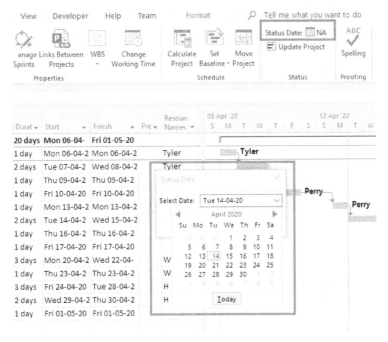

Figure 13.3 – Status Date dialog box

Before you track your project, it is imperative that you set the status date. This is important because this status date will be used in practically all of Project's tracking algorithms. If you forget to set the status date, then Project will default to the current date. In the case of small projects, such as in our case, it is perfectly fine to set the status date to the current date, as we have done so already. After you set the date, it will be displayed right on the menu bar, which is where it currently says **NA**.

> **Tip**
>
> By default, the status date line will not be visible on the Gantt chart. You can make it visible by setting a style and color for the status date line. To do this, go to the **Format** tab | **Format** group | **Gridlines** dropdown | **Gridlines** button | **Gridlines** dialog box | **Line to change: Status date**.

Simple techniques for project tracking

Project provides a wide array of methods you can use to track your project. You should choose a tracking method best suited for your project based upon the accuracy requirements of your project, time expendable on project updates, and complexities involved in both the project and updating techniques.

Percentage completion is an important concept to know about for the discussion that follows. It indicates how much of the task has been finished so far. We will use different techniques to tell Project the percentage completion of individual tasks. In other advanced situations, Project can algorithmically deduce percentage completion based on the other clues that we provide.

Let's suppose that you are handling a 10-person, 10-month, ten-million-dollar project with 200 tasks in your schedule. With a weekly status update cycle, you can normally expect between 20 to 40 updates to the schedule every week. Unless the update cycle is well planned and organized, it will be easy for the team to become overwhelmed by project tracking. In extreme cases, a team might end up spending 25% of their available time just on scheduled maintenance. It is important to keep this practical aspect in mind for the series of techniques we will begin to examine in the next section.

Context menu update technique

The simplest way to update individual task progress is to right-click on a task to bring up the contextual menu and mark the task as 100% complete. For now, we will only allow any task to be either at 0% or 100% complete. The advantage of this technique is that you can ask your team a fairly unambiguous question; that is, *Is the task complete or not?* Team members will only report back the tasks that are 100% complete. This is a useful strategy for Agile projects due to its simplicity. Refer to the following screenshot:

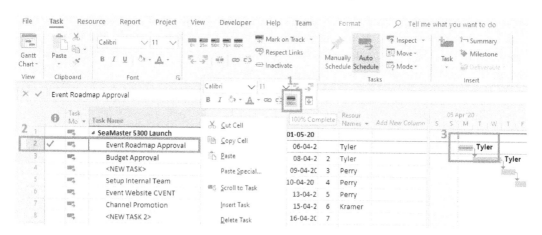

Figure 13.4 – Context Menu status update

There are a few important points to note from this screenshot:

1. The **100%** completion option is selected from the contextual menu.

2. Any task marked as 100% complete will get a prominent tick mark on the **Indicators** column.

3. Notice that the task bar in the **Gantt Chart** view now has a thin line running within it. This is to indicate the progress of the task. In the case of fully completed tasks, this line will run the full length of the task bar.

In this technique, we only allowed 100% completion of tasks, and completely ignored in-progress tasks. In practice, you can continue to update the whole schedule in this way. In the next section, we will allow for more a granular percentage completion of tasks.

Preset percentage complete technique

The next task, named **Budget Approval**, which has a 2-day duration, has been reported as 50% complete. There is an easy way to update such partial completion with a single button click within Project. Locate the preset percentage completion buttons on the **Task** tab | **Schedule** group. These preset buttons progress from 0% to 100% over increments of 25%. Select the task and click on the **50%** button to mark it as partially complete. Refer to the following screenshot:

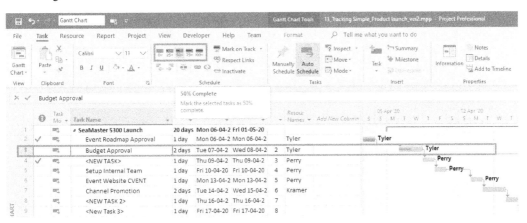

Figure 13.5 – Preset percentage completion options

There are some important points to note about this technique:

- Observe that the corresponding taskbar in the Gantt chart now has an inner line that only runs half the length of the taskbar, signifying 50% completion.

- Such estimations carry an implicit ambiguity. The percentage completion denoted by Project refers to the duration that was originally allocated. However, not all tasks can be meaningfully quantified as 25% complete or 50% complete. For example, what does it mean to have a budget approval that's 50% complete?

There is another inconsistency hidden within this technique. Note that since this task is only 50% complete, the remaining 50% is yet to be worked upon. This 50% is now scheduled to be executed *back in time*. You can confirm this with the current date line on the Gantt chart. In a later example, we will explore a technique we can use to resolve this inconsistency automatically.

The key advantage of this method is its relative ease of use, making this the most popular technique in actual practice.

The Mark on Track technique

Next up is a special feature known as **Mark on Track**, which allows you to quickly update tasks to their scheduled completion for the status date. Use this feature to update tasks that have followed the schedule *exactly as planned*. For example, if a task has completed 3 days out of the allowed 4 days, then it will be marked automatically at 75% completion. In the same vein, if the finish date of a task has elapsed, then the task will be marked as 100% complete. If a task has a start date in the future, it will remain unaffected at 0%.

The **Mark on Track** button can be accessed from the **Task** bar| **Schedule** group. Let's multi-select some tasks on line 4 and 5 and update them using the **Mark on Track** button. Refer to the following screenshot:

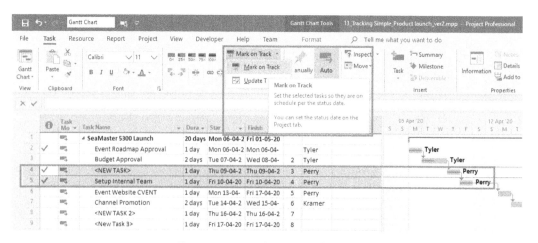

Figure 13.6 – Mark on Track feature

If your project is on track, then **Mark on Track** saves a lot of time. According to the scheduled dates on tasks, Project will autocalculate percentage completion from 0% to 100% automatically and update them. In the next section, we will see an extension of this logic with some added benefits.

Update Project technique

Imagine that, in the first update cycle, you had tracked several in-progress tasks to various stages of completion. In the next update cycle, if everything has been perfectly on track, then it is possible to automatically update all the tasks in progress instantly using the **Update Project** dialog box. This feature is located in the **Project** tab | **Status** group, as shown in the following screenshot:

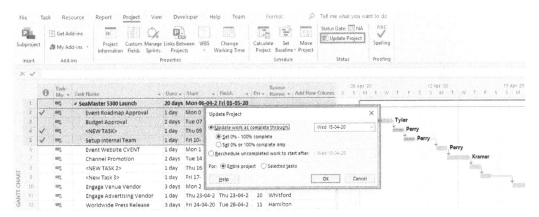

Figure 13.7 – Update Project feature

While it is possible to update the whole project quickly, there are two necessary conditions for its reliable usage:

- All the tasks to be updated should have obediently been on track with the scheduled dates.

- All the tasks should conform to the algorithmic percentage completion computed by Project.

Because of these conditions, this feature is more useful in small- to medium-sized projects with fewer accuracy requirements. On larger projects, use extreme diligence if you use this feature as the number of changes you make to the schedule can be overwhelming. In our running project, we will not apply this feature, and instead move ahead.

> **Pitfall**
>
> The **Update Project** dialog box has an advanced feature through which the entire project (or selected tasks) can be automatically rescheduled to a later date. Use this feature only if your project had halted completely for a few days, and now needs to be restarted again from a different starting date. Accidental usage of this feature can inadvertently impact a schedule in its entirety.

Advanced techniques for project tracking

So far, we have studied the simpler techniques of updating and tracking schedules, based only upon the estimated percentage completion of a task. They can be considered *simpler* because of the following practical reasons:

- Just using percentage completion for a task is almost never sufficient or realistic. For example, when a software developer says a task is 90% complete, it can mean that *they have used up 90% of the time allocated to the task*. Last week, if the developer reported 80% completion, then this week it has to be 90% complete. This can mean anything, and often does!

- So far, we have ignored what really happened with the execution details of the task. Was the task really started on time? Did some other task take up extra time and push all the other tasks on a team member's plate? Such incidents cannot be tracked.

So, now, the question is, *How can we track with factual information instead of potentially fictional information?* This is where **actuals** come into the picture. Team members can be asked for **Actual Start** dates, **Actual Duration** (worked on so far on a task), and **Remaining Duration** required to complete the task. These details can be acquired with or without the task's estimated percentage completion. In the following sections, we will discuss these advanced tracking techniques, but first, let's start with some advanced scheduling options that have to be specially enabled.

Advanced scheduling options

Hidden away within the **Project Options** dialog box, which you can access from the **File** tab, **Backstage** | **Options** button | **Project Options** dialog box | **Advanced** tab, are some special features that we will enable now. Refer to the following screenshot and replicate the information provided within your instance of Project:

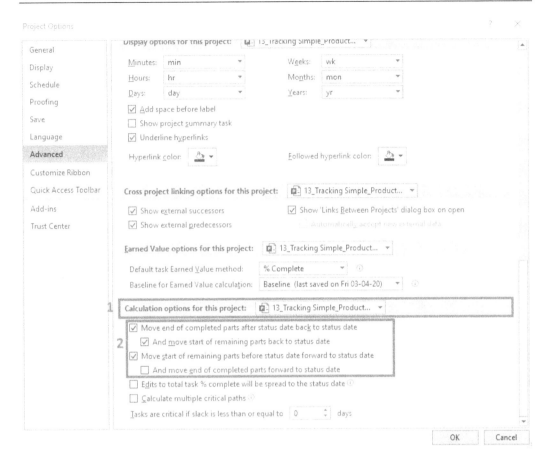

Figure 13.8 – Advanced scheduling options within the Project Options dialog box

There are a couple of important points to note about this screenshot:

1. These settings are applicable either to the *current project* or to *all new project files created*. Ensure that you make these changes only for the current project. The reason for this is that these settings will automatically adjust the schedule and it may not be what you want as the default behavior.

2. Enable the first three checkboxes, as shown in the preceding screenshot. They will be disabled by default. It is important to note that these options are only for tasks that are currently **in progress**. These settings will simply ignore tasks that you have updated in the past, or tasks that should have started but haven't been yet.

You are urged to read through the descriptive labels of these options as we will see them in action in the very next section.

Variable percentage complete technique

In this exercise, we will learn how to set a variable *percentage completion*. We will also see the effect of automatic schedule adjustment as a result of Project's advanced settings. For comparison, let's first start with the current state of our project, as shown in the following screenshot:

Figure 13.9 – Before applying advanced scheduling options

The task that we will update now is on line 6 and named **Event Website CVENT**. Double-click the task in the table to bring up the familiar **Task Information** dialog box. Against the simpler methods we had seen earlier, here, you can set the **Percent complete** variable. Refer to the following screenshot:

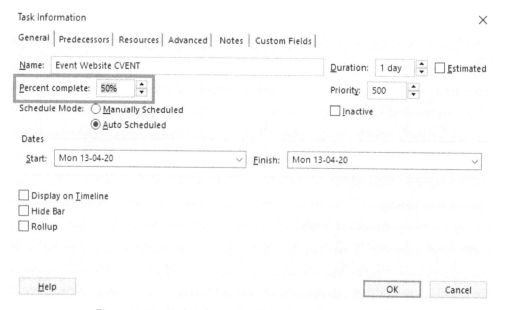

Figure 13.10 – Task Information dialog box – Percent complete

The effect of setting the task at 50% completion will have a radical impact on the schedule, as can be seen in the following screenshot:

	ⓘ	Task Mo ⌄	Task Name ⌄	Dura ⌄	Start ⌄	Finish ⌄	Pr ⌄	Resour Names ⌄
1		⏱	⊿ SeaMaster 5300 Launch	23.5 da	Mon 06-04-	Thu 07-05-2		
2	✓	⏱	Event Roadmap Approval	1 day	Mon 06-04-	Mon 06-04-2		Tyler
3		⏱	Budget Approval	2 days	Tue 07-04-2	Wed 08-04-	2	Tyler
4	✓	⏱	<NEW TASK>	1 day	Thu 09-04-2	Thu 09-04-2	3	Perry
5	✓	⏱	Setup Internal Team	1 day	Fri 10-04-20	Fri 10-04-20	4	Perry
6		⏱	Event Website CVENT	1 day	Mon 13-04-2	Fri 17-04-20	5	Perry
7		⏱	Channel Promotion	2 days	Fri 17-04-20	Tue 21-04-2	6	Kramer
8		⏱	<NEW TASK 2>	1 day	Tue 21-04-2	Wed 22-04-2	7	
9		⏱	<New Task 3>	1 day	Wed 22-04-2	Thu 23-04-2	8	
10		⏱	Engage Venue Vendor	3 days	Thu 23-04-2	Tue 28-04-2	9	Whitford
11		⏱	Engage Advertising Vendor	1 day	Tue 28-04-2	Wed 29-04-2	10	Whitford
12		⏱	Worldwide Press Release	3 days	Wed 29-04-2	Mon 04-05-2	11	Hamilton
13		⏱	Independent Media Release	2 days	Mon 04-05-2	Wed 06-05-2	12	Hamilton
14		⏱	Loopback to Product Database	1 day	Wed 06-05-2	Thu 07-05-2	13	Tabano

Figure 13.11 – After applying advanced scheduling options

There are several interesting points to note about the impact of updating our latest task to partial completion, detailed as follows:

- Note that the task we've updated (as 50% complete) has been split into two parts. The first part is completed, while the second part is yet to be worked upon.

- The incomplete part of the task has been pushed ahead of the status date. This makes perfect sense as the incomplete part could not have been worked upon on a backdate! This is a direct result of the **Move start of remaining parts before status date forward to status date** checkbox option that we set in the previous section.

- As a result of this task being pushed ahead, the whole schedule has been impacted. You can see that all the subsequent tasks on the table have been highlighted as a result of the change.

In the *Preset percentage complete technique* section, we set a task to 50% complete, but the impact was not as drastic. With the same advanced settings enabled, we will proceed with the next technique.

Percentage complete and remaining duration technique

In this technique, we will not only get the **percentage complete** from the team member, but also the time duration required to fully complete the task (that is, **remaining duration**). This is an effective technique if we wish to get a realistic estimate from the team.

For this exercise, we'll consider that the next task to be updated is on line 7, named **Channel Promotion**. This task was originally scheduled for a 2-day duration. But now, at the time of tracking the project, we find that this task has the following new aspects to be considered:

1. Task started ahead of time to recover from delays on the project

2. 70% of the task is completed

3. Another 2 days are required to complete the remaining parts of the task

From this, we can understand that our earlier planned estimations of this task were incorrect and that new task information has to be incorporated. To update this task, we will use a new interface called **Update Tasks**. This is available from the **Task** tab | **Schedule** group | **Mark on Track** dropdown | **Update Tasks**. Refer to the following screenshot:

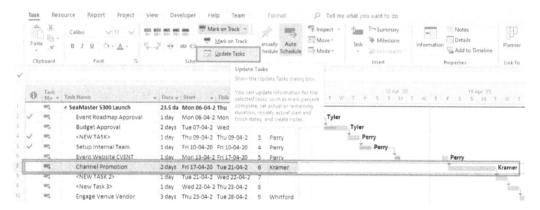

Figure 13.12 – Existing state of the task to be updated

The **Update Tasks** dialog box that opens up is the most powerful tracking tool that we have encountered so far. As can be seen in the following screenshot, a combination of data values can be used to automatically track the task:

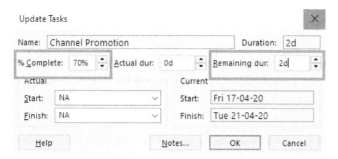

Figure 13.13 – Update Tasks dialog box

For this exercise, we will set the percentage completion to 70% and set remaining set the duration to 2 days. This much data is sufficient for Project to recalculate the duration and reschedule the task, as shown in the following screenshot:

#		Task Mo	Task Name	Dura	Start	Finish	Pre	Resour Names	05 Apr '20 S M T W T F S	12 Apr '20 S M T W T F S	19 Apr '20 S M T W
1			⊿ SeaMaster 5300 Launch	22.1 da	Mon 06-04-	Wed 06-05-					
2	✓		Event Roadmap Approval	1 day	Mon 06-04-2	Mon 06-04-2		Tyler	Tyler		
3			Budget Approval	2 days	Tue 07-04-2	Wed 08-04-2	2	Tyler	Tyler		
4	✓		<NEW TASK>	1 day	Thu 09-04-2	Thu 09-04-2	3	Perry	Perry		
5	✓		Setup Internal Team	1 day	Fri 10-04-20	Fri 10-04-20	4	Perry	Perry		
6			Event Website CVENT	1 day	Mon 13-04-2	Fri 17-04-20	5	Perry		Perry	
7			Channel Promotion	2 days	Wed 15-04-2	Mon 20-04-2	6	Kramer			Kramer
8			<NEW TASK 2>	1 day	Mon 20-04-2	Tue 21-04-2	7				
9			<New Task 3>	1 day	Tue 21-04-2	Wed 22-04-	8				
10			Engage Venue Vendor	3 days	Wed 22-04-2	Mon 27-04-2	9	Whitford			
11			Engage Advertising Vendor	1 day	Mon 27-04-2	Tue 28-04-2	10	Whitford			

Figure 13.14 – Task updated with percentage completion and remaining duration

Once again, in this case, the task has been split. This task was started ahead of its scheduled date, and the *completed* part of the task has been pulled behind the status date. This is a direct result of the **Move end of completed parts after status date back to status date** checkbox option, which we set in the previous section. Additionally, the *incomplete* part has also moved according to the **And move start of remaining parts back to status date** checkbox option.

In these last couple of exercises, we have seen the effects of Project's advanced scheduling options, coupled with different tracking techniques. Extreme diligence is required while using these advanced options since they can affect remote sections of the schedule, which will be very easy for a project manager to miss. For the upcoming exercises, we will proceed further after disabling the advanced scheduling options.

Actuals tracking technique

Before we proceed any further with the remaining tracking techniques, let's understand what is happening with our running project. New tasks were added in the previous chapter and tasks are running late in execution, as we have seen in this chapter. Both these factors have contributed to delays in our project. How do we quickly evaluate the current state of our project?

This is where our baselines will prove very handy. We can compare the current plan against the most recent baseline to get a rapid understanding of the situation. Refer to the following screenshot:

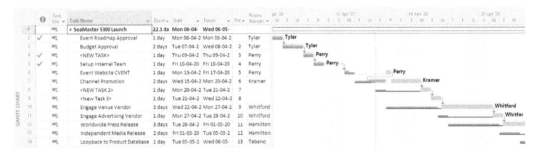

Figure 13.15 – Baseline comparison of the current project

To remedy this situation, we'll take some unconventional actions using our managerial influence. Assign the tasks on line 8 and 9 to emergency resources and get the tasks completed within the allocated duration of 1 day each. We will update the schedule with this information as our next exercise. We will use the *actuals* tracking method to do this.

The actuals tracking method uses zero fiction or estimation. Only the actual start dates, actual durations, and/or actual finish dates are used. The percentage completion calculated by Project will be as precise as possible. On the other hand, the tracking costs are much higher than normal since team members have to record all these parameters for every task.

Returning to our project, first, select the task on line 8 and, once again, open the **Update Tasks** dialog box from the **Task** tab | **Schedule** group | **Mark on Track** dropdown. Refer to the following screenshot:

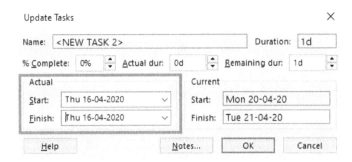

Figure 13.16 – Update Tasks dialog box

Since we know the actual start and finish of this completed task, we can directly enter it into the date fields available. After repeating the same process for the task on line 9, our project will have fully recovered. as can be observed in the following screenshot:

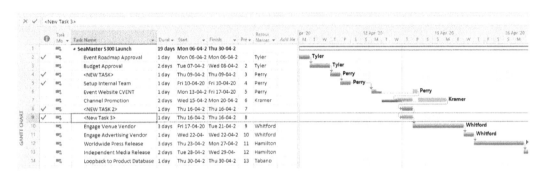

Figure 13.17 – Project update completed

Compared to the latest baseline plan, there is no variation in the project as a whole, and the tasks overlap the baseline on the Gantt chart. Sometimes, miracles happen on the project too!

There is more to come, and the best feature has been saved for last. Project provides the Swiss Army tool of tracking – the **Tracking Gantt Chart** view. We will examine this in the next section, now that we have seen all the other tracking techniques in good detail.

Using the Tracking Gantt Chart view

The **Tracking Gantt Chart** view is a special view that closely resembles our favorite normal **Gantt Chart** view, except that the first **Baseline** is included in the view. As can be seen in the following screenshot, this was the first baseline that was created when the project was started in *Chapter 12, Baselines – Techniques and Best Practices*:

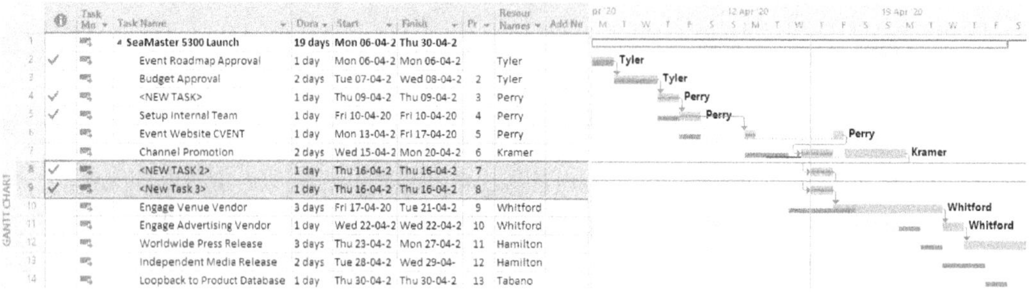

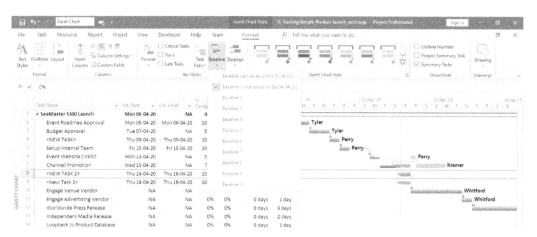

Figure 13.18 – Default Tracking Gantt Chart view

This is nothing special so far, until we change the current (**Entry**) table to the **Tracking** table. You can do that from the **View** tab | **Data** group | **Tables** drop-down button | select the **Tracking** table. Refer to the following screenshot:

Figure 13.19 – Tracking Gantt Chart view with Tracking table enabled

Notice that the latest baseline has now been brought into view just for completeness. As a reminder, this can be done from the **Format** tab | **Bar Styles** group | **Baseline** dropdown.

The specialty of this view configuration is that you now have access to all the tracking variables in a single table location, which can be dynamically updated using any of the techniques that we have learned about so far. For example, notice the **% Complete** column. If you enter 100% for a task, it will be immediately marked as completed.

Alternatively, you can choose to enter *percentage complete*, plus the *remaining duration*, and have Project compute the finish date. You can also mix and match your techniques for any task. However, it is highly recommended that you establish a single format of task data collation for the entire project and all resources. Feel free to experiment with this view for the remaining tasks in our project. In the next section, we will discuss yet another dimension of project tracking where we use *assignments* instead of *tasks*.

Assignment tracking

Remember that *tasks* logically become *assignments* when they are assigned to resources. That is, assignments are to be addressed from the resource's perspective. It is possible to track the project based upon assignments from the **Task Usage** view and the **Resource Usage** view. We have already encountered these views several times in the previous chapters.

However, assignment-based tracking is rarely used in practice due to a key drawback. It requires a high maintenance overhead of tracking every resource's daily work hours for the duration of the project. Such a system is only feasible with digital time tracking, which can be achieved with enterprise solutions such as Project Server. Due to this reason, we will not delve into this topic any further in this book.

With that, we will conclude our discussion of different tracking techniques available in Project. No matter what technique you apply within your own situations, there are some best practices of tracking that will greatly assist you. We'll discuss these in the next section.

Best practices for project tracking

Most teams view the project update cycle as extra work that doesn't directly contribute to the project's execution. It is up to the Project Manager to dispel this view. Here are some best practices to keep the update process as smooth as possible:

- Make the update cycle as painless as possible with cooperation from the entire team. A team meeting specifically for this purpose will go a long way in setting up project tracking success.

- Keep things simple. Choose the simplest tracking technique that your project can get by with in order to get realistic data and avoid fictional updates. *Percentage complete* and *remaining duration* should be the minimum data you collect.

- The project update cycle begins right from the very first week of execution. Every aspect of the update cycle, including the frequency of updates and the format, is to be trialed and fine-tuned before execution chaos ensues.

- If you have to share weekly update reports every Monday, ensure that you have finished collecting data from the team by the previous Friday. The intervening weekend can be a hidden buffer and will help collate stragglers' data.

- Use status meetings, Excel sheets, email, or any other medium to regularly collect tracking data.

- Be wary of a task that is perpetually *90% complete*. Most often, the update is fictional.

- Some projects track *work* instead of *duration*. In this case, the corresponding work fields, such as *actual work* and *remaining work,* are to be used. All the logic of this chapter will still hold. Project will use the basic work formula to calculate the actual duration and percentage completion as required.

- Not all metrics data is intended directly for the human eye, especially for large and complex projects! It is possible to export detailed schedule information for consumption by external systems. Specifically, in *Chapter 17, Project Reports 101*, we will discuss how intricate schedule tracking information can be exported to **Online Analytical Processing** (**OLAP**)-capable applications such as Microsoft Visio and Excel.

The bottom line is that practice makes perfect. A couple of update cycles can be utilized to establish a rhythm for the team. And with that, we've completed our discussion of project tracking.

Summary

The project tracking activity is a manager's bread and butter, especially during the execution of a project. And Project really shines in this department by providing many tools and features to aid tracking. So many techniques can be overwhelming for a brand-new user of Project, but this doesn't have to be the case. You can stick with the very simplest of techniques for a project or two, and only go to more advanced techniques as and when the situation demands it. This would be the best approach until you get a good grasp of the dynamics of tracking.

With this chapter, we have come to the end of this part of this book. In the next chapter, we start looking at the monitoring and control aspects of project management, as facilitated by Project. The concepts, techniques, tools, tips, and pitfalls we'll learn about in the upcoming part of this book will not be limited to any single phase of a project; they can generally be applied throughout the project, and will greatly enhance your confidence and skill with Project.

Section 5:
Monitoring and Control with Microsoft Project

While the project is in progress, the project manager will use Microsoft Project to monitor and control all the moving parameters of the project.

This section comprises the following chapters:

- *Chapter 14, Views, Tables, and Customization*
- *Chapter 15, Resource and Cost Management*
- *Chapter 16, Critical Path Monitoring and Advanced Techniques*
- *Chapter 17, Project Reports 101*

14
Views, Tables, and Customization

Welcome to this new part of the book, where we will focus on the **Monitoring** and **Control** process groups of project management. The topics we discuss going forward will be of a progressively advanced nature. **Monitoring** involves the mining of schedule data to glean valuable information. **Controlling** involves the analysis of trends and performance data to bring about improvements and appraise alternative plans. In this context, tables and views in Project provide a large spectrum of features and tools designed specifically to help you monitor and control your project from start to finish.

On an everyday basis, the project manager needs to disseminate project information to the stakeholders of a project. For example, every team member will want to know their critical-task responsibilities. The testing team wants to know what the big tasks are that are executed toward the end of the project. The integration team wants to know the active tasks this week and the tasks that are going to be completed next week. You want to know the tasks that have slipped and the tasks you can recover. All of this information can be extracted from a (well-maintained) schedule using the features provided within views in Project.

In this chapter, we are going to cover the following main topics:

- Gaining an advanced understanding of the internals of views
- Understand which views to use and when
- Deciphering tables and split-window views
- Sorting, filtering, and group data, with the help of several practical exercises
- Creating your own views using two techniques

Gaining an advanced understanding of views

Views are the principal user interface of Microsoft Project. Beginning in *Chapter 2, Fundamentals of Microsoft Project*, we have already explored more than 10 views in the book so far: Gantt Chart, Resource Sheet, Resource Usage, Task Usage, Team Planner, Timeline, Tracking Gantt, Task Board, Sprint Planning Sheet, Current Sprint Board, and Multiple Baselines Gantt, among others.

You will be aware that views provide a subset of the information contained in the project schedule. In this chapter, we will forge ahead to an advanced understanding of views. We take a top-down approach, beginning from the components of a view. Then we will move on to a classification of views followed by the innards of a view. Along the way, we will investigate powerful tools in Project to slice and dice schedule information. We will then finish the chapter by learning how to create our own custom views.

Types of view

All views can be classified under three major types, which are depicted as follows:

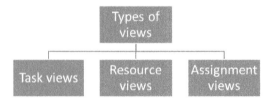

Figure 14.1 – Types of views

These three types of view are sufficient to present all available schedule data between them.

Views can be used to create, present, update, and delete data. In the next section, we will learn how views present data to the user.

Display formats used in views

Views present data to the outside world in several visual display formats. You can think of the display format as a particular visual style, applicable to the entire view. The following list describes the display formats that are used in a view:

- **Gantt Chart format**: This is, of course, the most popular display format, and it includes a table dynamically connected to a bar chart. Most views are based upon this format. Refer to the following representative screenshot for a comparison with other display formats:

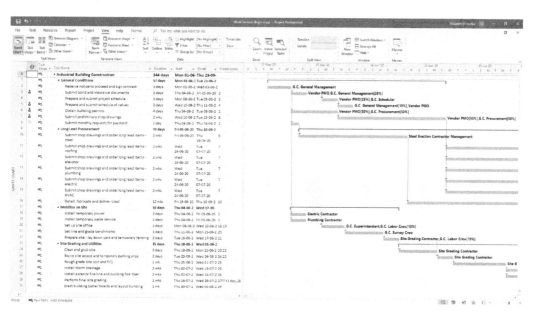

Figure 14.2 – Generic Gantt display format

- **Sheet format**: Views based on this format are composed entirely of a table area. The behavior of this table is similar to that of a spreadsheet. Such views are used to present information about tasks and resources and not assignments (as assignments will require additional time-phased or timeline-mapped information). Charts and diagrams are not a part of this view, as shown in the following screenshot:

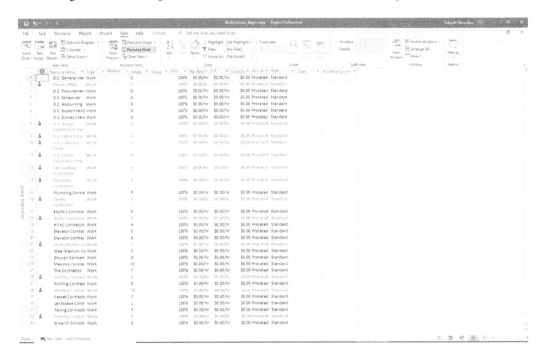

Figure 14.3 – Generic Sheet display format

- **Task Board (Kanban) format**: This design is the latest addition to Project's display format offerings. Such views are used in Agile-based project management. In this format, tasks can be dragged and dropped into configurable swim lanes. Refer to the following screenshot:

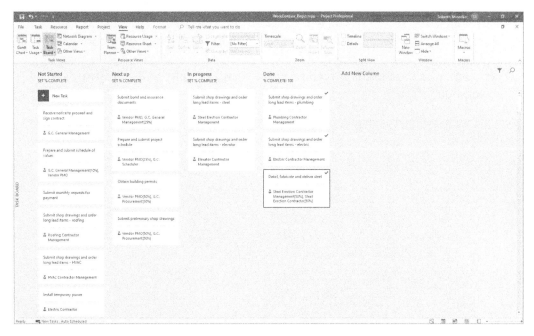

Figure 14.4 – Generic Task Board display format

- **Usage format**: This display format is used for assignment views, allowing both task and resource data analysis. The special feature of this format is the time-phased data shown on the right-hand side of the view. Refer to the following screenshot:

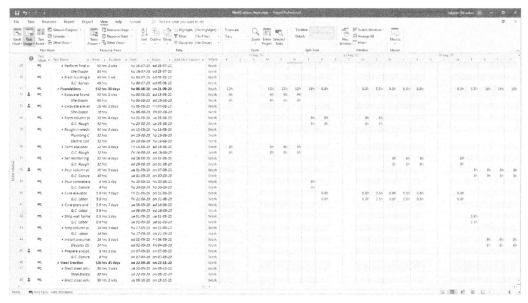

Figure 14.5 – Generic Usage display format

- **Form format**: Sometimes, you will want to work with peripheral data that is associated with a specific task or resource. Form display format views allow you to dynamically load peripheral data into additional forms. This format is always activated from the **Details** checkbox on the **View** tab. Refer to the following screenshot:

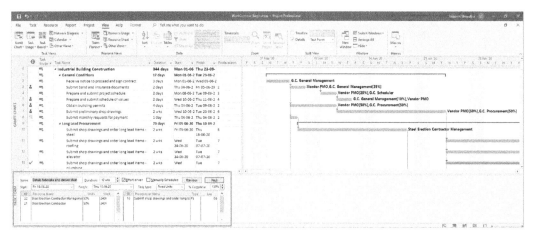

Figure 14.6 – Generic Form display format

- **Network Diagram format**: Views based on this format are entirely composed of a chart area. There are no tables in this view, as shown in the following screenshot:

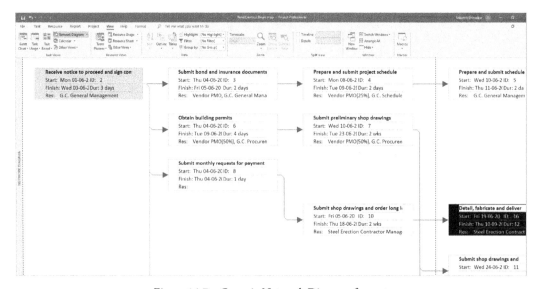

Figure 14.7 – Generic Network Diagram format

There are other one-off display formats, such as the **Graph** display format. **Calendar** view and **Timeline** view are examples of this display format. The workings of such formats are self-evident from their names, and we will not discuss them further. In the next section, we will learn which view is to be used in any given project situation.

> **Tip**
> The Gantt Chart is the default view every time you open Project. But this can be easily changed to any view of your choice by going to the **File** | **Options** | **General** tab | **Default view** dropdown. For example, you might change to a Task Board view in Agile-based projects.

Understanding which view to use and when

New users of Project are often overwhelmed and at a loss to decide which view is used when. This is because there are a lot of views available at your fingertips. You can follow a simple two-step process that you can use in any situation to always choose the perfect view:

1. Identify the entity that you want to work with—tasks, resources, or assignments.

2. The second step is to identify the suitable display formats that we discussed in the preceding *Display formats used in views* section.

With these two steps, you can work with a precise view that is catered to your specific needs.

Consider an example. Let's suppose that there is a problem with your project execution phase. Some of your team members are unhappy with the amount of work assigned to them. They complain of overwork. Meanwhile, a few others can handle more work. *Which view do we use to analyze this situation?* In this problem statement, the key words are *team members* and *work assigned*. Using the two-step process, we can easily identify what view we need:

3. As in the first step, you identify that the entity you want to view is **resources** (that is, team members).

4. In the second step, you identify the **usage** (that is, work assigned) display format. The perfect view for this format is the **Resource Usage** view. Using this view, you can pinpoint how much work is assigned to each resource on your project, and you can fine-tune the resource assignment accordingly.

To solidify this understanding and to provide a ready reference, we will now categorize all the major views *by utility* in the next sections.

Views to manage task data

You can manage task data by utilizing views of several different display formats. Most of the views in Project are related to task data. A few of the popular views that manage task data are detailed as follows, excluding the Gantt Chart view, which you already know well:

- **Other Gantt Chart views**: The common theme of these views is a dynamically coupled task listing on the left, accompanied by a bar chart on the right. The *Tracking Gantt* view and *Multiple Baselines Gantt* view are examples that we have seen earlier in this book. The *Leveling Gantt* view is another important example, which has advanced schedule analysis fields enabled. All of these views use the aptly named *Gantt Chart* display format.

- **Task Details form**: This is a split-window view that is used to manage tasks one at a time. Assigned resources and predecessor–successor relationships can be analyzed with such views, which are based upon the form display format. Other related views include the *Task Form* view and *Task Name Form* view.

- **Network Diagram view**: A rigorous analysis of the *schedule* can be performed by viewing it as a *flowchart*. This is a scientific technique that is classified as a network-analysis discipline. The Network Diagram view is designed specifically for this purpose. And no points for guessing that it uses the *Network Diagram* display format. There are some other views that are built for the same purpose, and they include the *Descriptive Network Diagram* view and the *Relationship Diagram* view.

After this, we move on to understand how resource data is managed in a view.

Views to manage resource data

Similar to task data views, Project also provides views designed specifically for resources. These are also available in different display formats. The most popular resource data views are detailed as follows:

- **Resource Sheet view**: This important view is the starting point to manage resources in your project. It is based on the sheet display format, as the name suggests, and it has no graphical component to the View.

- **Resource Graph view**: Here, resource information is displayed in a column graph. This view is especially useful for locating and debugging overallocation issues from a resource perspective.

Next, we move on to understand how assignment data is managed in a view.

Views to manage assignment data

The usage display format is designed specifically to manage assignment data. Remember that assignments are created when a resource is assigned to a task. There are two main perspective views (task and resource) to analyze assignment information, described as follows:

- **Task Usage view**: Assignments are listed, sorted by task. Work is displayed in a timesheet format on the right of the view.

- **Resource Usage view**: Assignments are listed, sorted by resource. Work is displayed in a timesheet format on the right of the view.

So far, we have learned about the high-level classification of views, based upon their data and utility. We looked at some heuristics that can be used to decide which views should be used when. In the next section, we will learn how to apply the advanced features of views in practical applications.

Advanced features of views

Every view in Project is constructed from four primary components, as depicted in the following diagram:

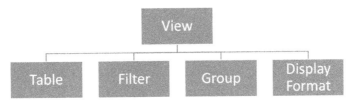

Figure 14.8 – Components of a view

It is important for us to understand the innards of a view if we are to derive the maximum benefit from the advanced concepts and features that we will learn about next.

Understanding tables

All views of Project are loaded with a default table, which is visible most of the time but is occasionally hidden. About 30 tables are prebuilt within Project. What many users of Project do not realize is that tables have a life even outside the boundary of a view, as we will shortly see in this section. But first, let's learn about some fundamental concepts of tables.

The most commonly used tables can be accessed from the **View** tab by clicking on the **Tables** drop-down button, as shown in the following screenshot:

Figure 14.9 – The popular tables of Project

There are a couple of further points to note about this screenshot, as follows:

- The **TASK USAGE** view is currently activated, as you can see on the left side of the screenshot.

- The table that loads by default is the **Usage** table. You can see that this table name has a check mark in the dropdown, indicating that it is currently being loaded on screen.

It is possible to change the active table of any view just by selecting an alternative table from the same dropdown that was shown in the preceding screenshot. Another way to change tables is to first click the **More Tables** link in the same dropdown. This will enable you to see every prebuilt table in Project, as shown in the following screenshot:

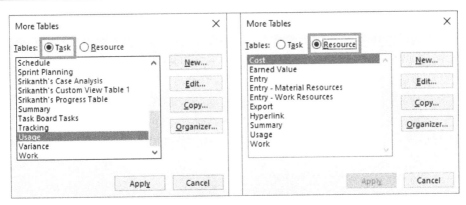

Figure 14.10 – The More Tables dialog box

The following are some important points to note about this screenshot:

- Note that tables are categorized under **Task** and **Resource**.

- You can select almost any table from these listings to change the default perspective of your view. If a table is inappropriate for the current view, the **Apply** button is grayed out, as you can see in the screenshot on the right, for the (**Resource**) **Cost** table.

For an example of changing tables, we will select the **Variance** table, as shown in the following screenshot:

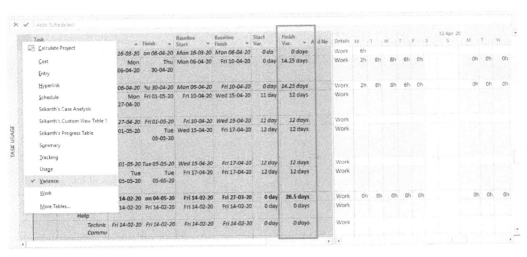

Figure 14.11 – Variance table loaded in the TASK USAGE view

This particular configuration of the view is especially useful to disseminate performance information, both from a task and resource perspective. For example, in the preceding screenshot, the **Finish Variance** column shows delays on all tasks, grouped by individual resources!

There is another important point to note about the behavior of tables. *If you modify a table within a particular view, it may impact other views too!* This is because a table exists as an entity outside the purview of any view. Let's see this in action with a simple exercise. Refer to the following screenshot:

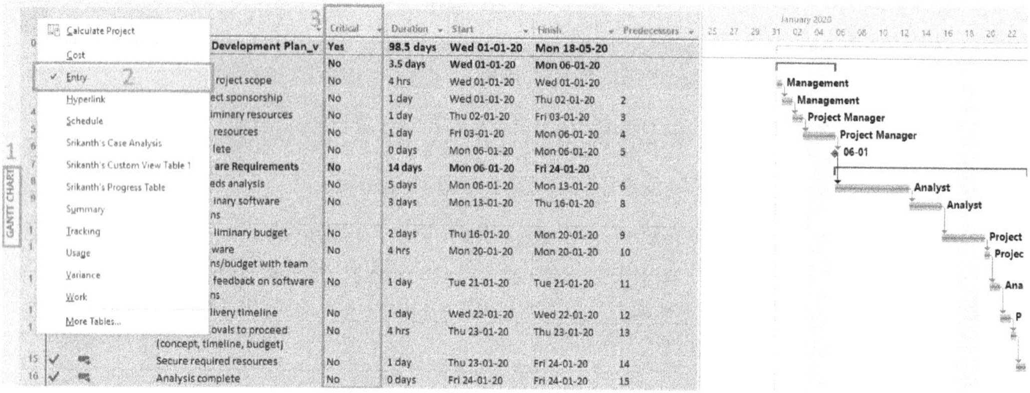

Figure 14.12 – New column added to the Gantt Chart view

There are three initial points to note about this exercise, as labeled in the screenshot:

1. The classic **GANTT CHART** view is active.

2. Correspondingly, the **Entry** table is loaded by default.

3. The view has been modified by adding a prebuilt column named **Critical** to the table.

Now, if we load the **TRACKING GANTT** view, would you expect the **Critical** column to show up there, too? Note that the **Critical** field is not visible in the **TRACKING GANTT** view by default. Refer to the following screenshot to see the resulting situation:

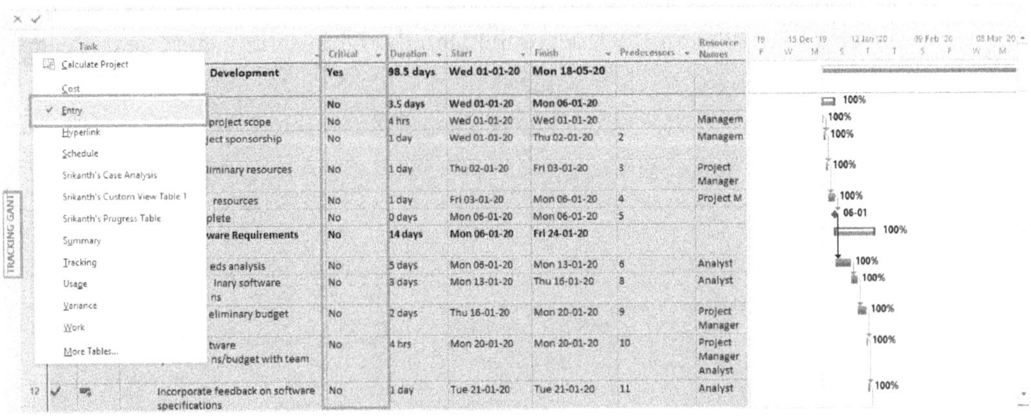

Figure 14.13 – The same new column appears in the Tracking Gantt view

As you can see in the screenshot, the newly included **Critical** column appears in the **TRACKING GANTT** view too. If you add, delete, or modify a column, other views will be impacted. Imagine that you are in a client status meeting, walking through a plan, and some internal variance information is unwittingly flashed on the screen! This behavior can startle users of Project, until we note that the two views, **GANTT CHART** and **TRACKING GANTT**, both use the same table—**Entry**. Simply put, modifications are carried from view to view when they share the same table.

Using these techniques, we can see the big picture presented by the view, using different perspectives. In the next section, we explore how to drill down into individual details of any specific task (or resource or assignment), *while retaining* the big picture presented in the view.

Details view (also known as the split-window view)

Project provides a powerful feature that allows a specific row in a table to be inspected in minute detail. This feature is called the **Details view**. Let's see this feature in action and learn about the various ways in which it can be used. The **Details view** can be enabled by going to the ribbon's **View** tab | **Split View** group | **Details** checkbox and clicking it. Refer to the following screenshot:

Figure 14.14 – Details view with Task Form enabled

There are a couple of interesting points to note:

- A split window appears in the bottom half of the working screen. A form-based display format is populated and the default view that loads is called the **TASK FORM**.

- The **Details** checkbox has an associated drop-down list, and it has been expanded in our screenshot. You can see that literally any view can be loaded in the split window below, but the special focus for split windows is the form-based views (such as the currently loaded **Task Form** view).

Form-based split-window views are useful for *cause-and-effect* analysis. For example, you can experimentally load different configurations for every parameter of the task and study its implications. But we are not limited to only the options shown here. There are other panels for you to choose, as shown in the following screenshot:

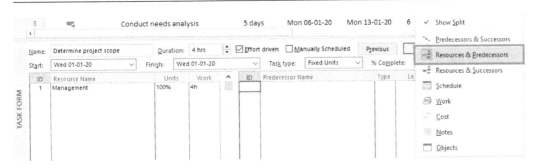

Figure 14.15 – Task Form panel options

In the current configuration of the **Task Form**, the **Resources & Predecessors** panel is selected. But any other configuration suitable for your analysis can be loaded, such as **Resources & Successors**.

Task Forms are not the only way to use split windows. You can load any other view of your choice to form powerful analysis view configurations. As an exercise, we will now see such a configuration. Refer to the following screenshot:

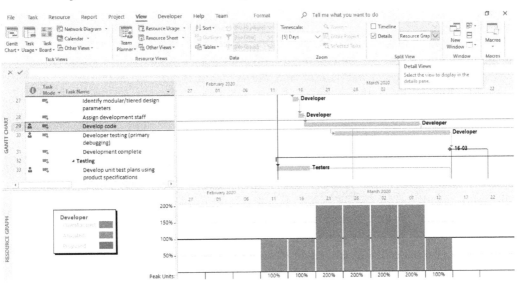

Figure 14.16 – Gantt Chart split window with Resource Graph

The preceding screenshot shows a configuration where the **GANTT CHART** view is used in a split window with the **RESOURCE GRAPH** view. The latter view, as you can deduce, is a view that does not incorporate a table and uses the graph display format. In this screenshot, overallocations are being analyzed, and you can see the precise point at which two overlapped tasks are causing an overallocation for a developer resource.

> **Tip**
>
> The fastest way to close a split window (and return to the full window view), is to double-click the boundary line between the two views. This technique works for both the **Timeline** view and **Details** split windows.

Remember that the split window on the bottom never controls the data! The upper main window always shows the big picture view, and the split window is for a drilldown. So, when you are designing a split window, make sure that the views are loaded in the correct location.

The primary functionality of the **Details** view is to drill down into schedule data, while retaining the big picture view on screen. But as we just saw in the last exercise, this same configuration can be conveniently used to load different views simultaneously (of different entities, such as task and resource), for a multidimensional analysis. We will now move on to even more data analysis features, such as the sorting, filtering, and grouping of schedule data, in the upcoming sections with practical applications.

Sorting of schedule data

One of the key activities *performed as part of the Monitoring and Controlling process group* is to analyze the schedule for improvements and evaluating different alternatives. We will now look at some exercises that demonstrate Project features for these activities.

You should identify tasks of the longest duration that finish toward the end of the project. Let's say that the testing team has asked you (the project manager) this question to better support the development team. This is our objective for the next exercise. Such tasks represent an inherent risk, and project managers like to identify such tasks to break them down further or add additional support to such tasks. Tables are prebuilt with sorting features into every column header, which we will explore for the first attempt at a solution.

Before we apply any sorting, it is always better to hide all Summary tasks in your table (you should hide the Summary task because they lose their contextual meaning when the sort order is changed). This can be done from the **Format** tab and in the **Show/Hide** group by unchecking the **Project Summary Task** and **Summary Tasks** checkboxes. Remember that hiding summary tasks has zero impact on the schedule. Refer to the following screenshot:

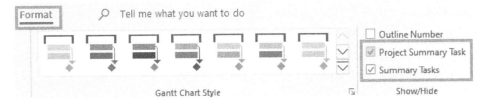

Figure 14.17 – Hiding Summary Tasks

We will now get a table without Summary tasks, but the task listing will still be indented as before. You should now notice that every column header of the table has a drop-down arrow. This is where the prebuilt table sorting options are available. Refer to the following screenshot, which shows the sorting options for several popular columns side by side:

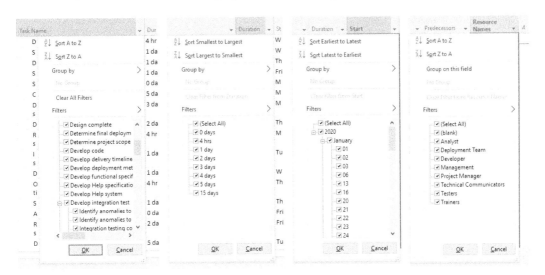

Figure 14.18 – Sorting options on different column headers of a table

There are the following important points to note about this screenshot:

1. The sorting option in each column header will vary according to the data presented by the column. There are *grouping* and *filtering* options here too, but we will ignore them for now and just focus on the *sorting* options.

2. The **Task Name** and **Resource Names** columns are essentially text fields, and so they present options for alphabetic sorting.

3. **Duration** is a numeric field, and sorting options are available from the smallest to the largest durations, and vice versa.

4. **Start** and **Finish** are date fields, and sorting options are available from the earliest to latest dates, and vice versa.

Returning to our exercise, the first part of our objective is to identify tasks of the longest duration. To achieve this, we will apply sorting in the **Duration** column and choose the **Sort Largest to Smallest** option. The resulting view is shown in the following screenshot:

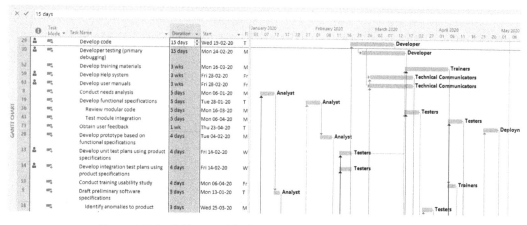

Figure 14.19 – Table sorted by Duration – Largest to Smallest tasks

In the screenshot, tasks have now been sorted by duration, with the largest tasks now appearing at the top of the table listing. There are another couple of important points to be observed:

- The Gantt Chart now resembles a bowl of spaghetti and is unusable in its present condition. This is fine for analysis purposes, and so we will ignore the Gantt portion of the view.

- Our objective has not been achieved yet because there is no way to easily identify the tasks *that finish toward the end of the project.*

At this stage, if you apply the second sort to the **Finish** column, then the first sorting is lost. So we need a method to apply more than one sorting order at the same time, and Project provides a nifty tool for just that. You can access it from the **View** tab by clicking **Data** group | **Sort** drop-down button | **Sort by** button. Refer to the following screenshot:

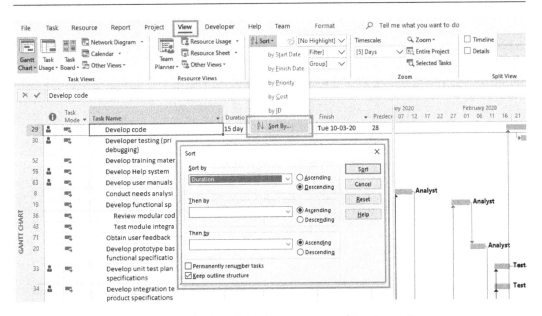

Figure 14.20 – The Sort dialog box presents multisorting options

The **Sort** dialog box presents an interface to apply a maximum of three simultaneous sorting orders, one by one. The structure is similar to constructing a SQL programming language query if you are familiar with database programming. You can first apply **Sort by** as your first field, **Then by** as the second field, and **Then by** again as the third field.

Note that the interface has properly identified that the table in question has already been sorted by the **Duration** field in **Descending** order. All we have to do now is to set the second sorting order. Refer to the screenshot for the final configuration of this interface:

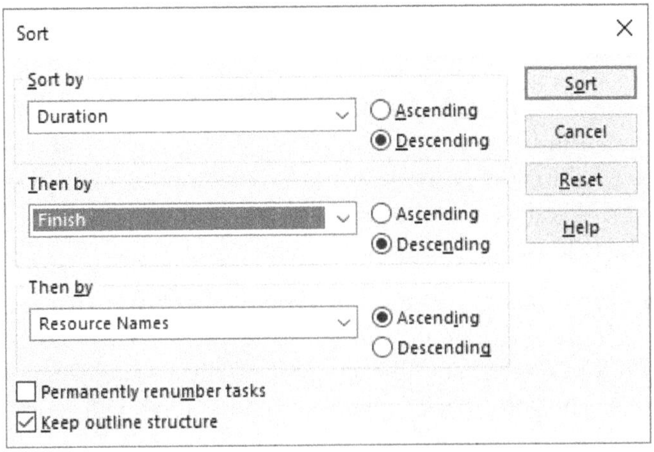

Figure 14.21 – Sorting configuration for the current exercise

The second sort order is set to **Finish** date in **Descending** order. Note that we have also set the third sort order (as an optional configuration) to **Resource Names**. This will additionally sort the result by resource, to our benefit. The final result of applying this full configuration is presented in the following screenshot:

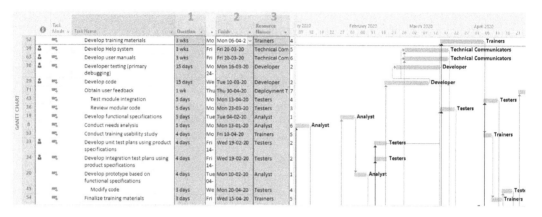

Figure 14.22 – Final sorting to achieve the exercise objective

Note that the final sort order is highlighted in the screenshot, in the column header. After such an analysis, you can optimize the schedule in several ways—say, by breaking the tasks into smaller and more manageable chunks. Or you might add other free resources to assist in the testing process. Overall, you can identify areas of the schedule where you have to be increasingly proactive. We will discuss several schedule-issue resolution techniques in *Chapter 16*, *Critical Path Monitoring and Advanced Techniques*.

This has been an example of how we can use Project's features to effect schedule improvements and evaluate alternatives.

There are a few other things that we should think about , such as the following:

- **How do we return to the normal, default view?** In any view, the default sorting is by field **ID**. Sometimes, you will be handed a view that has been sorted in a certain order, and you want to find the true sorting of the plan. Or you might have made a bunch of changes and want to get back to the normal view. In both cases, set the sort order to the field **ID**, in an **Ascending** direction.

- **What if I want to permanently alter the sequencing of my tasks according to my sort order?** In the **Sort** dialog box that we used in the previous exercise, as shown in *Figure 14.21*, enable the checkbox labeled **Permanently renumber tasks**. Be careful: there is no going back—all the tables and views will be affected.

Moving forward, we will inspect even more powerful features in the coming sections.

Filtering and highlighting information

Filters are another tool that is used in data analysis. The difference between sorting, filtering, and grouping is described in the following list:

- **Sorting** arranges all data according to a particular order—for example, *alphabetically*.

- **Filtering** hides (that is, *filters out*) unwanted data, and only returns data that you have asked for.

- **Grouping** categorizes all data according to certain criteria—for example, *active* or *inactive*.

We start by mentioning filters that are available in the column headers directly with an example of filtering tasks belonging to the **Deployment Team**.

A basic set of prebuilt filters are available directly in the table column header. For example, in the following screenshot, a prebuilt filter has been applied to the **Resource Names** column:

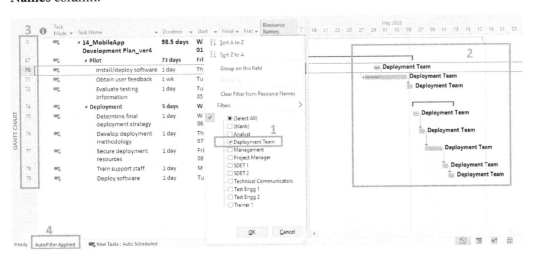

Figure 14.23 – Table column header filter applied for a specific resource

There are a few interesting points to note regarding this screenshot, as follows:

1. The filter has been applied to the schedule so that only tasks assigned to the **Deployment Team** are retained in the data. All other tasks are filtered out.

2. This is confirmed in the **GANTT CHART**, as you can only see tasks that have been assigned to the **Deployment Team**.

3. Note that the list of **ID** instances shows that many in the sequence are missing. If you are handed a view that looks like this, then this is the first clue that indicates that it has been prefiltered.

4. A message appears in the status bar alerting the user, labeled **AutoFilter Applied**.

Filters available in the table column headers are only the tip of the prebuilt-filter iceberg. In the following screenshot, you will see a list of the most commonly used prebuilt filters available by going to the **View** tab | **Data** group | **Filter** drop-down list:

Figure 14.24 – Prebuilt filters available from the dropdown in the View tab

A small treasure trove of prebuilt filters from the drop-down list can be instantly applied to your schedule, allowing you to cherry pick important data from your schedule. And this is not all it has to offer. Click on the **More Filters…** link to access approximately 60 more prebuilt filters. Refer to the following screenshot:

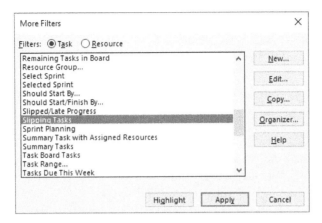

Figure 14.25 – More Filters dialog box

As the next simple exercise, we will apply a useful example of a prebuilt filter, called the **Slipping Tasks** filter. Slipping tasks in Project are defined as *those tasks that should have started, but have not started yet*. Additionally, their scheduled completion date has exceeded the baseline completion date. Such tasks are the ones that are currently delaying the project and should be identified during the **Monitoring** and **Controlling** processes. Refer to the following screenshot, where this prebuilt filter has been applied:

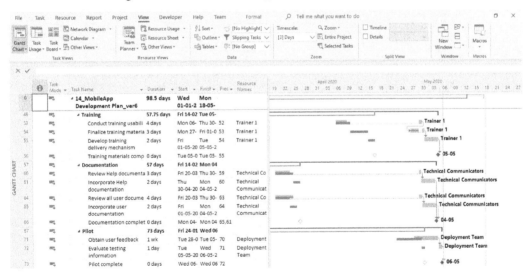

Figure 14.26 – Slipping tasks filter applied

In this screenshot, only the slipping tasks have been identified by Project. For verification, the **Baseline** is also shown in the **Gantt Chart** (from the **Format** tab | **Baseline** dropdown). It can be verified that the baseline finish dates for these tasks have been exceeded for their currently scheduled finish dates.

> **Important**
>
> If your schedule has not preserved the first baseline or has not been tracked periodically, then this filter will not return accurate results.

Project provides another feature called **Highlight** that is closely related to filters. This feature is available on the **View** Tab | **Data** group | **Highlight** dropdown, adjacent to **Filters**.

Using a filter returns only the tasks that we want; unwanted tasks are hidden by contrast, using a **Highlight** returns all tasks, but the wanted tasks are highlighted with a color and formatting of choice. Moreover, all the prebuilt *filters* within Project are also available for *highlights*. For example, refer to the following screenshot, where only the backlog tasks are highlighted:

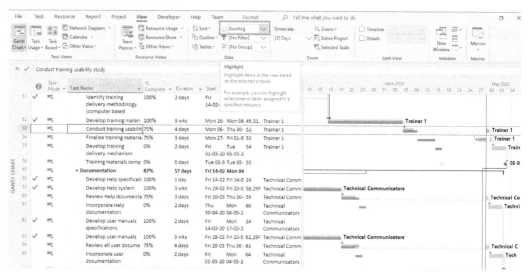

Figure 14.27 – Backlog tasks highlighted

Backlog tasks are those that are not yet complete. The **% Complete** column has been included in this view, just for a quick verification. For all other purposes, you can consider highlights as being very similar to filters, including the ability to create new highlights. After you are done experimenting, you can remove all highlighting by choosing the **[No Highlight]** option in the same **Highlight** dropdown. So far, we have studied sorting, filtering, and highlighting techniques; next, we move on to the grouping of tasks in Project.

Grouping project information

The **Group By** feature of Project is used for the categorization of schedule information. An additional advantage of this feature is that it additionally presents rolled-up summary information. We will see this in action in our next exercise.

As you might expect by now, the **Group By** feature, too, presents a large set of prebuilt criteria to be used, just like sorting and filtering. In the following screenshot, a popular prebuilt criterion called **Status** has been applied:

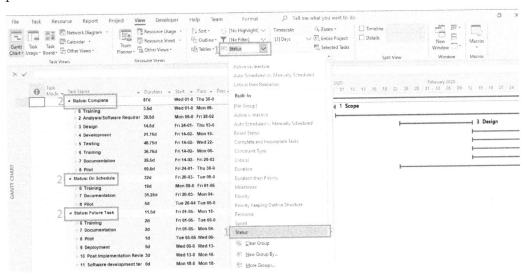

Figure 14.28 – Group by Status criterion applied

The points to note about this screenshot are as follows:

1. **The critical tasks? is a question Status** prebuilt criterion has been applied. The **More Groups…** link at the bottom of the dropdown will open a dialog box with more than 20 other prebuilt criteria options. You should be familiar with this dialog box interface by now.

2. **Task Name** has been grouped under the **Complete**, **On Schedule**, and **Future Task** categories. Other progress categories are not present in this particular sample project.

Let's consider one more example that you will relate to in your everyday project management. *Can every team member see their own critical tasks?* is a question that your team members will ask you during a team meeting. The solution to this query is a multilevel grouping that does not use an existing prebuilt criterion, so we will create our own **Group By** criteria for the next exercise.

Open the **Group Definition** dialog box by going to the ribbon's **View** tab | **Data** group | **Group By** dropdown | **New Group By** link. Refer to the following screenshot:

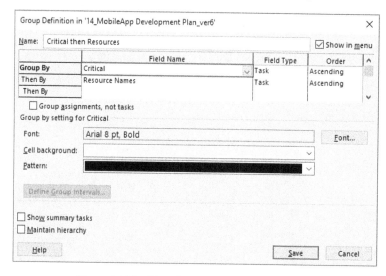

Figure 14.29 – New Group By criteria definition

The steps to create this new **Group By** criteria are as follows:

1. Start with the **Name** field and enter `Critical` then `Resources` Names or a suitable name of your choice to identify this criterion within Project.

2. We can apply a maximum of three separate criteria. In the first row's **Field Name** dropdown, select **Critical**. Similarly, set **Field Type** to **Task** and **Order** to **Ascending**.

3. Repeat for the second-row grouping: set **Field Name** to **Resource Names**, **Field Type** to **Task**, and **Order** to **Ascending**.

4. Optionally, you can customize the visual aspects for this new **Group By** criteria with new fonts and background colors.

The following screenshot shows the result of applying these newly designed criteria:

	Task Mode ▾	Task Name ▾	Duration ▾	Start ▾	Finis ▾	Prec ▾	Resource Names ▾
🛈		◢ Critical: No	89.75d	Wed 01-0	Tue 05-0		
		▷ Resource Names: No Value	86.25d	Mon 06-0	Tue 05-0		
		▷ Resource Names: Analyst	25d	Mon 06-0	Mon 10-		Analyst
		▷ Resource Names: Deployment Team	1d	Thu 30-04	Thu 30-0		Deployment Team
		▷ Resource Names: Management	31.5d	Wed 01-0	Thu 13-0		Management
		▷ Resource Names: Management,Project Manag	16d	Thu 23-01	Thu 13-0		Management,Proj
		▷ Resource Names: Project Manager	17d	Thu 02-01	Mon 27-		Project Manager
		▷ Resource Names: Project Manager,Analyst	0.5d	Mon 20-0	Mon 20-		Project Manager,
		▷ Resource Names: SDET 1	21.75d	Fri 14-02-	Mon 16-		SDET 1
		▷ Resource Names: SDET 2	15d	Wed 19-0	Tue 10-0		SDET 2
		▷ Resource Names: Technical Communicators	57d	Fri 14-02-	Mon 04-		Technical Commu
		▷ Resource Names: Test Engg 1	48.75d	Fri 14-02-	Wed 22-		Test Engg 1
		▷ Resource Names: Test Engg 2	4d	Fri 14-02-	Wed 19-		Test Engg 2
		▷ Resource Names: Trainer 1	57.75d	Fri 14-02-	Tue 05-0		Trainer 1
		◢ Critical: Yes	29.75d	Mon 06-0	Mon 18-		
		▷ Resource Names: No Value	8d	Wed 06-0	Mon 18-		
		◢ Resource Names: Deployment Team	11d	Tue 28-04	Wed 13-		Deployment Team
71	⬛	Obtain user feedback	1 wk	Tue 28-0	Tue 05-	70	Deployment Te
72	⬛	Evaluate testing information	1 day	Tue 05-0	Wed 06	71	Deployment Te
75	⬛	Determine final deployment strategy	1 day	Wed 06-	Thu 07-	73	Deployment Te
76	⬛	Develop deployment methodology	1 day	Thu 07-0	Fri 08-0	75	Deployment Te
77	⬛	Secure deployment resources	1 day	Fri 08-05	Mon 11	76	Deployment Te
78	⬛	Train support staff	1 day	Mon 11-	Tue 12-	77	Deployment Te
79	⬛	Deploy software	1 day	Tue 12-0	Wed 13	78	Deployment Te
		◢ Resource Names: Project Manager	3d	Wed 13-0	Mon 18-		Project Manager
82	⬛	Document lessons learned	1 day	Wed 13-	Thu 14-	80	Project Manager
83	⬛	Distribute to team members	1 day	Thu 14-0	Fri 15-0	82	Project Manager
84	⬛	Create software maintenance team	1 day	Fri 15-05	Mon 18	83	Project Manager
		◢ Resource Names: Trainer 1	18.25d	Mon 06-0	Thu 30-0		Trainer 1
53	⬛	Conduct training usability study	4 days	Mon 06-	Thu 30-	52	Trainer 1

Figure 14.30 – Critical by Resource with new Group By criteria applied

This is our solution, and now, with the help of this grouping that we just created, the project manager can quickly inform every resource of their critical-task responsibilities. Protecting the tasks on the critical path from slippage is the major concern of the **Monitoring** and **Control** processes.

> **Pitfall**
>
> Do not mistakenly assume that all tasks on the critical path will be grouped under the **Critical** category. Finished tasks are not considered critical by Project. The logic behind this reasoning is simple. If a task is 100% complete, then it can no longer impact the project finish dates, and so it is no longer critical to the schedule. You need only focus on the *in-progress* and *upcoming* tasks on the critical path.

At any point in time, to remove all applied grouping, apply the [**No Group**] criteria. With this discussion, we conclude our journey of sorting, filtering, highlighting, and grouping through project data, gleaning important information for the success of our projects. Next, we will explore techniques to create our own custom views.

Creating custom views

We have now come full circle with our discussion of Project views. We can apply everything that we have learned so far in this chapter to create new views that are perfectly suited for our own projects. Let's explore two techniques to create custom designed views. Remember that views are constructed from specific instances of tables, filters, groups, and display formats. So, a new view can be designed from the bottom up, designing each of the components that make up your new view. Refer to the following diagram:

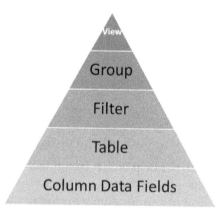

Figure 14.31 – A pyramid design showing the construction of a new view

It is best to build a view by starting from the bottom of the component pyramid and moving up, shaping our data as we reach the completion of our view.

In the next sections, we will create a new view from the solution achieved by our previous exercise.

Creating a new view from a current view

With this simple technique, you first modify an existing view to achieve the desired results. Then you save the onscreen configurations (of the *data fields*, *table*, *filter*, and *group*) into a new view. Refer to the following screenshot:

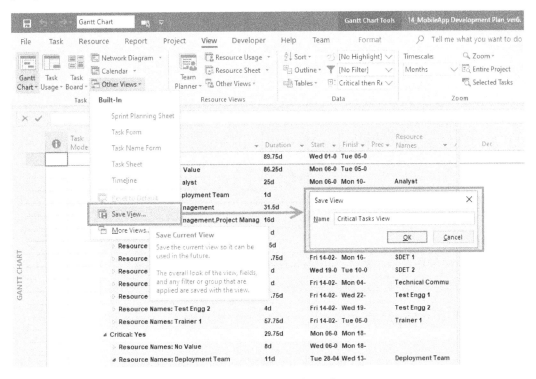

Figure 14.32 – Creating a new view from the current screen

The **Save View…** link is available from multiple locations all over the ribbon menu, wherever the view-choosing dropdowns are present. In our case, they are located under the **View** tab | **Task Views** group | **Other Views** drop-down button. The new view you create will behave exactly like all of the other prebuilt views of Project.

Creating a new view from scratch

A more robust technique of view creation involves creating new components of the view first. You design and save a new table, a new filter, and a new group, and then bring them all together into a new view. Any or all of these components can be reused from prebuilt entities shipped with Project. Refer to the following screenshot:

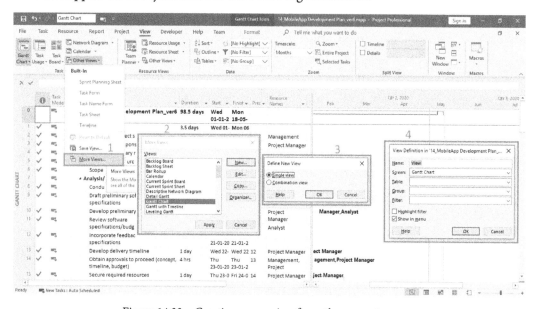

Figure 14.33 – Creating a new view from the current screen

The steps to create a new view from the **View Definition** dialog are described as follows:

1. Start from the **More Views…** link located under the **View** tab | **Task Views** group | **Other Views** drop-down button.

2. In the **More Views** dialog box, click the **New** button. This will open the **Define New View** dialog box.

3. Decide upfront whether your view will be a split-window view. For simplicity, we have chosen a single-window view format. You can configure the same for split-window views too.

4. In the following **View Definition** dialog box, you can individually select all the view components of your choice. You can proceed to further customize your views if you choose and save when you are done.

Any new view that you create will simply be categorized as a custom view by Project, and it will be available from all of the same locations in which you access your other workhorse views. With this discussion of creating custom views, we now conclude our full-circle discussion of Project views. We have applied everything that we have learned so far in this chapter to create custom views that are tailor-made for our own projects.

Summary

We have concluded our journey into the world of Project views and tables. We started this chapter with a deconstruction of existing views. Then, we explored every component in detail—tables, detailed split windows, filters, groups—to mine our schedule data for gems of information. Finally, everything we learned was brought together to create new custom views. With your own custom views, you do not have to spend hours massaging reams of data to find critical information for your project. This is crucial for projects whose schedules run into thousands of lines.

In the next chapter, we will take a similarly detailed journey into advanced resourcing concepts and tools within Project. We also discuss project-costing features that are built within Project. Resourcing and project costs are tightly coupled, and both topics are addressed from a monitoring and control perspective.

15
Resource and Cost Management

Projects have complex resourcing requirements. If there is no competition for a resource, then it is doesn't need to be managed; for example, the dedicated laptop of an employee need not be explicitly managed. All other resources are to be acquired at a suitable time on the schedule and released at project closure. For example, people, machinery, materials, and budgets have to be carefully orchestrated among competing project demands and need to be managed.

Resourcing is inextricably linked to cost since resources cost money. It is imperative for all competitive organizations to monitor and control project costs. You will encounter a wide variety of modality while costing resources. For example, some of your team members might be full-time employees, while others may be consultants. Some others may be part of a vendor team with different costing mechanisms. There may be fixed costs for some tasks and one-time licenses that need to be acquired.

Microsoft Project provides built-in features to accommodate a wide spectrum of resourcing and costing requirements for standalone projects. This chapter provides a deep exploration of Project's resourcing and costing techniques, which we'll discover through a new hands-on project. However, to manage resources and costs for multiple simultaneous projects at the enterprise level, you should be connected to a Project Server solution. You will learn how to precisely model the resourcing needs of your project and their associated costs by using a wide spectrum of tools, techniques, and best practices. You will also learn how to analyze project costing at different levels of granularity, starting from the project levels, while drilling down all the way to individual tasks and individual resources.

In this chapter, we are going to cover the following main topics:

- Different resource types and how to deploy them to our project
- A costing framework implemented in Project
- How to create a project budget in Project
- Learning about different costing techniques for different resource types
- Learning about different analysis techniques for the project plan
- Let's get started!

A deeper understanding of resources and costs

We have used basic resource concepts extensively in all the hands-on projects we've covered so far; that is, every time we assigned a task to a person. We also studied the fundamentals of resource management in *Chapter 5, Resource Management with Microsoft Project*.

In this chapter, we will learn about the advanced features of resource management within Project. Resourcing is tightly integrated with the costing abilities of Project. *Costing* can be calculated based on any financial terms used commonly in real-life situations. Some examples of this include a standardized rate of pay for full-time employees, one-time fees for services rendered, fixed costs for licenses, raw material costs, or even variable charges such as airfare ticket costs and hotel booking charges. These different costing techniques are mapped to the resource types classified within Project. Refer to the following screenshot:

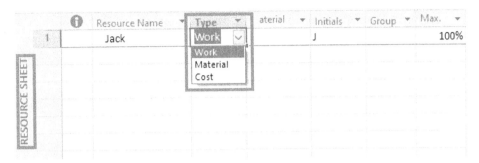

Figure 15.1 – Three types of resources within Project

Remember that the **RESOURCE SHEET** view, as shown in the preceding screenshot, is the central location for managing resources within Project.

Project classifies all resources under three fundamental types, as shown in the preceding screenshot – **Work** resources, **Material** resources, and **Cost** resources. Each of these resource types will be explained in the upcoming sections.

> **Pitfall**
>
> You cannot manage resources that are *shared* among multiple projects from within standalone versions of Project. This is an enterprise-level feature available only from the Microsoft Project Server family of products. Specifically, Project has a feature called **Build Team from Enterprise**, which allows access to a central database of organization-level shared resources. We will not discuss Project Server features in this book.

The Work resource type

Resources assigned to the project on the *basis of time* are called *work resources*. The people that are assigned to a project – that is, everyone on your project team – are *work resources* within Project. So far in this book, all the resources we've used in our hands-on projects have been work resources. Similarly, any other resource that is competing for temporal usage among more than one project is also to be considered as a work resource. Some examples in the construction industry include heavy machinery such as excavators and tunnel-boring machines. Time-shared supercomputers are also work resources.

It is recommended that you follow along and get hands-on to understand these concepts better.

Fire up Project and start with a blank project file. We will combine the exercises that follow into a hands-on project later on. Refer to the following screenshot to create three new **Work** resources within the **RESOURCE SHEET** view:

Figure 15.2 – Three Work resources created

The following are a few important points to be noted about this screenshot:

- By default, every resource you create will begin its life as a **Work** resource in the **Type** column. This is perfectly fine for the current exercise. If you want a different resource type, you will have to manually change the resource type, *post facto*.

- Ignore the column labelled **Material** for now, as it is not relevant to Work resources.

- The **Initials** column is an optional label that can be used as an abbreviation of the resource name. This is best used to declutter views from long resource names on task bars.

- The **Group** column is also an optional label, best used as a view filter for analysis. The first two resources we've created are categorized into the **Tech** group, while the third resource is categorized into the **Consultant** group.

- The **Max.** column actually stands for **Maximum Units**, expressed as a percentage. This denotes the number of units of a specific resource made available to the project. This field refers to the same **Units** parameter in **Basic Work Formula**, which we discussed extensively in *Chapter 4, Underlying Concepts of Microsoft Project*. Remember that **100%** in this column means 1 unit of assigned work in a day, which is defaulted to 8 hours. In the same vein, 50% implies 4 hours/day, while 200% implies 16 hours worked in a 24-hour day.

- The **Base** column implies the base calendar that's been applied to the specific resource. This is also the location for you to set the resource calendar.

We will learn about the other columns, such as **Std. Rate**, **Accrue**, and others, a little later in this chapter. For now, let's proceed and create new resources of the *Material resource*.

The Material resource type

Resources that are *consumed* by your project during execution are known as *Material resources*. **Material** resources are assigned to the project on the *basis of quantity*. For example, in a civil construction project, the **Material** resources would be cement, bricks, stone, steel, and so on. The logic is that these materials will be consumed by your project and the same material will not be available for your next project. This is in contrast to work resources, which will be available for another project too. Continuing with our exercise, create two **Material** resources, as shown in the following screenshot:

	Resource Name	Type	Material	Initials	Group	Max.	Std. Rate	Ovt.	Cost/Use	Accrue	Base
1	Senior Developer	Work		SD	Tech	100%	$0.00/hr	$10.00/hr	$0.00	Prorated	Standard
2	Tech Lead	Work		TL	Tech	100%	$0.00/hr	$0.00/hr	$0.00	Prorated	Standard
3	Architect Consultant	Work		AC	Consultant	100%	$0.00/hr	$0.00/hr	$0.00	Prorated	Standard
4	Monitoring Software	Material	Annual Lice	M	Software		$0.00		$0.00	Prorated	
5	Cloud API Webservice	Material	Unlimited	CAW	Software		$0.00		$0.00	Prorated	

Figure 15.3 – Two Material resources created

The key points to note about this screenshot are as follows:

- Any number of **Material** resources can be created for your project, but you will have to explicitly set their resource type to **Material** from the **Type** dropdown.

- The **Material** column is an optional label used to specify the units of usage for the specific material. For example, if you were using cement, the label you use could be **tons** or **bags**. Similarly, if printing ink was being used in your project, you would typically specify **carton** in this column.

- The **Group** column was explained earlier, in the previous section.

- The **Max. Units** column is not applicable for **Material** resources. It is used exclusively for work resources.

- An important point to note is that **Material** resources will not be associated with any calendars in the **Base** column.

Material resources are always allocated in terms of units of usage; for example, *2 bags of cement*. Project is intelligent enough to compute fractional amounts, which means you can allocate 0.5 bags of cement too. Sometimes, it is not possible to predict the exact cost of a project's expense. For such situations, we can use the third resource type of Project, known as *Cost*.

The Cost resource type

Cost resources are used for project situations that demand one-off expenditure; for example, when a project is launched with a press release party. Cost resources include any out-of-pocket expenditure such as airfares, hotel stays, taxi fares, and others. Continuing with our exercises, two new **Cost** resources need to be added to the **RESOURCE SHEET** view, as follows:

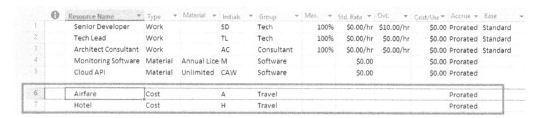

	Resource Name	Type	Material	Initials	Group	Max.	Std. Rate	Ovt.	Cost/Use	Accrue	Base
1	Senior Developer	Work		SD	Tech	100%	$0.00/hr	$10.00/hr	$0.00	Prorated	Standard
2	Tech Lead	Work		TL	Tech	100%	$0.00/hr	$0.00/hr	$0.00	Prorated	Standard
3	Architect Consultant	Work		AC	Consultant	100%	$0.00/hr	$0.00/hr	$0.00	Prorated	Standard
4	Monitoring Software	Material	Annual Lice	M	Software		$0.00		$0.00	Prorated	
5	Cloud API	Material	Unlimited	CAW	Software		$0.00		$0.00	Prorated	
6	Airfare	Cost		A	Travel					Prorated	
7	Hotel	Cost		H	Travel					Prorated	

Figure 15.4 – Two Cost resources created

There are no special columns for the **Cost** resource. However, the behavior of **Cost** resources will be special, as we will see in the *costing* exercises.

Basics of costing in Project

Now that we have understood the three types of resources in Project, we can construct an elaborate project costing framework. Remember that even though Project provides a variety of costing features, it cannot replace dedicated accounting software.

To make the best use of Project's costing features, it is critical that you understand certain guidelines and limitations of tracking the costs within Project, as we'll discuss in the upcoming sections.

Costing versus pricing

Project can help with the *costing* of a project, but not *pricing*. *Cost* is incurred by you to execute the project, while *price* is what the customer pays. Accordingly, you can expect to plan and track your costs with Project, but you cannot expect to build an invoicing framework with Project, as this is to do with pricing. Users who clearly understand this difference will be saved a lot of frustration while working with financials on Project.

Costing is based on resourcing

Every resource can optionally be associated with a cost. This is true for all three types of resources – **Work** resources, **Material** resources, and **Cost** resources. When such a resource (with an associated cost) is assigned to a task, the cost gets accrued to the resulting assignment. Such *assignment* costs are rolled up into summary tasks. Finally, all the summary tasks get rolled up into the **Project Summary Task** view.

In this way, costs will bubble up from the individual task level to the summary task level, all the way up to the whole project. We will now learn about all the intricacies of costing with Project by using different types of resources within a hands-on project.

Project for this chapter

Case Scenario: You are the CEO of a start-up that builds enterprise-level customer care software. Every customer site installation is a project for your team. Such a simple deployment project is shown in the following screenshot:

		Task Name	Durati	Start	Finish	Predecessors
0		⊿ **Software Deployment Project**	**15 days**	**Mon 11-05-20**	**Fri 29-05-20**	
1		⊿ **Design Training**	**5 days**	**Mon 11-05-20**	**Fri 15-05-20**	
2		Doc Walkthrough	2 days	Mon 11-05-20	Tue 12-05-20	
3		Design Review	3 days	Wed 13-05-20	Fri 15-05-20	2
4		Design Complete	0 days	Fri 15-05-20	Fri 15-05-20	3
5		⊿ **Offshore Training (BANGALORE)**	**5 days**	**Mon 18-05-20**	**Fri 22-05-20**	
6		Strategy Meeting	2 days	Mon 18-05-20	Tue 19-05-20	4
7		Database side	1 day	Wed 20-05-20	Wed 20-05-20	6
8		Code Configuration	2 days	Thu 21-05-20	Fri 22-05-20	7
9		Offshore Complete	0 days	Fri 22-05-20	Fri 22-05-20	8
10		⊿ **Onsite Training (PARIS)**	**5 days**	**Mon 25-05-20**	**Fri 29-05-20**	
11		Server setup	2 days	Mon 25-05-20	Tue 26-05-20	9
12		Database setup	2 days	Wed 27-05-20	Thu 28-05-20	11
13		Code setup	1 day	Fri 29-05-20	Fri 29-05-20	12
14		Project Complete	0 days	Fri 29-05-20	Fri 29-05-20	13

Figure 15.5 – Project task list for this chapter

If you have been following along with the resource creation exercises so far, use the same blank project to create the schedule shown in the preceding screenshot. If not, you can start with a blank project. Link the tasks with the clues provided in the **Predecessors** column. When you have created the task list, the **GANTT CHART** view should resemble the following screenshot:

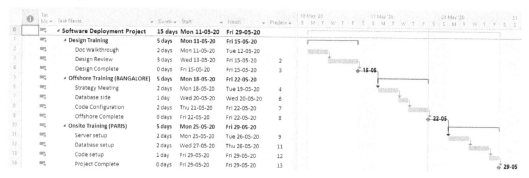

Figure 15.6 – The GANTT CHART view for our hands-on project

There are some salient points to note about this schedule:

- The total duration of the project is 3 weeks (15 days)

- The first week is for project groundwork and can be identified under the **Design Training** heading.

- The second week is for **Offshore Training** conducted remotely, by an external consultant. This will involve a domestic travel cost.

- The third week is for **Onsite Training**, conducted at a customer office in **PARIS**. This will involve an international travel cost.

- None of the tasks have been assigned a resource yet. However, there are several special resource costing requirements for this project, all of which we will uncover as we construct the project in the following sections.

Our project objectives are to do the following:

- Create a (rough) *budget* for the project

- Create a (detailed) *costing plan* for the project

Do not confuse the *budget* with the *baseline*. The baseline is analogous to a snapshot of your schedule at a particular point in time. The budget is a summary of planned expenditures.

Creating a Project budget

Budgets can include estimates for both *cost* and *work*, though the focus of this chapter will only be on *costing*, purely for brevity. Everything that we model for cost in this section can be replicated equivalently for work. We will begin by creating a budget for our project. Setting a tentative budget for the project will help you negotiate a project price with the customer. You can only create a rough, approximate budget with Project. This should suffice for small- and medium-sized projects. Creating a budget with Project involves a specific series of steps, as follows:

1. Begin by creating two new Cost resources, as shown in the following screenshot:

	Resource Name	Type	Material	Initials	Group	Max.	Std. Rate	Ovt.	Cost/Use	Accrue	Base
1	Senior Developer	Work		SD	Tech	100%	$0.00/hr	$0.00/hr	$0.00	Prorated	Standard
2	Tech Lead	Work		TL	Tech	100%	$0.00/hr	$0.00/hr	$0.00	Prorated	Standard
3	Architect Consultant	Work		AC	Consultant	100%	$0.00/hr	$0.00/hr	$0.00	Prorated	Standard
4	Monitoring Software	Material	Annual Lice	M	Software		$0.00		$0.00	Prorated	
5	Cloud API Webservice	Material	Unlimited	CAW	Software		$0.00		$0.00	Prorated	
6	Airfare	Cost		A	Travel					Prorated	
7	Hotel	Cost		H	Travel					Prorated	
8	BudgetTravelCost	Cost		B						Prorated	
9	BudgetConsultantCos	Cost		B						Prorated	

Figure 15.7 – Two new Cost resources created

As shown in the preceding screenshot, we have created **BudgetTravelCost** and **BudgetConsultantCost** as two new cost resources in the **RESOURCE SHEET** view.

2. As the next step, we have to inform Project that these cost resources will be used specifically for budgetary purposes in our project. This is the critical step as Project will not allow ordinary resources for budget calculations. Double-click on the **BudgetTravelCost** resource to open the **Resource Information** dialog box, as shown in the following screenshot:

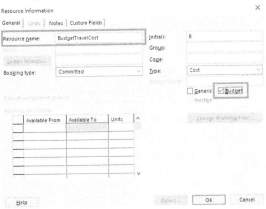

Figure 15.8 – Budget checkbox in the Resource Information dialog box

The **Budget** checkbox has to be enabled for both newly created resources, one after another. By doing so, we tell Project that the resource is to be used only for budgetary purposes. For the sake of brevity, we will refer to such resources, which have been enabled for budgetary calculations, as *budget resources*.

3.   Now that we have created our budget resources, they have to be assigned to the project before monetary values can be allocated. Moreover, the project's budget can only be assigned to **Project Summary Task**. Refer to the following screenshot:

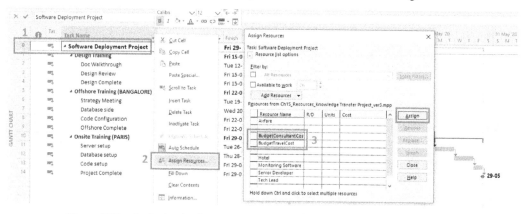

Figure 15.9 – Assigning budget resources using the Assign Resources dialog box

The following steps explain how to assign the budget resources to your project:

1.   Remember that **Project Summary Task**, at row 0, is a special feature that is always available to you as a hidden row and can be made visible from the **Format** tab.

2.   Right-click on **Project Summary Task**, open the **Assign Resources** dialog box, and assign **BudgetTravelCost** and **BudgetConsultantCost** to **Project Summary Task**. We cannot set the monetary value in this dialog box. That is the next step.

> **Note**
>
> Only budget resources can be assigned to **Project Summary Task** by design. Other normal resources cannot be assigned to it.

The next part of the process is to assign monetary values to our budget resources. This can only be achieved from any assignment-based view. The easiest way to do this is from the **Task Usage** view. Refer to the following screenshot:

Task Name	Fixed Cost	Fixed Cost Accrual	Budget Cost	Total Cost	Baseline	Variance	Actual	Remaining
0 ◢ Software Deploym	$0.00	Prorated	$20,000.00	$1,300.00	$0.00	$1,300.00	$0.00	$1,300.00
BudgetTravelCos			$10,000.00					
BudgetConsulta			$10,000.00					
1 ◢ Design Training	$0.00	Prorated		$1,300.00	$0.00	$1,300.00	$0.00	$1,300.00
2 Doc Walkthrou	$300.00	Prorated		$300.00	$0.00	$300.00	$0.00	$300.00
3 Design Review	$1,000.00	Prorated		$1,000.00	$0.00	$1,000.00	$0.00	$1,000.00
4 Design Comple	$0.00	Prorated		$0.00	$0.00	$0.00	$0.00	$0.00
5 ◢ Offshore Training	$0.00	Prorated		$0.00	$0.00	$0.00	$0.00	$0.00
6 Strategy Meetir	$0.00	Prorated		$0.00	$0.00	$0.00	$0.00	$0.00
7 Database side	$0.00	Prorated		$0.00	$0.00	$0.00	$0.00	$0.00
8 Code Configura	$0.00	Prorated		$0.00	$0.00	$0.00	$0.00	$0.00
9 Offshore Comp	$0.00	Prorated		$0.00	$0.00	$0.00	$0.00	$0.00
10 ◢ Onsite Training (P	$0.00	Prorated		$0.00	$0.00	$0.00	$0.00	$0.00
11 Server setup	$0.00	Prorated		$0.00	$0.00	$0.00	$0.00	$0.00
12 Database setup	$0.00	Prorated		$0.00	$0.00	$0.00	$0.00	$0.00
13 Code setup	$0.00	Prorated		$0.00	$0.00	$0.00	$0.00	$0.00
14 Project Comple	$0.00	Prorated		$0.00	$0.00	$0.00	$0.00	$0.00

Figure 15.10 – Assigning budget monetary values in the Task Usage view

The following steps explain how to assign monetary values to your budget resources:

1. Change the table displayed to the **Cost** table. This table is specially designed for managing project costs.

2. Add the **Budget Cost** column. This column is not visible by default.

3. Assign $10,000 for both budget resources, as shown in the preceding screenshot.

4. Congratulations – your project's budget has now been set!

> **Tip**
> The work equivalent of the **Budget Cost** column is the **Budget Work** column. You can allocate a work budget to create a cost budget for the project using the exact same technique described here.

So far, we have only created a tentative budget for our project. In the next section, we will continue with our project to see how this budget will pan out against an actual resource-based detailed costing plan.

Costing of work resources

Projects that need greater diligence in monitoring and control will choose to implement a project costing plan. It is your choice whether to cost your project or not. There is a great deal of flexibility available in costing, as we will see in the upcoming sections. Choosing to reflect a higher costing realism will incur a significant increase in your activities as a project manager. In the next section, we will begin with costing techniques for work resources by using the simplest use cases possible.

Standard rate of pay

For any work assignment, the cost will be calculated by a basic formula: *Standard rate of pay * hours worked*. You can specify the rate of pay using any mode that's used in your organization – hourly, daily, monthly, or yearly. Refer to the following screenshot, where the **Std. Rate** column has been now filled in for the work resources we created earlier:

❶	Resource Name	Type	Material	Initials	Group	Max.	Std. Rate	Ovt.	Cost/Use	Accrue	Base
1	Senior Developer	Work		SD	Tech	100%	$50.00/hr	$0.00/hr	$0.00	Prorated	Standard
2	Tech Lead	Work		TL	Tech	100%	$12,500.00/mon	$0.00/hr	$0.00	Prorated	Standard
3	Architect Consultant	Work		AC	Consultant	100%	$800.00/day	$0.00/hr	$50.00	Prorated	Standard

Figure 15.11 – Set standard rates of pay for work resources

There are a few points to note about this screenshot, as follows:

- **Senior Developer** is an internal full-time employee who has been assigned a standard rate of **$50.00/hr**.

- **Tech Lead** is also an internal full-time employee, and has been assigned a standard rate of **$12,500.00/month**.

- **Architect Consultant** is an external consultant who charges a standard rate of **$800.00/day**.

- The overtime rate of payment can be set in the **Ovt** column. This will rely on the calendar set in the **Base** column. Needless to say, overtime hours should be configured in the calendar for this to work. For the sake of brevity, we will not focus on overtime.

No matter how you approximate the standard rate of pay, Project will make the necessary costing calculations intelligently. You can observe this in the following screenshot, where assignments have been made on the **GANTT CHART** view:

❶	Tas M	Task Name	Durati	Budget Cost	Cost	Start	Finish	Predec	Resource Names
0		⊿ Software Deployment Project	15 days	$20,000.00	$9,125.00	Mon 11-05-20	Fri 29-05-20		BudgetConsultan
1		⊿ Design Training	5 days		$3,125.00	Mon 11-05-20	Fri 15-05-20		
2		Doc Walkthrough	2 days		$1,250.00	Mon 11-05-20	Tue 12-05-20		Tech Lead
3		Design Review	3 days		$1,875.00	Wed 13-05-20	Fri 15-05-20	2	Tech Lead
4		Design Complete	0 days		$0.00	Fri 15-05-20	Fri 15-05-20	3	
5		⊿ Offshore Training (BANGALORE)	5 days		$4,000.00	Mon 18-05-20	Fri 22-05-20		
6		Strategy Meeting	2 days		$1,600.00	Mon 18-05-20	Tue 19-05-20	4	Architect Consultar
7		Database side	1 day		$800.00	Wed 20-05-20	Wed 20-05-20	6	Architect Consultar
8		Code Configuration	2 days		$1,600.00	Thu 21-05-20	Fri 22-05-20	7	Architect Consultar
9		Offshore Complete	0 days		$0.00	Fri 22-05-20	Fri 22-05-20	8	
10		⊿ Onsite Training (PARIS)	5 days		$2,000.00	Mon 25-05-20	Fri 29-05-20		
11		Server setup	2 days		$800.00	Mon 25-05-20	Tue 26-05-20	9	Senior Developer
12		Database setup	2 days		$800.00	Wed 27-05-20	Thu 28-05-20	11	Senior Developer
13		Code setup	1 day		$400.00	Fri 29-05-20	Fri 29-05-20	12	Senior Developer
14		Project Complete	0 days		$0.00	Fri 29-05-20	Fri 29-05-20	13	

Figure 15.12 – Project costs added up from work resources

The following are a few important points to note about this screenshot:

- The **Cost** column and the **Budget Cost** column have been added to the default **Entry** table in this view.

- Every assignment now has the **Cost** field automatically computed by Project based on the resource's standard rate of pay, times the assignment work hours.

- For all of these monetary calculations, Project will rely on the default values configured for monthly (160), weekly (40), and daily (8) work hours.

- Just for practice, you are urged to verify the cost computations independently.

Work resources are the most common resources used on a project, and the computations we have seen so far have been straightforward. However, for even more complex situations, a variable rate of pay is possible, as we will see in the next section.

Variable rate of pay

The standard rate of pay for a work resource can be further configured. Let's see how:

1. Double-click on any resource in the **RESOURCE SHEET** view to pull up the **Resource Information** dialog box.

2. In the **Costs** tab, a variable rate of pay by *effective date* can be configured, as shown in the following screenshot:

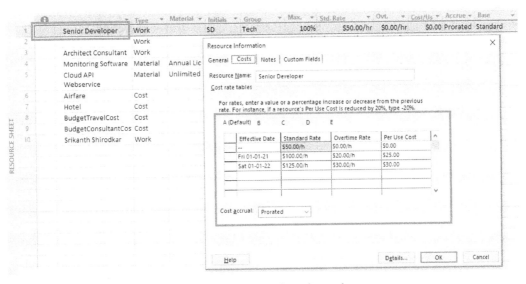

Figure 15.13 – Variable rate of pay for work resources

Such a variable rate of payment is used in the following use cases:

- **Senior Developer** is paid a standard rate of **$50.00/h** through December 31 of the current year. After that, they are promoted to **$100.00/h** as the standard rate of pay.

- For overtime hours, the standard rate can be incremented by a specified monetary value, such as an additional **$25.00/h**, and so on.

- A variable pay per use can also be deployed. This is a one-time extra payment per assignment, over and above the normal computed cost. We will explore this concept for material resources in the next section.

- There can be multiple combinations of the previous three configurations too, as can be specified in the individual rows of the **Resource Information** dialog box.

So far, we have observed work resources from both a standard and variable rate of payment model. In the next section, we will give the same treatment to material resources.

Costing of material resources

Material resources are calculated based on *units of usage*. For example, if a bag of cement costs $20, then five bags, when consumed by an assignment, will cost $100. Sometimes, material resources will incur an additional one-time additional cost. Continuing with the same example, an additional cost of $75 is incurred for delivering the cement bags. These one-time costs can be clubbed under the **Cost/Use** column. While these were some simple examples, we will see some more costing variations in our hands-on project. We will start with the most common use case of variable material costs in the next section.

Variable costs

The first material resource in our project is **Monitoring Software**, for which costs are now attached in the **RESOURCE SHEET** view, as shown in the following screenshot:

	Resource Name	Type	Material Label	Initials	Group	Max.	Std. Rate	Ovt.	Cost/Use	Accrue	Base
1	Senior Developer	Work		SD	Tech	100%	$50.00/hr	$0.00/hr	$0.00	Prorated	Standard
2	Tech Lead	Work		TL	Tech	100%	$12,500.00/mon	$0.00/hr	$0.00	Prorated	Standard
3	Architect Consultant	Work		AC	Consultant	100%	$0.00/hr	$0.00/hr	$0.00	Prorated	Standard
4	Monitoring Software	Material	Annual License	M	Software		$500.00		$99.00	Start	
5	Cloud API Webservice	Material	Unlimited	CAW	Software		$0.00		$1,000.00	Start	

Figure 15.14 – Variable cost for material resources

There are a few important points to note about this material costing, as follows:

- The cost of the monitoring software (material resource) is $500 per license. This is specified in the **Std. Rate** column.

- However, there is an additional one-time fixed media cost of **$99.00**. No matter how many licenses are purchased, the media cost will not change.

- This entire material resource cost can be paid immediately when an assignment is made. In other words, the cost accrues at the beginning of the assignment. This is the reason why the **Accrue At** column is now set to **Start**. In other cases (say, work resources) where a monthly cost is incurred, the cost will be accrued *pro rata*.

With these costing configurations in place, we will now create an assignment. Refer to the following screenshot:

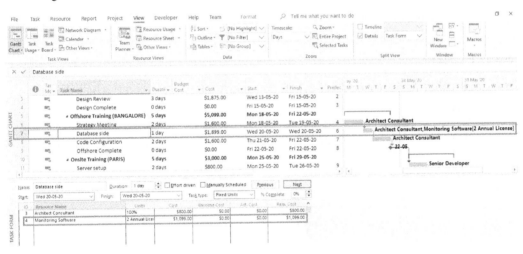

Figure 15.15 – Assignment of a variable cost material resource

In this screenshot, the **GANTT CHART** view is loaded in the main display window. Let's take a look:

- A split window configuration has been created by the **Details** checkbox being enabled in the **View** tab.

- In the secondary window, the **Cost** panel is loaded in the **TASK FORM** view. The task named **Database side** is selected for inspection. This task had been assigned a *work resource* in the previous section with an associated cost of $800 (that is, 8 hours of work at the rate of $100 per hour).

- Additionally, we have now attached a cost resource, **Monitoring Software**, to the same task. We will analyze this second assignment, with reference to the split window in the preceding screenshot, as follows:

- Two licenses for the software have been purchased, as shown in the **Units** column. Observe that this is the same text string from the **Material** column in the **RESOURCE SHEET** view.

- The cost of this material resource assignment is $1,099. This is the sum of the two licenses ($500 + $500), plus the one-time cost per use of $99.

- The **total cost** of the assignment is $1,899. This is the sum total of all the individual costs ($800 work resource cost, plus $1,099 material resource cost).

This example shows how a complex costing use case can be constructed from the flexibility of the different resource types. We will see another variation in the next section, where a fixed cost material resource can be utilized.

Fixed costs

Our second material resource is **Cloud API Webservice**. It is costed on the **RESOURCE SHEET** view, as shown in the following screenshot:

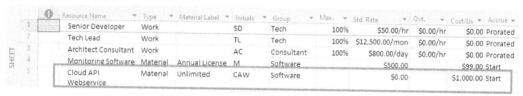

Figure 15.16 – Fixed cost for material resources

There are a few important points to note about this material costing, as follows:

- This software license is purchased under a one-time, unlimited lifetime access fee of **$1,000.00**. There are no other charges of any kind.

- To represent this licensing structure, **Std. Rate** is costed for **$0.00** and, correspondingly, the one-time **Cost/Use** column is set to **$1,000.00**.

Let's inspect this fixed-cost resource assignment while it's in action, as shown in the following screenshot:

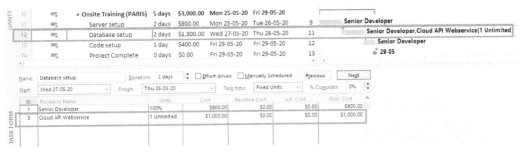

Figure 15.17 – Assignment of a fixed-cost material resource

The split-window view configuration is exactly the same as the one shown in the previous example. Let's analyze the fixed-cost assignment:

- One unit of software has been purchased, as shown in the **Units** column.

- The cost of this assignment is **$1,000.00**. This is the sum of the standard rate ($0) and the fixed cost per use ($1,000).

- The total cost of the assignment is $1,800. This is the sum total of all individual costs ($800 work resource cost and $1,000 material resource cost).

With this technique, we have costed a one-time fixed cost material resource. In the next section, we will examine cost resources.

Costing of cost resources

There are some unique features of cost resources compared to the other resource types:

- The monetary values of cost resources are determined only at the time of assignment.

- The same cost resources can have different monetary values for different assignments.

- Logically, the cost resources are not tied to work like **Word** and **Material** resources are.

Two cost resources have already been created in our hands-on project, as shown in the following screenshot:

		Resource Name	Type	Material Label	Initials	Group	Max.	Std. Rate	Ovt.	Cost/Us	Accrue	Base
1		Senior Developer	Work		SD	Tech	100%	$50.00/hr	$0.00/hr	$0.00	Prorated	Standard
2		Tech Lead	Work		TL	Tech	100%	$12,500.00/mon	$0.00/hr	$0.00	Prorated	Standard
3		Architect Consultant	Work		AC	Consultant	100%	$800.00/day	$0.00/hr	$0.00	Prorated	Standard
4		Monitoring Software	Material	Annual License	M	Software		$500.00		$99.00	Start	
5		Cloud API Webservice	Material	Unlimited	CAW	Software		$0.00		$1,000.00	Start	
6		Airfare	Cost		A	Travel					Start	
7		Hotel	Cost		H	Travel					Start	
8		BudgetTravelCost	Cost		B						Prorated	
9		BudgetConsultantCos	Cost		B						Prorated	

Figure 15.18 – Cost resources in our project

Notice that cost resources will not have a cost value assigned to the **Std. Rate** column in the **RESOURCE SHEET** view, where they are defined. The reason for this is that costs such as airfares, hotel prices, conference rooms, and others fluctuate. The actual cost can only be known at the time of booking. Similarly, airfares to a domestic location will be significantly less than international travel (unless you are in Europe, perhaps). Now, let's see cost resources in action.

Fixed costs for resource usage

There are two travel costs associated with our hands-on project. The first case is a domestic flight for **Offshore Training** in **BANGALORE**. The associated task will be **Strategy Meeting**. We will continue to use the same split window view configuration as in the previous examples, as shown in the following screenshot:

Figure 15.19 – First assignment for the Airfare cost resource

Notice that an **Airfare** cost of **$1,000.00** is assigned to the **Strategy Meeting** task in the split window. You can also see this cost appear on the **GANTT CHART** view on the main display window. The cost is to be entered only after the resource has been assigned in the **Cost** panel of the **TASK FORM** view.

Now, we will proceed to assign the same **Airfare** cost resource once again to another task. This assignment is to signify international travel for the **Server setup** task, which is scheduled as a part of **Onsite Training** in **PARIS**. Refer to the following screenshot:

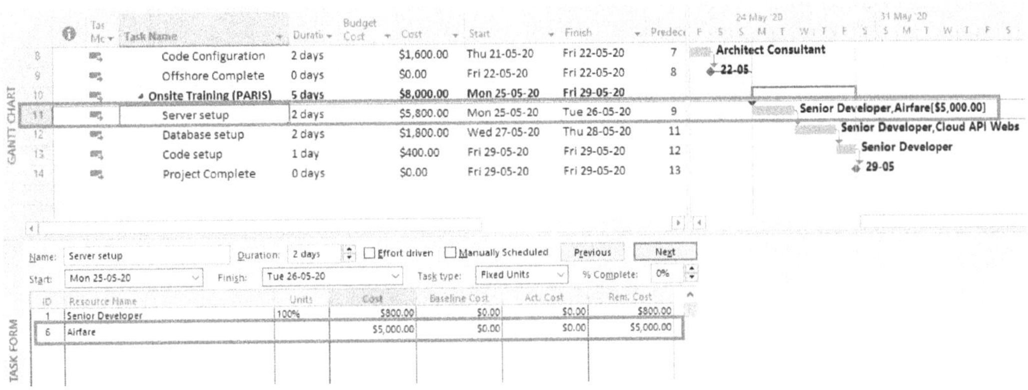

Figure 15.20 – Second assignment for the Airfare cost resource

This time around, the airfare costs have shot up to **$5,000.00** as it is an international fare. As can be verified from this exercise, the same cost resource was allocated different cost values as the situation demanded.

However, once the cost resource is assigned, it cannot be further modulated either by units of time or usage. This is the reason cost resources are considered fixed for a specific resource usage. In the next section, we will consider an extension of the same logic; that is, a fixed cost as applied to a *task* instead of a resource.

Fixed costs for task usage

Sometimes, you might want to attach a fixed cost to a task, without any of the hassle of creating a specific cost resource. For example, a small bonus is attached to a task for successfully completing the difficult code setup that was required by the customer. Project provides a quick and simple technique we can use to add such fixed task costs. Refer to the following screenshot to see this technique in action:

Figure 15.21 – Fixed cost assigned to a task

There are some important points to be noted from the preceding screenshot, as follows:

- Project provides a column called **Fixed Cost**, which has been inserted into the **GANTT CHART** view.

- Enter the fixed cost for the task of your choice.

- Observe that since this is a task-level cost, you are able to enter the value directly into the **Entry** table of the **GANTT CHART** view. This is contrary to the other costs in the previous exercises, where assignment was mandatory to enable costing or different assignment views were used.

Fixed costs for a task is like a cheat code for project costing. You can quickly attach a cost to the task directly, without integrating it with a resource. It is also the cause of frequent confusion while costing, as these costs do not show up by default in assignment views. Use them with caution and appropriate diligence.

> **Pitfall**
> Fixed costs do not get rolled up totals at the summary task levels – not even at the whole project level! This is because it is possible to add a fixed cost even for summary tasks. If, for some reason, your costs are not adding up, ensure that you enable the **Fixed Cost** column and then reverify the totals.

With this exercise, we have completed our hands-on project. We started by learning how to create a rudimentary budget for our project. This was followed up by constructing an elaborate cost plan for the project in order to employ all the different fixed and variable costing techniques available in Project. In the next section, we will look at some different analysis techniques we can use for project costs.

Analyzing costing using different views

Once you have created a budget and a cost plan for the project we've discussed in this chapter, the best practice is to proceed with **baselining** and **tracking**, as you would normally do. As a result, the following two additional benefits will accrue for your project:

- Your baseline will contain costing data for all future references.

- When you track project work progress periodically, costs will also get updated automatically based on the changes that are made to the work's progress.

Project cost analysis is a critical aspect of monitoring and controlling a project. The following screenshot shows our current hands-on project, which has now been baselined. Our work progress has also been updated to the current date:

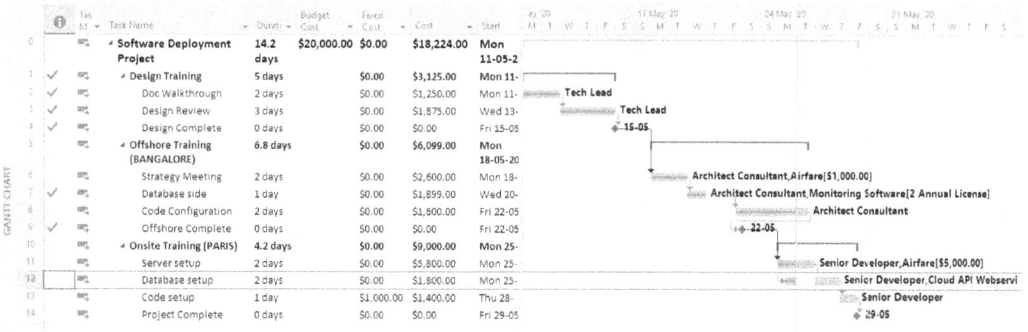

Figure 15.22 – Current project baselined and progress updated

For the remainder of this chapter, we will progressively drill down into the different levels of costing analysis views. We will use a top-down approach, beginning with the current state of our project schedule.

Project-level cost analysis views

Project Summary Task is the absolute first point of reference to be used for project cost totals. We have already enabled it for all the exercises in this chapter. Remember to include the **Fixed Cost**, **Cost**, and **Budget Cost** columns in the **GANTT CHART** view as they will be hidden by default.

The next quick reference tool for the entire project is the **Project Statistics** interface. This is available from the **Project** tab | **Project Information** button | **Project Information** dialog box | **Statistics** button. Refer to the following screenshot:

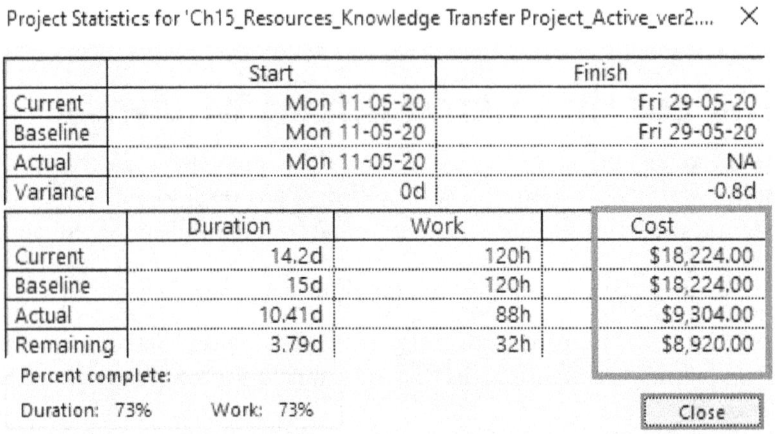

Project Statistics for 'Ch15_Resources_Knowledge Transfer Project_Active_ver2....   ✕

	Start		Finish
Current	Mon 11-05-20		Fri 29-05-20
Baseline	Mon 11-05-20		Fri 29-05-20
Actual	Mon 11-05-20		NA
Variance	0d		-0.8d

	Duration	Work	Cost
Current	14.2d	120h	$18,224.00
Baseline	15d	120h	$18,224.00
Actual	10.41d	88h	$9,304.00
Remaining	3.79d	32h	$8,920.00

Percent complete:

Duration: 73%   Work: 73%   Close

Figure 15.23 – Current project quick statistics

Project Statistics provides an excellent quick reference to the overall costing details of the project. The actual and remaining costs are calculated automatically, based on project progress tracking, and it is only an extrapolation of the actual and remaining work data. In the next section, we will dig one level deeper into the assignment cost details.

> Pitfall
>
> The **Cost** column (in the **GANTT CHART** view) and the **Total Cost** column (in other views) are exactly the same – they're just labelled differently in different views. This is a source of frequent confusion and frustration during cost analysis for users who are not aware of this fact.

Assignment-level cost analysis view

The **TASK USAGE** view provides the best interface for assignment cost analysis, with the **Cost** table applied instead of the default **Usage** table. Refer to the following screenshot, which shows the aforementioned view configuration:

TASK USAGE

	Task Name	Fixed Cost	Budget Cost	Total Cost	Baseline	Variance	Actual	Remaining	Details	11	16	21	26	June 2020 31	05
0	◢ **Software Deploym**	**$0.00**	**$20,000.00**	**$18,224.00**	**$18,224.00**	**$0.00**	**$9,304.00**	**$8,920.00**	Work	40h	24h	24h	32h		
	BudgetTravelCos		*$10,000.00*						Work						
	BudgetConsulta		*$10,000.00*						Work						
1	◢ **Design Training**	**$0.00**		**$3,125.00**	**$3,125.00**	**$0.00**	**$3,125.00**	**$0.00**	Work	40h					
2	◢ Doc Walkthro	$0.00		$1,250.00	$1,250.00	$0.00	$1,250.00	$0.00	Work	16h					
	Tech Lead			*$1,250.00*	*$1,250.00*	*$0.00*	*$1,250.00*	*$0.00*	Work	16h					
3	◢ Design Review	$0.00		$1,875.00	$1,875.00	$0.00	$1,875.00	$0.00	Work	24h					
	Tech Lead			*$1,875.00*	*$1,875.00*	*$0.00*	*$1,875.00*	*$0.00*	Work	24h					
4	Design Comple	$0.00		$0.00	$0.00	$0.00	$0.00	$0.00	Work						
5	◢ **Offshore Training**	**$0.00**		**$6,099.00**	**$6,099.00**	**$0.00**	**$4,459.00**	**$1,640.00**	Work		24h	9.6h	6.4h		
6	◢ Strategy Meetir	$0.00		$2,600.00	$2,600.00	$0.00	$1,600.00	$1,000.00	Work		16h				
	Architect Co			*$1,600.00*	*$1,600.00*	*$0.00*	*$1,600.00*	*$0.00*	Work		16h				
	Airfare			*$1,000.00*	*$1,000.00*	*$0.00*	*$0.00*	*$1,000.00*	Work						
7	◢ Database side	$0.00		$1,899.00	$1,899.00	$0.00	$1,899.00	$0.00	Work		8h				
	Architect Co			*$800.00*	*$800.00*	*$0.00*	*$800.00*	*$0.00*	Work		8h				
	Monitoring			*$1,099.00*	*$1,099.00*	*$0.00*	*$1,099.00*	*$0.00*	Work		2				
8	◢ Code Configura	$0.00		$1,600.00	$1,600.00	$0.00	$960.00	$640.00	Work			9.6h	6.4h		
	Architect Co			*$1,600.00*	*$1,600.00*	*$0.00*	*$960.00*	*$640.00*	Work			9.6h	6.4h		
9	Offshore Comp	$0.00		$0.00	$0.00	$0.00	$0.00	$0.00	Work						
10	◢ **Onsite Training (P**	**$0.00**		**$9,000.00**	**$9,000.00**	**$0.00**	**$1,720.00**	**$7,280.00**	Work			14.4h	25.6h		
11	◢ Server setup	$0.00		$5,800.00	$5,800.00	$0.00	$400.00	$5,400.00	Work			8h	8h		

Figure 15.24 – Assignment-level cost analysis with the Task Usage view

As we can see, the individual costs for every assignment can be analyzed from this view. All the relevant cost columns are included within the **Cost** table. Remember that the **Total Cost** column that's displayed in this table is exactly the same as the **Cost** column in the **GANTT CHART** view. In the next section, we will see the appropriate view for cost analysis at the task level.

Task-level cost analysis view

The **TASK SHEET** view is the most appropriate view for analyzing costs at a task level, once again with the **Cost** table applied (instead of the default **Entry** table). This is a simple and straightforward view, without a chart or time-phased component for it. Refer to the following screenshot:

TASK SHEET

	Task Name	Fixed	Budget	Total Cost	Baseline	Variance	Actual	Remaining	Add New Column
0	◢ **Software Deploym**	**$0.00**	**$20,000.00**	**$18,224.00**	**$18,224.00**	**$0.00**	**$9,304.00**		
1	◢ **Design Training**	**$0.00**		**$3,125.00**	**$3,125.00**	**$0.00**	**$3,125.00**		
2	Doc Walkthrou	$0.00		$1,250.00	$1,250.00	$0.00	$1,250.00		
3	Design Review	$0.00		$1,875.00	$1,875.00	$0.00	$1,875.00		
4	Design Comple	$0.00		$0.00	$0.00	$0.00	$0.00		
5	◢ **Offshore Training**	**$0.00**		**$6,099.00**	**$6,099.00**	**$0.00**	**$4,459.00**		
6	Strategy Meeti	$0.00		$2,600.00	$2,600.00	$0.00	$1,600.00		
7	Database side	$0.00		$1,899.00	$1,899.00	$0.00	$1,899.00	$0.00	
8	Code Configura	$0.00		$1,600.00	$1,600.00	$0.00	$960.00	$640.00	
9	Offshore Comp	$0.00		$0.00	$0.00	$0.00	$0.00	$0.00	
10	◢ **Onsite Training**	**$0.00**		**$9,000.00**	**$9,000.00**	**$0.00**	**$1,720.00**	**$7,280.00**	
11	Server setup	$0.00		$5,800.00	$5,800.00	$0.00	$400.00	$5,400.00	
12	Database setup	$0.00		$1,800.00	$1,800.00	$0.00	$1,320.00	$480.00	
13	Code setup	$1,000.00		$1,400.00	$1,400.00	$0.00	$0.00	$1,400.00	
14	Project Comple	$0.00		$0.00	$0.00	$0.00	$0.00	$0.00	

Remaining (Remaining Cost)
The remaining scheduled expense that will be incurred in completing the remaining scheduled work.
Remaining Cost = (Remaining Work * Standard Rate) + Remaining Overtime cost

Figure 15.25 – Task-level cost analysis with the Task Sheet view

Similar to task-level costing analysis, we can also review costing at the resource level. This will be covered in the next section.

Resource-level cost analysis view

Those of you who are astute will now be able to surmise that, for a resource-level cost analysis, the most suitable view is the **RESOURCE SHEET** view, with the **Cost** table applied (instead of the default **Entry** table). Refer to the following screenshot:

	Resource Name	Cost	Baseline Cost	Variance	Actual Cost	Remaining
1	Senior Developer	$2,000.00	$2,000.00	$0.00	$720.00	$1,280.00
2	Tech Lead	$3,125.00	$3,125.00	$0.00	$3,125.00	$0.00
3	Architect Consultant	$4,000.00	$4,000.00	$0.00	$3,360.00	$640.00
4	Monitoring Software	$1,099.00	$1,099.00	$0.00	$1,099.00	$0.00
5	Cloud API Webservice	$1,000.00	$1,000.00	$0.00	$1,000.00	$0.00
6	Airfare	$6,000.00	$6,000.00	$0.00	$0.00	$6,000.00
7	Hotel	$0.00	$0.00	$0.00	$0.00	$0.00
8	BudgetTravelCost					
9	BudgetConsultantCost					

Figure 15.26 – Resource-level cost analysis with the Resource Sheet view

This view presents all the resources mapped to their corresponding cost data in a concise, fast-to-grok view. Notice that the budget costs do not appear in the resource-level views, and that makes perfect sense. In the next section, we will discuss how costing values can be extrapolated in a baseline view.

Baseline cost comparison analysis

A *baseline versus current plan* with costing information can be very useful for status meetings with stakeholders. Such a view can help us make critical engineering decisions on the future course of a project. Refer to the following screenshot:

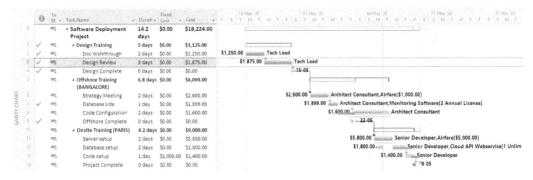

Figure 15.27 – Baseline Gantt Chart comparison with costs displayed

The baseline comparison, with costs displayed, can be useful for understanding the monetary impact of delays on a project. Both the baseline and the type of cost data displayed can be configured from the **Format** tab. In the preceding screenshot of the project, the **Cost** (total cost) data field is displayed, but you can also display any other relevant data; for example, remaining costs on a task. Knowledge of these cost analysis views will help the project manager effectively pinpoint costing issues, and perhaps even suggest probable solutions.

With this, we have completed our analysis of the different views for costing and, by extension, concluded our discussion of resourcing and costing management.

Summary

We started this chapter by gaining a deep understanding of how resources and costs are inextricably connected and must be managed together. Then, we explored different resource types that you can apply to your project to get deeper realism in your schedules. Then, we explored all the major types of resource costing situations that are normally encountered in project management. Finally, we concluded this chapter with a bouquet of views that will help you drill into different levels of costing information with a top-down approach. The hands-on project in this chapter should have enabled you to approach costing in Project with confidence.

In the next chapter, we will cover even more advanced tools and techniques that are useful for monitoring and controlling projects. The topics we'll cover will be an amalgamation of important project management concepts and the corresponding techniques. This will include resolving difficult scheduling and costing problems.

16
Critical Path Monitoring and Advanced Techniques

A project in execution is often under several forms of external and internal pressure, which can derail it. These include scope creep, inflationary costs, competing resource commitments, risks, issues, and quality concerns. These factors can ultimately cause schedule slippage, budget overrun, resource overallocation, and quality issues. The project manager should use different monitoring and control techniques to minimize the impact of these factors on the schedule.

Critical Path Method (CPM) is the scheduling methodology of choice used in Project. A robust understanding of the CPM empowers the project manager to absorb and dampen the impact of external and internal pressures, as we will investigate in this chapter. Furthermore, we will also revisit the topic of overallocation, looking at some advanced features provided by Project with the aid of practical exercises.

In this chapter, we are going to cover the following main topics:

- The underlying logic of CPM
- Techniques to shorten the project from a project management perspective
- Lag and lead times of a project
- Advanced overallocation resolution techniques
- A strategic approach to resolving scheduling issues

So by the end of this chapter, you will have understood the significance of CPM as implemented by Project, the benefits derived by applying CPM in your schedule, and also the risks of overallocations if you deviate from the critical path.

A deeper understanding of the critical path

Let's begin with a quick and practical recap of the critical path concept. Any project schedule can be represented as a network of tasks, from the start to the finish of the project. The critical path is the longest path of tasks on the schedule. By virtue of being the longest path, the critical path will determine the end date of the project.

Efficient monitoring and control of a schedule in execution often include the following:

- Identifying tasks that need special protection against delays and risk. These are the tasks on the critical path.
- Identifying and analyzing alternative paths in the schedule for comparative analysis. This can help, for example, when you want to shorten the project duration.
- Identifying tasks in the schedule that have a certain *play* or buffer. That is, identify those tasks that can be delayed without impacting the whole schedule. This can help, for example, in absorbing changes to the project.

All of these skills first require a foundational understanding of the concept of **slack**. Slack is the topic of discussion in the next section.

What is slack?

Slack is the amount of time a task can be delayed without having an impact on the project. Slack is also referred to as *float* and can be positive, zero, or even negative. To understand this concept better, consider the following screenshot:

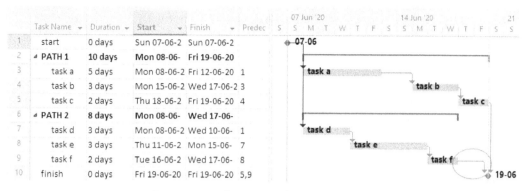

Figure 16.1 – Illustration of slack in a project

There are a few interesting points to note about this project:

- Observe that there are two parallel paths (**PATH 1** and **PATH 2**) in the schedule. Parallel sequencing of tasks is a common (and important) design feature of schedule network analysis.

- **PATH 1** has a duration of **10 days**, and **PATH 2** has a duration of **8 days**.

- Both paths start from and finish at the same milestones. Even then, the overall project duration is really determined by the longer path, **PATH 1**.

- **PATH 2** has 2 days of slack. A floating time period within a schedule is a slack. From the screenshot, we can see that it is possible to delay **task f** (the predecessor) by a maximum of 2 days without impacting the project's end date. In fact, any preceding tasks can be delayed without impacting the entire schedule.

We can understand from this that slack is a concept relevant both at the task level and at the path level. Based on this understanding, we can classify slack into two categories. Refer to the following screenshot, where we can differentiate the two types of slack:

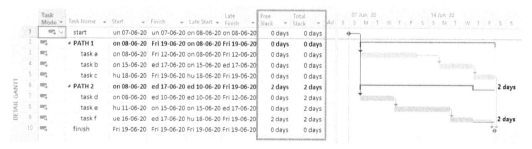

Figure 16.2 – Free Slack and Total Slack identified in the DETAIL GANTT view

As seen in the preceding screenshot, the **DETAIL GANTT** view with the schedule table configuration is the best-suited view for analyzing slack on your schedule. It includes the **Free Slack** and **Total Slack** columns, as highlighted in the screenshot:

- **Free Slack**: This is the amount of time that a *task* can be delayed before it runs into the next task. In our example, only **task f** has free slack (of 2 days) before it bumps into the milestone task named **finish**.

- **Total Slack**: This is the amount of time a *path* can be delayed before it impacts the end date of the whole project. In the **DETAIL GANTT** view, **Total Slack** appears as a thin teal-colored line.

Slack represents the flexibility of your schedule. Not all tasks have slack, and in the next section, we will discuss tasks that have no slack.

What is a critical task?

Tasks with no slack are called **critical tasks**. Any slippage on tasks with no slack will immediately impact the project's end date. Therefore, critical tasks are critical for the integrity of your schedule. Within Project, the important special conditions that trigger a task to be classified as critical are as follows:

- Any task with zero slack (this is obviously the most common condition).
- Any task with the **Must Start On** (**MSO**) or **Must Finish On** (**MFO**) date constraint.
- Any task with the **As Late As Possible** (**ALAP**) scheduling constraint, when scheduling in the forward direction from a start date. It is not recommended to schedule from the reverse order finish date, but in such a situation, the equivalent **As Soon As Possible** scheduling constraint on a task will classify it as critical.

Critical tasks are liable to impact the project's end date. Therefore, due diligence is prescribed to manage critical tasks during the following common project situations:

- New requirements added to the scope
- Overallocation resolution
- Budget and cost adjustments
- General maintenance and optimization of the schedule

The bottom line is that you should choose to modify a non-critical task with available slack instead of a critical task (if and when you have the luxury of such a choice).

> **Tip**
> Completed tasks are not classified as critical in Project. Once a task is completed, it can no longer impact the schedule for the rest of the project.

So, then, how do we monitor this? This is where the critical path comes in.

What is the critical path?

A series of critical tasks that determine the finish date of the project is the *critical path*. Logically, this will also be the longest path in the schedule. The critical path is dynamic in nature and can change during the execution of the project. There are several situations that might change the dynamics of the critical path, and the most common ones are mentioned as follows:

- New requirements might create a longer path in the schedule, thereby becoming the new critical path.

- When a task is marked as complete, it will no longer belong to the critical path, thereby changing the critical path.

It is best practice to always design your schedule with a single critical path for logical, mathematical, and practical reasons. All such best practices have been captured in a methodology called CPM, discussed in the next section.

What is CPM?

CPM is a methodology for scheduling tasks. As the name suggests, CPM is conceptually built around the critical (longest) path of a schedule. The time it takes to execute the critical path will be the same as that of the whole project. Microsoft Project is built around CPM as the central algorithm. In practice, CPM is used with another technique, called **Program Evaluation and Review Technique** (**PERT**). This second technique provides the mathematical framework to calculate schedule timings algorithmically.

Project does not insist that you schedule with CPM. The proof of this statement is that we have a chapter dedicated to Agile methodologies in this book: *Chapter 10, Executing Agile Projects with MS Project*. Agile is agnostic to any scheduling techniques such as CPM within a timebound sprint. But if you understand CPM (slack, critical tasks, and critical path), then the machinations of Project will not mystify you.

> **Pitfall – Multiple Critical Paths**
>
> If a schedule has multiple finish points, then it will have multiple critical paths, one for each different finish point. However, it is highly recommended that you design your schedule to always have a single finish point.

In the next section, we will investigate different applications of CPM concepts, to achieve an important goal of shortening the project duration.

Techniques to shorten the project

The project manager is often asked to deliver a project quicker than it will actually take to finish the project. At other times, there are delays, and the project manager must find ways to compress the schedule and recover from the slippage. Fortunately, there are some well-understood techniques of project management that can be applied to compress the schedule. It must be understood that all such compression techniques will incur an extra cost to the project, directly or indirectly. Furthermore, all schedule compression techniques will revolve around the concept of the critical path, and we will discuss three techniques briefly in the following sections.

Shortening the critical path (crashing the project)

Since the critical path determines the duration of the project, shortening the critical path will result in an earlier project finish date. This technique is commonly called *crashing a project*. To achieve this result, we can consider all possibilities, such as the following:

- Assigning additional resources to the critical tasks

- Assigning overtime work on the critical path

- Breaking up larger sized critical tasks to allow simultaneous work (with additional resources)

- Overlapping dependent tasks where possible (this is called *lead* time, and we will discuss it the *Applying lead and lag time* section)

- Increasing schedule flexibility by removing or modifying constraints (both date and schedule constraints)

These are only some of the tips that you can use to shorten the critical path, and your own business domain logic and specific project conditions might allow other ways to crash the project.

Increasing parallel paths (fast-tracking the project)

The second generic technique to compress the schedule is to overlap critical tasks, rather than follow a linear sequential path. This technique is commonly called *fast tracking a project*. The major assumption here is that your schedule logic will allow such parallel processing, at least for some sections of the critical path. The tasks that have been serialized purely based on resource availability should be the ones to be considered first for parallel execution.

The major concern with this approach is the risk introduced by parallel processing for critical tasks with logical dependencies. Fast-tracking should only be considered if all such risks can be efficiently managed.

Resource reallocation

In this third technique of schedule compression, the focus is on the *resources* of the project. Normally, during the estimation process, the average productivity of a resource is considered to derive an estimate. However, there may be hidden strength that can be leveraged during a crunch period to compress the schedule. This is the essence of the resource reallocation technique.

The strategies commonly applied in this technique include the following:

- Skilled resources are reassigned to critical tasks, rather than non-critical tasks.

- Resources from completed critical tasks are reassigned new critical tasks.

- Prior experience is leveraged for reusable design and components.

- Temporary staff can be engaged in the project.

Crashing, fast-tracking, and resource reallocation are three generic techniques of schedule compression that revolve around the critical path of a project. It is recommended that you read up more about these and practice schedule compression, as it is an invaluable skill.

We will conclude this discussion on schedule compression, with the following notable points:

- One or all of these techniques can be applied to the schedule.

- There is no guarantee that any of these techniques will deliver desired results in every given project situation.

- Additional risk is always introduced with schedule compression, no matter the specific technique involved. Proceed only if the risk can be managed.

- Additional cost is often incurred with schedule compression, no matter the specific technique involved.

Techniques to shorten the project schedule rely heavily on the presence of slack. However, slack is not something imposed by the requirements of the project. Slack is an incidental entity in the schedule. In contrast to slack, there will be other times when an intentional waiting time has to be enforced. For example, after a wall has been painted, some time is allocated for the paint to dry before the second coat is applied.

In the next section, we will learn how Project allows us to enforce time intervals between dependent tasks.

Applying lag and lead time

In contrast to naturally occurring slack, we also come across situations where the project manager *intentionally* injects a period of time into the schedule, because it is required (or demanded) by the nature of the project. Let's consider some examples to clearly understand this concept:

- In the civil construction industry, after concrete has been cast, it will be allowed to cure for a period of time. The succeeding task cannot be started during this curing time.

- After an employee joins the company, they are typically allowed to acclimatize to the new work environment before being assigned to a task.

Such an *intentional* time delay between the predecessor and the successor tasks is called **lag** and can easily be introduced into the schedule using Project. Consider the following screenshot of a schedule, which we will now use for our exercises:

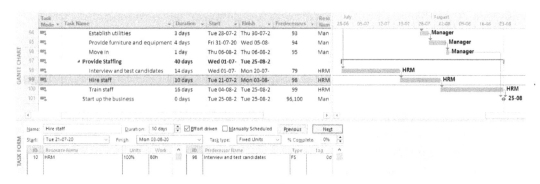

Figure 16.3 – Schedule before application of lag

There are a few points to note about this screenshot before we start our exercises:

- Under the **Provide Staffing** summary header, notice the three tasks that will be used for the lag and lead exercises, namely the one with task ID **98**, **Interview and test candidates**, task ID **99**, **Hire staff**, and task ID **100**, **Train staff**.

- All three tasks are on the critical path, as can be observed from the special color of the taskbars.

- The detailed split window has been enabled with the **Resources and Predecessors** panel, which is displayed on the bottom half of the screen.

At this point in the project, it is now realized that a *lag* of 3 days is required after the **Interview and test candidates** task and before the **Hire staff** task. These 3 days can be represented as a lag in our schedule, as depicted in the following screenshot:

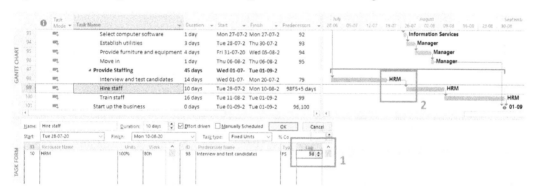

Figure 16.4 – After application of the lag period

The steps to add lag are as follows:

1. Ensure the successor task is selected in the main window and pertinent details are shown in the split window, **TASK FORM**. In the **Lag** column, enter 5 days. Only when you click the **OK** button is the change affected. Also, note that lag (or lead) is always applied to the successor task.

2. Observe the lag representation on the Gantt chart. The link arrow has been elongated over the lag days.

We have successfully applied a lag duration at this point. Because the task was on the critical path, the finish date of the entire project has been pushed forward.

The opposite of lag is a *lead*. Lead is denoted in a negative time period. To recover the 5 days of lag in the schedule, it has now been decided to have an early (lead) start to the **Train Staff** task. When a lead period of - 5 days is added to our exercise schedule, an overlap is created between the predecessor and successor tasks. This can be observed in the following screenshot:

Figure 16.5 – After application of the lead period

The steps to add a lead period are as follows:

1. Ensure the successor task is selected in the main window and pertinent details are shown in the **TASK FORM** split window. In the **Lag** column, enter - 5 days. Notice the overlapped tasks in the **GANTT CHART** area. The **Train staff** task will now start 5 days before the predecessor is scheduled to complete. This logically means that training will begin even before all the staff is hired, presumably in shorter batches. You can also observe that the lag and lead effectively cancel each other out on the schedule impact. At this stage, there is no change to the original schedule finish date.

2. Observe the introduction of overallocation on the tasks concerned. This is obviously the result of tasks now being overlapped while assigned to the same resource. This overallocation can be resolved easily by assigning one of the tasks to a different resource.

There are several techniques to resolve overallocation in Project, as we have studied in this book so far. We should choose a resolution technique that has the least impact on the critical path to minimize the impact on the project's finish date. This point is important to remember and obvious to understand. Stated in other words, while resolving overallocation, we should minimize the impact of our modifications by choosing to work on tasks with slack.

In the next two sections, we will now learn about two of the advanced overallocation tools provided by Project, with the critical tasks in perspective.

> **Information**
> **Finish-to-Start (FS)** and **Finish-to-Finish (FF)** dependencies are mostly the relationships that utilize a lag and lead period.

Advanced overallocation resolution techniques

The powerful scheduling engine within Project is based on CPM. We will now inspect two algorithms that are included in this framework from an overallocation and critical path perspective. These algorithmic techniques are like a double-edged sword because they can harm your schedule if used unwittingly.

The resource leveling technique

Resource leveling is a broad project management technique to optimize resource utilization on a project. In the context of Project, resource leveling often narrows down to resolving resource overallocation. Project provides an automatic and algorithmic-driven tool to level resources. We will study this tool, called **Level Resource**, in action with an exercise. Refer to the following screenshot:

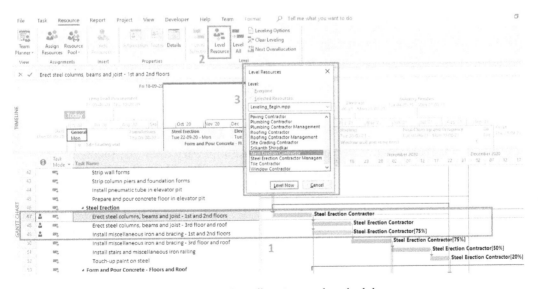

Figure 16.6 – Overallocation on the schedule

The important points to note about this screenshot are as follows:

- Tasks with IDs **47**, **48**, and **49** have an overallocation and they are all assigned to the same resource, **Steel Erection Contractor**. It is important to also notice that task **49** is not on the critical path, but the other tasks – **47** and **48** – are on the critical path. This is the reason for their different coloring on the Gantt chart.

- The **Level Resource** button is accessible from the **Resource** tab | **Level** group. This tool opens the **Level Resources** dialog box.

- Select the resource to level in the listing provided. In our case, the resource is **Steel Erection Contractor**. It is possible to select and level multiple resources at once.

The aftereffect of applying the **Resource Level** tool is shown in the following screenshot:

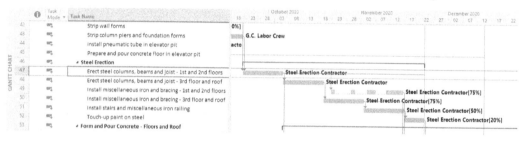

Figure 16.7 – Overallocation resolved by resource leveling

The important points to note about this screenshot are as follows:

- The overallocation has been resolved.

- Only task ID **49** has been impacted. This task was the only one not on the critical path and had slack. Project's algorithm has intelligently deduced the least impact to the project's finish date and acted accordingly.

- Task ID **49** has been delayed and split within its inherent slack to resolve the overallocation. Task delay and split are the two methods used by the **Level Resource** tool.

Even though this example appeared perfect and straightforward, there are plenty of caveats to using an algorithmic approach to resolving overallocation. These limitations are discussed in the next section.

Caveats to using the resource leveling tool

The resource leveling tool is perfectly usable for small projects and to analyze one resource at a time.

But there are some concerns when it is applied to medium or complex projects with many resources to be managed; let's see what these are:

- Not all automatic resolutions will be to your liking. Just by looking at the modified task, it is not possible to deduce the entire logic of the automatic resource leveling in the previous screenshot. Analysis of the complete schedule is required to manually deduce the reasoning of the algorithm. This situation is compounded when multiple resources are resolved over long schedules simultaneously. It will be difficult to identify all the changes made.

- Too many splits (created by the tool) are not productive, as common sense dictates. There is a well-understood *switching cost* to be paid with every task split. This is the time it takes to switch context from task to task, mentally and physically.

- It is not easy to delay any task just because of available slack. Often, your team members will resist an algorithmic approach to delaying and splitting their tasks!

These issues can be alleviated to some extent by configuring the underlying leveling algorithm. The **Resource Leveling** dialog box has the configuration options and is accessible from the **Resource** tab | the **Level** group | the **Leveling Options** button. Refer to the following screenshot:

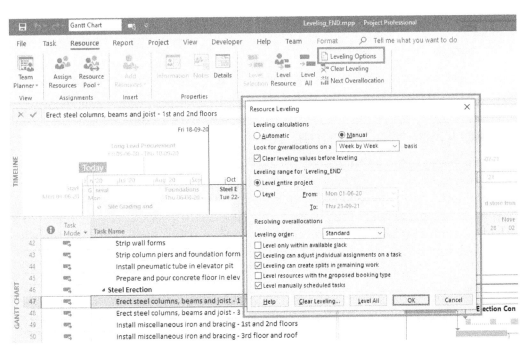

Figure 16.8 – The Resource Leveling dialog box

There are three sections to this dialog box interface, which are explained as follows:

- The first section is for the **Leveling calculations** options. **Manual** mode is selected by default and it is wise to let this be. **Automatic** calculations will attempt to resolve the entire schedule and all resources automatically, one resource after the other. This results in a cumulative impact of modifications and is not recommended for new users.

   Look for overallocations on a is an important dropdown, as it will decide the granularity of overallocation alerts. You are recommended to use a frequency that is smaller than your reporting frequency here. In our exercise schedule, the project runs over a year, and so a proportional **Week by Week** frequency is chosen.

- The second section is for the **Leveling range** options. Retain the default **Level entire project** option so that all assignments of a resource over the entire project is inspected.

- The third section is for the **Resolving overallocations** options. You are urged to read through these options and experiment with their behavior before altering the defaults in your projects.

It can be concluded that the **Level Resource** tool is best used as an analysis tool for one resource at a time. In practice, this tool works great with some additional tweaking to the assignments after the tool is applied. This assignment tweaking is done in consultation with the concerned team members.

In the next section, we will discuss yet another such automatic tool that works great for analysis and tweaking.

The work contour technique

When work is assigned to a resource, a convenient assumption that is normally made is that the resource works a flat 8 hours per day on the task for the number of days assigned. This is a perfectly reasonable assumption to make for all the calculations and estimations of the project. But the ground reality will often be different. For example, work might start slowly, peak in the middle, and taper off at the end. Such a descriptive loading of work is called a **work contour**. All assignments default to a flat work contour.

The work contour of an assignment can be customized to resolve overallocation. Refer to the following screenshot, which shows an overallocation in the project that we will resolve using work contours:

Figure 16.9 – Overallocation on the schedule

Notice the overallocation toward the end of the schedule, which we will resolve in this exercise using work contours. Notice the following:

- Task ID **142** has a duration of 2 days and is on the critical path.

- Task ID **143** has a duration of 1 day and is not on the critical path.

Work contours are applied to *assignments* (not tasks or resources), so change the view to **TASK USAGE**. Refer to the following screenshot:

Figure 16.10 – The TASK USAGE view shows overallocated assignments

The **TASK USAGE** view shows the cause of overallocation in our schedule. The **Vendor PMO** resource is loaded to **16** hours of work on a particular day! We will attempt to resolve this overallocation by changing the work contour of both the assignments concerned, such that the overall work is balanced.

Double-click on the first offending assignment to bring up the **Assignment Information** dialog box, as shown in the following screenshot:

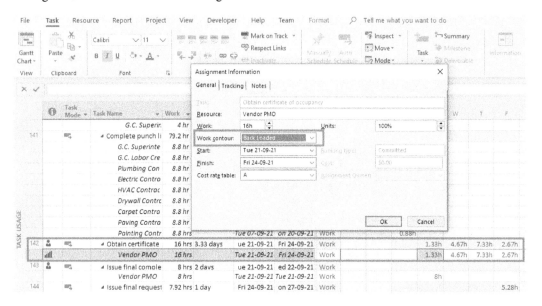

Figure 16.11 – The Back Loaded work contour applied to the first assignment

There are a few interesting points to note about this screenshot:

- The first assignment (task ID **142**) is configured with a **Back Loaded** work contour. As a result, the duration of the assignment has increased to **3.33** days.

- Observe the corresponding change to the work hours assigned to each of these days on the right-hand side section of the view. It is important to note that these numbers can be manually tweaked for even better results.

- Also, notice the special icon in the **Indicators** column to represent a **Back Loaded** work contour.

- The overallocation is not yet resolved and we will proceed to modify the second assignment too.

> **Tip**
> Microsoft Project provides eight different predesigned work contour shapes: **Flat** (default), **Back Loaded**, **Front Loaded**, **Double Peak**, **Early Peak**, **Late Peak**, **Bell**, and **Turtle**. The names are descriptive enough to understand the shapes, but it will help to experiment hands-on with some dummy assignments before using them on your projects.

Using the same technique, change the work contour of the second assignment to **Early Peak**. Refer to the following screenshot:

	Carpet Contra	8.8 hrs	Tue 07-09-21	on 20-09-21	Work		0.88h			
	Paving Contra	8.8 hrs	Tue 07-09-21	on 20-09-21	Work		0.88h			
	Painting Contr	8.8 hrs	Tue 07-09-21	on 20-09-21	Work		0.88h			
142	⊿ Obtain certificate	16 hrs 3.33 days	Tue 21-09-21	Fri 24-09-21	Work			1.33h	4.67h	7.33h	2.67h
	Vendor PMO	16 hrs	Tue 21-09-21	Fri 24-09-21	Work			1.33h	4.67h	7.33h	2.67h
143	⊿ Issue final comple	8 hrs 2 days	Tue 21-09-21	ed 22-09-21	Work			5.6h	2.4h	
	Vendor PMO	8 hrs	Tue 21-09-21	ed 22-09-21	Work			5.6h	2.4h	
144	⊿ Issue final reques	7.92 hrs 1 day	Fri 24-09-21	on 27-09-21	Work					5.28h
	G.C. General	2.64 hrs	Fri 24-09-21	on 27-09-21	Work					1.76h
	Vendor PMO	2.64 hrs	Fri 24-09-21	on 27-09-21	Work					1.76h
	G.C. Accountin	2.64 hrs	Fri 24-09-21	on 27-09-21	Work					1.76h

Figure 16.12 – The Early Peak work contour applied to the second assignment

When the second assignment is also modified with a different work contour, the overallocation is finally resolved.

Caveats to using the Work Contours tool

Work contours are algorithm-driven, and there is no special intelligence applied other than the redistribution of work on the assignment. Important caveats to be noted are as follows:

- Almost every time, work contours will increase the duration of the assignment.

- Do not attach any special significance to the contour shape apart from work distribution. In short, *if it works, use it.*

- After you apply the work contour, it is fine to manually tweak the assignment for the best fit.

Both the resource leveling and the work contour techniques are algorithmically driven. Understanding the strengths and weaknesses of these automatic tools will go a long way in their effective use during challenging periods of a project. In the next section, we will examine such a project with scheduling troubles, using many of the different techniques that we have learned so far.

Resolving scheduling problems

Even diligently run projects can run into scheduling issues. These issues should be highlighted by the monitoring and control processes of project management. When you face scheduling problems, a simple but effective course of action will be as follows:

1. Evaluate where the schedule stands now (using Project).

2. Identify the source of the problem (using Project).

3. Identify where in the schedule you can act (using Project).

4. Do the necessary action (outside Project).

Let's examine these steps in action, with the help of an exercise schedule. This schedule has been baselined and suitably tracked to simulate a project in execution that has run into trouble. Refer to the following screenshot:

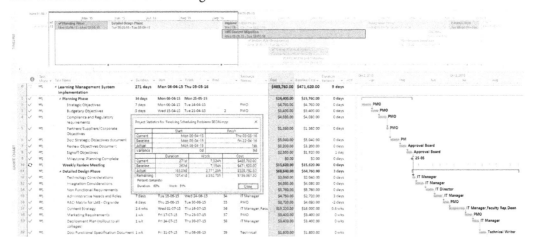

Figure 16.13 – A medium-sized project facing problems in execution

This is the schedule for an **Information Technology** (**IT**) project to implement a learning management system at a university. We will begin with the following observations:

1. The project statistics dialog box indicates that the project will last approximately 15 months, has 50 person-months in effort, and has a planned cost of half a million USD.

2. The schedule has already overshot the baseline finish dates by approximately 1 month, after the last tracking update was conducted.

3. On a positive note, the project has a robust baseline for both schedule and cost.

4. The schedule has been tracked frequently, and the integrity of the progress update information can be relied upon.

5. Most importantly, if the project did not have a baseline and it was not tracked, then any detailed analysis would not be possible.

Once we get this basic understanding of the project, we want to identify where the schedule slippage has originated and grown. The view best suited for this analysis is the **TRACKING GANTT** view. Refer to the following screenshot:

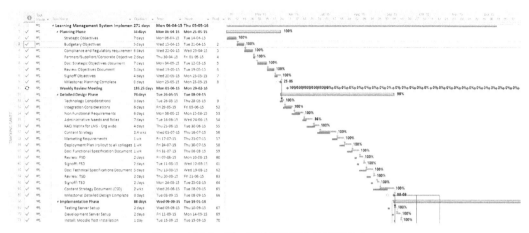

Figure 16.14 – The TRACKING GANTT view

The **TRACKING GANTT** view presents baseline information as an additional thick gray bar underlying the taskbar. From this preceding screenshot, the following can be observed:

- The project had been on track for the initial 2 months of the project.

- A small slippage on the critical path started from the **detailed design phase**.

- Slippage continues to cumulatively increase, as the project enters into the **implementation phase**.

- An attempt to recover lost time would have been ideal before the project entered implementation, but there is no evidence it has been performed.

Continuing with the **TRACKING GANTT** view analysis, the latter part of the schedule is shown in the following screenshot:

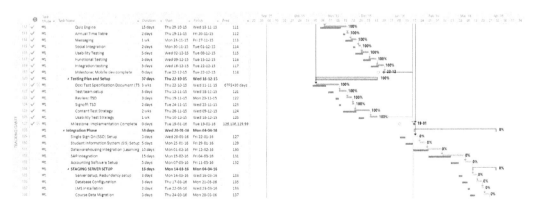

Figure 16.15 – The TRACKING GANTT view continued

From this screenshot, the following can be observed:

- Multiple parallel paths of execution in the schedule has helped control slippage.
- The project is tracked up to the **integration phase**, where it currently stands.

We can now use some prebuilt filters to identify areas of the schedule where we can act. The first filter we will use, **Late Tasks**, is also the most commonly used one. This filter will identify tasks that have started (*in progress*) but have exceeded their baselined estimates. Refer to the following screenshot:

Figure 16.16 – Tasks that have started (in-progress) but are running late

Some of these tasks have been running late for a long time. The project manager can investigate whether there is a significant obstacle to completing these late tasks. Sometimes, tasks are not updated or are abandoned and end up on the late tasks filter. In all cases, these are the tasks that demand the attention of the project manager.

For projects that are running behind schedule, it helps to rally the team members around a new date to collectively push for a reduction in the overall slippage in the project. The **Should Start By** filter can help with this, and is applied in the following screenshot:

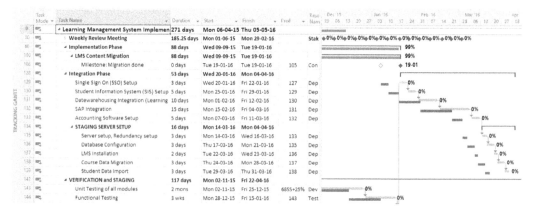

Figure 16.17 – The Should Start By filter applied

In this screenshot, we can see the tasks that are scheduled to have commenced but are dormant now. The project manager can talk to these resources individually to understand how the project can be brought back on track. Finally, the last filter that we will use in this exercise is the **Work Overbudget** filter. Refer to the following screenshot:

Figure 16.18 – The Work Overbudget filter applied

The **Work Overbudget** filter identifies tasks that require more work than was initially estimated. It is possible that these tasks are underestimated or improperly scoped, or the resource might need extra training and guidance. In all cases, these tasks need extra attention from the project manager.

Even with our brief analysis, we have seen how the source of problems can be identified, and where remedial action can be taken in the schedule. It is important to remember that a wealth of project information is only available to the diligent project manager who has baselined and tracked the project periodically!

Summary

We started this chapter with an understanding of CPM, which is the scheduling methodology of choice used in Project. Knowledge of slack, critical tasks, and the critical path allows the project manager to create and manage a truly flexible schedule. We also briefly touched on standard schedule compression techniques, such as project fast tracking and crashing. You are advised to learn more about these techniques and practice them. Finally, we concluded this chapter with two advanced algorithmic overallocation resolution techniques, always keeping the critical path in perspective.

In the next chapter, we will explore a wide assortment of built-in dynamic reports that are shipped with Project. These reports are graphical, and you will not need any third-party software to generate them. All the hard work you put into creating and managing the project schedule will come to fruition in the next chapter, with beautiful and impressive reports!

17
Project Reports 101

Every status report you send out to the world should say a story about your project journey. It should highlight where you are in your journey at the moment. Additionally, you may add how far you have come and where you are going to next. Depending on the audience, you will use different parameters to showcase and use different graphs. The first beneficiary of good reports is always the project managers themselves!

Project is shipped with powerful predesigned reports, broad dashboards, and more than a dozen other analytical reports for export, all out of the box. As long as you keep the progress updated on your schedule, you will have access to these professionally designed reports at the click of a button. These reports will suffice for most projects, with minimal tweaks. In this chapter, we will discuss these bouquets of reports, readily available as a gift to you in Project. In a later chapter, we will cover other advanced concepts of modifying existing reports, creating new reports, and sharing report templates with the world.

In this chapter, we are going to cover the following main topics:

- Understanding Project's reporting framework architecture
- Creating effective and data-driven **View-Table** reports
- Leveraging dozens of attractive prebuilt **graphical** reports
- Learning to export dozens of prebuilt **visual** reports to Excel and Visio
- Revising project status reporting best practices

Introduction to Project's reporting framework

There are several types of reports that a project manager will share during the course of a project – for example, feasibility reports, quality and testing reports, risk assessment reports, and resource reports. In the context of this book, the *report* we are referring to is the **project status report**. The status report is chosen as it is frequent and periodic and touches upon all aspects of project execution – schedule, resources, costs, quality, and more.

The primary objectives of a status report are the following:

- To communicate timely and periodic progress *(updates since the previous status report)*

- To set expectations on timeframes and quality *(publish relevant dates and numbers)*

- To highlight the issues you are battling today and risks in the future *(seek help and resources if required)*

- To alert everyone on upcoming milestones and deliverables *(prepare to test and integrate deliverables)*

- To predict the future of the project *(arrival dates of deliverables)*

There are many other beneficial soft objectives to be achieved with a status report too:

- To showcase your team's hard work to the world

- To showcase your own skills as a project manager, with crisp, precise, and professional-looking reports

The good news is that Microsoft has spared no expense in perfecting a set of reports that can help you achieve all of these objectives. Let's check them out!

Salient features of Project reports

There are specific advantages to using Project's reporting framework. The reports have the following features:

- **Dynamic**: As long as you keep the progress updated on your schedule, the reports are immediately available to you, without the need to update them manually. If you were using Excel, PowerPoint, or similar tools to create your report graphs and tables, then you would spend a considerable amount of time updating the numbers manually for every reporting period. With Project, the latest schedule data is used automatically, and updated reports are always available to you.

- **Self-contained**: There is no need for any third-party applications to create your reports with Project. If you are looking to analyze large amounts of schedule data, Project facilitates this with report exporting options.

- **Flexible**: What you share on the report will depend on the audience, and Project provides something for all stakeholders. For example, your team will want hard data, and senior stakeholders want graphical summarized data.

Project is designed for a very broad spectrum of reporting options. We will discuss this aspect in the next section.

Reporting architecture in Project

There are three distinct categories of project status communication in Project, as follows:

1. **View-Table reports**: You can print directly from the views and tables to create quick but efficient reports.

2. **Graphical reports**: You can use Project's crown jewel reporting framework, originally marketed under the moniker of **Graphical Reports**. This category is the main theme of the current chapter. These reports include an element of graphs and charts, which make them user-friendly and universally attractive.

3. **Visual reports**: For users who seek data-intensive reports for large projects, Project builds a seamless bridge to other software applications capable of **Online Analytical Processing (OLAP)** features.

Do not attach much significance to the naming of these reporting categories; all of them can include graphical and visual elements.

> Tip
>
> OLAP is a dated acronym, but the functionality it represents is still very relevant. Without getting technical, it will suffice to understand that OLAP *cubes* are a lightweight alternative to transactional databases. In the context of this book, OLAP technology enables us to crunch numbers better than Project is designed to handle.

Without further ado, let's examine each of the different reporting mechanisms of Project, starting with the simplest technique in the next section.

View-Table reports

You can directly print views as they appear on your screen to be used as a report. Such simple but effective reports are specifically useful for internal team meetings, as you will be able to present data with none of the abstractions used for the consumption of external teams. As discussed extensively in *Chapter 14, Views, Tables, and Customization*, use groups, filters, highlights, tables, and additional data columns to create reports custom-designed for the agenda of your team meeting.

Let's consider an example where you would use a **View-Table** printed report. Imagine that you are off to the weekly team status meeting and you need a report of every team member's current status on the project. It should include all of the tasks that they have each completed, tasks in progress, and the remaining duration for each task. Refer to the following screenshot, which shows such a report:

ID		Task Mode	Task Name	Duration	Start	Finish	Pred	Resource Names
			Resource Names: No Value	**239d**	**Fri 20-12-19**	**Thu 19-11-20**		
			Resource Names: Approval Board	**8d**	**Wed 11-12-19**	**Fri 20-12-19**		**Approval Board**
7	✓		Review Objectives Document	5 days	Wed 11-12-19	Tue 17-12-19	6	Approval Board
8	✓		Signoff Objectives	3 days	Wed 18-12-19	Fri 20-12-19	7	Approval Board
			Resource Names: Architect	**64.25d**	**Thu 09-04-20**	**Wed 08-07-20**		**Architect**
31	✓		Database design	5 days	Thu 09-04-20	Wed 15-04-20	30	Architect
32	✓		Doc: Upgrade Strategy Document (USD)	5 days	Thu 16-04-20	Wed 22-04-20	31	Architect
47			Automated and Manual Communications setu	5 days	Wed 01-07-20	Wed 08-07-20	45	Architect
			Resource Names: Content Team	**41.25d**	**Thu 21-05-20**	**Fri 17-07-20**		**Content Team**
39			Courses Upload	10.25 days	Thu 21-05-20	Thu 04-06-20	37	Content Team
40	✓		Courses Structuring	4 days	Thu 04-06-20	Wed 10-06-20	39	Content Team
41			Courses Support Material Upload	3 days	Wed 10-06-20	Mon 15-06-20	40	Content Team
43			Course Space Creation	5 days	Mon 15-06-20	Mon 22-06-20	41	Content Team
44			Course Pages	4 days	Mon 22-06-20	Fri 26-06-20	43	Content Team
49			Course Release Strategy	3 days	Tue 14-07-20	Fri 17-07-20	48	Content Team
			Resource Names: Content Vendor	**80d**	**Thu 16-04-20**	**Wed 05-08-20**		**Content Vendor**
62			Migrate SCORM Content	10 days	Thu 16-04-20	Wed 29-04-20	61	Content Vendor
63			Vendonr: New Content Creation	60 days	Thu 30-04-20	Wed 22-07-20	62	Content Vendor
64			Vendor: New content Upload	10 days	Thu 23-07-20	Wed 05-08-20	63	Content Vendor
65			Milestone: Migration done	0 days	Wed 05-08-20	Wed 05-08-20	64	Content Vendor
			Resource Names: Deploy Team	**165d**	**Thu 02-04-20**	**Wed 18-11-20**		**Deploy Team**
28	✓		Testing Server Setup	2 days	Thu 02-04-20	Fri 03-04-20	26	Deploy Team
29	✓		Development Server Setup	2 days	Mon 06-04-20	Tue 07-04-20	28	Deploy Team

	Task	Inactive Summary	External Tasks
	Split	Manual Task	External Milestone
Project: Learning Management	Milestone	Duration-only	Deadline
Date: Thu 20-08-20	Summary	Manual Summary Rollup	Critical
	Project Summary	Manual Summary	Critical Split
	Inactive Task	Start-only	Progress
	Inactive Milestone	Finish-only	Manual Progress

Page 1

Figure 17.1 – A print-friendly View-Table report

This report is printed from the **GANTT CHART** view (**File | Print**). Observe that it highlights the tasks of each resource on the project. Additionally, it shows the progress of each task, the (*projected*) remaining duration of each task that is in progress, and, as a bonus, the slack is shown for each task! This report is perfectly suited for a team status meeting.

You can replicate this report for your own use with the following configurations:

- The **GANTT CHART** view with the **Tracking** table is used, instead of the default **Entry** table.

- Show and rearrange any additional columns of your choice (such as the **Total Slack** column).

- Group the table data with the **Resource** criteria (the **View** ribbon tab | the **Data** section | the **Group By** dropdown).

Notice, in the preceding screenshot, that Project prints a legend at the end of every page by default. This default legend is just wasted space when you do not need the Gantt chart in your report and can be easily removed. Refer to the following screenshot for steps to remove the legend from the printed report:

Figure 17.2 – Modify or delete the default legend on print reports

The steps to remove the default legend are as follows:

1. Enter the backstage view from the **File** tab on the ribbon. Select the **Print** tab.

2. Click the **Page Setup** link.

3. The **Page Setup** dialog box opens up. Click on the **Legend** tab.

4. Select the **None** radio button option to remove the page legend from the report.

> **Tip**
>
> A picture speaks a thousand words. Learn to use a screen capture tool to copy and paste images into your different communications, such as email. Screenhunter is an example of a free and lightweight tool that you can use to capture parts of your screen.

There is, however, a pitfall here. The Gantt chart will not make much sense when groups and filters are applied to views. Do not use such a modified Gantt chart for analysis in meetings, as it will be difficult and messy to use.

View-Table print reports, as we have seen, are great for data-driven meetings. In the next section, we will learn about more attractive predesigned reporting features.

Graphical prebuilt reports

The **Graphical Reports** feature is the crown jewel of Microsoft Project. If you have followed all the best practices of schedule management, then graphical reports provide a fantastic medium to tell the story of your project. A set of more than 20 predesigned reports are shipped out of the box with Project. The design interface of these reports has been a major hit with users and has not changed much since its launch in 2013. However, new reports are added and existing reports become more polished. The report categories and the number of prebuilt reports are as follows:

- **Costs**: 5
- **In Progress**: 4
- **Resources**: 2
- **Dashboards**: 5
- **Task Boards**: 5

Each of these prebuilt reports is accessible from the **Report** tab in Project:

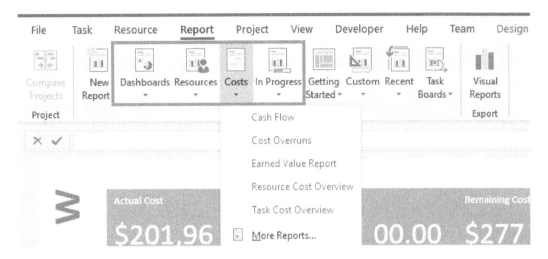

Figure 17.3 – The Report tab houses all the prebuilt reports

For the sake of brevity, the access path is not repeated later in the chapter.

Oftentimes, project managers limit the usage of graphical reports only to the five dashboards available. In the upcoming sections, we will briefly discuss all the major prebuilt reports with ample project data. The objective of the following discussion is to serve as a ready reference for the prebuilt reports.

Perfect reports do not happen on their own. The preconditions for great reports are as follows:

- **WBS best practices**: The top-level tasks of your schedule are used for analysis. We have covered these in *Chapter 6, Work Breakdown Structure – the Single Critical Factor*.

- **Baseline best practices**: A baseline created at the end of the planning stage and before the execution stage should exist in your schedule to study all variances. Refer to *Chapter 12, Baselines – Techniques and Best Practices*.

- **Progress tracking best practices**: Your schedule should be realistically and periodically tracked to reflect up-to-date progress information. Refer to *Chapter 13, Project Tracking Techniques*.

With this understanding of requisite best practices, we are ready to look at the individual reports. All the reports that we see in this chapter are from a single project schedule that has followed the aforementioned best practices.

Cost reports

The financial aspects of your project are abstracted in the **Costs** reports category. There are five prebuilt reports that we will inspect briefly, starting with the **CASH FLOW** report in the next section.

The CASH FLOW report

The **CASH FLOW** report showcases a high-level view of money transfer within your schedule. It also presents the remaining costs present on-hand (liquidity) in your project. Refer to the following screenshot:

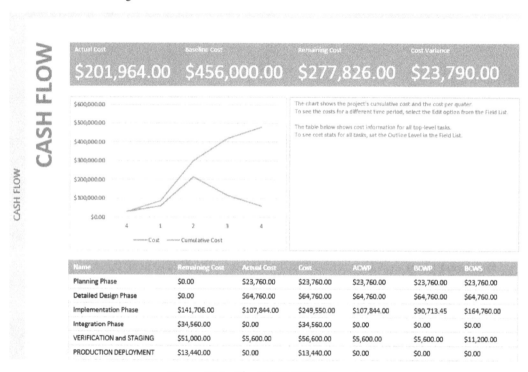

Name	Remaining Cost	Actual Cost	Cost	ACWP	BCWP	BCWS
Planning Phase	$0.00	$23,760.00	$23,760.00	$23,760.00	$23,760.00	$23,760.00
Detailed Design Phase	$0.00	$64,760.00	$64,760.00	$64,760.00	$64,760.00	$64,760.00
Implementation Phase	$141,706.00	$107,844.00	$249,550.00	$107,844.00	$90,713.45	$164,760.00
Integration Phase	$34,560.00	$0.00	$34,560.00	$0.00	$0.00	$0.00
VERIFICATION and STAGING	$51,000.00	$5,600.00	$56,600.00	$5,600.00	$5,600.00	$11,200.00
PRODUCTION DEPLOYMENT	$13,440.00	$0.00	$13,440.00	$0.00	$0.00	$0.00

Figure 17.4 – The CASH FLOW report

Observe that the table at the bottom of the screenshot shows the phase-wise distribution of costs in the project. This design is possible here because the report is programmed to show the costs of tasks at the highest level of the hierarchy (top-level tasks). In our case, these are summary tasks. By design, the summary tasks are named after the major phases in our schedule. Use this design model to get the most intuitive reports.

The Cost Overruns report

A cost *overrun* is said to exist when the *actual cost* exceeds the *planned cost*. The cost overrun report highlights the cost variance for top-level tasks, and for associated resources too. Refer to the following screenshot:

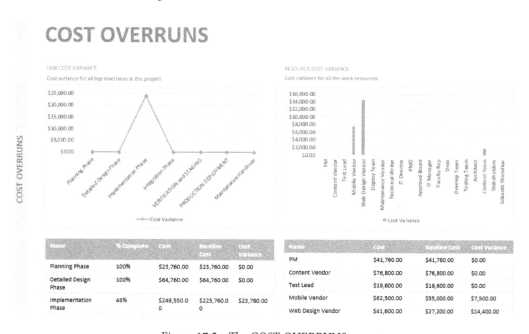

Figure 17.5 – The COST OVERRUNS report

As can be understood from the preceding report screenshot, the **implementation phase** is the cause of all overruns currently on the project. From a resource perspective, the two resources, **Mobile Vendor** and **Web Design Vendor**, contribute all the current cost overruns on the project.

The EARNED VALUE report

Earned Value Management (**EVM**) is a powerful project management technique to assess and forecast progress on a schedule. The **EARNED VALUE** report is designed for practitioners of this technique and it relies heavily on accurate costing data existing in your schedule to be able to forecast future trends on your schedule. Refer to the following screenshot, which shows this report:

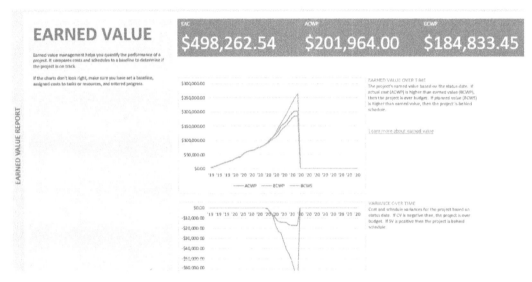

Figure 17.6 – The EARNED VALUE report

The EVM theory is beyond the scope of this book, and it has a separate learning curve. Whether you are already a practitioner or not, this report will add significant value to your project analysis.

The RESOURCE COST OVERVIEW report

This report is comprised of a chart that shows the cost status for all work resources (which includes people and any machinery) in the project. The associated costing details are included in an adjoining table:

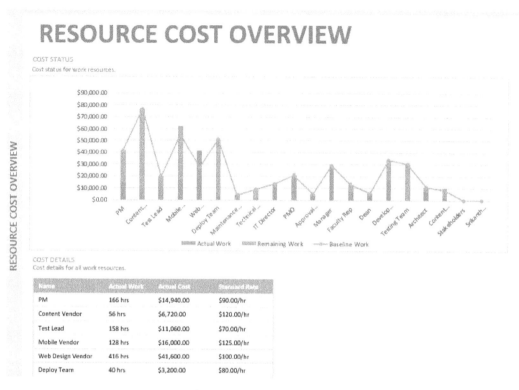

RESOURCE COST OVERVIEW

COST STATUS
Cost status for work resources.

Actual Work   Remaining Work   Baseline Work

COST DETAILS
Cost details for all work resources.

Name	Actual Work	Actual Cost	Standard Rate
PM	166 hrs	$14,940.00	$90.00/hr
Content Vendor	56 hrs	$6,720.00	$120.00/hr
Test Lead	158 hrs	$11,060.00	$70.00/hr
Mobile Vendor	128 hrs	$16,000.00	$125.00/hr
Web Design Vendor	416 hrs	$41,600.00	$100.00/hr
Deploy Team	40 hrs	$3,200.00	$80.00/hr

Figure 17.7 – The RESOURCE COST OVERVIEW report

The **TASK COST OVERVIEW** report is similar to the **RESOURCE COST OVERVIEW** report, except that the costs for top-level tasks are considered, instead of resources.

The In Progress reports

The current schedule-related information of your project is categorized under the **In Progress** reports. A total of four reports are available here.

The CRITICAL TASKS report

This is a listing of the current critical tasks on the schedule. Any delay in these tasks will result in the slippage of the entire schedule:

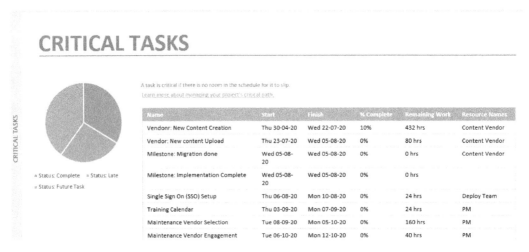

Figure 17.8 – The CRITICAL TASKS report

The LATE TASKS report

This report is a listing of all tasks whose actual start or finish is later than the scheduled start or finish dates:

Figure 17.9 – The LATE TASKS report

The MILESTONE report

Milestones are tasks with zero duration. They are used to denote significant events in the schedule. The **MILESTONE** report lists the delayed, upcoming, and successfully completed milestones on the schedule:

Figure 17.10 – The MILESTONE report

The SLIPPING TASKS report

Slipping tasks are those that are taking longer to complete than first anticipated. The scheduled finish dates of slipping tasks will be later than their baseline finish dates:

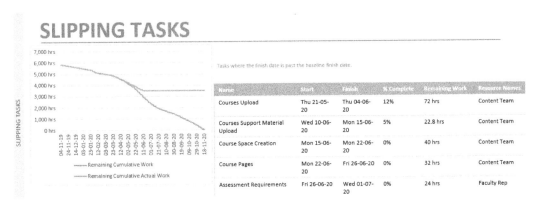

Figure 17.11 – The SLIPPING TASKS report

Resource reports

The **RESOURCE OVERVIEW** report is a comprehensive report that shows the work status of everyone on your project team. At a quick glance, the actual work and remaining work is cumulatively displayed. The included table is used to view the remaining work hours of every resource:

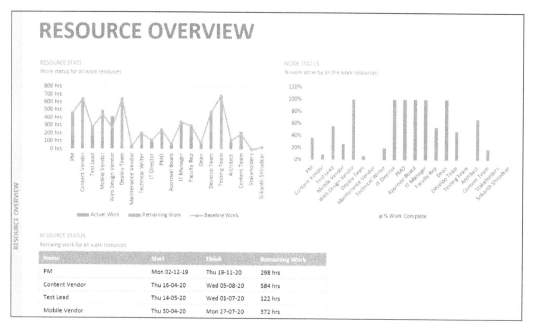

Figure 17.12 – The RESOURCE OVERVIEW report

There is another prebuilt resource report called **OVERALLOCATED RESOURCES**, which displays the actual work and remaining work for overallocated resources.

Dashboard reports

Dashboards are a popular reporting format designed to present key performance indicators over a broader area in a visually attractive way. In Project, the five dashboards are the most commonly used graphical reports and can encapsulate reporting of the entire project. We will start our discussion of dashboards with the **BURNDOWN** report.

The BURNDOWN dashboard

Burndown charts present **baselined work** against **finished work** and **remaining work**. Gaining massive popularity with practitioners of the Agile methodology, they are useful tools for analysis, no matter which project management methodology is employed:

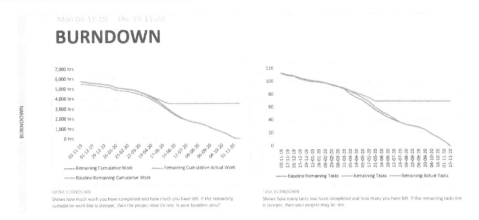

Figure 17.13 – The BURNDOWN dashboard report

The **BURNDOWN** dashboard includes the work burndown and task burndown charts. These charts are useful for making predictive estimations regarding the completion of a project.

The COST OVERVIEW dashboard

A high-level view of the entire project's monetary aspects is presented in the **COST OVERVIEW** dashboard. The actual cost and remaining costs are highlighted against the percentage completion of the entire project. Additional charts display the project progress versus costs incurred and the cost status of all the top-level tasks:

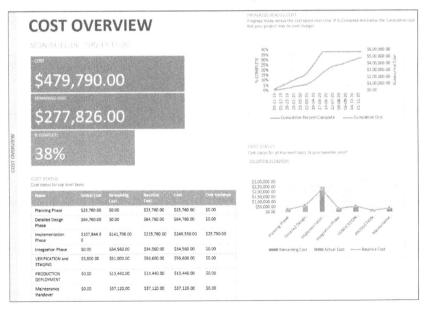

Figure 17.14 – The COST OVERVIEW dashboard report

The included table in this dashboard also shows the cost variance in numeric format, and this is a useful addition to the dashboard.

The WORK OVERVIEW dashboard

The **WORK OVERVIEW** dashboard paints a picture of the project with the perspective of the work involved. This dashboard helps the project manager answer the following key questions:

- How many working hours remain on hand to complete the project?
- How much work remains on each of the top-level tasks in the schedule?
- For every resource, what are the available work hours?

Here is the dashboard view:

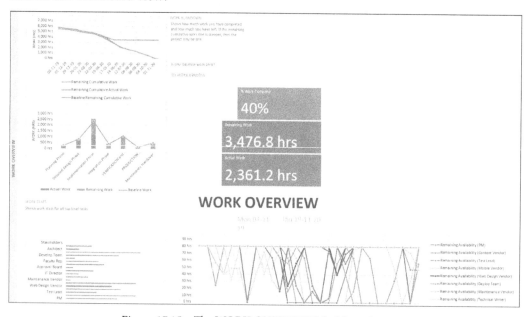

Figure 17.15 – The WORK OVERVIEW dashboard report

We have already seen the work burndown chart that is included in this dashboard. This chart helps the project manager predict the working hour requirements to finish the project, in combination with the other data presented in this dashboard.

The PROJECT OVERVIEW dashboard

Saving the best for last, the **PROJECT OVERVIEW** dashboard tells the high-level story of the entire project. This report is best used to answer the following questions:

- What is the overall status of the project? What is the status of the key deliverables of the project?

- What are the next upcoming events (milestones due) that the stakeholders should prepare for?

- What issues exist in the schedule execution (late tasks)?

Here is how this dashboard appears:

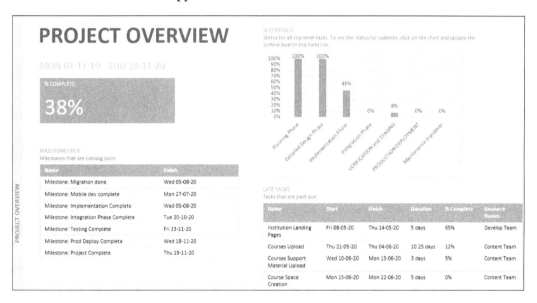

Figure 17.16 – The PROJECT OVERVIEW dashboard report

It must be noted that all of the reports that we have seen so far do not need a single edit to show perfectly credible schedule information. This point vouches for the usability of graphical reports. However, the schedule design also plays a big part in optimal reports. The schedule itself was baselined, a proper WBS-derived hierarchical tasks list was used, and the schedule was updated to the reporting periods. But there are limitations to the graphical reports, as we will see in the next section.

Limitations of graphical reports

As mentioned in the preceding section, there are a couple of limitations to graphical reports:

- Modifications to the prebuilt reports (for example, to add a new data column) require an additional learning curve. This will be discussed in *Chapter 19*, *Advanced Custom Reports and Templates*.

- Graphical reports can get clunky on larger-sized projects. If your project exceeds three dozen or more resources or top-level tasks, a lot of charts start overlapping each other. In general, you will face design issues with the report.

On larger-sized projects, graphical reports are generally not sufficient. Higher accuracy of predictions (particularly the project finish date) is required for larger and more complex projects, where the stakes are higher. We will investigate reports that require better number-crunching abilities in the next section.

Visual (OLAP) reports

Project provides a method to package schedule data for usage by external OLAP-capable tools. The external tools are mainly Microsoft's Excel and Visio, but they can be any compatible application. The exported packages themselves are called *visual reports*. Refer to the following screenshot, in which the **Visual Reports** button is grouped under the **Export** section of the **Report** tab:

Figure 17.17 – The Visual Reports dashboard

The exported data will be prepackaged into a report *template* design of your choice, hence the name *visual* report. This process can be best understood by an exercise. Open the **Visual Reports** dialog box, as shown in the following screenshot:

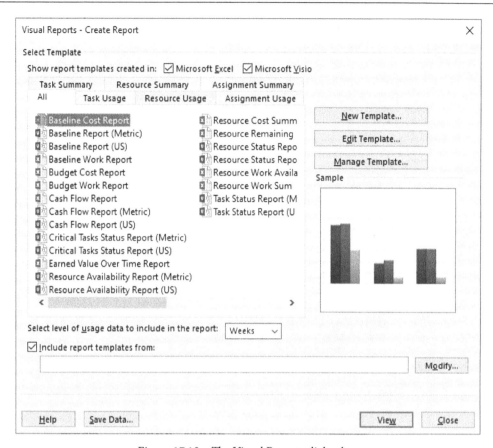

Figure 17.18 – The Visual Reports dialog box

The steps to create a visual report are explained as follows:

1. Select an (existing) report template to export data. When you open the dialog box, all the available reports for both Excel and Visio are displayed. For our exercise, **Baseline Cost Report** is chosen. This is an Excel report.

2. We will retain all the other defaults, and the export function starts when the **View** button is clicked. Project creates the *OLAP cubes* (a lightweight database) of export data.

The data is automatically transferred to Excel without your intervention. Excel pops up with the report, as shown in the following screenshot:

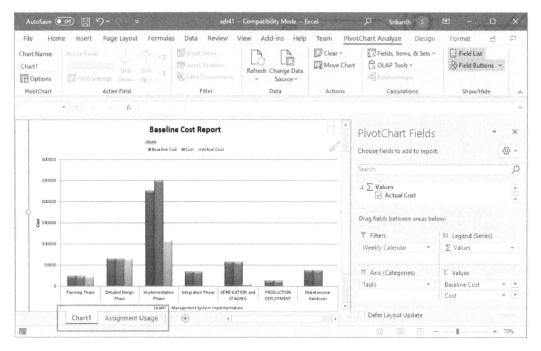

Figure 17.19 – The Baseline Cost Report visual

Project exports the data intelligently into **PivotChart** and **PivotTable** format, intelligible to Excel. Notice that there are two tabs in the new spreadsheet created. The **Chart1** tab is opened by default and displays the **PivotChart** format.

The other tab will contain schedule information in numeric data, in the **PivotTable** format of Excel. Refer to the following screenshot:

	A	B	C	D	E	F
1	Weekly Calendar	All				
2						
3			Data			
4	Task	Task 1	Baseline Cost	Cost	Actual Cost	
5	Learning Managemen	Planning Phase	23760	23760	23760	
6		Detailed Design Phase	64760	64760	64760	
7		Implementation Phase	225760	249550	107844	
8		Integration Phase	34560	34560	0	
9		VERIFICATION and STAGING	56600	56600	5600	
10		PRODUCTION DEPLOYMENT	13440	13440	0	
11		Maintenance Handover	37120	37120	0	
12	Learning Management System Implementation Total		456000	479790	201964	
13	Grand Total		456000	479790	201964	
14						

Figure 17.20 – The baseline cost report

More than 20 such reports, including those for consumption by both Excel and Visio, are presented out of the box by Project! All of these reports are customizable from within the respective applications.

For a holistic completion of this chapter, we will briefly revise some project management best practices for status reporting in the next section.

Best practices for status reporting

Effective reports are created with good presentation skills. Effective reports communicate better to the stakeholder and make project management much easier. Here are some simple aspects of an effective report:

- Keep it simple. Start with an executive summary for busy stakeholders.

- Understand your audience. Create different reports for different meetings, as necessary. For example, your CEO will not be interested in the task-level issues of the project, which is used for your team meetings.

- Timing is everything. Status reports are like newspapers and should be delivered promptly. Even the best reports lose value when delayed.

- Set proper expectations on all project parameters. Do not be tempted to promise more than what is baselined for your project.

- Brevity is valued. If you are presenting the report, practice to get the timing right. Keep spare some of the available time for questions and clarifications.

- Create a template for your status reports. Project's dynamic reports help you create and share the report faster.

These are just a few pointers in the right direction. There will also be several other domain-specific reporting practices that will add great value to reports.

Summary

Reports are supremely important for projects. The project manager should communicate that the project is in safe hands to all the stakeholders of the project, from the top to the bottom of the corporate totem pole. Reports can help negotiate valuable resources for your team and help influence important project decisions.

In this chapter, we have seen a wide spectrum of reporting options from Project. Closest to the level of the actual schedule is the **View-Table** reports, which are printed directly from customized views. At a higher level is a slew of attractive predesigned **graphical** reports. Finally, for larger projects with number-crunching abilities are **visual** reports. We have seen all of these reports function for the same project exercise schedule, without any major tweaking required. You have learned how to use the right report for the right situation. With the conclusion of this chapter, we also end the current section of this book focused on the *monitoring and control* aspects of project management.

Continuing on, we will start a new section of the book that will focus on *project closure*. In the next chapter, we will learn how to review schedules created with Project. We will learn, with examples, about many of the most common schedule design problems that exist in practice. We will also learn about the critical organizational advantages of using Project's template file architecture.

Section 6: Project Closure with Microsoft Project

Now we have come to the final stages of the project life cycle. This section will explain techniques by which the work of this project can be packaged in order to be used in other projects, or even across the entire organization.

This section comprises the following chapters:

18
Reviewing Projects and Creating Templates for Success

Welcome to this new and final part of the book. Here, we discuss how to gracefully close a project, whether or not its key objectives have been met. The normal tendency of developers is to close the project with a celebration, file the documents, and throw away the key. In this chapter, we will see how the process of closing a project systematically can add exponential value to your next project and to the organization. Our focus will be on the tools provided by Project that are used during the closing stages of a project.

Project closure is the time for introspection. It is the time to look back at the good, so-so, and bad aspects of the project that we are in the process of winding up. A project closure review is performed to analyze the schedule. Project provides two tools to draw conclusions from this schedule data and learn lessons from them. These lessons can be converted into templates in Project, for the benefit of future projects.

In this chapter, we are going to cover the following main topics:

- Introduction to the project closing phase

- Common error patterns in Project usage

- Importance of the Project Closure reviews

- Scheduling analysis tools in Project (to compare multiple projects and baselines)

- Introduction to templates in Project (global templates and project templates)

- Creating a new template for your organization

Introduction to the project closing phase

The **Closing Process Group** is the lightest process group within the **Project Management Body of Knowledge (PMBOK)** book, with a single process called the **Close Project phase**. As we will see in this chapter, being lightweight does not take away any of its importance. We tend to not pay much attention to the closure of small and personal projects. This tendency can lead to the same trivialization of closure, even with commercial projects. Improper or insufficient project closure can lead to some well-known risks, such as the following:

- **The never-ending project**: So many change requests have taken place in this project that the original scope is forgotten. The project is no longer financially profitable, but the resources cannot be released.

- **The suspended project**: The original stakeholder left the customer's company without a replacement, leading to difficulty in closing the project.

- **The orphaned project**: The project was executed successfully but is not in use now because it was not handed over efficiently to the customer (say, without a training and maintenance plan).

As testament to PMBOK's farsightedness and wisdom, we can note that the Close Project or Phase process applies to both individual phases of the project and to the whole project too. In the context of this book, we will focus on the closure of the whole project rather than the smaller constituent phases.

So, how do we go about closing a project? The following steps capture the essence of a project closure, no matter the size or domain of a project:

1. **Perform a review**: Conduct the *project closure review*. Project provides two superlative analysis tools that are especially useful during the project closure review. These tools are discussed later in the *Project Closure Review* section.

2. **Sign-off documents**: As the project manager, you might work with various departments of both your own organization and the client's. The **Project Management Office** (**PMO**), Quality Assurance, and Finance will be the relevant departments to work with for most projects during the closing stages.

3. **Release resources**: New projects are in the pipeline and project resources are to be productively re-engaged. You will release the resources, with appropriate performance feedback and further training needs.

4. **Transition to maintenance**: You might be obligated to train the maintenance team and/or perform other support activities. So now is the time to prepare for maintenance.

Performing the project closure review is critical for the future success of your project, and for your own journey as a project manager.

In this chapter, we will discuss some practical aspects of reviewing a project. The critical lessons from the closure review meeting can be a valuable legacy for the organization. They can be inherited by all future projects and hence can add exponential value to the organization. Project's **Template** concept is specially designed for this exact purpose. Project closure lessons are captured through a project template for use by other projects.

Reviews have shown that people who are new to Project tend to make the same patterns of errors along their learning curve. It will benefit us greatly to recognize these common design errors so that they can be avoided in our own work. We will discuss these common error patterns in the next section.

Common error patterns in Project

Learners of any new skill will tend to go through the same patterns of learning, as well as the same patterns of committing errors. If these pitfalls can be identified by a new learner, they can also be avoided. We will now see a series of schedule examples, each of which showcases a specific error pattern. You should bear in mind the following points when going through the examples in this chapter:

- It is important to visually identify the discrepancies discussed as *patterns*.

- Our examples will be simple, but the same error patterns can also be found in large and complex projects.

- Your attention should only be on the highlighted aspect in the screenshot; other details of the schedule are not relevant to the discussion.

- Error patterns can compound and are often found together.

The diligent reader who has worked through the book from the beginning will be able to recognize these patterns, as they have been discussed earlier in different contexts. All the error patterns are categorized as originating from either *sequencing* or from *scheduling*, as described in the next two subsections.

Sequencing error patterns

During the planning phase, you will go from the hierarchical tree structure of the WBS to the linear task list used in Project. At this point in time, it is easy for sequencing bugs to creep into the schedule, even with seasoned project managers. Such sequencing errors are discussed in the following list:

- **Abandoned tasks**: Every task in the task list should be linked. Tasks with neither predecessors nor successors are called abandoned tasks. Refer to the following screenshot:

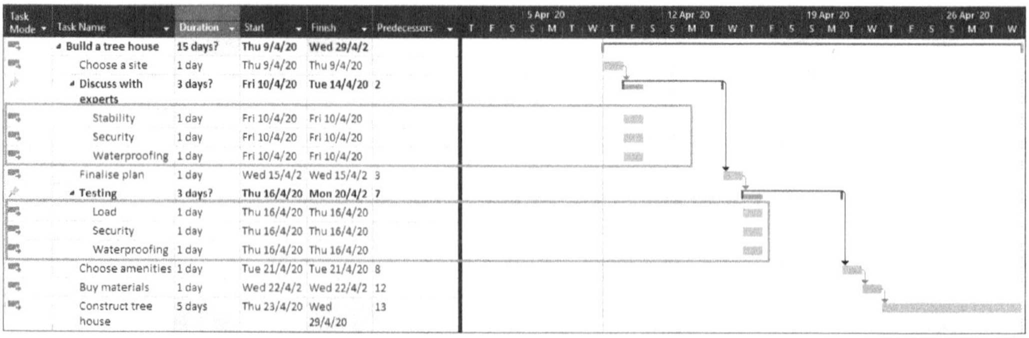

Figure 18.1 – Abandoned tasks

Abandoned tasks do not contribute to scheduling logic. In the screenshot, you can see two sets of abandoned tasks with neither predecessors nor successors. Such tasks run a wide gamut of risks, from being overlooked for execution, to being overallocated when discovered.

- **Jumbled sequencing**: In Project, the task list should be ordered chronologically. Even though this ordering is not enforced in Project, failure to do so will result in schedules that are confusing and difficult to follow. Such a schedule is seen in the following screenshot:

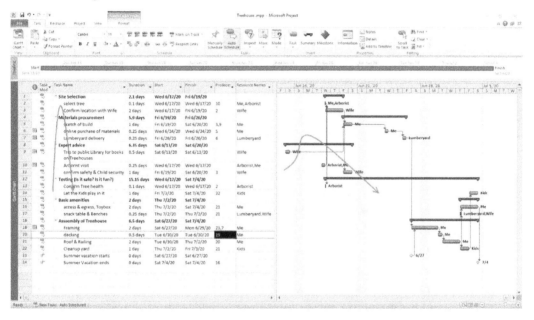

Figure 18.2 – Jumbled sequencing of tasks

To understand this error pattern, go through the tasks one by one *chronologically* on the Gantt chart, starting with the task that is scheduled first. You will find yourself going up and down the corresponding task list. Even though this error is cosmetic and is not catastrophic in nature, it can introduce errors by confusing the people assigned to the tasks. This error greatly reduces the readability and usability of your schedule.

- **Complicated sequencing**: Redundant (aka *dummy*) links on the network diagram of your schedule tend to add complexity exponentially. Look at the complexity of linking in the following screenshot:

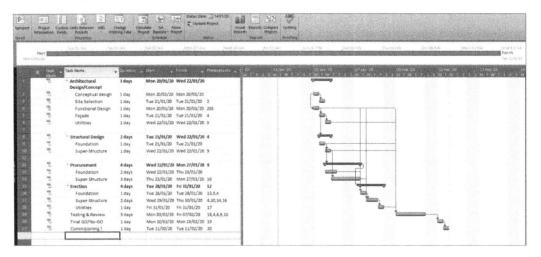

Figure 18.3 – Complicated sequencing of tasks

Many links in this schedule are redundant and can be removed with some understanding of *network theory*. After the network diagram of your schedule has been created, it is necessary for you to simplify the schedule with the removal of redundant links.

- **Disjointed sequencing**: Sequences of tasks disconnected from the main network can cause errors in schedule calculations and resource planning. They tend to get overlooked in the execution phase of the project. Refer to the following screenshot:

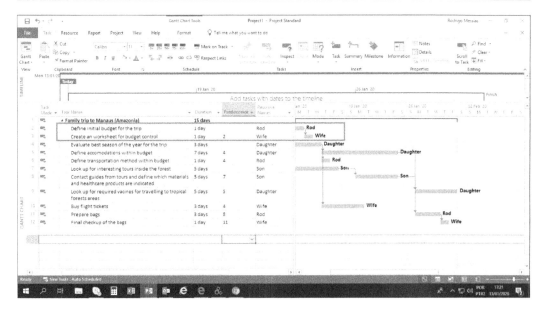

Figure 18.4 – Disjointed sequencing of tasks

In this schedule, a small disjointed set of linked tasks can be observed at the top of the schedule. Such disjointed sequences undermine the effectiveness of Project's scheduling algorithms because they are unaffected by the changes to the critical path (the longest path) on the project.

- **Stack sequencing**: In this type of error pattern, the schedule typically has several starting points and it is assumed that too many resources can work in parallel. The schedule is stacked with multiple tasks starting together early, as shown here:

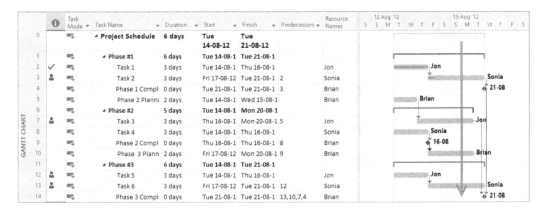

Figure 18.5 – Stack sequencing of tasks

The main issue with such a stacked set of tasks is that it can be overly ambitious in nature. There is neither slack in the schedule, nor a meaningful critical path. Overallocations will be in abundance on such schedules.

These five types of sequencing error can all be resolved by adopting additional best practices of *iterative design* and *multiple reviews*.

Scheduling error patterns

The errors that we discussed prevent you from leveraging the full power of Project's scheduling engine. These scheduling errors will impair the ability to mitigate project risks with schedule slack and to optimize the utilization of your resources. A practical knowledge of network analysis, the **Critical Path Method** (**CPM**), and its implementation in Project, will prevent all the errors discussed in this section, as shown in the following list:

- **Constrained complexity**: If you manually adjust the date of any (automatic mode) task, a date constraint is immediately added to the schedule by Project. The task gets *hard-coded* to that date, thereby greatly reducing the flexibility of your schedule. Refer to the following screenshot, which shows an all-too-common example:

⊿ **Project Definition**		5 days	Mon 12/16/19	Fri 12/20/19	
Business Reqt Sprecs Review		1 day	Mon 12/16/19	Mon 12/16/19	Manager
Software Reqt Specs Review		1 day	Tue 12/17/19	Tue 12/17/19	Manager
System Test Plan Creation		1 day	Wed 12/18/19	Wed 12/18/19	Manager
Infra Planning and Setup - including Bugzilla		1 day	Thu 12/19/19	Thu 12/19/19	Manager
Milestone - Definition Complete		1 day	Fri 12/20/19	Fri 12/20/19	Manager
Date constraints					
⊿ **System Design**		4 days	Fri 12/20/19	Wed 12/25/19	
Integration Test Plan		1 day	Fri 12/20/19	Fri 12/20/19	Team Lead
Acceptance (incl. Sanity) Test Plan		1 day	Mon 12/23/19	Mon 12/23/19	Team Lead
Integration Review		1 day	Tue 12/24/19	Tue 12/24/19	Team Lead
Sanity Testing Review		1 day	Wed 12/25/19	Wed 12/25/19	Team Lead
Implementation		1 day	Thu 12/26/19	Thu 12/26/19	T1
⊿ **Component Test Plan**		2 days	Fri 12/27/19	Mon 12/30/19	
Component Test Plan Review		1 day	Fri 12/27/19	Fri 12/27/19	T1
Milestone - Plans ready		1 day	Mon 12/30/19	Mon 12/30/19	T1

Figure 18.6 – Too many constraints in the schedule

In this example, practically every task has a constraint. This fact indicates that the user was unaware of Project's automatic scheduling and has manually adjusted the dates (with great care!), *before* linking them.

- **Fractured Critical Path**: Microsoft Project is best suited to CPM, and a failure to use this design will deprive the user of the scheduling power of Project. In the following screenshot, there are many scheduling issues that you will be able to identify, but the lack of a critical path will be the most glaring issue:

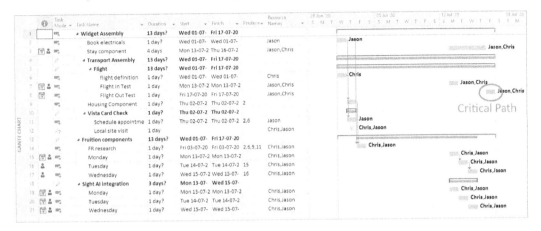

Figure 18.7 – A fractured critical path

In this schedule, a single unlinked task is identified as the critical path by Project because it is the last to finish.

- **Summary task linking**: Summary tasks can be linked in Project, but doing so introduces several complexities into the schedule, including resource overallocations and circular logic. The following screenshot shows an example of summary tasks linked erroneously:

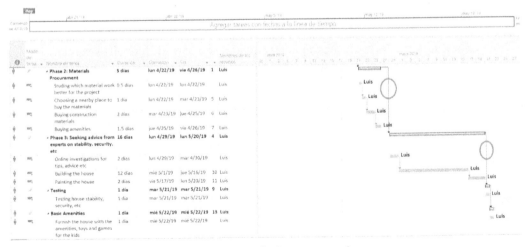

Figure 18.8 – Linked summary tasks

In this example, you can observe that the summary tasks are assigned resources. This is a bad practice too, as it can result in overallocation warnings and errors in the resource usage calculations. It should be noted that the Project Management Institute's guidebook *Practice Standard for Scheduling* advises against the linking of summary tasks.

- **Manual scheduling**: Project used manual scheduling task mode for new projects by default until the 2016 version. This caused many new users to construct complex schedules completely in manual mode. As you will be aware, it is a best practice to reduce manual mode usage to the absolute minimum. Refer to the following screenshot for an example of accidental manual task usage:

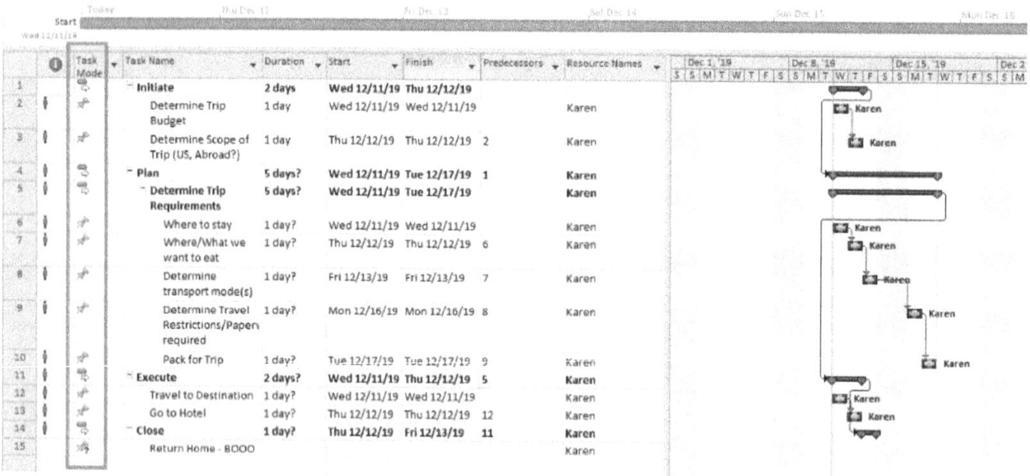

Figure 18.9 – Manual tasks

From the 2019 version onwards, the default task mode has been changed to automatic task mode. In the example screenshot, you can additionally see many design errors, including the linking of summary tasks and a stacked sequencing of tasks.

- **Unassigned tasks (and resources)**: When a schedule contains hundreds and thousands of tasks, it is a common human error to mis-assign one or two tasks to the appropriate resources. But this can potentially add chaos to the project, especially during crucial junctions. The schedule should be carefully reviewed for unassigned tasks before you create a baseline. You can perform this check conveniently with Project's **No Resources Assigned** filter criteria. This filter is accessible from the **View** tab| **Data** group | **More Filters** dialog box.

These were some of the most common, well-known, and highly visible patterns to look out for in the schedule. Setting the project calendar and seeking stakeholder approval of the schedule are a couple of additional good practices that are often missed by new users. Every one of these errors could (and should) have been caught in the design review before execution stage. Reviews are extremely important in preventing missteps during the entire project life cycle.

In the next section, we will discuss a special type of review performed during the final stages of the project.

Understanding the project closure review

The project closure review can add exponential value to your organization. The lessons learned from one finished project can be leveraged to benefit all future projects. For this reason, efficient organizations have a meticulous analysis of all aspects of the project during the project closure review. A top-down approach is used for the analysis, starting with the project's stated objectives, then proceeding to cover every project process, human resource, the costing, schedules, budgets, and any other extraordinary events. However, the key objective will be to understand the following:

- Were the project objectives achieved?
- What went right/wrong?
- What can be improved?
- How can we leverage the lessons that we learned from the project?

Project provides two superlative features that are especially useful during the project closure reviews. In the next section, we will study the first of these tools, which allows the comparison of two different physical Project files.

Project comparison report tool

As a best practice, project managers should save different versions of the project file under a document version control tool, or mechanism. Since Project uses a proprietary file format, you cannot compare different versions of the file using a generic file comparison tool. But fear not since Project ships with a tool exactly for this requirement.

Refer to the following screenshot, which demonstrates usage of the **Compare Projects** feature:

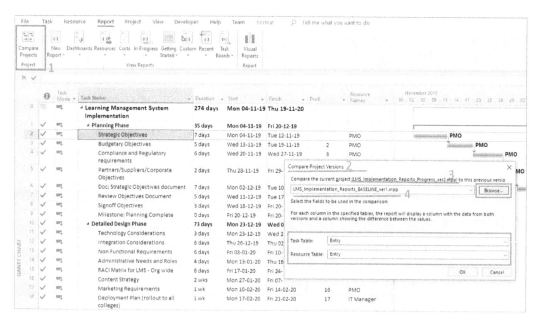

Figure 18.10 – Compare Project Versions dialog box

The steps required to compare two separate project files (versions) are as follows:

1. Click on the **Compare Projects** button, located in the **Report** ribbon tab under the **Project** group. The **Compare Project Versions** dialog box will open up. Note the current file name mentioned on the label at the top.

2. Use the **Browse** button to locate a second file. An earlier version of the current file is then loaded, as shown in the example screenshot.

3. Only the task and resource information are compared in the comparison tool, and you can choose the respective tables for each parameter. The **Entry** table is prepopulated by default, and in most cases this will be sufficient. Assignment information is not compared with this tool. Assignment information is compared with the Multiple Baselines Gantt view discussed in the next section of this chapter.

The comparison report is created in a new (physical) Project file. As can be predicted, the comparison report is really a clever split-window view implemented by Project. Refer to the following screenshot:

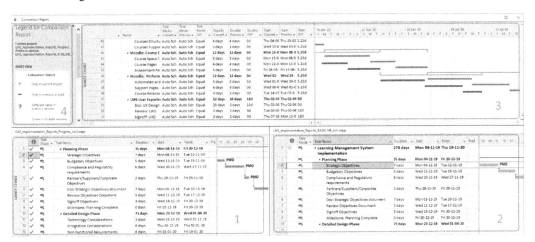

Figure 18.11 – Comparison report

The labeled sections of this screenshot are shown in the following list:

1. The file from which the report is generated is in the bottom-left split window.

2. The file that is loaded for comparison is in the bottom-right split window.

3. The main comparison report is shown in a classic Gantt chart.

4. A side panel in the top left shows the *legends* used in the Gantt comparison chart. You must refer to this panel for the colors and shapes used to interpret the Gantt chart.

The comparison table will contain data from both versions with one column for each parameter from each file, and an additional column showing the differences. Refer to the following screenshot:

ID	Name	Task Mode Curr	Task Mode Prev	Task Mode Diff	Duration: Current	Duration: Previous	Duration: Diff	Start: Current	Start: Previous
37	Course Landing	Auto S	Auto S	Equal	4 days	4 days	0d	Fri 15-05-	Fri 15-0
38	◢ Moodle: Course D	Auto S	Auto S	Equal	17.25 days	12 days	5.25d	Thu 21-05	Thu 21-
39	Courses Upload	Auto S	Auto S	Equal	10.25 days	5 days	5.25d	Thu 21-05	Thu 21-
40	Courses Structu	Auto S	Auto S	Equal	4 days	4 days	0d	Thu 04-06	Thu 28-
41	Courses Suppor	Auto S	Auto S	Equal	3 days	3 days	0d	Wed 10-0	Wed 03
42	◢ Moodle: Course C	Auto S	Auto S	Equal	12 days	12 days	0d	Mon 15-0	Mon 08
43	Course Space C	Auto S	Auto S	Equal	5 days	5 days	0d	Mon 15-0	Mon 08
44	Course Pages	Auto S	Auto S	Equal	4 days	4 days	0d	Mon 22-0	Mon 15
45	Assessment Re	Auto S	Auto S	Equal	3 days	3 days	0d	Fri 26-06-	Fri 19-0
46	◢ Moodle: Perform	Auto S	Auto S	Equal	12 days	12 days	0d	Wed 01-	Wed 24
47	Automated and	Auto S	Auto S	Equal	5 days	5 days	0d	Wed 01-0	Wed 24
48	Support Pages	Auto S	Auto S	Equal	4 days	4 days	0d	Wed 08-0	Wed 01
49	Course Release	Auto S	Auto S	Equal	3 days	3 days	0d	Tue 14-0	Tue 07-
50	◢ LMS User Experier	Auto S	Auto S	Equal	52 days	34 days	18d	Thu 02-04	Thu 02-
51	Doc: UX Design	Auto S	Auto S	Equal	23 days	5 days	18d	Thu 02-04	Thu 02-
52	Review: UXD	Auto S	Auto S	Equal	2 days	2 days	0d	Tue 05-05	Thu 09-
53	Signoff: UXD	Auto S	Auto S	Equal	2 days	2 days	0d	Thu 07-05	Mon 13
54	Custom Theme	Auto S	Auto S	Equal	2 wks	2 wks	0d	Mon 11-0	Wed 15
55	Department-w	Auto S	Auto S	Equal	1 wk	1 wk	0d	Mon 25-0	Wed 29
56	Logo and Brand	Auto S	Auto S	Equal	5 days	5 days	0d	Mon 01-0	Wed 06

Figure 18.12 – Interpretation of the comparison report

Note the following columns, as highlighted in the preceding screenshot:

1. **Duration: Current**

2. **Duration: Previous**

3. **Duration: Difference**

The function of each column is explained by its name. Data from each file is collated side by side and an additional column presents their difference. It is important to note that only row values with a difference are reported (basically, this report is not a data consolidation of the two files).

The report that is generated can be saved in a new file for a permanent reference, exactly like a normal schedule file. Just as a matter of good practice, you should name the file appropriately as a comparison report (and not just a schedule). In the next section, we will discuss another tool that is used for comparative analysis.

Baseline comparison tool

When we move on from creating a detailed task-by-task analysis, the next step will be to perform an analysis of the big-picture view of the project. The **Multiple Baselines Gantt** view provides a big-picture analysis. We have covered this view in detail in *Chapter 12, Baselines – Techniques and Best Practices*. For now, consider a quick scenario in which this view is used during project closure.

Scenario: A project is finally drawing to a close after two major change requests. Three baselines are to be compared to understand the individual impact of every change request to the schedule. The three baselines to be compared are as follows:

1. **Baseline**: Created during the *scope baselining* process of the project, just before the start of project execution.

2. **Baseline 1**: Schedule has been modified for the first time with a change request during project execution. New tasks have been added and other tasks have been modified.

3. **Baseline 2**: Schedule has been modified for the second time with another change request.

Refer to the following screenshot, which demonstrates this scenario analysis performed with the **Multiple Baseline Gantt** view:

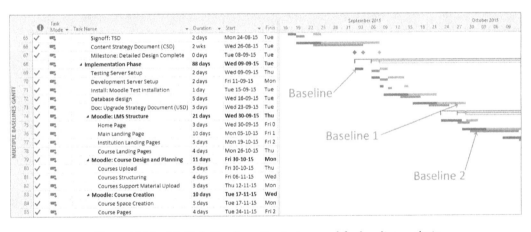

Figure 18.13 – Multiple Baselines Gantt view used for baseline analysis

By default, only the first three baselines are displayed in this view. To add more baselines to the analysis, you will just have to add bar style formatting for the other baselines of your choice. This is so just by design, as explained in *Chapter 12, Baselines – Techniques and Best Practices*, in the *Multiple baselines issue and its resolution* section.

So far, we have learned about the powerful tools for closure analysis provided by Project. Analysis leads to us learning valuable lessons about the project we are concluding. The next question will be how to pass on these lessons to the next generation of projects.

Templates for success

Templates are a fundamental concept that we see everywhere in real life. For example, a ruler is often the first template we encounter as young students. The ruler is a template for straight lines. Similarly, children use cookie-cutter templates to make quick and easy shapes with play dough. These are examples of the simplest forms of templates.

With Project, you can transform your successfully completed project into a template for future projects. For example, an architect might create different project templates for homes, offices, institutions, leisure spaces, and retail shops. Inside these templates, they might include their own signature style of project execution. They may also include the valuable lessons from reviews of previous projects.

Organizations of all domains, shapes, and sizes use templates. For example, your organization might have different templated forms to be filled for travel, material procurement, quality assurance, and so on.

In the remainder of this chapter, we will discuss how templates are implemented in Project, how they contribute to project success, and how we can create our own templates.

For now, let's see how we use templates in Project.

Templates in Project

The concept of a template is central to Project, and it ships with several prebuilt templates for your convenience. Templates were first introduced in *Chapter 2, Fundamentals of Microsoft Project*. Throughout this book, you have been using the **Blank Project** template to create new files for our hands-on exercises.

There are two types of templates within Project, as follows:

- **Global Template**: This is the central storage repository of every view, table, calendar, report, and filter that is shipped with Project.

- **Project Template**: This is also a repository, and it is used to *extend* the global template. It can additionally hold task, resource, and assignment information.

From a usage perspective, the global template helps store and share new project elements that you create. We will explore this perspective in *Chapter 19, Advanced Custom Reports and Templates*. The focus in this chapter will be on local *project templates*. The project template *inherits* (that is, it has access to) everything from the global template and can also contain schedule information. Creating your own project templates provides significant benefits to you and your organization, as discussed in the next section.

Benefits of templates

Exploratory projects are hard to size and estimate because of the unknown factors involved. But you can jumpstart the next similar project by leveraging on the success and lessons of the earlier project schedule. The previous project's schedule information becomes the new **template**! The benefits that you reap from creating and using a template are as follows:

- **A better understanding of the real work involved**: Consider the situation where a customer has missed a critical requirement, or some tasks turned out to be much more complicated than expected. Or perhaps some third-party software libraries did not behave as promised and a different library had to be identified. These lessons can now be added into the template's activity list so that the next project manager will benefit from them.

- **A better understanding of the real costs involved**: Just as the actual project work is better understood after a closure review, the associated resourcing and costs are also fully apprehended. The template can store generic resource names and their indicative costs to the company.

- **Ability to build and scale the schedule rapidly**: Assume that one successful project leads to three similar projects for your company. Using the template reduces the planning time required from $3x$ to x, with a few caveats.

- **Enforce a certain methodology in the organization**: Project templates can be a boon for organizations and domains driven by exacting quality standards, enforced by regulation. For example, if certain testing is mandatory for a project, then it can be represented as a milestone in the template.

As you might have guessed by now, in Project, the project template is (almost) a standard project file, saved with a different file extension. There is some curation of the actual data involved with a template. We will learn about this in the next section.

Creating a new template for your organization

When you decide to turn your existing project schedule into a template, the first question to ask is, *Who is the intended audience of this template?* If the audience is outside your department or organization, for example, you might choose not to reveal the resourcing (and costing) information. Of course, the more detailed the template, the better it may help the next generation of projects.

Let's create a new template as an exercise. The following screenshot shows a schedule to implement an online open source learning-management system for a large university:

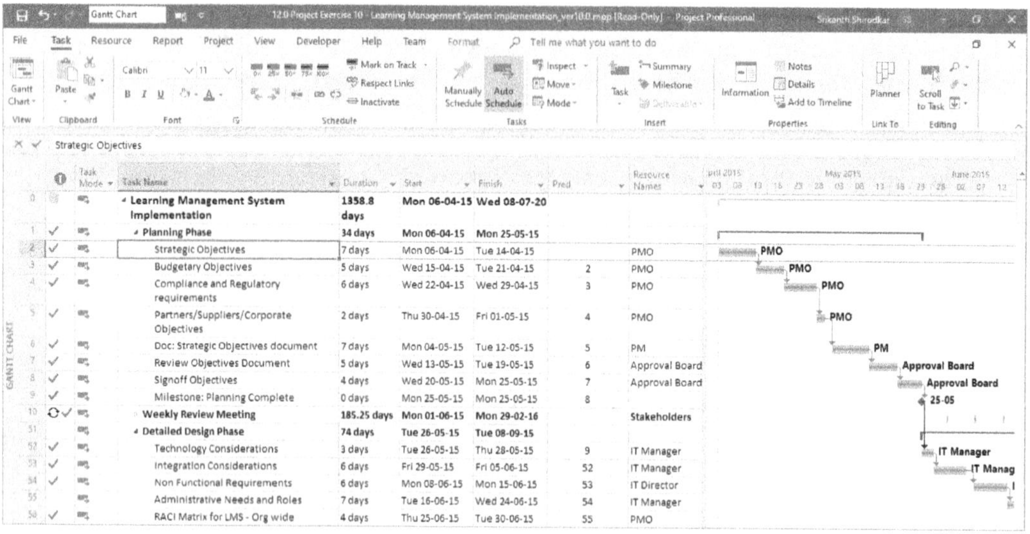

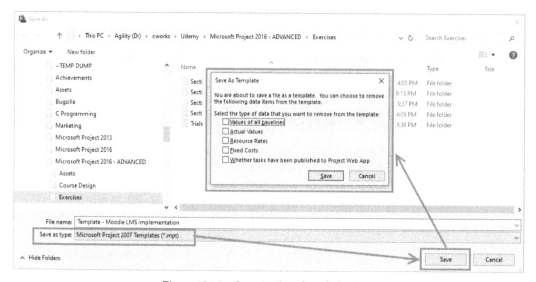

Figure 18.14 – A normal schedule is used to create a new template

Let's say that you want to create a project template from your earlier successful schedule because your organization is flooded with new business from the marketplace.

Start by navigating to the familiar **Save As** dialog box by going to the **File** ribbon menu and clicking the **Save As** button. Refer to the following screenshot:

Figure 18.15 – Save As Template dialog box

The steps to create a new template are as follows:

1. Choose to save the file with an MPT file extension in the **Save As Type** drop-down list box.

2. Click the **Save** button. You would normally expect the file to just be saved without any further interaction, but instead, the **Save As Template** dialog box opens up.

3. All data that is in the original project schedule file will be saved to the template *except* the elements selected in the checkbox. For example, you may choose to remove the **Resource Rates** by selecting the appropriate checkbox.

4. As a best practice, annotate the template liberally with the lessons that you learned from previously successful projects using the **Notes** data field (available for all tasks, resources, and assignments separately).

You can now create a new project schedule from the saved template by opening it directly from the file explorer. Templates can be shared with your colleagues and perhaps even industry peers. Templates are a great way to share your expertise with the world and make contributions to your domain knowledge. I intend to build a repository of templates that are accessible to all my readers and students; please learn and contribute on www. learngood.in. Several organizations commercialize domain-specific templates too, which can be used directly for your own business purposes.

Summary

Microsoft Project has a steep learning curve but reading this book will have helped you surmount this with ease. New learners tend to commit the same patterns of errors, and in this chapter, you have learned to identify these patterns. Now, you will have the ability to avoid these patterns in your own work and recognize them in other schedules that you will review. All such error patterns should be identified and ironed out systematically during project reviews, throughout the project life cycle.

The project closure review process has great significance in your journey as a practitioner of project management. In this chapter, we have learned about the tools to reviewing both the big-picture view (multiple baselines) and the detail-oriented view (project comparison report) for usage during the closing stages of the project. The lessons gleaned from the closure review can be packaged effectively into project templates for the benefit of the organization.

In the next chapter, we will revisit the concept of templates. We will learn how to create advanced customized reports and share them with the world through global templates.

19
Advanced Custom Reports and Templates

If you are already a skilled user of reporting with Excel and PowerPoint, then you will find Project's report customization features to be a garden of delight. If you are not, then this chapter will get you up and running fast.

In the previous chapter, we only studied the wide variety of prebuilt reports readily available out of the box with Project. Already, I expect you might have played around with the reports a bit, and a lot of questions will have come to your mind. This chapter will seek to answer those questions.

In this chapter, we are going to cover the following main topics:

- Understanding the logic of Project's reporting architecture
- Modifying existing prebuilt reports
- Creating new custom reports
- Saving reports to a global template to enable sharing

- Loading reports from a global template
- Understanding the best practices for global templates

Introduction to customized reports

We studied a multitude of prebuilt reports available to us in Project in *Chapter 17, Project Reports 101*. There are three fundamental categories of report communications in Project, detailed as follows:

- **View-Table reports**: These are lightweight reports created (usually printed) from combinations of views and tables, mostly for consumption by the internal project team.

- **Graphical reports**: These are the prebuilt reports most popularly showcased by Project practitioners. They are dynamic, intuitive, and visually attractive. These reports are mostly suited for client meetings or similar. This category is the main theme of the current chapter.

- **Visual reports**: These reports allow you to export prebuilt report templates to applications capable of better number-crunching, such as Microsoft Excel.

In this chapter, we will first learn how to modify (or tweak) existing reports to suit our needs. Then, we will proceed to create custom-designed graphical reports. We will finally conclude by learning techniques to share and reuse our custom reports with the world.

> Pitfall
>
> Always perform your report modification experiments on a backup file, never on the same file you use to report to your stakeholders. It is easy to break a report with an accidental click. This is not advised, especially if you have just an hour to go to the next meeting!

Let's begin with an understanding of Project's reporting architecture. We will learn just enough to create customized reports on our own!

Understanding Project's reporting architecture

When you begin editing any of Project's graphical reports, you might find that it has an array of buttons and options that resemble the cockpit of a fighter plane! But when you actually begin to use the reporting features, the complexity begins to vanish. This is because the interface closely resembles the charting options available in other Microsoft Office products such as Excel and PowerPoint. Fortunately for us, all your WYSIWYG charting skills are transferrable to Project.

The following points are to be understood before we start our customizing reports exercises:

- All the data columns that you can access within the normal functioning of Project are available to you within the reporting framework too. Some extra data fields are available for the higher versions of Project that map to the additional features available.

- Any graphical report is made up of four fundamental components – the data fields, filters, groups, and a display format. The astute among you will be able to detect the similarities to the *views* architecture. Views are made up of table columns, filters, groups, and display formats.

- The display format for a graphical report can be any combination of charts, tables, or a textbox.

- Mathematically speaking, charts can be made up of tables, figures, or graphs. Graphs display the mathematical visual relations of datasets. In Project, the terms *charts* and *graphs* are used interchangeably, just for the sake of intuitive user experience.

> **Tip**
> Learn how to identify column names accurately from the (multitude of) views that we have discussed in this book. Every chapter includes an explanation of the data types behind the table columns. This skill will be invaluable while modifying existing reports or creating new ones. It will also be helpful in fixing broken reports!

All the graphical reports in Project are directly hooked to your project data. Every week, when you update the project status, all your reports will have automatically changed as well! We will understand the consequences of this dynamic design in the next section.

Understanding dynamic reports

Imagine a scenario where you are presenting the project costs to your company's board. Your report has a week-by-week project cost breakdown for the previous year. During the presentation, the CEO asks for a *monthly* breakdown of the costs to compare with their own monthly outlay. If you are using Project to make the presentation, you can instantly (dynamically) present the data requested. For a detailed explanation and examples of how this works, refer to *Chapter 17*, *Project Reports 101*. As we will find out later in this chapter, you can also do a whole lot more.

> **Pitfall**
>
> Dynamic reports are a double-edged sword, as it is easy to accidentally break a report. A pragmatic project manager will probably refrain from dynamically changing data during a presentation. Expectations have to be carefully managed when presenting reports to key stakeholders.

Proceeding with this same scenario, we will learn how to modify existing reports in the next section.

Modifying an existing report

We will start with a simple exercise and slowly decipher the intricacy involved. Project ships with a lot of graphical reports, but often, you will want to tweak the report to suit your own style of reporting.

First, we will load the **COST OVERVIEW** dashboard report from the **Report** tab | the **Dashboards** drop-down button | the **Cost Overview** report button.

On this dashboard, **PROGRESS VERSUS COST** is an important graphical report that compares *project completeness* against *costs incurred* along the project timescale:

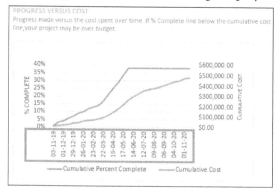

Figure 19.1 – The PROGRESS VERSUS COST graph

The following are a few important points to note about this graph:

- The **Cumulative Percent Complete** data field is plotted on the left vertical axis.

- **Cumulative Cost** is plotted on the right vertical axis, with its values in dollars.

- A *weekly* timescale is plotted on the horizontal axis, completing the graph. Notice that the timescale is hard to interpret and is better understood with a *monthly* timescale.

As soon as you click anywhere on the graph, a new panel will dock to the edge of the work area, as shown in the following screenshot:

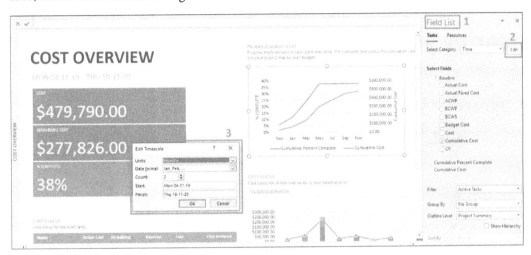

Figure 19.2 – The PROGRESS VERSUS COST graph

There are some salient points to be noted about this screenshot:

1. A new *panel interface* titled **Field List** is shown anytime you click on a dynamic report. If the panel does not show up for you, right-click on any graph and you will be able to toggle the panel visibility on and off. Take a moment to observe this panel. Notice that this panel has two tabs—one for the **Task** fields and another for the **Resource** fields. This is followed by a listing of all the fields available for the graph. At the bottom of the panel are options to filter, group, and outline data.

2. Notice the **Select Category** dropdown at the top of the panel. This dropdown is to select the horizontal axis of our graph (or table) and the current graph has **Time** as the horizontal axis. Click on the **Edit** button to format the timeline as per our requirements.

3. The **Edit Timescale** dialog box pops up and you can now set **Units** to **Months** (instead of the default option of **Weeks**). There are also multiple **Date format** choices available, and we will choose a short format as shown in the screenshot.

It will usually take a moment or so for the graph to automatically update itself to your formatting choices, depending on the size of the data being plotted. When the data is refreshed, our objective for this simple exercise has been accomplished.

Now that we have been gently introduced to the report customization interface of Project, it is time to take on more challenges. We will proceed to build out some new and interesting graphical reports of our own in the next section.

Creating your own custom report

Let's explore how to create a brand-new custom report. From the **Report** ribbon tab, click on the **New Report** drop-down button. There are four easy-to-understand templated options presented, as shown in the following screenshot:

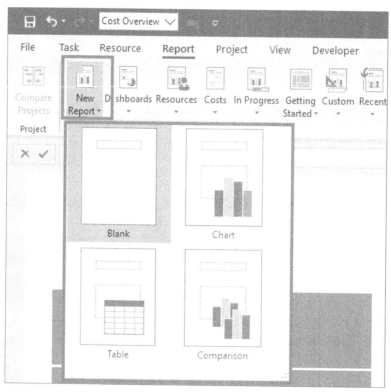

Figure 19.3 – Options to create a new report

We will choose a blank report template for our next exercise. This will act as an empty canvas for us to paint our reporting stories.

The other choices are intuitive to understand and there is not much of a difference between them because you can add any chart or table to any of the report templates. The **Comparison** report template, however, is different and used to compare two Project *files*, as explained in *Chapter 18, Reviewing Projects and Creating Templates for Success*, in the *Project comparison report tool* section.

You will then be prompted to name your new report, and it is good practice to name it so that it is easily identifiable as a custom report. In the next section, we will add a simple but useful table to highlight the cost variance from a resourcing perspective.

A new report – resource cost balancing table report

If you are tracking costs in Project, then it will be productive to analyze cost variance by resource. This becomes essential when you are working with external vendors and consultants. Even more so when you have a tight budget and must decide when *done is better than perfect* regarding features delivered by specific resources. Refer to the following screenshot:

Figure 19.4 – Inserting a new table for our report

There are some important points to observe in this screenshot, as follows:

1. Notice the new tabs, **Table Design** and **Layout**, added to the ribbon. These allow you to customize the look and feel of the table. However, since those interfaces are intuitive and exactly like those found in other Microsoft Office products, we will gracefully slide over discussing those in any greater detail. You can explore those features later.

2. When you insert a brand-new table, it will be prepopulated with a few default fields. The currently selected fields are **Name** (the task name), **Start**, **Finish**, and **% Complete** (percentage complete).

3. Correspondingly, notice that at any given time on the fields panel, the same currently selected fields will be displayed for your quick reference.

All we must do now is select these four data fields. For our table, we do not want any data fields from the **Tasks** tab in the panel. So, first uncheck all the currently selected fields. Then, enable the **Resources** tab and check that the following fields are included:

-   **Name** (that is, the resource name)
-   **Work**
-   **Actual Work**
-   **Cost Variance**

We have included the **Work** and **Actual work** fields to analyze the quantity of work done on the project in comparison to the cost variances incurred. Similarly, you may want to add more data fields to help you make critical decisions on your project. The final table that we create will resemble the following screenshot:

Resource Cost Balancing

Name	Work	Actual Work	Cost Variance
Web Design Vendor	416 hrs	416 hrs	$14,400.00
Mobile Vendor	500 hrs	128 hrs	$7,500.00
Content Team	234 hrs	43.2 hrs	$1,890.00
PM	464 hrs	166 hrs	$0.00
Content Vendor	640 hrs	56 hrs	$0.00
Test Lead	280 hrs	158 hrs	$0.00
Deploy Team	640 hrs	40 hrs	$0.00
Maintenance Vendor	40 hrs	0 hrs	$0.00
Technical Writer	200 hrs	40 hrs	$0.00
IT Director	112 hrs	112 hrs	$0.00
PMO	248 hrs	248 hrs	$0.00
Approval Board	64 hrs	64 hrs	$0.00
IT Manager	344 hrs	344 hrs	$0.00
Faculty Rep	296 hrs	160 hrs	$0.00
Dean	80 hrs	80 hrs	$0.00
Develop Team	480 hrs	226 hrs	$0.00
Testing Team	680 hrs	0 hrs	$0.00
Architect	120 hrs	80 hrs	$0.00
Stakeholders	0 hrs	0 hrs	$0.00

Figure 19.5 – Resource cost balancing table report

In this exercise, we have learned how to manipulate data fields. We have learned how to locate, select, and deselect data fields that appear in our reports. We will extend these learnings by creating a visually attractive bar graph-based report in the next section.

A new report – resource work variance bar graph report (plus costs too!)

The previous exercise focused on *cost variance*, and now we will focus on *work variance*. In the same new custom report that we created in the previous example, click on the **Chart** button, located in the **Insert** group of the **Design** ribbon tab. The **Insert Chart** dialog box will open up, as shown in the following screenshot:

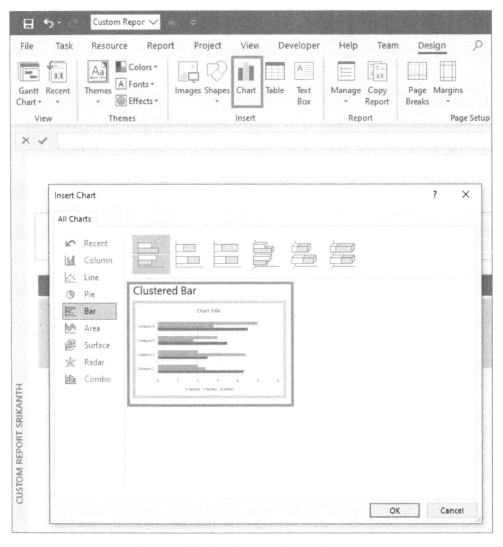

Figure 19.6 – Creating a new bar graph report

You can observe from this screenshot that the **Insert Chart** dialog box allows you to create a wide variety of column, line, pie, and bar graphs, as well as other mathematical models too. For our exercise, we will select the **Clustered Bar** graph report, as highlighted. Let's see how the final report will look in the following screenshot:

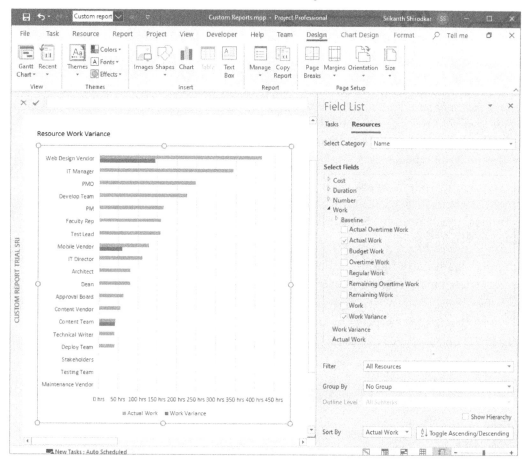

Figure 19.7 – Resource work variance graphical report

The steps to create this report are as follows:

- When you create a graph for the first time from the **Insert Chart** dialog box, it will be prepopulated with two default fields—**Actual Work** and **Remaining Work**—from the **Tasks** tab. First, these default fields will have to be deselected. Proceed further to select the **Actual Work** and **Work Variance** fields from the **Resources** tab, as shown in *Figure 19.7*.

- Change the sorting order so that resources that have done the most work (**Actual Work**) appear at the top. To do this, select the **Actual Work** criterion in the **Sort By** dropdown. Use the **Toggle Ascending/Descending** button until you get the right sorting order.

We have now completed our second exercise. The next exercise is even more interesting as we will use some special fields of Project that we have not discussed in the book so far.

Earned Value Management (EVM) report

If you are already familiar with the famous EVM technique of performance monitoring, then you will find this exercise especially interesting. If you are not already familiar with the EVM project management technique, there are excellent primers available on the web, which we will not replicate here.

For this exercise, with just a few clicks, we will *recreate* an existing graphical report from Project's repository, called the **Earned Value Over Time** report. You can locate the original report from the **Report** tab | the **Costs** drop-down button | the **Earned Value** report.

Using all the same techniques as explained in the previous two exercises, create a new line graph, as shown in the following screenshot:

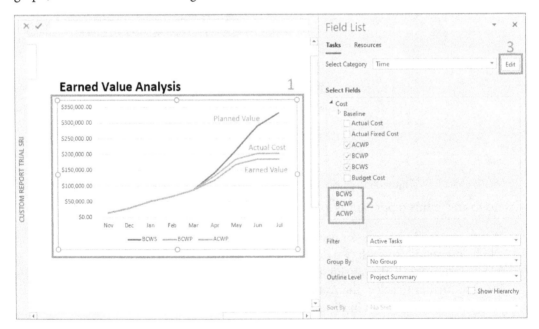

Figure 19.8 – The Earned Value Analysis report

The steps to create this new graph report are as follows:

1. Insert a simple line graph using the **Chart** button, located in the **Insert** group of the **Design** ribbon tab. The result is shown in the preceding screenshot.

2. Remove the prepopulated default fields from the newly created line graph. Instead, select the fields labeled **ACWP**, **BCWP**, and **BCWS** from the **Tasks** tab. Note that we have not discussed these data fields in the book so far. The significance of these fields will be explained shortly in this section.

3. Edit the timeline to set the last tracked date of the schedule. In our exercise, this has been set to July 1.

Incidentally, there are multiple sets of acronyms used in different EVM texts. This is a frequent cause of confusion for EVM practitioners. These EVM acronyms can be correspondingly recognized in Project terminology as follows:

- **Planned Value (PV)**: This is also known as **Budgeted Cost of Work Scheduled (BCWS)**. This is the baseline cost of total work on the schedule. To use this value, your project should be completely budgeted and baselined.

- **Actual Cost (AC)**: This is also known as **Actual Cost of Work Performed** (ACWP). The actual cost is derived from the progress-updated schedule, as on the *status date*.

- **Earned Value (EV)**: This is also known as **Budgeted Cost of Work Performed (BCWP)**. This is the real value derived from the work performed, as on the *status date*.

Notice that the baselining, resource costing, and frequently updating both the status date and schedule progress are a big part of EVM.

Congratulations! We have recreated an existing graphical report of Project and come to the end of our custom report creation exercises.

The customized reports that we create reside within the same project file and are always available to be used within that schedule. *But how do we leverage our custom-designed charts on other projects?* This is the question that we will resolve through the remainder of this chapter.

Understanding the global template

Custom-developed reports are to be considered as an asset of your organization. You should be able to leverage not only your own earlier custom reports but also those shared by other managers too.

Reports and other assets are shared through Project's global template. Remember that there are two types of templates within Project: *project-level local templates* and *global templates*. In *Chapter 18*, *Reviewing Projects and Creating Templates for Success*, we studied the usage of project-level local templates as a blueprint to successfully launch new projects. In this chapter, we will focus on using global templates to share custom reports.

Project templates follow an object-oriented inheritance architecture, as represented in the following diagram:

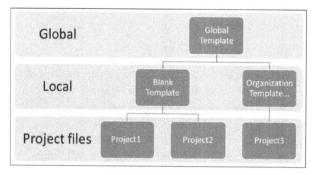

Figure 19.9 – Template architecture in Microsoft Project

When you create custom reports (new or modified), they are initially only available inside the same file. If you want to make your reports available across an organization, you must save it to the **global template**. This can be understood from the preceding diagram.

Global templates are just repositories and little more. Every time Project is started, it will access the global template to load a variety of information, as detailed in the next section.

What is stored in the global template?

It is easy to surmise now that every defaulted value in Project is stored in the global template. Here is a listing of all the definitions and values stored in the global template:

- All the basic prebuilt calendar, view, and table definitions
- All prebuilt report definitions
- All prebuilt filter and group definitions
- All custom field definitions for tables and views
- All the default behavioral settings from the **Project Options** dialog box

There are some other aspects stored in the global template too, such as any macros that you record or program. Import and export maps are also stored in global templates, so they are available across all your projects by default.

Everything that we have discussed so far will be prepackaged into the global template out of the box. You can extend this functionality by storing your own customized elements so that they are accessible to other projects too. Let's see some aspects of this in the next section.

Copying into and from the global template

Project provides a simple and robust tool to manage the global template. This tool is called **Organizer** and is in the form of a dialog box. You can access **Organizer** from the backstage view. Click on the **File** tab on the ribbon to open the backstage, then click on the **Info** tab | the **Organizer** button. Refer to the following screenshot:

Figure 19.10 – Organize Global Template

Before we proceed any further with **Organizer**, there is an important point to be understood. You have now opened the hood of your precious Ferrari, so to speak. It is possible to accidentally delete or rename entities that are used in the functioning of Project. Or you might do the same to your company-designed reports. Let's understand the interface closely before proceeding any further. Refer to the following screenshot:

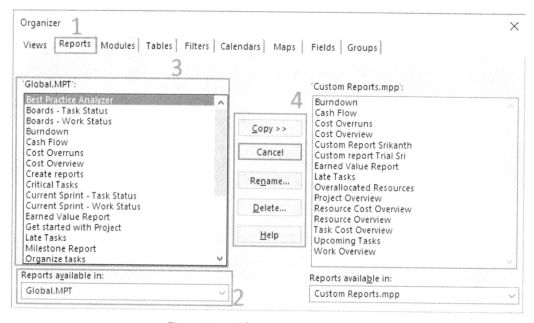

Figure 19.11 – The Organizer dialog box

There are a few important points to notice about this interface, as follows:

1. A series of tabs are present at the top of the dialog box. Each tab represents an important entity in Project, which are available to work with **Organizer**. The tab currently selected is **Reports**.

2. Any two Project files, whether it is a normal file with the * . MPP extension or a template file with the * . MPT extension, can be loaded into **Organizer**. The first file is loaded from the drop-down list on the left. By default, the **Global.MPT** file (that is, the global template) is loaded here first.

   For other normal files or templates to show up on this drop-down list, they must first be opened within the main Project application.

3. Since the **Reports** tab is currently selected, all the reports available in the loaded file are shown in the list box on the left.

4. A set of action buttons are available in the middle. They allow you to copy, rename, and delete any entities that you select. The same interface is mirrored on the right too, where a second file can be loaded up.

To *copy* a custom report that you have created from your project to another project, select the report name from the list box and click on the **Copy** button. The report will be copied to the other file intelligently in the correct direction. This same technique can be applied to all other entities, such as views and filters.

It is also possible to *rename* and *delete* any of the other entities using the same set of action buttons. Exercise extreme caution as you can accidentally delete (or rename) any of favorite entities, such as the **GANTT CHART** view! Continuing with the same discussion, here are some best practices for the usage of **Organizer** and templates in general:

*   Always create a backup of the `Global.MHT` file before using **Organizer**. It is your insurance against accidents.

*   If an accident occurs and you delete a Project prebuilt entity from the global template, you can copy it back in from your backup file. If you are required to reinstall your Project application, it is best to contact Microsoft Office support in all cases.

*   A pitfall here is that from the latest version of Project onward, all new views, tables, and other entities are saved to the global template by default. This automatic save is not advised, as the global template will quickly bloat up with your experimental views (and other entities) that you create. It is recommended that you disable this setting by going to the **Project Options** dialog box | the **Advanced** tab and unticking the **Automatically add new views, tables, and groups to the global** checkbox.

*   You cannot copy tasks into the global template! If you need to do that, use the local project template technique, as discussed in *Chapter 17, Project Reports 101*.

Organizer is a wonderful tool to manage the multitude of entities across your files. You can conveniently share this knowledge with your friends and peers who use Project.

Summary

This chapter has been all about leveraging your different skills and learnings to maximize benefit for future projects. You can reuse your Excel and PowerPoint skills to create customized graphs on attractive reports.

As you get more experienced and fluent with Project, you will accumulate a variety of clever views and impressive reports that are customized to your clients' expectations. The global template is where you can accumulate this knowledge to be reused. Caution should be exercised when working with the global template.

In the next chapter, we will conclude this book. We have journeyed through the entire life cycle of a project, with Project as a faithful ally. Project has its quirks, but your efforts in schedule management always bear fruit. In the next chapter, we will explore how you can leverage all your learning with continuous practice.

20
Book Conclusion and Next Steps

Welcome to the final chapter of this book. Congratulations on reaching the end of the marathon journey of Project. You are now within touching distance of the finish line.

There are many ways of working successfully with Project. You will eventually evolve your own way of using Project. Your own way of working with Project needs to be customized to your business domain and project complexities. This book has been my humble attempt to teach a method that works with Project's default behaviors, values, assumptions, and algorithms with the least possible friction. Your hands-on participation while reading this book will have prepped you to apply everything you have learned so far to the outside world.

The intention of this chapter is to present a final big-picture view of Microsoft Project applied to project management. We will now connect the project phases and process groups to everything that you have learned about Microsoft Project.

In this chapter, we are going to cover the following main topics:

- Big-picture mapping of Microsoft Project features to PMBOK-based process groups
- Overall best practices, pitfalls, concepts, and techniques mapped to the project life cycle
- Next steps

The complete Project roadmap

Throughout this book, the priority has been on Microsoft Project. In this chapter, we will instead focus on the project life cycle and map Project to it. This chapter will answer the question, *how will an experienced practitioner use Project across the entire project life cycle?* We are not interested in discussing the nitty-gritty details of ribbons, buttons, and dialog boxes, although we will provide the references for you to find the detailed discussions of these topics. Rather, our interest now is to put together all the best practices, pitfalls, tools, tips, techniques, and concepts in this book together for a big-picture view of common practice when working with Project in the real world.

Initiating with Project

Initiating processes constitutes the *honeymoon period* of a project. The pragmatic project manager will strive to set the correct expectations for all stakeholders. For the rest of the project, the project manager will strive to uphold these expectations, all the way to the successful closure of the project.

The following are some considerations to bear in mind when working with Project during the initial processes of a project:

- Understand and use the Basic Work Formula (*Duration = Work / Units*) for all your estimation and sizing calculations. This simple formula is the bedrock upon which Project performs a multitude of calculations involving tasks, resources, assignments, calendars, tracking, and so on. It will also help you demystify automatic scheduling behavior. Refer to *Chapter 4, Underlying Concepts of Microsoft Project*, in the *Understanding the Basic Work Formula* section.

- Always use the **Automatic** mode when scheduling tasks. Explicitly ensure that this is correctly set in your instance of Project.

  Manual scheduling can be used on any task if sufficient details are not known in the initiating stages; however, these unknown details should be resolved before the project enters execution stages.

- Use *generic resource names* to create time, cost, and scope estimations. Later, these can be seamlessly replaced in the schedule during the planning phase when actual resources are assigned to the project.

- Budget (costs and resources) can be planned for the entire project by assigning budget resources to the **Project Summary Task**. Refer to the *Creating a Project budget* section in *Chapter 15, Resource and Cost Management*, for more information.

- Match the project calendar to the working conditions of your organization during the initiation phase. Other calendars at resource and task level can be configured in the planning phases when required.

- Use the **Resource Sheet** view as the central location to manage your resources. Even though you can add and manage resources from other views and dialog boxes, refrain from doing so as they will introduce hard-to-detect bugs in resource management.

- It is important for you to understand the *default values* and *default behaviors* of Project as a first step, as they have been carefully designed to cater to the vast majority of project management use cases that you will encounter. These default values have been carefully highlighted over the course of this book.

The time spent on initiating a new project is a great opportunity to ensure a win-win situation for all the stakeholders involved. As the project manager, you have the responsibility to ensure that your team is neither overworked nor underworked.

Planning with Project

The planning stage is an exciting stage because the project manager takes complete command of the project when the initiation stage is completed and the execution stage is yet to start. From a Project perspective, your key objective in this planning stage is to create an *effective* schedule that can be executed by your team. The following are the overall considerations that you need to bear in mind when working with Project during the planning phases of a project:

1. Depending on the size and complexity of your project, you should decide on your integration strategy with Project.

   For example, if it is less than 10 person-months in size, then you probably do not need all of the power of Project's scheduling and tracking features, or the added complexity and costs involved in using Project.

   Similarly, you can plan and track schedules in Project with or without *resource allocation* or *costs*.

   If you want to manage a portfolio of projects with shared resources, consider Microsoft's cloud-based enterprise offerings. Project is not suited to managing portfolios.

2. Always start your planning by setting the project **Start Date**. You will then be able to make predictions during the initiation stage, such as *if we launch the project before June this year, then delivery can happen by August of next year*.

456 Book Conclusion and Next Steps

3. Schedule in reverse chronology.

4. **Scope** translates to **WBS**, which translates to **Task List** (Activities), which then translates to **Schedule**. This finally translates to awesome reports and promotions!

5. It is very important that you organize your task list, as it improves the usability of the schedule that you must manage for the entire project life cycle.

   Three popular techniques to organize schedules are discussed in the *Organizing Tasks to create a Schedule* section of *Chapter 7, Tasks – under the Microscope*.

6. *How realistic will the schedule be?* You can use special dependencies like SS, FF, and FS to convey incremental realism in your schedule. But there is an extra cost to be paid for executing these special dependencies (an engineering trade-off). This cost will be due to extra communications, extra training, and other costs to monitor and control the special dependencies. Only if the costs are trivial or manageable should the incremental realism be implemented in your schedule. One way of working is to use these special dependencies and date constraints only when they are mission-critical to the project.

7. Gain an understanding of the **Critical Path Method**. Use the flexibility of **slack** in your schedule with the power of automatic scheduling. Slack can be designed in the schedule during the planning phase. Its impact is discussed in later stages; refer to *Chapter 16, Critical Path Monitoring and Advanced Techniques*, for more information.

8. *Costing* is inextricably linked to *resourcing* in Project since resources cost money. It is possible to plan and build a realistic model of project costs using the different resource types of Project—work, material, and cost resources. Each of these three types provides flexible methods to plan project costs.

9. The common denomination of most errors is *overallocation*, directly or indirectly. If work is underestimated or is not detailed enough, then the result is overallocation somewhere along the project, usually at the last possible moment. If a team member is inexperienced or the user market has shifted from Android to Apple, then the change still leads to overallocation. *This is the reason that we should watch out for the overallocation indicator in Project.*

10. It is the project manager's responsibility to make the schedule readable, understandable, and maintainable. An aesthetically designed schedule goes a long way in satisfying these nonfunctional requirements. Refer to *Chapter 9, Extended Customization – Tasks and Gantt Formatting* for a complete discussion on this topic.

At the end of the planning phase, your schedule should be analogous to a *highly detailed manual* on how to execute the project successfully.

Executing with Project

We now enter the tactile execution of the project. These are the overall considerations that need to be accepted when working with Project during the execution processes of a project:

1. Begin by creating the first **Baseline** of your project. This baseline shows the original estimation and planning of the project.

2. Establish the tracking technique to be used for the project. This involves answering the following questions:

   - How much accuracy will be captured in tracking the schedule?

   - How will progress information be captured from the team? The considerations, techniques, and best practices for project tracking are discussed in *Chapter 13, Project Tracking Techniques*.

3. Overallocations can creep into the schedule when the project is in execution. For example, this can be due to increased scope, a resource leaving the company, or just because life happens! There are several techniques discussed in *Chapter 11, Overallocation – the Bane of Project Managers*, that specifically handle these situations holistically.

4. If your project does not require the complete rigor of the **Critical Path Method**, then consider using the **Agile** features of Project. Agile methodologies offer a flexible and adaptive *alternative* to the traditionally rigid Waterfall methodology. A great deal of flexibility is available for you to create your own hybrid model with Project that is perfectly suited for your business domain. Refer to *Chapter 10, Executing Agile Projects with MS Project* for a discussion on Kanban and Scrum-based tools.

5. A powerful and detailed analysis of project costs can be performed during execution, at different granularities—project level, assignment level, task level, resource level, and baseline level. Refer to the *Analysis of costing using different views* section in *Chapter 15, Resource and Cost Management*.

6. Project tracking activity is the bread and butter of the manager, especially during the execution stages. This allows the project manager to know precisely where they stand in the schedule on any given day. A multitude of simple and advanced techniques of tracking, along with best practices, are presented in *Chapter 13, Project Tracking Techniques*.

The many project tracking techniques of Project can be overwhelming for a brand-new user during the execution phases. But it need not be so. Begin with the simplest of techniques for a project or two. Proceed to more advanced tracking techniques as and when the situation demands it. Tracking is what generates the data required for the **Monitoring and Control** processes of the project, which we will discuss in the next section.

Monitoring and controlling with Project

Monitoring involves the *mining of schedule data* to glean valuable information. **Controlling** involves the *analysis of trends and performance data* to bring about improvements and to evaluate alternative plans. Project provides a large spectrum of features and tools designed specifically to help you monitor and control your project from start to finish. These controls are located within the views and tables framework.

The following are the overall considerations to bear in mind when working with Project during the monitoring and controlling processes of a project:

- Project's primary interface is the **view**. Even reports are just views. Views are constructed from a logical and robust framework of four primary components: table, filter, group, and display format. A solid understanding of these four components allows you to effortlessly slice and dice your schedule data.

- You can create and leverage views customized to your organization and business domain. You can then save and share these customized views using the global template. Refer to the *Templates for success* section in *Chapter 18, Reviewing Projects and Creating Templates for Success*.

- Constantly monitor the critical path and protect it from risks and delays.

- There are three well-known techniques to shorten the project duration, called *fast tracking*, *crashing the project*, and *resource reallocation*. Each of these techniques has its own pros and cons (that is, engineering trade-offs). Application of these techniques can be made relatively easier with Project. Refer to the *Techniques to shorten the project* section in *Chapter 16, Critical Path Monitoring and Advanced Techniques*.

Fully powered status reports using Project's graphical reports feature are only possible when you have done the following:

- Used WBS to create your task list (refer to *Chapter 6, Work Breakdown Structure - the Single Critical Factor*).

- Designed the organization of your tasks (refer to *Chapter 7, Tasks - under the Microscope*).

- Created a baseline (refer to *Chapter 12, Baselines – Techniques and Best Practices*).

- Set the status date (refer to the *Relevance of the status date* section in *Chapter 13, Project Tracking Techniques*).

- Tracked progress periodically (refer to *Chapter 12, Baselines – Techniques and Best Practices*).

- If you have missed any of these steps, then your reports will be suboptimal.

- Recognize that reports are views! Use the same logic that we used to create custom views to create new reports and manipulate existing ones. Refer to *Chapter 14, Views, Tables, and Customization – A Deeper Understanding* for more information.

You can mine your schedule data, both baseline and in-progress, for gems of information. This will support your monitoring and controlling the process groups.

Closing with Project

Closure is the time for introspection. It is the time to look back at the good, medium, and bad aspects of the project we are closing. A project closure review is performed to analyze the schedule. Project provides two tools to glean lessons from the schedule data—the **project comparison report** and the **multiple baseline comparison report**. These learnings can be converted to templates in Project for the benefit of future projects.

The following are the overall considerations to bear in mind when working with Project during the closing processes of a project:

- Learn to critically evaluate schedules. Specifically, you should be able to identify error patterns in the schedule by visual inspection. Reviewing techniques and tools are discussed in the *Common error patterns in Project* section in *Chapter 18, Reviewing Projects and Creating Templates for Success*.

- Use the template architecture of Project to the fullest. This will allow you to carry over the lessons and work from previous projects into your new projects! There are two types of template in Project—the **project template** and **global template**. Templates are just normal files and serve as repositories for project data. Use the project template to store activities and the structure. Use the global template to store *customized entities*, such as custom views, reports, tables, filters, groups, and so on.

- A formal **project closure review** helps you to identify and implement your template strategy.

New learners (*of any skill*) tend to commit the same patterns of error. In this book, you have learned to identify these patterns. You can avoid these error patterns in your own work, and you can also recognize it in other schedules that you will review. All such error patterns should be identified and ironed out systematically during project reviews, throughout the project life cycle.

Next steps

Congratulations! You have arrived at the end of this book through diligence and hard work. Now is the time to translate all that you have learned into project success. Here are the next steps to take:

- As the saying goes, *practice makes perfect*. You have learned about all of the tools to practice the techniques we have covered perfectly. If you have not been working on the chapters in this book, then I urge you to start recreating the simple examples. You can find new assignments that I give to my students periodically on the website www.learngood.in.

- Review project schedules from anywhere that you can get them—from your company, from colleagues, and from your extended network.

- *Sharpen the saw*: Study and leverage project templates from your organization, industry, and business domains.

- Share your own templates and schedule plans! Be careful to sanitize them first by removing named resources and any business-critical information. Be generous, but exercise due diligence.

- Connect with the author on LinkedIn. I would love to hear your experiences with project management and Microsoft Project.

A final summary

Just a short while after I started writing this book, the world was rocked by the global pandemic that began in 2019. As I conclude this book now, nations are scrambling to reduce the catastrophic loss of human life. Project managers are working globally behind the scenes, building new hospitals and new facilities to manufacture ventilators and other pieces of medical infrastructure. In the medical industry, they are also working on projects to discover and manufacture vaccines on a never-before-seen scale. The race is on to vaccinate the planet. Corporate working conditions have also changed, with *working from home* now the current global normal.

Now more than ever, we need to adopt tools like Microsoft Project and put them to hard work. Thank you for choosing to learn from this book. It has been a pleasure to journey with you into the world of Microsoft Project and project management. No effort will be spared to keep this book updated in future editions.

Appendix A: Using This Book as a Textbook

Several colleges offer project management as a higher education course and match it strategically with Microsoft Project. This book will be an excellent match for your syllabus because it maps to the core project management process groups and concepts, as well as the project life cycle. If you want to use this book as a textbook for your own institution, course, or learners, you are welcome to do so.

Specific advantages to using this book include the following:

- Incremental complexity. It starts from the simplest topics and projects and gradually progresses to advanced topics.

- Features and techniques introduced exactly as needed in real-life practice.

- Learning content is equally distributed over the entire project life cycle.

- Advanced topics are neatly segregated and can be made optional – for example, the chapter on advanced custom reports, or the chapter on the inner workings of views.

In the following table, I share an outline of the whole book to help in your pedagogical design. It can act both as a *ready reference* and as a mapping to desired *educational outcomes*:

Book Structure	Learning Objectives
Full Book	The 20 chapters in total are divided are into 6 parts, as follows: • PART 1: Primer to Project Management (Chapter 1) • PART 2: Project Initiation (basic level) • PART 3: Project Planning Like a Pro! (intermediate level) • PART 4: Project Execution (intermediate level) • PART 5: Monitoring and Control (advanced level) • PART 6: Project Closure (advanced level)
Parts of the book	Chapter-wise mapping to parts of the book is as follows: • **PART 1**: *Chapter 1, Project Management – The Essential Primer* (A primer to *project management*, with a recap of the core concepts required for this entire book) • **PART 2**: *Chapter 2, Fundamentals of Microsoft Project, Chapter 3, Initiating Projects with Microsoft Project, Chapter 4, Underlying Concepts of Microsoft Project, and Chapter 5, Resource Management with Microsoft Project* (*initiating process groups* along with providing a high-level but complete overview of Project functionality) • **PART 3**: *Chapter 6, Work Breakdown Structure – The Single Critical Factor, Chapter 7, Tasks – Under the Microscope, Chapter 8, Tasks – Under the Microscope, and Chapter 9, Extended Customization – Task and Gantt Formatting* (WBS with a detailed overview of Project usage for *planning process groups*) • **PART 4**: *Chapter 10, Executing Agile Projects with MS Project, Chapter 11, Overallocations – the Bane of Project Managers, Chapter 12, Baselines – Techniques and Best Practices, and Chapter 13, Project Tracking Techniques* (Agile with a detailed overview of Project usage for *executing process groups*)

Book Structure	Learning Objectives
	• **PART 5**: *Chapter 14, Views, Tables, and Customization – A Deeper Understanding, Chapter 15, Resource and Cost Management, Chapter 16, Critical Path Monitoring and Advanced Techniques*, and *Chapter 17, Project Reports 101* (Views with a detailed overview of Project usage in *monitoring and control process groups*) • **PART 6**: *Chapter 18, Reviewing Projects and Creating Templates for Success, Chapter 19, Advanced Custom Reports and Templates*, and *Chapter 20, Book Conclusion and Next Steps* (custom reports with a detailed overview of Project usage in *closing process groups*) WBS, Agile, advanced views, and custom reports can be considered as supplementary or optional topics for a deeper understanding. They can be opted out if taught elsewhere in a different course, or if time does not permit.
Chapters for each part	Each chapter has a clear focus and learning objectives are stated on the starting page. Every example is designed to be hands-on with replicable exercises (projects). Every exercise is followed by a discussion of the preconditions and postconditions. Every chapter is designed to be self-contained with minimal dependencies on other chapters or external downloads. As we get to the advanced sections, the trainer can create larger examples as suitable for their teaching purposes. This is to avoid any potential copyright infringement. It is my intention to provide extra learning assignments and other tools on my website (`www.learngood.in`). Stay connected!
Topics of each chapter	All topics in a chapter are threaded into a story-telling narrative. This is to increase the engagement of the learner and to introduce features in the same way as encountered in real-life situations. Throughout the book, readers are encouraged to follow along as practice cements book learning.

Book Structure	Learning Objectives
Blended learning design	An optional flipped-classroom model for teaching can be utilized for teaching this course.
	In this model, students read the chapters on their own before the class is conducted. In the classroom, the lesson is only summarized, and hands-on exercises are practiced with the instructor. Students use the valuable face-to-face time to clarify doubts.
	The personal learning aspect can be supported by a learning management system that also delivers assessments.
Best practices, tips, tricks, and pitfalls	Industry-based latest teachings are delivered through special topics, which are interspersed liberally throughout the book.

Appendix B: Available Fields Reference

Views, tables, and reports generally present only a small subset of all the data fields available in a project. In this discussion, we will understand the structure of these hundreds of predefined data fields available in Project.

It is possible to program custom-built tools using Microsoft Office's scripting languages and these data fields. Without further ado, let's begin with a classification of the available fields.

We will not repeat the most common data fields here and will only focus on some of the other useful fields. This is not a complete listing, but only a small and useful subset, to be used as a ready reference:

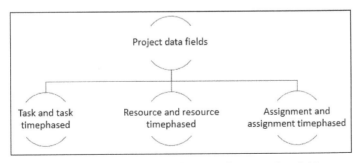

Figure B.1 – Classification of Microsoft Project data fields

Some fields are Project Professional-specific. Also, there are data fields specifically related to the enterprise features of Project, which we will not be covering in this appendix.

Task fields – a small curated subset

#	Field	Description
1	Active	You can enable and inactivate tasks from this field. Inactive tasks will not affect the overall schedule. Useful for schedule impact analysis and to study alternative task paths.
2	Actual Cost	Shows incurred costs for work already performed.
3	ACWP Similarly, other associated fields are **BCWP**, **BCWS**, **CV**, and **EAC**.	**Actual Cost of Work Performed (ACWP)**, used in earned value calculations.
4	Assignment Units	Shows how many units of the assigned resource are allocated to a task.
5	Baseline Budget Cost (and **Baseline Budget Work** is similar)	Shows planned budget for budget cost resources. Remember that budget resources can be assigned only to a project summary task.
6	Baseline Start (You can extrapolate similarly, for **Baseline Finish**, **Baseline Duration**, and **Baseline Work**.)	Displays the planned start date for a task (or assignment) after the first baseline is saved. (This applies to the slot labeled Baseline.)
7	Baseline 1 to 10 Start (and similarly for the other baseline common fields)	These fields are used to store the Baseline 1 through Baseline 10 data fields.
8	Complete Through	Shows the progress of a task (based upon the actuals that have been tracked).

#	Field	Description
9	Cost	Displays the total estimated cost for a task, based on costs already incurred for work performed plus the costs planned for the remaining work.
		Note: When the project has not yet been tracked, it will only contain the starting estimate of the task cost.
10	Cost Variance (similarly, for **CV%**)	Displays the difference between the baseline cost and total cost for a task. CV% shows the cost variance in percentage form.
		These fields can also be applicable for a resource or assignment too.
10	Critical	Yes/no indication of whether the task is on the critical path. If a task has slack, it will not be critical.
11	Duration Variance	The difference in the duration of the baselines
12	Early Start (and similarly for **Early Finish**)	Shows the earliest date that a task could possibly start.
		This is an algorithmically computed field based on the early start dates of the predecessors and other constraints, as applicable in the schedule.
13	Estimated	This is a flag that indicates whether the task's duration is just an estimate.
		Remember that the default duration for a task newly created is set to 1. Remember to have no such tasks when you go for a baseline.
14	Fixed Cost Accrual	You can set how the fixed cost will be accrued to a task – either at the start, or prorated, or at the end of the task.
15	Free Slack	Indicates how much the task can be delayed without impacting successor tasks.
16	Ignore Resource Calendar	This field can be enabled to forcibly ignore the resource calendar constraints on a task.

#	Field	Description
17	Milestone	This is a flag field that indicates whether a task is a milestone or not. By default, Project sets this flag when you make the task duration 0 (zero) days. However, you can explicitly set this flag to make non-zero tasks as milestones! Be wary about the schedule impacts.
18	Remaining Cost	Displays the (algorithmically calculated) expense that will be incurred to finish the task. This will be based on remaining scheduled work.
19	Remaining Work	Shows the work hours required to finish the task.
20	Start Variance	Shows the difference between the baseline start date and the current scheduled start dates.

Resource fields – a small curated subset

#	Field	Description
1	Assignment	This is a flag field that indicates whether the specific row in the table is an assignment (and not just a task or resource row).
2	Available From (and similarly for **Available To**)	Displays the starting date from when a resource is available for work at specified units.
3	Can Level	This is a flag field that you can set to allow a resource to be algorithmically leveled or not.
4	Cost Per Use	Displays the cost that accrues every time the resource is used. For every task that the resource is assigned to, a cost is accrued. This is only available for work resources (people, machinery, and other equipment).
5	Finish	Displays the date on which the resource is scheduled to complete all their work in the schedule. This is usually the finish date of the last task in the resource's assignments.

#	Field	Description
6	Leveling Delay	Displays the leveling delay time applied because of resource-leveling.
7	Max Units	Displays the maximum percentage (or resource units) the resource is available to the schedule.
8	Overallocated	This is a Boolean yes/no field that indicates if the resource has been assigned more work than their computed capacity (required to complete the tasks assigned).
9	Peak	Displays the maximum units the resource is assigned at any point in the schedule.
10	Remaining Work	Displays the estimated work hours required for the resource to complete all the tasks assigned to them.

Assignment fields – a small curated subset

#	Field	Description
1	Assignment Units	Displays the total units of resource assignments allocated to a task.
2	The Baseline 0 to 10 Cumulative Work field (and similarly for the **Baseline 0 to 10 Remaining Cumulative Work** field)	This is a relatively new field added to Project. It is best used when more than one baseline has been set to compare the resource's complete work assignment over time.
3	Overallocation (for the Assignments field)	If any of the resources allocated to an assignment is overallocated, then this field will be set.
4	WBS	Displays an alphanumeric code used to uniquely identify a specific task in the WBS hierarchical tree structure.
5	Work Contour	Displays the contour shape chosen to load the resource allocated to a task.

These are only a subset of all the available fields. Getting familiar with Project's data fields will allow you to create efficient custom views and attractive reports with ease.

Appendix C: Keyboard Shortcuts

A keyboard shortcut is a multi-key combination (pressed together) that performs certain commands instantly. This bypasses the need for you to lift your hand from the keyboard and navigate over to the ribbon, spending more time searching for an icon from tab to tab. This happens to all of us.

In this context, keyboard shortcuts provide a fast and alternative way to perform the same command from the keyboard directly. You will be perfectly familiar with the *Ctrl + C* and *Ctrl + V* shortcuts to *copy* and *paste*, respectively. Shortcuts improve productivity and help retain your *flow* when working on complex schedules. They can also be useful to users with vision and mobility challenges.

Learning to use even the simplest of these keyboard shortcuts will deliver instant gains in your work. I will present a curated list of some shortcuts that you can memorize and use quickly.

The most common commands and their shortcuts are as follows:

Command	Shortcut
Save file	*Ctrl + S*
New file	*Ctrl + N*
Edit field	*F2*
Menu bar	*Alt* (followed by arrow navigation)
Open file dialog box	*Ctrl + F12*
Find	*Ctrl + F*
Undo	*Ctrl + Z*

This is the promised small set of commands that will really boost your productivity:

Command	Shortcut
Link tasks	*Ctrl + F2*
Unlink tasks	*Ctrl + Shift + F2*
Assign resource	*Alt + F10*
Task/resource/assignment information	*Shift + F2*
Remove all filters	*F3*
Field settings	*Alt + F3*
Reset sort order (to ID)	*Shift + F3*
Navigate print preview	*Alt + arrow key*
Indent task	*Alt + Shift + right arrow key*
Outdent task	*Alt + Shift + left arrow key*
Jump to next dialog control	*Tab*
Add new task	*Insert*
Delete row (beware: the delete is instant, with no warning!)	*Ctrl + minus* (only on the numeric pad)
Scroll to task	*Ctrl + Shift + F5*
Copy screen to clipboard image	*Alt + Prt Sc* (the print screen button)

Appendix D: Glossary

8/80 rule of WBS: This is a rule of thumb used in the context of breaking down work from the scope into the schedule. Refer to *Chapter 6, Work Breakdown Structure – the Single Critical Factor*.

Accrue (field): Resource cost can be accrued either at the beginning of a task or as the work progresses (prorated), or at completion. The default value is `Prorated`. The primary location of this field is the **Resource Sheet**. Refer to *Chapter 5, Resource Management with Microsoft Project*.

Actuals: This is an important detail of schedule progress tracking and can apply to work, cost, and overall progress. Before project execution is tracked, the actuals will only be planned (estimated) values. Refer to *Chapter 13, Project Tracking Techniques*.

Assignment: Allocation of a resource (this could be a person, machinery, equipment, or even a budgeted cost) to execute a task.

Automatically scheduled tasks: This is the recommended operating mode for tasks in Project. Tasks can be either automatically scheduled or manually scheduled. The start times of these tasks are adjusted at runtime by Project, among other algorithmically driven behavior.

Backstage view: This is a common user interface accessible across Microsoft Office product offerings from the **File** tab. Refer to *Chapter 1, Project Management – the Essential Primer*.

Basic work formula: This simple formula is the bedrock upon which Project performs a multitude of calculations involving tasks, resources, assignments, calendars, tracking, and more. Refer to *Chapter 4, Underlying Concepts of Microsoft Project*.

Base calendar: Project ships with three base calendars, named **Standard**, **24 Hours'**, and **Night Shift**. Refer to *Chapter 4, Underlying Concepts of Microsoft Project*.

Baseline: The original schedule with only estimates that is saved for future comparison with the schedule in execution is called the baseline. Refer to *Chapter 12, Baselines – Techniques and Best Practices*.

Calendar: A fundamental entity of Project, calendars are used to configure the working times of tasks and resources, and for the entire project.

Constraint: A limitation set on the start or end of a task date. There are eight different date constraints possible in Project, and the default constraint is **As Soon As Possible** (**ASAP**). Refer to *Chapter 8, Mastering Link Dependency and Constraints*.

Contour: Time-phased loading of work on a resource can follow one of the several standard contour shapes. Work contours can be used to resolve the overallocation of resources. Refer to *Chapter 16, Critical Path Monitoring and Advanced Techniques*.

Cost: Cost is an important aspect of project management, and forms one of the sides of the iron triangle of projects. Refer to *Chapter 1, Project Management – the Essential Primer*.

Cost resource: Cost resources are used for project situations that demand one-off expenditure. Cost resources include any out-of-pocket expenditure, such as airfare, hotel stays, and taxi fare. Refer to *Chapter 15, Resource and Cost Management*.

Critical (field): This is a task-related data field. **Yes/No** indication is displayed, indicating whether the task is on the critical path. If a task has slack, it will not be critical. Refer to *Appendix B, Available Fields Reference*.

Critical path: A series of critical tasks that determines the finish date of the project is the critical path. The critical path is dynamic in nature and can change during the execution of the project. Refer to *Chapter 16, Critical Path Monitoring and Advanced Techniques*.

Critical Path Method (**CPM**): CPM is a methodology for scheduling tasks and is conceptually built around the critical (longest) path of a schedule. Refer to *Chapter 16, Critical Path Monitoring and Advanced Techniques*.

Critical task: Tasks with no slack are called critical tasks. Any slippage on tasks with no slack will immediately impact the project end date. Refer to *Chapter 16, Critical Path Monitoring and Advanced Techniques*.

Deliverable: A project can be thought of as a deliverable. This big and final project deliverable can then be broken up into a series of smaller deliverables all along the execution route. Refer to *Chapter 6, Work Breakdown Structure – the Single Critical Factor*.

Dependency: A relationship between two tasks is called a dependency. It is represented as a link between the tasks, signifying one as the predecessor and the other as the successor task. There are four types of dependencies defined in Project. Refer to *Chapter 8, Mastering Link Dependency and Constraints*.

Driving predecessors: For any task in a schedule, a sequence of linked predecessors is called the driving predecessors of the task. Refer to *Chapter 8, Mastering Link Dependency and Constraints*.

Duration: The estimated working time required to execute a task. Refer to *Chapter 2, Fundamentals of Microsoft Project*.

Effort: Also known as work, it is measured by the number of hours required to execute a particular task. Refer to *Basic work formula* in this glossary. Also refer to *Chapter 4, Underlying Concepts of Microsoft Project*.

Effort-driven: Most tasks are effort-driven, which is when more resources are added to execute the task, and the associated duration to finish the task decreases. However, some tasks will not be effort-driven (for example, events, seminars, and virtual conferences). Refer to *Chapter 7, Tasks – under the Microscope*.

Entry table: This is the most popular data entry table in Project, and is a component of the most popular view – the **Gantt Chart** view. Refer to *Chapter 2, Fundamentals of Microsoft Project*.

Field: Corresponds to a single data cell in the Project table. Project fields are represented as data columns in tables. Refer to *Appendix B, Available Fields Reference*, for a curated list of available fields in Project.

Filter: Filters are a component of views in Project. Filtering hides (that is, filters out) unwanted data, and only returns data that you have asked for. Refer to *Chapter 14, Views, Tables, and Customization*.

Fixed cost: An unchanging budget allocated to execute the task, different from resourcing costs. Refer to *Chapter 15, Resource and Cost Management*.

Fixed duration: A type of task that will take a fixed span of time to execute, irrespective of the resource parameters associated. For example, the curing of concrete takes a fixed amount of time. Refer to *Chapter 4, Underlying Concepts of Microsoft Project.*

Fixed units: A type of task where you have a predecided number of people (or machinery) working on a specific task. This is a common situation in real life, and in fact, you can note that this is the default setting as set by Project. Refer to *Chapter 4, Underlying Concepts of Microsoft Project.*

Fixed work: This task type is when the amount of a task's total effort is known and fixed upfront. These tasks are very common in actual practice and often form the bulk of your tasks in a project. Refer to *Chapter 4, Underlying Concepts of Microsoft Project.*

Flexible constraints: There are eight types of constraints in Project in a progressive spectrum of inflexibility. ASAP and ALAP are the most flexible constraint types in Project. Refer to *Chapter 8, Mastering Link Dependency and Constraints.*

Free slack: Also just called slack, this is the amount of time a task can be delayed without having an impact on the project. Slack is also referred to as float and can be positive, zero, or even negative. Free slack is always positive. Refer to *Chapter 16, Critical Path Monitoring and Advanced Techniques.*

Gantt Chart view: The most popular and default view of Project (based on the Gantt model of schedule representation). Refer to *Chapter 2, Fundamentals of Microsoft Project.*

Global template: This is the primary predefined template in Project. It is a repository for all the predefined views, tables, filters, and groups shipped with Project. Refer to *Chapter 19, Advanced Custom Reports and Templates.*

Group: Tasks or resources can be grouped as per specific grouping criteria. This is an essential component of views in Project and several predefined criteria for grouping are shipped with Project. Refer to *Chapter 14, Views, Tables, and Customization.*

Group (resource field): This is a resource data field, optionally used to group resources for organizational purposes (for example, into teams or departments). Refer to *Appendix B, Available Fields Reference.*

Import: Bring data into Project using the **Import** wizard tool. The common data formats used to import data are as an Excel workbook, XML, and CSV. Refer to *Chapter 7, Tasks – under the Microscope.*

Inflexible constraint: There are eight types of constraints in Project in a progressive spectrum of inflexibility. **Must Start On** (**MSO**) and **Must Finish On** (**MFO**) are the most inflexible constraint types in Project. Refer to *Chapter 8, Mastering Link Dependency and Constraints.*

Interim plan: A lightweight alternative to the baseline. The interim plan stores only the task's start and finish dates. Refer to *Chapter 12, Baselines – Techniques and Best Practices*.

Lag (time): An intentional time delay between the predecessor and the successor tasks is called lag and can be easily introduced into the schedule using Project. Refer to *Chapter 16, Critical Path Monitoring and Advanced Techniques*.

Lead (time): A negative lag is also called lead time. It denotes overlap of dependent tasks. Refer to *Chapter 16, Critical Path Monitoring and Advanced Techniques*.

Link: A dependency between two tasks is denoted in the Gantt chart, with a directional arrow called a link. Refer to *Chapter 2, Fundamentals of Microsoft Project*.

Manually scheduled task: These tasks are fully scheduled by the project manager and are not automatically adjusted by Project algorithms. Manual scheduling mode should be an exception in your working model of Project. Refer to *Chapter 2, Fundamentals of Microsoft Project*.

Material resources: Resources that are consumed by your project during execution are called material resources. For example, in a civil construction project, the material resources would be cement, bricks, stone, steel, and so on. Refer to *Chapter 15, Resource and Cost Management*.

Max. units (resource field): This data field displays the maximum percentage (or resource units) the resource is available to the schedule. Refer to *Appendix B, Available Reference Fields*.

Milestone: A milestone is used to represent a significant event in the project schedule. Any task can be marked as a milestone automatically by setting it to 0 (zero) duration. Also refer to *Milestone (field)* in *Appendix B, Available Reference Fields*. Refer to *Chapter 7, Tasks – under the Microscope*.

Negative lag (aka negative slack): A negative lag is also called lead time. It denotes overlap of dependent tasks. Refer to *Chapter 16, Critical Path Monitoring and Advanced Techniques*.

Network Diagram view: This view uses the network diagram display format, and a rigorous analysis of the schedule can be performed by viewing it as a flowchart. Refer to *Chapter 14, Views, Tables, and Customization*.

Night Shift base calendar: This is a base calendar shipped with Project, useful to design a shift-based working-hours calendar for your schedule. Refer to *Chapter 4, Underlying Concepts of Microsoft Project*.

Non-critical task: Any task that is not on the critical path (and potentially has free slack). Refer to *Chapter 16, Critical Path Monitoring and Advanced Techniques.*

Notes (field): These fields can be associated with a task, resource, or assignment. It is used to hold free-form comments (in text format). Refer to *Appendix B, Available Reference Fields.*

Organizer: This is a simple and robust tool to manage the global template. Refer to *Chapter 19, Advanced Custom Reports and Templates.*

Overallocated (resource field): This is a Boolean **Yes/No** field that indicates if the resource has been assigned more work than their computed capacity (required to complete the tasks assigned). Refer to *Appendix B, Available Reference Fields.*

Phase (project management term): The life of all projects, of any size, can be described as a series of phases that together make up the project management life cycle.

Plan (project management term): A sequence of tasks to execute the project. In the context of this book, this is the same as a schedule.

Predecessor (task): The controlling task in a dependency relationship with another task is called the predecessor. Refer to *Chapter 8, Mastering Link Dependency and Constraints.*

Project: A project is a temporary and unique endeavor with defined objectives. It has a clear, time-bound start state and end state. It is not repetitive and will have an exploratory nature to it. This exploratory nature usually means both higher returns and higher risks. Refer to *Chapter 1, Project Management – the Essential Primer.*

Project calendar: This is (a base calendar) used to calculate all working times for the project. Refer to *Chapter 4, Underlying Concepts of Microsoft Project.*

Project summary task: This is a predefined summary task for the entire project. It is always located at row 0 (zero) of any table or view that you can apply in Project. Refer to *Chapter 7, Tasks – under the Microscope.*

Recurring task: Tasks that repeat with an established frequency. Weekly meetings are a common example of recurring tasks. Refer to *Chapter 7, Tasks – under the Microscope.*

Relationship: Also called a dependency between two tasks. There are four fundamental types of relationships between tasks – FS, FF, SS, and SF. Refer to *Chapter 8, Mastering Link Dependency and Constraints.*

Reports: Project is shipped with powerful predesigned reports, broad dashboards, and more than a dozen other analytical reports for export, all out of the box. Refer to *Chapter 17, Project Reports 101.*

Resource: Tasks are executed by resources. This can be people, machinery or equipment, or even budgeted costs associated with the execution of the task. Refer to *Chapter 15, Resource and Cost Management*.

Resource calendar: The calendar of working times customized to a specific resource. Refer to *Chapter 4, Underlying Concepts of Microsoft Project*.

Resource leveling: Overallocations can be resolved using a combination of task splits and task delays. This technique is called resource-leveling. Refer to *Chapter 16, Critical Path Monitoring and Advanced Techniques*.

Ribbon interface: The common tabbed user interface available in all the Office product offerings. Within tabbed headers, related buttons and links are grouped together for easy access.

Risk: The possibility of something happening that might negatively affect the costs, schedule, resources, or other parameters of a project. Refer to *Chapter 1, Project Management – the Essential Primer*.

Scheduling algorithm: The scheduling logic used in Project's scheduling engine. That is, the underlying mathematical foundation for the scheduling logic used in Project, encapsulated within algorithms in Project's scheduling engine. Refer to *Chapter 2, Fundamentals of Microsoft Project*.

Scope: The complete set of deliverables promised by a project. This can consist of functional and non-functional requirements. Refer to *Chapter 1, Project Management – the Essential Primer*.

Sequence: Tasks ordered chronologically to execute a deliverable. Refer to *Chapter 18, Reviewing Projects and Creating Templates for Success*.

Slack: Slack is the amount of time a task can be delayed without having an impact on the project. Slack is also referred to as float and can be positive, zero, or even negative. Refer to *Chapter 16, Critical Path Monitoring and Advanced Techniques*.

Sort: Any technique of ordering the rows in a table or view. Several prebuilt sorting options are packaged in Project with the ability to create new sort orders. Refer to *Chapter 14, Views, Tables, and Customization*.

Split: A technique of pausing a task for a while, and then resuming it after some time has elapsed. Refer to *Chapter 13, Project Tracking Techniques*, and *Chapter 16, Critical Path Monitoring and Advanced Techniques*.

Stakeholder: Stakeholders are those people, groups, or organizations that will be impacted by your project. Refer to *Chapter 1, Project Management – the Essential Primer*.

Standard base calendar: The default base calendar packaged with Project. This will have an 8 AM–5 PM working day, Monday through Friday. You can customize the calendars as per your own working conditions. Refer to *Chapter 4, Underlying Concepts of Microsoft Project*.

Status date: The date that you collect project information from your team, or the date until when your tracking information is accurate, is called the status date. This has to be explicitly set to keep your tracking information accurate. Refer to *Chapter 13, Project Tracking Techniques*.

Subtasks: The constituent tasks of a summary task. The parameters (duration, work, and costs) of subtasks are rolled up into the summary task. Refer to *Chapter 7, Tasks – under the Microscope*.

Successor (task): The task that is driven by the predecessor in a dependency relationship with another task is called the successor. Refer to *Chapter 8, Mastering Link Dependency and Constraints*.

Summary task: The summary task, despite its name, is not really a task. It is primarily a feature to organize the schedule. Refer to *Chapter 7, Tasks – under the Microscope*.

Table: Tables are a fundamental constituent entity of Project. All views and reports of Project are loaded with a default table, mostly visible but occasionally hidden. Refer to *Chapter 14, Views, Tables, and Customization*.

Task: Also called an activity, these are the smallest units of work on a project. Refer to *Chapter 7, Tasks – under the Microscope*.

Task calendar: The calendar associated with a specific task. This calendar will determine the working hours for the execution of the task. Refer to *Chapter 4, Underlying Concepts of Microsoft Project*.

Task ID (field): The unique identifier applied to tasks in a schedule. These appear in the far-left column of views – for example, within the entry table of the **Gantt Chart** view. Refer to *Chapter 2, Fundamentals of Microsoft Project, Chapter 6, Work Breakdown Structure – the Single Critical Factor*, and *Chapter 7, Tasks – under the Microscope*.

Task type: Tasks can be classified under three fundamental types (in the context of the basic work formula). These three types are fixed units (default), fixed duration, and fixed work. Refer to *Chapter 4, Underlying Concepts of Microsoft Project*.

Template: A design feature of Project that serves a dual purpose – as a storage repository of Project entities (such as views, tables, and reports), and secondly, as a tool to reuse earlier schedule design. Refer to *Chapter 18, Reviewing Projects and Creating Templates for Success*, and *Chapter 19, Advanced Custom Reports and Templates*.

Time: This is one of the three major constraints of a project, the other two being cost and scope. Refer to *Triple constraints of a project* in this glossary. Also refer to *Chapter 1, Project Management – the Essential Primer*.

Timeline view: Introduced in the 2010 version of Project, this is a graphical view often used in a split window configuration with the **Gantt Chart** view. Refer to *Chapter 3, Initiating projects with Microsoft Project*.

Time-phased fields: Fields whose values are distributed over time. These fields might be in the context of tasks, resources, or assignments. Usage views such as the **Task Usage** view utilize time-phased fields. Refer to *Chapter 11, Overallocation – the Bane of Project Managers*, and *Chapter 14, Views, Tables, and Customization*.

Timescale: Time represented in a horizontal scale, used in a wide variety of views in Project. This is accompanied by scrolling bars and zoom controls to easily adjust the granularity of the view. Refer to *Chapter 2, Fundamentals of Microsoft Project*.

Total slack: The total amount of time a task can be delayed without having an impact on the project. It is also referred to as just slack or float, and it can be positive, zero, or even negative. Refer to *Chapter 16, Critical Path Monitoring and Advanced Techniques*.

Tracking: This is a major responsibility of the project manager. Tracking is done to measure the progress of a project. It involves analysis, collating progress information from the team, and updating the schedule with the progress information. Refer to *Chapter 13, Project Tracking Techniques*.

Triple constraints of a project: This is an essential concept of project management. Every project in real life is bound by three constraints (time, cost, and scope). The triple constraint concept explains the interplay of these constraints on a project. Refer to *Chapter 1, Project Management – the Essential Primer*.

Under allocation: Under-utilization of resources. This is a situation where any resource is allocated less work than their capacity within the working hours to execute it. Refer to *Chapter 11, Overallocation – the Bane of Project Managers*.

Units: This is the measure of resources allocated to a specific task, measured by percentage in Project. Refer to *Basic work formula* in this glossary. Also refer to *Chapter 4, Underlying Concepts of Microsoft Project*.

Variance (fields): The deviation from the original planned estimate and the actual tracked value. Variances are tracked in different data fields, such as the Cost Variance field, the Work Variance field, Start Variance and Finish Variance, and so on. Refer to *Chapter 16, Critical Path Monitoring and Advanced Techniques*.

View: Views are the principal user interface of Microsoft Project. All views can be classified under three major types: task views, resource views, and assignment views. Refer to *Chapter 14, Views, Tables, and Customization.*

Work: The effort required to execute a task. Work can be associated with a task, a resource, or an assignment. It is a part of the basic work formula. Refer to *Chapter 4, Underlying Concepts of Microsoft Project.*

Work Breakdown Structure (WBS): The WBS is a breakdown of the project into smaller deliverables to achieve the project scope. The WBS is the critical bridge between the scope and schedule. Refer to *Chapter 6, Work Breakdown Structure – the Single Critical Factor.*

Work resources: Resources assigned to the project based on time are called work resources. The people assigned to a project – that is, everyone on your project team – are work resources in Project. Refer to *Chapter 15, Resource and Cost Management.*

Other Books You May Enjoy

If you enjoyed this book, you may be interested in these other books by Packt:

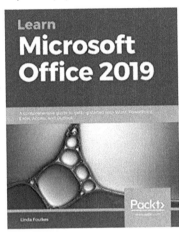

Learn Microsoft Office 2019

Linda Foulkes

ISBN: 978-1-83921-725-8

- Use PowerPoint 2019 effectively to create engaging presentations
- Gain working knowledge of Excel formulas and functions
- Collaborate using Word 2019 tools, and create and format tables and professional documents
- Organize emails, calendars, meetings, contacts, and tasks with Outlook 2019
- Store information for reference, reporting, and analysis using Access 2019
- Discover new functionalities such as Translator, Read Aloud, Scalable Vector Graphics (SVG), and data analysis tools that are useful for working professionals

Learn Power Query

Linda Foulkes

ISBN: 978-1-83921-971-9

Convert worksheet data into a table format ready for query output

- Create a dynamic connection between an Access database and Excel workbook
- Reshape tabular data by altering rows, columns, and tables using various Power Query tools
- Create new columns automatically from filenames and sheet tabs, along with multiple Excel data files
- Streamline and automate reports from multiple sources
- Explore different customization options to get the most out of your dashboards
- Understand the difference between the DAX language and Power Query's M language

Leave a review - let other readers know what you think

Please share your thoughts on this book with others by leaving a review on the site that you bought it from. If you purchased the book from Amazon, please leave us an honest review on this book's Amazon page. This is vital so that other potential readers can see and use your unbiased opinion to make purchasing decisions, we can understand what our customers think about our products, and our authors can see your feedback on the title that they have worked with Packt to create. It will only take a few minutes of your time, but is valuable to other potential customers, our authors, and Packt. Thank you!

Index

Printed in the USA
CPSIA information can be obtained
at www.ICGtesting.com
JSHW072331170724
66548JS00001B/2